SCIENCE AND SALVATION

SCIENCE
AND
SALVATION

Evangelical Popular Science Publishing
in
Victorian Britain

Aileen Fyfe

THE UNIVERSITY OF CHICAGO PRESS

Chicago and London

Aileen K. Fyfe is a lecturer in the history of science at the
National University of Ireland, Galway.

The University of Chicago Press, Chicago 60637
The University of Chicago Press, Ltd., London
© 2004 by The University of Chicago
All rights reserved. Published 2004
Printed in the United States of America
13 12 11 10 09 08 07 06 05 04   1 2 3 4 5
ISBN: 0-226-27647-3 (cloth)
ISBN: 0-226-27648-1 (paper)

Library of Congress Cataloging-in-Publication Data

Fyfe, Aileen.
Science and salvation: evangelical popular science publishing in
Victorian Britain / Aileen Fyfe.
p.   cm.
Includes bibliographical references (p.) and index.
ISBN 0-226-27647-3 (cloth: alk. paper)—ISBN 0-226-27648-1 (pbk.: alk. paper)
1. Religion and science—Great Britain—History—19th century.   2. Religious Tract
Society (Great Britain)—History—19th century.   3. Science publishing—Great
Britain—History—19th century.   4. Evangelicalism—Great Britain—History—
19th century.   I. Title.

BL245 .F94   2004
261.5'5'094109034—dc22   2003017513

To Jean Kennedy
and to the memories of George Kennedy
and Amy and William Fyfe,
my grandparents

Contents

Illustrations

Figures

TABLES

EXHIBITS

Abbreviations

BBA   British Biographical Archive

BFBS   British and Foreign Bible Society (f. 1804)

DEB   Dictionary of Evangelical Biography

DLB   Dictionary of Literary Biography, vol. 106: "British Literary Publishing Houses"

DNB   Dictionary of National Biography

LCM   London City Mission (f. 1835)

LMS   London Missionary Society (f. 1795)

OED   Oxford English Dictionary

RLF   Royal Literary Fund (f. 1788). The Royal Literary Fund archive has been microfilmed by World Microfilms. References to RLF archives take the following form:
>   RLF 1385.3, Martin to RLF, 14 April 1852
>   i.e., RLF file 1385, item 3, a letter from Martin to the RLF, dated 14 April 1852

RTS   Religious Tract Society (f. 1799). Since 1935, the society has been known as the United Society for Christian Literature (USCL). The USCL/RTS archives are on deposit at the School of Oriental and African Studies, London. References to RTS archives are as follows:

USCL/RTS Add.	Additional Deposit
USCL/RTS CCM	Copyright Committee Minutes
USCL/RTS Corr.	Correspondence
USCL/RTS ECM	Executive Committee Minutes
USCL/RTS FCM	Finance Committee Minutes
USCL/RTS Publ.	List of New Publications
RTS Report	Annual Report

SDUK Society for the Diffusion of Useful Knowledge (1826–46). The
SDUK archives are held at University College, London.

SPCK Society for Promoting Christian Knowledge (f. 1698)

ZS   Zoological Society (of London, f. 1826). References to ZS archives
are as follows:
    ZS MC   Minutes of Council
    ZS MMC   Minutes of Museum Committee

Acknowledgements

ALL BOOKS OWE much to those that have come before, in methodological and stylistic terms, as well as in the direct debts that are acknowledged in footnotes. Equally, all books owe a great deal to many people other than the writer whose name appears on the title page. Here I can attempt only to acknowledge the most obvious of those contributions.

This entire project would clearly have been impossible without the archives of the Religious Tract Society, and the assistance of Rosemary Seton and her team at the School of Oriental and African Studies. I am also grateful to Alwyn Marriage (then general secretary of RTS) and Adrian Brink (managing director of Lutterworth Press), who roped me into helping with the Society's bicentenary celebrations and made me feel that I was not alone in my interest in RTS history. Brian Alderson and Pat Garrett at the Children's Book History Society were crucial in making sure that the bicentenary conference happened, thus bringing lots of RTS enthusiasts together. I also had a most productive day in the archives of the Zoological Society of London, and thank Michael Palmer for his assistance on that occasion.

My thanks to the following for allowing me to use material in their possession: the Royal Literary Fund; the Syndics of Cambridge University Library; the United Society for Christian Literature (formerly Religious Tract Society); and the Zoological Society of London.

I also thank the library staff at Cambridge University Library, the Bodleian Library, the British Library, and the National Library of Scotland. Their friendly efficiency in fetching rare books and responding to queries proved essential to this project. Gina Douglas at the Linnean Society and Sarah Strong at the Royal Geographical Society made friendly and helpful responses to my queries, unearthing tiny pieces of biographical information that helped to flesh out the biographies of two of my writers.

If archives and libraries made the project possible, funding was equally important in making sure that I could be the person to undertake it. The research for this book has been supported by the University of Cambridge Research Maintenance Fund (1996–98), the British Federation of Women Graduates

(1998), the Arts and Humanities Research Board (1998–2000), and the National University of Ireland, Galway (2001). The Centre for Research in Arts, Social Sciences and Humanities at the University of Cambridge gave me a base for the months leading up to the preparation of the final manuscript, and the National University of Ireland generously provided funding for the index.

Colleagues in the Department of History and Philosophy of Science, University of Cambridge, have heard about this project for several years now, and I am grateful to them all for their support and curiosity, as much in the coffee room as in the seminar room. Several people have read parts of this project in various forms, and I thank John Brooke, Geoffrey Cantor, Bernie Lightman, and Simon Schaffer for their constructive comments. I deeply appreciate the efforts of Anne Secord and Jon Topham, who both read the entire manuscript, and the constructive comments of the publisher's readers.

One of the curiosities of writing a book about a mid-nineteenth-century publishing house is that I now know a vast amount about how publishing used to work. It's a little different these days, of course. But writers would still fail to find an audience if it were not for their editors and publishers, and I am grateful to Susan Abrams for being enthusiastic about this project, and encouraging me not to write a straight book-of-thesis. I also appreciate the efforts of Alan Thomas and Jennifer Howard in taking over from Susan and shepherding this book through the publication process.

Morag and Alastair Fyfe not only provided the support and care that all young researchers need, but were invaluable in helping with odds and ends of research related to Glasgow and the family history of some of those about whom I write. Paul Smith has listened to my discoveries, worries, and inspirations over the course of this project with patience and interest. That is deeply appreciated, as are his careful readings of the manuscript.

The final acknowledgement must be to Jim Secord, who encouraged this project from its early stages, and who, even now, can still get excited about it. That is a truly valuable support.

SCIENCE AND SALVATION

Introduction

IN THE mid-1840s, a devout schoolteacher suffered a spiritual crisis. Mrs. Sarah Pugh had decided to read George Combe's *The Constitution of Man in Relation to External Objects* (1828).[1] She hoped that its explanation of the laws of nature would help her to understand her pupils' different aptitudes for learning. She was also curious to discover whether scientific views of the human mind were compatible with her Christian faith. The inexpensive "People's Edition" of Combe's work, issued in 1835, had become a best-seller, with an unprecedented forty thousand copies sold within a year. The success had concerned many Christian commentators because *Constitution of Man* could be read as suggesting that natural laws were more important than divine or moral laws.[2] Sarah's first impressions, however, were favourable. She became convinced that "the science of Phrenology has truth for its basis," and that reading the bumps on the skulls of her pupils would help her to understand their innate talents and limitations. Then she reached the ninth chapter, "On the Relation between Science and Scripture," and her mind was "painfully exercised." She read the chapter over and over again. The problem, she would later write, was that "Many of the views *seemed* to be at variance with Revelation. I could not disbelieve the evidence of my senses on the one hand, nor relinquish my hold of Scripture truth on the other. To recede, appeared to be folly; to advance, madness."[3]

Sarah Pugh now had a difficult decision to make. She had been con-vinced by phrenology—it "had given me more light and assistance than I had

---

1. Nothing is known about Mrs. Pugh other than that her own initials were "S.D." and her husband's name was John. See title page and preface of Pugh, *Phrenology Considered.* However, of the twenty-one recorded marriages of a John Pugh to a woman with the initial "S" in the fifteen years prior to 1846, seventeen were to a "Sarah."

2. van Wyhe, *Phrenology and Victorian Scientific Naturalism;* Cooter, *Cultural Meaning of Popular Science.*

3. Pugh, *Phrenology Considered,* 7.

obtained from any other source"—but she was desperately unwilling to give up her faith. "I laid the book aside for many months. I searched the Scripture diligently. I wept and prayed. . . . 'Perish the knowledge of science,' I thought, 'if it can only be obtained by the abandonment of my hopes for eternity!'" Yet she was still unable to convince herself to give up either phrenology or faith. She began to study the writings of other phrenologists, including those of William Newnham, who shared her commitment to an evangelical form of Christianity. Finally, she read *Constitution of Man* again, determined to decide for herself how much "appeared to me to be in accordance with Revelation, and what seemed otherwise, that I might feel satisfied whether his opinions were really opposed to the Scriptures, or merely independent of and distinct from them." She eventually followed Newnham in deciding that phrenology could indeed be reconciled with evangelical faith.[4]

Sarah's hopes for eternity had thus been saved, but it had been a long and traumatic process. Her experience illustrates the two central concerns that are the subject of this book. First, in the mid-nineteenth century the sciences were increasingly being perceived as opposed to religious faith, but this was something that many Christians worked to overcome, convinced that, when properly considered, the claims of science and salvation would be perfectly complementary. Second, cheap print allowed more people than ever before to read about new developments in the sciences. While this might be useful educationally, it could also be profoundly unsettling. Sarah Pugh began reading about phrenology with a firm evangelical faith, but by the end of the work she was left in a quandary. The temptation to accept phrenology and abandon her faith was very strong, and it took months of mental debate, coupled with an extensive reading programme, before she was able to develop a compromise position that included both systems. This was precisely why evangelical Christians were so concerned about the expansion of cheap publishing in the middle of the nineteenth century, and why the sciences were one of the areas of most concern. Sarah Pugh was a well-educated reader with a strong personal faith and access to the additional literary resources she needed—and yet she almost succumbed to the temptation.[5] Just imagine what cheap books on the sciences might do to less prepared readers!

In this book I explore the relationship between science and religion, specifically the religious reaction to the perceived threat posed by cheap science

---

4. Ibid., 8.

5. Compare the experience of Mary Smith, reading *Vestiges of the Natural History of Creation*, in James A. Secord, *Victorian Sensation*, 15–17.

publishing in the middle of the nineteenth century. The significance of religious faith in the history of European science is already well known.[6] In the case of nineteenth-century Britain, in particular, much has been written on the transformation of the sciences into professionalised, organised, specialist disciplines during the course of the century, and this is seen as going hand in hand with the story of the separation of science from religion as each developed into a profession.[7] The sciences are regarded as moving from a highly religious state with no clear criteria for measuring expertise, to one that is professional and mostly secular. This book does not intend to challenge that story, but it starts from the observation that such narratives do not take account of the ways in which science and faith related to one another outside the restricted community of specialists. Historians have been concerned with the development of professional science, so they tell the story largely from the point of view of men of science. This book approaches the question from the point of view of a religious community, and examines popular, rather than expert, science. I take as a premise that the history of popular science and religion need not be the same as that of expert science and religion, and get to the root of the issue by concentrating on the period when popular science publishing, in its secular and Christian variants, was developed.

Evangelicals are Protestant Christians particularly committed to the Bible's message of salvation through faith in Christ, seeking as part of the practice of their faith to help as many people as possible to share in that salvation. The commitment to the Bible has, for some groups at some points in history, come into conflict with scientific discoveries. Evangelicals in the mid-nineteenth century, however, did not consider the sciences, in themselves, to constitute a danger to the faith and salvation of the nation. Although many of their works were on the relatively conservative areas of natural history, rather than newer sciences such as physiology, it becomes clear that these evangelicals were not worried by the discoveries of geology, phrenology, and nebular astronomy. All of these sciences were quite conformable with faith, as long as they were properly interpreted.[8] The manner of interpretation was, of course, the bone of contention. When works such as *Constitution of Man* or, even worse, the anonymous *Vestiges of the Natural History of Creation* (1844) presented the

---

6. Lindberg and Numbers, *God and Nature;* Brooke, *Science and Religion;* Brooke and Cantor, *Reconstructing Nature.*

7. Turner, "Victorian Conflict between Science and Religion"; Ben-David, *Scientist's Role in Society;* Desmond, *Huxley: The Devil's Disciple;* Desmond, *Huxley: Evolution's High Priest.*

8. This was the evangelical version of what Topham calls "safe science." See Topham, "Science and Popular Education in the 1830s."

sciences in a framework that appeared to remove any role for God in the world, and perhaps even denied his initial act of creation, then evangelicals got worried. Works that omitted all mention of God were almost as dangerous as the atheistic ones that openly attacked belief in God and gloried in religious infidelity.[9] Secular works were less overtly shocking to believers, but they had the insidious potential to convince their readers that the sciences could be adequately and completely understood without reference to religion.

It is important to appreciate that evangelicals in the mid-nineteenth century were not usually concerned about the specific scientific discoveries themselves; rather, they were worried about what they regarded as the distorting manner in which those discoveries were represented to a wider reading public. Educated Christian readers could be expected to recognise and reject the atheistic or secular framework of potentially dangerous works by realising that the evidence could also be arranged in a different manner, and recasting it in a Christian framework. This is what Sarah Pugh was ultimately able to do with her reading of *Constitution of Man*. However, when such works were read by less educated, or less faithful, readers, they could be dangerous, and this was why they were attacked by evangelicals. Readers who did not have intellectual safeguards might be seduced by the cosmic romance of *Vestiges* into believing that new scientific discoveries could be interpreted only in an anti-religious manner, and they might end up unbelievers as a result. Effectively, evangelicals thought it was irresponsible to the spiritual health of the nation to publish atheistic or secular works on the sciences that might end up in the hands of unprepared readers.

The religious response was to produce alternative works of Christian popular science, thereby creating a genre that survived the secularisation of professional science.[10] I am therefore approaching the science–religion debates from a fresh angle, by examining the public understanding of science as opposed to that articulated by experts through their published papers. *Science and Salvation* is not concerned with eminent men of science, nor even with particularly well-known clergymen. I seek a wider scope by attempting to gauge attitudes to the sciences and faith as held by laypeople.

I also wish to move the history of the relations between science and religion into the practical sphere. Although the importance of practice has been increasingly recognised in the history of science and in the history of religion

---

9. On overtly atheistic works, see Desmond, "Artisan Resistance."

10. Lightman, " 'The Voices of Nature' "; Lightman, "The Story of Nature"; Lightman, "The Visual Theology of Victorian Popularizers."

in recent years, it has yet to have much effect on histories of the intercon-nection of science and religion.[11] Thus, although this book will consider the intellectual aspect of evangelicals' attitudes to science and faith, it will con-centrate on the effects those attitudes had in a more practical arena. Deciding how the demands of science and salvation should best be reconciled was not simply a mental exercise. It had implications for how one should act in the world. This is obvious in the case of those men of science in the late nine-teenth century who lost their faith, and thus stopped going to church. It is less obvious for those in the earlier part of the century who decided that faith and the sciences were in harmony. For evangelicals, faith encompassed everything. The Reverend Edward Bickersteth quoted Moses to remind his readers that religious beliefs affected every moment of their lives, including the most mundane activities: "[Thou] shalt talk of them when thou sittest in thine house, and when thou walkest by the way, and when thou liest down, and when thou risest up" (Deuteronomy 6:6–7).[12] Given this all-pervading influence of religious conviction, we should not think of the sciences as being something that could be separated from faith, or that could, potentially, be in conflict with it. Evangelicals lived and worked within a theological frame-work that included the sciences just as much as organised activities such as church-going.[13]

The subjects of this book are a group of evangelical middle-class men and women, all of whom were involved with the Religious Tract Society. Like all the Society's members, they believed strongly in the saving grace of Christ's sacrifice on the cross, and they wished to help other people on the road to salvation by teaching them about Christ's Atonement for the sins of mankind. These particular men and women were part of the Religious Tract Society's programme of popular science publishing, which meant that they had to articulate for a public audience their understanding of the proper relationship between evangelical faith and new developments in the sciences. Their attitudes to the sciences were thus manifested not only in an intellectual position on the relationship between science and faith, but in a great deal of activity—writing, editing, printing, and publishing. This can be seen in the decision to publish Christian popular science at all, and in a science writer's decision to write for the Religious Tract Society in particular.

---

11. On science as practice, see Pickering, *Science as Practice and Culture.* On religion as practice, see Williams, *Religious Belief and Popular Culture.*

12. Bickersteth, *Domestic Portraiture,* xiv.

13. A similar approach is taken in Hilton, *Age of Atonement,* 7.

The involvement of my subjects in writing and publishing makes it easier to find out about their views, but their attempts to convert their readership to their own view of the sciences and faith make their opinions significant. The initial conception of that readership was as an audience comprising members of the working and lower-middle classes as well as the "educated families" of the country. The existence of a "mass audience" was just beginning to be recognised in the 1840s, and it was frequently perceived as a crowd of different sorts of people rather than as the homogeneous mass that we tend to think of today.[14] Despite this recognition of heterogeneity within the mass audience, the Religious Tract Society still hoped to be able to reach the varied constituents with the same product. As will become evident in the course of this book, these evangelicals were not as successful as they would have wished. Like many of their contemporaries, they bemoaned the difficulty of getting cheap print to the working classes. Nevertheless, they were more successful than most and, of the nonfiction publishers, came the closest to reaching that mass audience.

Until recently, evangelicals rarely appeared in histories of science and religion, because of the tradition that identifies evangelicals as opponents of rational enquiry. This has emerged from the emphasis placed by many historians on natural theology, since it illustrates so well the widespread harmony—rather than conflict—between science and religion in the first half of the nineteenth century.[15] The most familiar aspect of natural theology is the argument for design. As set out in William Paley's oft-reprinted *Natural Theology* (1802), it claimed that all the intricate mechanisms and contrivances found in nature, from the human eye to the elephant's trunk, were striking evidences of design.[16] Since Paley could not imagine any convincing explanation for the existence of design other than the existence of a designer, these mechanisms and contrivances in the natural world were taken as proof of the existence of God the Creator. Paley also felt it possible to prove some of the attributes of God, such as his personality, unity, and benevolence, from the natural world. From that position, one could regard the Revelation found in the Bible as

---

14. Klancher, *English Reading Audiences*, 77–97; Anderson, *Printed Image*, 9.

15. In particular, see Young, *Darwin's Metaphor*. See also Brooke, "Natural Theology and the Plurality of Worlds"; Brooke, "Natural Theology of the Geologists"; Topham, "'An Infinite Variety of Arguments.'"

16. Gillespie, "Divine Design"; Fyfe, "Reception of William Paley's *Natural Theology*"; Fyfe, "Publishing and the Classics."

offering additional information about God's relationship with his people, and the duty mankind owed to God.[17]

Close links between religion and the investigation of nature remained almost universal in Britain until the middle of the nineteenth century, and for some individuals, for even longer. As historians have recently begun to realise, however, that does not mean that everyone continued to subscribe to a Paleyan version of natural theology.[18] Among those who accepted that science and religion complemented each other, there was significant divergence between those who believed that nature could prove the existence of God (as Paley contended) and those who based their faith on Revelation but nevertheless regarded nature as a divine creation worthy of study. For the latter group, whose members had a theological understanding of nature but did not accept natural theology in its strict sense, the investigation of nature could still be an important devotional exercise, a means of learning more about the works of the God of Scripture, and a confirmation of his foresight and care for his creatures.[19] By the middle of the nineteenth century, this was the majority position, and relatively few people still accepted the claims of natural theology.

Evangelicals of the mid-nineteenth century based their faith on Revelation. For them, it was missing the point of faith to attempt to ground Christianity on a rational proof of God's existence.[20] They rejected natural theology when it was used in that way, which is why historians who concentrate primarily on natural theology have tended to ignore evangelicals. Now that historians of science have begun to pay more attention to other theologies of nature, evangelicals are beginning to re-appear.[21] Many evangelicals were deeply interested in the natural world, and a few were actively involved in its investigation, seeing their efforts as an investigation of God's work.[22] They did not deny that God's hand could be seen in nature and welcomed Paley's

---

17. An introduction to these themes can be found in Brooke, *Science and Religion;* Brooke and Cantor, *Reconstructing Nature.*

18. On the variety of natural theologies, see Topham, "Science, Natural Theology, and Evangelicalism," esp. 141; Topham, "'An Infinite Variety of Arguments.'"

19. The distinction between "natural theology" and "theology of nature" was made by Brooke and Hooykaas, *New Interactions between Theology and Natural Science,* but it did not receive significant attention until recently.

20. On evangelicals and science, see Bebbington, "Science and Evangelical Theology."

21. Livingstone, Hart, and Noll, *Evangelicals and Science;* Astore, *Observing God.*

22. For examples, see Astore, "Observing God"; Astore, *Observing God;* Sivasundaram, "'Nature Speaks Theology.'"

book for providing so many striking examples, but this was always considered a devotional exercise, something that would illustrate and deepen their faith rather than provide a foundation for it.

Like many other Christians, these evangelicals made use of the metaphor of the "two books": God had written two books, that of his Word (the Bible) and that of his Works (nature, and sometimes also the historical record). Although evangelicals gave precedence to the Bible as the basis of their faith, they did not doubt that the book of nature was also written by God, and argued that the common authorship of the two books made it impossible for them to disagree. One of the Religious Tract Society writers expressed the common view when he wrote "there is only one source of truth, so we need not be under any alarm lest human research should discover facts at variance with the word of God. It cannot be that truth should oppose truth." Nevertheless, the same writer acknowledged that it is possible that "so many links are wanting in our chain of knowledge, that we have to wait in all humility till these are supplied, before we can take in the grand ideas which are dawning upon us."[23] In other words, it may not yet be obvious how the two books are to be reconciled, but that they will be so is not in doubt. Despite this, evangelicals were always careful to point out the inadequacies of natural theology, for, fascinating and worthy though it was, the study of nature could not teach mankind anything about those central aspects of evangelical faith: atonement and salvation. Paley had been able to deduce the benevolence of God the Creator, but he had nothing to say about Christ the Redeemer.[24]

Another reason for the lack of attention paid by historians of science to evangelicalism is the high profile of subgroups who would accept scientific discovery only when it could be reconciled with literalist interpretations of the Bible. The early-twentieth-century conservative American Protestants who also bore the label "evangelical" are obvious examples, but there were also nineteenth-century groups who can be portrayed as being "anti-science," such as the Scriptural Geologists.[25] Recent work in the history of evangelicalism has increasingly stressed that evangelicalism was a broad-spectrum

---

23. [Charles Tomlinson], *British Nation*, 62.

24. On the reception of Paley, including evangelical reactions, see Fyfe, "Reception of William Paley's *Natural Theology*."

25. On American evangelicals, see Numbers, *The Creationists;* Livingstone, Hart, and Noll, *Evangelicals and Science*, particularly the essays in section 3. On British scriptural geologists, see Mortenson, "British Scriptural Geologists"; Roberts, "Geology and Genesis Unearthed."

movement, and one that changed over time. Twentieth-century American evangelicals were significantly different from their mid-nineteenth-century predecessors in Britain and America. Within the mid-nineteenth-century context, the more radical subgroups of evangelicalism were in a minority.[26] They happen to have received significant amounts of attention from historians charting the fortunes of evangelicalism because of their influence on later generations.[27] The majority of mid-nineteenth-century British evangelicals did not insist on the exact and invariable wording of the Bible, expect an imminent apocalypse, or claim to speak in tongues. They believed in the need for activism to improve the religious and social conditions of the world, and thus prepare the way for Christ's second coming; and they took a practical, and often liberal, approach to questions of biblical interpretation. Evangelicalism was in its heyday in mid-nineteenth-century Britain, and it was these moderate evangelicals who were predominant. If we want to consider evangelical attitudes to the sciences in the mid-nineteenth century, therefore, we should not focus exclusively on a small minority of intellectual evangelicals.

Following this reassessment of the importance of natural theology and the recognition of the varieties of evangelicalism, this book seeks a deeper and more sympathetic understanding of the ways in which evangelicals related to and responded to scientific enquiry. It shows how moderate evangelicals engaged directly with cheap publishing to avoid abandoning the field to those of a neutral or explicitly atheistic disposition. Thus there emerged a significant group of evangelical writers, editors, and publishers who both came to terms with the sciences and developed a new concept of the relationship between the sciences and faith that was to inform their publications. Only a few of these people had any claim to scientific expertise, but many of them were committed students of the sciences—of botany, zoology, astronomy, and geology, in particular—and were extremely knowledgeable in their fields.

My contribution to the history of science and religion emerges from a focus on the world of cheap publishing in the middle of the nineteenth century.[28] The histories of publishing, authorship, and reading have attracted a great deal of attention from scholars in the last two decades, providing

---

26. Hilton, *Age of Atonement;* Bebbington, *Evangelicalism in Modern Britain.*

27. As, for example, in Bebbington, *Evangelicalism in Modern Britain,* chap. 3.

28. For the earlier part of the nineteenth century, see Topham, "Beyond the 'Common Context'"; Topham, "Science, Natural Theology, and the Practice of Christian Piety." For midcentury, see Astore, *Observing God.*

a focus for much interdisciplinary work by historians, literary scholars, and bibliographers.[29] While most of the earliest research focused on the canonical works of European literature, especially in the early modern period, interest in book history is now spreading to historians of science and to historians of religion.[30] In contrast to most of the existing studies, I do not focus on well-known books (such as the Bible, or works by famous scientists). Rather I use popular publishing as a way to uncover the attitudes of nonexperts. This offers access to the positions adopted by the middle-class publishers and writers, and illustrates the sort of material that was available to working-class readers attempting to create their own positions on science and religion.[31]

Protestantism's emphasis on access to the Bible meant that its followers had a long-standing interest in literacy and publishing.[32] British evangelicals were no exception, and in addition to seeing print as an aid to devotion, they were alert to the possibilities it offered for evangelising. From the 1780s, they were trying to improve literacy rates among the working classes by providing basic instruction in the Sunday schools. By the 1790s, they were setting up missionary organisations to convert the heathen at home and abroad, and virtually all of these organisations relied on some form of print—such as tracts, posters, and Bibles—to assist the missionaries in their programmes of outreach. The evangelical determination to provide print for those less certain of salvation than themselves continued into the nineteenth century, and organisations such as the Religious Tract Society and the British and Foreign Bible Society became adept at using the latest publishing technologies and distribution methods to achieve their goals. With the exception of itinerant hawkers, these societies were virtually the only sources of cheap print at the beginning of the nineteenth century.

Yet, by the second quarter of the nineteenth century, evangelicals had lost their effective monopoly on cheap print. There were various radical attempts

---

29. On methodologies of book history, see Darnton, "What Is the History of Books?"; Adams and Barker, "A New Model." For nineteenth-century examples, see Jordan and Patten, *Literature in the Market Place;* Raven, Small, and Tadmor, *Practice and Representation of Reading;* Erickson, *Economy of Literary Form.*

30. On book history and the sciences, see Johns, *Nature of the Book;* James A. Secord, *Victorian Sensation;* Frasca-Spada and Jardine, *Books and the Sciences;* Topham, "Scientific Publishing and the Reading of Science." On book history and religion, see Howsam, *Cheap Bibles;* Wosh, *Spreading the Word;* Nord, "Economics of Religious Publishing"; Raven, *Free Print and Non-Commercial Publishing,* chaps. 6–8.

31. For existing studies of working-class reading (which say little about religion), see Vincent, *Bread, Knowledge and Freedom;* Rose, *Intellectual Life.*

32. Ian Green, *Print and Protestantism;* O'Brien, "Publishing Networks."

to produce cheap newspapers or political pamphlets for the working classes in the 1810s and after, but these routinely fell foul of the law and were short-lived.[33] From the late 1820s, however, a wider range of more long-lasting attempts to reach the working classes began. Initially, the publishers who became involved were those who shared the evangelicals' desire to improve the working classes through the use of cheap print, but who saw this in terms of secular instruction. W. & R. Chambers of Edinburgh and the Society for the Diffusion of Useful Knowledge both produced cheap instructional works on the sciences, history, and geography that avoided contemporary politics and religion. The success of some of these efforts alerted even more publishers to the possibility of larger audiences. In contrast to both the secular and religious publishers of earlier days, many of the publishers who began to specialise in cheap publishing in the 1840s had no philanthropic ambitions at all. For them, cheap print was simply a commodity, a means of making money. Print had no spiritual, or even educational, value.

At best, this new sort of cheap publishing could be seen as harmless. Those who read its productions were certainly wasting time that might have been better spent, but, as one commentator pointed out, "the reading of trashy fiction is a better form of excitement than dram-drinking."[34] At worst, cheap publishing could be dangerous to its readers. Fictitious stories could normalise immoral behaviour, historical works might undermine the history of Christianity, and scientific works could attack the existence of God. Those works that were considered to be potentially corrupting included the atheistic, the politically radical, and the pornographic, but the category was ultimately extended to include any work that assumed a secular tone. According to evangelicals, secular writing might appear neutral, but it was in reality an agent of the enemy, encouraging its readers to believe they could dispense with religion.

While it was hardly the first time that immoral or error-ridden works had been published, the difference now was that they were being published at a price that made them far more widely accessible. The working classes might have become literate, but they were assumed to be childlike in their inability to discriminate between reliable authoritative works and mere speculation (or worse). Publications that had been of relatively little concern when the typical print run was barely five hundred copies or so became much more

---

33. Desmond, "Artisan Resistance."
34. [Masson], "Present Aspects and Tendencies," 181.

problematic if they were read by five thousand or fifty thousand people. Some of the penny periodicals of the 1850s even had circulations approaching five hundred thousand. While the sceptical or potentially corrupting works had been confined to the wealthier classes, they had not been a significant threat to the nation, as such readers were assumed to be sufficiently discerning to reject or resist their temptations. But once a work became available to a wider audience, there was the risk that unsophisticated readers would succumb to its blandishments and sink into error, depravity, or sin.

Circulations had increased tenfold, if not a hundredfold, largely because of the industrialisation of the book trade. It was not just that more publishers were involved in cheap publishing, or that they were making more of an effort. They were aided by the latest developments in steam printing machines and railway distribution. As we will see, print had been transformed into the first of the mass media. This meant that although the proportion of cheap publications that involved radical politics, unorthodox religion, or pornography was far smaller than the proportion of relatively harmless fiction, the higher circulations meant that the absolute number of dangerous publications was larger than ever before.

By the 1840s and 1850s, it had become clear that cheap literature was not necessarily educational or wholesome, but might as easily be erroneous, immoral, or downright corrupting. For evangelicals, this was not good news. They regarded the printing press as a divine gift for spreading the word of God. It was due to the press that "the word of the Lord has had free course and been glorified. The darkness, superstition, and despotism of the middle ages can never return."[35] The apparent multitudes of secular, immoral, and corrupting publications were a prostitution of that gift. During the 1840s and 1850s, therefore, evangelicals had to decide how to respond to these changes and to rethink their own publishing programmes in response to the new competition. It was far too spiritually dangerous to "leave the whole extensive field of historical and scientific literature to the devil," but what could be done?[36] The French government had attempted to censor cheap publications due to very similar concerns, but British Christians agreed that this was not a realistic approach, let alone one in keeping with their cherished concept of liberty.[37] A Religious Tract Society writer contended that, in

---

35. Pearson, *Infidelity*, 477.

36. "Notice of objections," *Christian Spectator* (1841): 91.

37. This affair, and the British reaction, is described in [Masson], "Present Aspects and Tendencies," at 177–81.

contrast to the situation in Roman Catholic countries, "There is no need to denounce the discoveries of science, or to prohibit the reading of books in which those discoveries are made known. A corrupt church, which fears and abhors the progress of enlightenment, may resort to these devices; but the Bible Christian is not afraid of the progress of human knowledge."[38] Evangelicals were convinced that, in a free competition, Good would win out against Evil. Thus, the solution had to lie, not in the constraint of the less desirable sections of the press, but in the increased activity of the moral and Christian press, with a particular emphasis on the sciences. The result was one of the least expensive and most widely available popular science series of the midcentury.

I begin in this book by explaining why the popular science publications of the 1840s were seen as such a threat to faith. I also introduce the Religious Tract Society, which was the largest of the evangelical publishers and, as such, was expected to lead the attack on the dangerous cheap publications. This attack had to be based on true knowledge, the definition of which reveals evangelical attitudes to knowledge. The works of science already on the market exemplified a range of approaches to presenting scientific knowledge, from the explicitly atheistic, to the secular, to some form of Christian tone. The Religious Tract Society had to decide whether any of these potential models were worth emulating, and whether its own version of Christian tone would prove effective against the opposition. Christian tone had to convince readers that the sciences did not imply the exclusion of faith—it had to provide them with a spiritual worldview that not only incorporated the sciences but was strong enough to withstand any future encounters with neutral or infidel works. The effectiveness of this strategy was dependent on the interaction between narrative voice and reader, and this will be seen in action through a close reading of one of the new publications, *British Fish and Fisheries* (1849).

Christian tone would be of no use if it did not reach its readers. This involved finding manuscripts that were written in a suitable style—not only Christian, but also sufficiently easy to understand—and then producing them cheaply enough to make them accessible to their intended readers. The Religious Tract Society gradually discovered, however, that price alone was not enough and that more attention to distribution channels was needed to reach working-class readers. This discussion also illustrates some of the tensions

---

38. [Charles Tomlinson], *British Nation*, 62.

inherent in the Religious Tract Society's work, as it strived to be both an efficient commercial organisation and an evangelical charity. Similar tensions are apparent among the Society's writers. Religious publishers were highly dependent on their writers to produce material written in a suitably Christian tone, and they often presented them as people with a spiritual vocation for writing. This disguised the reality of these writers' lives, in which money and physical toil played a much greater part than the imagery would suggest. The writers appear relatively late in my account, which should help to emphasise the anonymity of the majority of the publications. Nineteenth-century readers of *British Fish* did not know who wrote it, and I would like my readers to retain that sense of uncertainty for as long as possible. It is also the case that it was publishers who were the motive forces behind the expansion of popular publishing in the 1840s, and this is something that an overemphasis on writers as creative agents tends to ignore.[39]

I argue in this book that evangelicals were not opposed to the sciences but did worry about the manner in which the sciences were presented and interpreted. This is the key theme of the final chapter, which examines more closely the ways in which evangelicals themselves could vary their presentations of the sciences to suit different audiences. I consider two evangelical writers on the sciences: Thomas Milner on astronomy and geology, and William Martin on zoology. Both wrote extensively for the Religious Tract Society, but also regularly published with other houses. These writers certainly had some creative freedom in their relationships with publishers, and chose their projects to suit their current situations. But they were both also very experienced in adapting their writing style to the needs of their publishers. Publishers' constraints may have been tacit, but if writers did not produce what was wanted, they would not get paid. Neither Milner nor Martin could afford that, and each became extremely adept at manipulating the presentation of the same material for different contexts.

On one level, *Science and Salvation* demonstrates that evangelicals were very closely involved with and knowledgeable in the sciences, particularly in the area of popular publishing, and, as such, I hope to make a significant contribution to the developing literature in the history of science and evangelicalism. At a more fundamental level, I hope this book contributes to the cultural study of science by examining the relationship between science and

---

39. For those who do wish to know more about the writers, and other RTS staff mentioned, there is a biographical appendix.

faith in an unusually wide context, by concentrating on popular rather than expert science. Expert men of science and professional ministers and theologians were not the only people who had to think about how new discoveries related to their personal faith. Rather, this was a matter of concern to a wider educated public, as the products of the industrial printing press brought a knowledge of the sciences and novel questions relating to salvation to an ever-expanding audience.

I

The Threat of Popular Science

IN 1853, the Reverend Thomas Pearson, an evangelical minister from North Berwick, Scotland, won a prize offered by the Evangelical Alliance for his essay *Infidelity: Its Aspects, Causes and Agencies.* In this work, Pearson outlined the main varieties of religious infidelity, starting with outright atheists but including all those who ostensibly accepted the tenets of Christian faith but made no effort to live their lives accordingly. The prize was not offered, however, merely for a description of the ways in which men denied themselves the opportunity of salvation. The crucial part of the essay was the explanation of the causes and agencies of infidelity, which led to a discussion of ways in which unbelief could be attacked and defeated. Of the agencies that Pearson implicated in the spread of infidelity, the printing press was identified as the worst culprit of all.

Pearson noted, "The age in which we live, is unprecedented for the cheapness and abundant supply of its literature. The huge costly tomes which were within reach of comparatively few of our ancestors, have given place to the small and low-priced volume which is accessible to all."[1] This was certainly the cause of much good, as Pearson acknowledged, but it was also a cause for concern. Cheap print had become more influential than the pulpit, because "Millions who listen, week after week, to the living voice of the preacher, are daily fed by the press; and millions more are only accessible by its instrumentality, and to them it is the great teacher."[2] As a consequence, "Speculations, decidedly hostile to true religion and to man's best interests, are no longer confined to the upper and more refined classes of society; but they have descended through the many channels opened up by the prolific press, to the reading millions of the present time."[3] The implication here was that ideas that were relatively harmless when limited to the "upper and more refined

---

1. Pearson, *Infidelity*, 478. 2. Ibid., 473. 3. Ibid., 478–79.

classes" could become dangerous when they reached the "reading millions." It was partly a question of scale, but there was also an assumption that the so-called refined classes would be educated enough to identify and reject unfounded speculations, while other readers might succumb to its temptations.

Cheap print gave more people access to instructive, educational, and religious publications, yet concerns about its dangers were expressed by commentators across the political and religious spectrum. Evangelicals like Pearson were certainly not the only people to be worried, but they were vocal about their concerns and, more importantly for our story, were particularly active in their attempts to do something about it. All sorts of publications, from fiction to history, could be regarded as problematic, but the sciences were a particular concern. Popular publishing therefore offers us a unique opportunity to examine the involvement of evangelicals in the sciences. Their commitment to intervention meant that they were not merely commenting on the sciences from an intellectual position, but were actively engaged in creating an evangelical framework for the sciences.

THE THREAT OF POPULAR SCIENCE PUBLISHING

Thomas Pearson had highlighted two areas of particular concern for religious faith, the first of which was literature. Evangelicals are often represented as disapproving of fiction, but many were in fact happy to read the "great" works of literature, including William Shakespeare and Walter Scott.[4] They did worry that the perusal of fiction took up valuable time that ought to have been spent on more useful activities, and they were deeply concerned by the moral tone (or lack of such) apparent in much fiction. Pearson's concerns about "literature" were largely about contemporary fiction, particularly that produced by third-rate writers and published in penny magazines for the entertainment of the masses. Plenty of commentators from less religious viewpoints despaired of the absence of literary, educational, or spiritual value in this sort of literature. A writer in the *British Quarterly Review* in 1855 declared it to be "trash and garbage . . . which subsists in virtue of its adaptation to the lowest order of literary taste and appetite."[5] The problem was that, with no controls but those of the market, "the great competition in the press naturally tempts its conductors to minister to the public tastes whatever these be."[6]

---

4. Rosman, *Evangelicals and Culture*, chap. 8.
5. [Masson], "Present Aspects and Tendencies," 170.
6. Pearson, *Infidelity*, 479.

Pearson's second area of concern was publications on the sciences. As with all nonfiction, some scientific books could be labelled "trash and garbage" due to their poor execution and their contents of "unmitigated platitude—error and superstition being distinct ingredients."[7] There was a more specific problem with the sciences, however, particularly with the manner in which they were presented to a nonspecialist audience. For example, at the time Pearson was writing, the anonymous best-seller *Vestiges of the Natural History of Creation* (1844) was without doubt one of the most obvious candidates for evangelical ire.[8] It had been widely criticised by men of science for its errors and misrepresentations of scientific discoveries and for presenting speculative theories as certain, as well as condemned from a religious viewpoint for weaving discoveries together into speculative philosophical schemes that did not involve God.[9] The Cambridge geologist Adam Sedgwick memorably described the work as a "rank pill of asafoetida and arsenic, covered with gold leaf," claiming that its attractive exterior concealed atheistic sentiments as dangerous as a foul-smelling poison.[10] The problem was that *Vestiges* was a gripping read and created a fascinating tale of progressive development using sciences such as nebular astronomy, geology, and phrenology. Reliance on these sciences made it possible to imply that progressive development and change could happen in the natural world without divine intervention, which gave the term "progress" radical religious and political implications.[11] Indeed, one of the strongest critiques against *Vestiges*, particularly once its errors had been corrected, was that it left little or no space for the God of Christianity.

One had only to look at the situation in France to appreciate how easily the sciences could be tied to a non-Christian framework. There, the ancient system of monarchy and Church had been dismantled in the Revolution of 1789–93, and eminent men of science such as the astronomer and mathematician Pierre-Simon Laplace could openly propose cosmological systems that did not include God.[12] Great Britain was, of course, a different country, and it had not experienced a revolution like that in France. Until the middle of the nineteenth century, the majority of Britain's men of science were still

---

7. [Masson], "Present Aspects and Tendencies," 170.
8. James A. Secord, *Victorian Sensation,* chap. 8.
9. On the responses to *Vestiges,* see ibid., pt. II.
10. Quoted in James A. Secord, "Behind the Veil," 187.
11. Schaffer, "Nebular Hypothesis."
12. For introductions to the changes in French science, see David Knight, *Age of Science;* Russell, *Science and Social Change.*

Christians, and many were in fact clergymen.[13] Their personal faith was not at issue, but general publications on the sciences did not necessarily reflect the beliefs of the experts. In the late eighteenth and early nineteenth centuries, the potential impact of any radical publications had been restricted, since most printed matter was so expensive that it was unlikely to get into the hands of potentially rebellious working men. The few exceptions, such as the second part of Thomas Paine's *Rights of Man* (1791–92) or the illegal reprints of French works of science produced by radical printers in the 1810s and 1820s, were the target of legal prosecutions.[14] It was understood, then, that works of science that appeared to support religious infidelity would be a significant threat to the faith of the nation if they were widely available. And, in the 1840s, much more widely available is exactly what these works became, which is why concerns about the power and influence of the press became so much more widespread.

Yet it is important to realise that while evangelicals condemned the overall worldview of *Vestiges,* they did not necessarily condemn the specific sciences of nebular astronomy, geology, or phrenology. As we have already seen, Sarah Pugh eventually reconciled phrenology with her evangelical faith. One of the writers she found helpful was William Newnham, who argued in a work written in 1847 (as part of the series to be discussed later) that "No right-thinking person can doubt that the brain is the organ of mind." The question at issue was "whether the said doctrines, established as true in themselves, may not have been perverted and misapplied so as to produce serious errors and consequences of a painful nature."[15]

Similarly, geology and nebular astronomy were no threat when rightly interpreted. Thomas Milner, another of the writers to be more fully discussed later, had no trouble with the concept that the earth was older than the six thousand years calculated by seventeenth-century biblical scholars. He accepted that the earth was significantly older than mankind and that it had undergone change during the course of its history. For Milner, this was evidence of God's foresight in preparing the earth for the arrival of man. Furthermore, in books written both before and after *Vestiges* (in 1843 and 1846), Milner contended that even the nebular hypothesis, famously linked with Laplace, would be no threat to religion if it were proved true. Supporters

---

13. Morrell and Thackray, *Gentlemen of Science.*

14. On the association of science with radicalism, see Jacyna, "Immanence and Transcendence"; Desmond, "Artisan Resistance."

15. Newnham, *Man,* 156.

of the nebular hypothesis argued that modern astronomy demonstrated that change had occurred in the heavens, as diffuse, gaseous nebulae gradually developed into solar systems such as our own, and that this took place without the help of God. Milner argued that such development might indeed have taken place, but it was an illustration of the way in which God had exercised his creative power, and not a proof that he had not done so at all. Thus, for evangelicals, the sciences of progress were not a threat to faith as long as they were properly interpreted.

"If the press be a powerful agency for good," wrote Thomas Pearson, "it is unquestionably a powerful agency for evil also. . . . It is ceaselessly sending forth publications of almost every shape and character, like the sand by the sea-shore for number, which must be assigned to the account of evil."[16] In this sentiment, Pearson and the *British Quarterly* found themselves in rare agreement with the most senior Roman Catholic in Britain.[17] Evangelicals tended to regard Cardinal Nicholas Wiseman with loathing, yet, only a year after Pearson's essay, while addressing an audience at the Educational Exhibition of the Society for Arts, Wiseman condemned "those publications which at present creep—which I may rather say crawl—in their own slime on the surface of the earth, and . . . insinuate themselves into the peaceful and happy domestic circle, and there introduce pain, and ruin, and death." He accepted that exterminating these "reptiles" would be impossible, but urged that an antidote be provided in the form of sound wholesome literature.[18] The problem was one of controlling the undesirable publications without restricting the flow of wholesome and respectable cheap publications. As Pearson said, "Out of the same mouth proceedeth blessing and cursing, and this fountain sends forth sweet water and bitter. . . . We can very well hold that the press does more good than evil, and yet maintain that the evil is fearfully great."[19] Censorship was not an option for a country proud of its libertarian traditions. When Wiseman proposed an antidote, he was suggesting fighting back in kind, using the press to unmake what it had wrought. While men of science often found it easier to criticise popular works than to do something about them—according to the *Westminster Review*, men of science generally "disdain to popularise science"[20]—there were plenty of Christians who were

---

16. Pearson, *Infidelity*, 477–78.

17. On anti-Catholic feeling, see Wolffe, *Protestant Crusade*.

18. Wiseman's lecture at the Society of Arts Educational Exhibition, 1854, quoted in [Masson], "Present Aspects and Tendencies," 178.

19. Pearson, *Infidelity*, 477–78.

20. "Review of *Kosmos* and *Vestiges*," *Westminster Review* 44 (1845): 153.

willing to get actively involved with the popular press. Although Wiseman had envisaged doing so from a Roman Catholic perspective, it was actually his archenemies, the Protestant evangelicals, who were best suited to fight this battle, having been experts for more than half a century in the use of the cheap press for missionary purposes.[21]

EVANGELICALISM AND THE RELIGIOUS TRACT SOCIETY

Evangelicalism had its roots in the eighteenth-century revivals associated with John Wesley and George Whitefield. By the early years of the nineteenth century, it had become a significant religious force in Britain. Methodism had emerged as a new denomination, the Congregationalists (or Independents) and the Baptists had largely become evangelicals, and there were substantial parties of evangelicals within the (Presbyterian) Church of Scotland and the (Episcopalian) Church of England. These groups all laid great emphasis on the reality of Original Sin and the Fall, and the necessity of accepting Christ's sacrifice on the cross as Atonement for the sins of mankind. Conversion (that is, the conscious acceptance of that sacrifice) was a life-changing moment and the mark of true evangelical faith. Evangelicals believed that faith in the Atonement was their sole route to salvation.[22]

During the eighteenth century, evangelicals had been a minority with great ambitions to influence the religious opinions of the rest of the country, and ultimately the world. By the second and third generations of evangelicalism, in the decades leading up to 1850, the characteristics of the movement had begun to change. Evangelicalism had become part of mainstream, middle-class life. A young man rebelling against his upbringing was now more likely to abandon evangelicalism than embrace it.[23] On the fringes, there were charismatic figures like Edward Irving, whose followers expected an imminent apocalypse and claimed to speak in tongues. Moving farther afield, one might be inspired by John Henry Newman and his followers, who meditated on the historic links between the Church of England and the Church of Rome, and whose Oxford Movement shocked evangelicals by reintroducing ritual, imagery, decoration, and Gothic architecture into the English

---

21. Knickerbocker, "Popular Religious Tract"; O'Brien, "Publishing Networks"; Nord, "Evangelical Origins of Mass Media."

22. Bebbington, *Evangelicalism in Modern Britain*, chap. 1.

23. Ibid., chap. 3. For an example of rebellion against evangelical upbringing, see Edmund Gosse, *Father and Son*.

Church. Equally, one might move in the opposite direction and abandon Christian faith altogether, becoming a Freethinker (or atheist). There were children of evangelical families who followed all of these routes.

The evangelical movement never attained complete control of British religious belief, but it came closer than any other candidate during the nineteenth century. Even those who would not have subscribed to the particular doctrinal beliefs of evangelicalism found themselves influenced by it. Government thinking on issues from political economy and financial rectitude to factory and educational reform was affected by evangelical attitudes to money and personal (spiritual) development.[24] Late-nineteenth-century social work movements grew out of organisations founded for evangelical purposes, while even the rhetoric of such famous non-Christians as Thomas Henry Huxley owed much to evangelical styles of preaching.[25] Equally, evangelical campaigns to prevent postal or railway services desecrating the Sabbath had the potential to affect everyone in Britain, no matter what their personal beliefs. Some of the best-known contemporary references to evangelicals in literary works reflect this desire to interfere with other people's lives, as exemplified by Charles Dickens's righteous do-gooders Mrs. Jellyby and Mrs. Pardiggle. Although some modern commentators have difficulty reconciling the image of evangelicals as interfering kill-joys with their role as social reformers, for nineteenth-century evangelicals, these were all coherent parts of a life devoted to being active in the cause of Christ.

One reason for the evangelicals' national prominence was their propensity for forming organisations to achieve their goals. Some of these organisations had political ambitions, most famously to bring an end to slavery within the British empire, but evangelicals also campaigned to improve factory working conditions, reduce working hours, and preserve the sanctity of the Sabbath. Their emphasis on faith meant that evangelicals were extremely keen to help other people have conversion experiences of their own, and to welcome them (back) to the fold. Hence, their enthusiasm for overseas missionary organisations to introduce Christianity in heathen parts of the world, and their distribution of tracts (fig. 1.1) and creation of domestic visiting societies to reach those in spiritual need within Britain. Reading the Bible and other

---

24. On political economy, see Hilton, *Age of Atonement*, pt. I. On business attitudes, see ibid., pt. II; Garnett, "'Gold and the Gospel.'"

25. Bebbington, *Evangelicalism in Modern Britain*, chap. 4; on social work, see Donald M. Lewis, *Lighten Their Darkness*, chap. 9; on Huxley, see Desmond, *Huxley: Evolution's High Priest*.

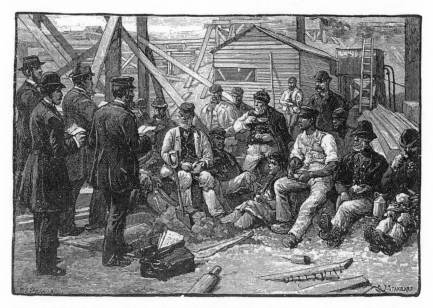

Figure 1.1. Distributing tracts to the navvies. From Samuel G. Green, *Story of the Religious Tract Society,* opp. 81.

religious works was usually seen as a crucial step in acquiring a saving faith, so evangelicals were also at the forefront of attempts to organise Sunday schools, and latterly day schools, to educate the children of the working classes and give them an opportunity to know Christ.

Although this description makes evangelicalism seem a unified, coherent movement, it was actually extremely diverse. It drew members from virtually all of the main Protestant churches. Roman Catholics were always excluded, since they were regarded as being totally in thrall to their priests, rather than making personal decisions based on their own reading of Scripture. Protestants who showed too much affinity with Rome, such as the Tractarians of the Oxford Movement, were also excluded. Unitarians were equally undesirable, although in their case it was because they had taken rational religion too far, and denied the divinity of Jesus Christ. Within the broad group of Protestants who were evangelicals, one of the key divisions concerned the timing of Christ's second coming and the thousand-year reign of peace (the Millennium). There were those who believed that the second coming was nigh, and preached of imminent apocalypse, to be followed by the Millennium. These premillenarians were a minority, although their juicy quotations appear frequently in the historical literature. When historians of science find evangelical opposition to such new scientific ideas as phrenology, geology, and evolution, they frequently come from these more extreme fringes.[26] The majority of mid-nineteenth-century evangelicals, however, were postmillenarians, believing that the apocalypse would happen after the thousand years of peace, rather than before. Postmillenarians believed that Christ would not return until the earth and its peoples had been made ready.[27] This was why they (in contrast to premillenarians) were so actively involved in projects that contributed to the evangelisation of the entire world. These activities were not motivated simply from a desire to improve the lot of their fellow men, but from a desire to bring about the Millennium.

Even though the majority of evangelicals shared this commitment to postmillenarianism, there were plenty of differences among them, starting with the obvious ones of geography and social class. Most evangelicals were from the middle classes and had ambitions for the evangelisation of the working classes and the reform of the upper classes.[28] Nonetheless, there were major social differences between a factory owner from the burgeoning industrial city of Manchester and a gentleman's son studying for ordination at King's College, Cambridge. To take a degree at Cambridge, the student had to profess himself a member of the Church of England. Northern factory owners, on the other hand, frequently came from Nonconformist backgrounds—that is, from one of those denominations (such as Congregationalism or Baptism) whose members refused to conform to the doctrines, practices of worship, and method of governance of the established Church. These differences of religion combined with their social differences meant that the northern factory owner probably took a liberal line on political issues, while the Cambridge student was most likely to support conservative positions. Nevertheless, since party politics as we know them had not yet developed, these political divisions could be relatively fluid.

Even where political affiliations were not at issue, Church governance and doctrine frequently divided evangelicals who had so much else in common. Even among the Nonconformists, the Baptists distanced themselves from other denominations by their refusal to accept the efficacy of child baptism,

---

26. Evangelicals appear as opponents to phrenology in van Wyhe, "Phrenology's Nature," chap. 4; as opponents to evolution in James A. Secord, *Victorian Sensation*, chap. 8. The marginality of the scriptural geologists within evangelicalism is clear in ibid., 177; and in Stilling, "Scriptural Geology."

27. Hilton, *Age of Atonement*, 10; Bebbington, *Evangelicalism in Modern Britain*, chap. 3.

28. Primitive Methodism had unusually high support among the working classes, but even it had plenty of middle-class support. See Bebbington, *Evangelicalism in Modern Britain*, 110–11.

while Presbyterians and Congregationalists disagreed fundamentally over the appropriate systems of administration and authority for churches. And the thorny issue of the legitimacy of state-established churches frequently made cooperation difficult between Church of England evangelicals and those from the Baptist or Congregationalist traditions. Despite all this, one of the features of British evangelicalism in the 1840s was the increasing success of an impulse toward cooperation and pan-evangelical unity.[29]

Pan-evangelical unity had been attempted in earlier decades, but even relatively successful organisations had trouble mediating the tensions that arose between members of different denominations and politics.[30] In the 1840s, however, changing political alignments following Prime Minister Robert Peel's repeal of the protectionist Corn Laws meant that all evangelicals, within and without the Church, were likely to support the liberal point of view, thus temporarily removing the political differences among them. The growing number of perceived threats to Protestantism also prompted evangelicals to unite in common opposition, for instance, against proposed political concessions to Unitarians, against the Oxford Movement, and especially against Roman Catholics. Pope Pius IX's decision in 1850 to reestablish the English hierarchy of Roman Catholic bishops, under the leadership of Cardinal Wiseman (as Archbishop of Westminster), provoked a great deal of outspoken Protestant antagonism to what was seen as "Papal Aggression."[31] The formation of the Evangelical Alliance in 1846 was an attempt to build something more permanent out of pan-evangelicalism, but most of the unity was short-lived.[32] Of the major religious societies of the day, many were organised on denominational lines. The two main exceptions were the Religious Tract Society (RTS, 1799) and the British and Foreign Bible Society (BFBS, 1804). Of these, the RTS was particularly successful at making its interdenominational membership work.[33] Without such management, it could not have become the largest evangelical publisher of general Christian literature in the middle and late nineteenth century.

In the 1790s, evangelicals had organised the principal overseas missionary societies: the Baptist Missionary Society (1792), the London Missionary Society (LMS, 1795), and the Church Missionary Society (1799). By the

---

29. R. H. Martin, *Evangelicals United;* Donald M. Lewis, *Lighten Their Darkness.*

30. For instance, see Howsam, *Cheap Bibles;* R. H. Martin, *Evangelicals United,* chaps. 3–4.

31. R. H. Martin, *Evangelicals United;* Donald M. Lewis, *Lighten Their Darkness;* Wolffe, *Protestant Crusade.*

32. Wolffe, "Evangelical Alliance."

33. R. H. Martin, *Evangelicals United,* chap. 8.

Figure 1.2. The kitchen of a lowly lodging house in London. These were the sorts of people whom evangelicals felt to be in need of salvation. From Mayhew, *London Labour and the London Poor,* i, opp. 258.

end of the decade, however, it was recognised that there were many people nearer to home who needed evangelising every bit as much as those the LMS was trying to convert in the South Seas (fig. 1.2).[34] It was this recognition that led to the foundation of the RTS. At the LMS annual meeting in 1799, the Reverend George Burder of Coventry drew the attention of members to the needs of the heathen at home. As "Bible Christians," evangelicals placed great emphasis on the ability to read the Scriptures and had been among the strongest supporters of the nascent Sunday school movement in the 1780s, which taught elementary reading skills to the children of the working classes.[35] By the time Burder addressed the LMS, the Sunday schools were already regarded as a success, and it was claimed that "thousands who would have remained grossly illiterate, hav[e] through the medium of Sunday-schools been enabled to read."[36]

Quantifying that assurance is difficult, particularly because most estimates of literacy rates are based on the ability to sign the marriage register, while

---

34. On the LMS involvement in the South Seas, see Sivasundaram, "'Nature Speaks Theology.'"

35. Laquer, *Religion and Respectability.*

36. *Evangelical Magazine* 7 (1799): 307.

the skills of reading and writing were not as closely linked as they now are. Marriage registers suggest that 60 percent of late-eighteenth-century males and around 40 percent of females were literate, and that by 1800, female literacy had risen to around 50 percent.[37] Male literacy appears not to have risen until a decade or so later. Such estimates disguise all regional, social, and urban/rural variation, but they also almost certainly overestimate the levels of functional literacy. People able to sign their names may well have been more likely to be able to read than those who could not, but they need not have been very literate. It was one thing to be able to spell out the words on a poster, but quite another to be able to read a textually complex work such as the Bible. As far as evangelicals were concerned, literacy levels among the working classes were not good enough, and the Sunday schools were improving their chances of salvation by allowing them to read about Christ's atoning sacrifice.

George Burder's point was that there was very little reading material available to most of these Sunday scholars. If reading the Bible was a difficult task for most of them, it was unlikely that they would do it very often. And the only other publications that were likely to be found in working-class homes in the late eighteenth century were the inexpensive wares of the peddler: chapbooks, ballads, and execution broadsides (fig. 1.3). Compared with the Bible, such works used simpler language, were more likely to have pictures, and had more interesting subject matter.[38] It therefore seemed likely that former Sunday school pupils would exercise their literacy skills on works their teachers regarded as rubbish, rather than attempting to save their eternal souls. Burder argued that it was a duty "of growing importance widely to diffuse such publications as are calculated to make that ability [to read] an unquestionable privilege."[39] Some private individuals, Burder included, had already experimented with the production and distribution of religious tracts, but it was a time-consuming and expensive process, difficult to sustain for a long period. Even the indefatigable Anglican writer Hannah More had given up her series of "Cheap Repository Tracts" after three years.[40] The LMS members decided that the solution was to set up a society dedicated to producing and distributing cheap tracts. There were already some tract societies

---

37. Schofield, "Dimensions of Illiteracy."

38. On such literature, see Neuburg, *Popular Literature*; Ó Ciosáin, *Print and Popular Culture*.

39. *Evangelical Magazine* 7 (1799): 307.

40. On the tracts, see Knickerbocker, "Popular Religious Tract," chap. 3. On More, see Stott, *Hannah More*; M. G. Jones, *Hannah More*; Spinney, "Cheap Repository Tracts."

Figure 1.3. A ballad seller offers his wares. These are "long songs," three songs printed on a long sheet of paper, the sales of which depended "on the veritable cheapness and novel form" in which they were produced. From Mayhew, *London Labour and the London Poor*, i, opp. 222.

in existence, most obviously the Society for Promoting Christian Knowledge (SPCK, 1698), but theirs was to be a different sort of organisation.[41] First, it was to be interdenominational, whereas the SPCK was firmly linked to the Church of England. Second, the SPCK concentrated on the publication of materials for members of the Church, but Burder wanted a society that would publish for people who were not members of any church.

The new Religious Tract Society was founded in May 1799, with a treasurer, a secretary, ten committee members, and four rules.[42] The committee was to organise the printing of tracts, which would be paid for and distributed by members. The tracts were to be exhortative, presenting simple stories illustrating the vital importance of faith in the Atonement. It was hoped that they would act as "silent messengers," able to reach places where human agents would be rejected.[43] Within a few years, the Society's subscription lists included at least some lay and clerical members of the Church of England, the Church of Scotland and the Secession Church, the Baptist churches, the Independent churches, and the Countess of Huntingdon's Connexion, as well as Methodists, Lutherans, and members of the Society of Friends.[44] By the 1810s, the RTS began to receive significant support from the Church of England, which not only made it more successfully interdenominational than the LMS, but increased the subscription income substantially. By excluding Roman Catholics and Unitarians, and carefully defining the scope of its activities, the RTS was able to manage the tensions among its members successfully enough to avoid the problems of some of the other would-be pan-evangelical societies.[45]

For its first two decades, the RTS was run by a committee assisted by one paid member of staff. Its depository shared premises with a china and earthenware shop in London's Paternoster Row. It was a tiny organisation in comparison with the overseas missionary societies or the BFBS. Even though

---

41. On tract societies around 1800, see Knickerbocker, "Popular Religious Tract."

42. The foundation of the RTS was announced in the *Evangelical Magazine* 7 (1799): 307. For the history of the RTS, see William Jones, *Jubilee Memorial*; Samuel G. Green, *Story of the Religious Tract Society*; Hewitt, *Let the People Read.* A brief history for the bicentenary was prepared by Aileen Fyfe, the United Society for Christian Literature and Lutterworth Press, and published in the celebratory brochure produced by the USCL, *Two Hundred Years of Christian Publishing* (1999), 13–20.

43. On the efficacy of tracts, see Donald M. Lewis, *Lighten Their Darkness*, chap. 6.

44. William Jones, *Jubilee Memorial*, 152–53.

45. R. H. Martin, *Evangelicals United*, 160, 168.

the RTS grew throughout the century, it remained small in relation to these other societies, as the annual incomes illustrated in figure 1.4 indicate. The overseas missionary societies, the BFBS, and the SPCK all enjoyed large memberships who contributed significant financial support. These societies' incomes from subscriptions and donations far outstripped that of the RTS. For instance, over 60 percent of the BFBS income came from such sources, while subscriptions and donations to the RTS accounted for only about 10 percent of its income.[46] The RTS's total income approximated that of the bigger societies solely because of the success of its sales programme. That success could also be seen in the changing fortunes of the Society's premises. In 1844, the RTS built a new depository in the heart of the London

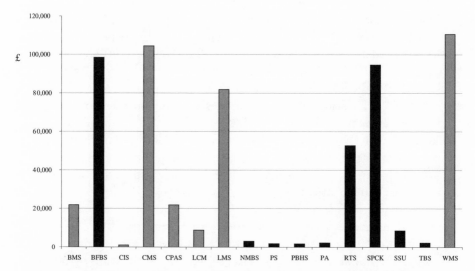

Figure 1.4. Annual income of some religious societies in 1844, from figures printed in *Christian Spectator* (June 1844), 63. Societies represented in black have income from both sales and benevolent sources; those in grey obtain all their income from benevolent sources. The societies are *BMS*, Baptist Missionary Society; *BFBS*, British and Foreign Bible Society; *CIS*, Christian Instruction Society; *CMS*, Church Missionary Society; *CPAS*, Church Pastoral-Aid Society; *LCM*, London City Mission; *LMS*, London Missionary Society; *NMBS*, Naval and Military Bible Society; *PS*, Peace Society; *PBHS*, Prayer Book and Homily Society; *PA*, Protestant Association; *RTS*, Religious Tract Society; *SPCK*, Society for Promoting Christian Knowledge; *SSU*, Sunday School Union; *TBS*, Trinitarian Bible Society; *WMS*, Wesleyan Missionary Society.

---

46. On BFBS auxiliaries and their contributions, see Howsam, *Cheap Bibles*, 39–46; RTS figures from William Jones, *Jubilee Memorial*, app. V.

Figure 1.5. The Depository of the Religious Tract Society, by John Tallis, ca.1846 (published 1847), at 56 Paternoster Row, London. The RTS demolished several existing buildings to build this large neoclassical building in 1844. This building contained the shop and warehouse. The Society also had premises at nearby 65 St. Paul's Churchyard, where the committee meetings were held.

publishing district around St. Paul's cathedral (fig. 1.5). Its neoclassical style carefully eschewed the contemporary fad for Gothic and its connotations of High Churchmanship. The *Illustrated London News* described the depository as follows:

> The interior of the building will be fitted up plainly and substantially, in every respect, as a warehouse. On the ground floor, one continuous room, the entire length of the building [120 feet], will serve as a shop and country department, in which it is important to have a supply of every work on the society's catalogue in all their various bindings; for this purpose, a vast extent of wall room is required; and, in order to render the entire height (about 14 feet) available to this end, there will be a light iron gallery. On each floor, except the shop, there is a small tram-road from end to end, to convey the work from any part of the premises to a hopper at the east-end of the building, which communicates with every floor.[47]

47. *Illustrated London News*, 24 February 1844, 118.

The RTS was still run by a committee, the members of which were extremely active, often sitting on several subcommittees as well as the executive committee; some attended RTS-related meetings several times a week. As almost all were professionals with their own affairs to look after, this indicates the strength of their commitment to the Society and its mission. Yet the extent of the Society's operations had become such that not even the most enthusiastic volunteers could have run it efficiently. The bulk of the work was now done by the sixty paid employees, overseen by the three senior officers: the editor, the superintendent, and the corresponding secretary.

The RTS was a significant force in the British religious landscape. It eventually supplied publications to virtually all the domestic and overseas missionary organisations, of whichever denomination, indicating the centrality of its operations to evangelical activity. It supplied tracts for city missionaries working in London and Liverpool, but it also published foreign language tracts (in more than a hundred languages by 1850) for use in the overseas mission fields. On a more local level, there was a network of auxiliary tract societies across the country, whose members were involved in tract distribution in their home towns and in fund-raising for the parent Society. All the auxiliaries were supposed to remit subscriptions to the London headquarters in return for reductions on the price of tracts they ordered for their own distribution efforts.[48] Of the four hundred auxiliary societies listed in 1850, barely a quarter made such a contribution, and we can assume that these were the most active societies. It is clear from the map in figure 1.6 that the auxiliaries in the industrial areas of Yorkshire and Lancashire made by far the greatest contributions, providing striking evidence of the strong evangelical and philanthropic spirit that flourished in the large industrial cities. These were the places where wealth was being created, but also where there was a clear need for the activities of organisations such as the RTS. As we shall see, it was from the north of England that the impetus came that led to the Society's involvement in popular science publishing.

While the Society's networks were important for placing it at the heart of the British religious scene, its publications had an even greater impact. The original mission of the RTS had been the supply and distribution of religious tracts to the sorts of people who passed through the Sunday schools, in other words, the working classes. All the early publications were short pamphlets (perhaps four, eight, or sixteen pages stitched together) with a

---

48. William Jones, *Jubilee Memorial*, 183–85; Knickerbocker, "Popular Religious Tract," 146–47.

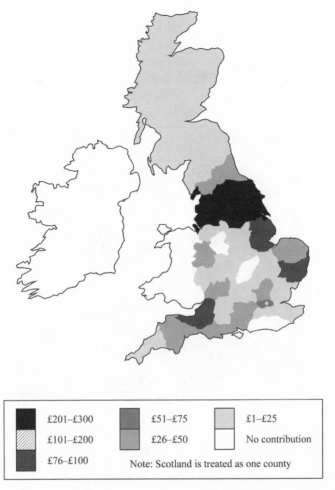

	£201–£300		£51–£75		£1–£25
	£101–£200		£26–£50		No contribution
	£76–£100		Note: Scotland is treated as one county		

Figure 1.6. Financial contributions made by auxiliary societies in each county to the RTS in London in the financial year, 1849–50. Total contributions that year were £1,440. From figures printed in RTS Report (1850): 148–49.

clear religious message, such as that illustrated in figure 1.7. These were produced in print runs of tens of thousands, and usually sold in bulk to local tract auxiliary societies, or to city missionary societies, who left them in pubs, shops, and houses in the hope that they would be accepted where the missionary himself was not.[49] The early RTS may have been small,

---

49. Donald M. Lewis, *Lighten Their Darkness*, 131–49.

TO RAILWAY LABOURERS.

MY FRIENDS—A deep concern for your welfare in this life and for eternity, leads me to write this short address to you. I have been employed among you as a missionary Scripture-reader for a long time, and my great object has been to seek your happiness. I cannot, therefore, think of the dangers to which you are exposed, both in regard to your bodies and your souls, without much grief and anxiety. Your labours are of so hazardous a nature, that it may be said of you as the apostle said of himself, you are " in deaths oft ;" a fall of earth, or many other accidents, may in a few moments destroy any one of you. But

THE RELIGIOUS TRACT SOCIETY, INSTITUTED 1799;
56, PATERNOSTER ROW, AND 65, ST. PAUL'S CHURCHYARD.

Figure 1.7. Religious tract no. 646 (1850). This was a twelve-page tract, with the typical eye-catching picture on the front cover, selling for 3*s.* per hundred. By midcentury, tracts were being targeted at specific groups, such as sailors, emigrants, and railway labourers.

but its expectations were great. By the mid-1820s, it had already issued no fewer than 44.5 million copies of 280 different tracts. By 1850, it had issued over 450 million copies of 5,300 different publications. Over 19 million of those issues, and almost 200 of the new publications, had been in the previous year alone.[50] Thus, even though there were only around 4,500 subscribers to the Society at midcentury (whereas the SPCK had 15,000 subscribers), the RTS publication programme enabled it to reach hundreds of thousands of people, and quite probably millions.[51]

By midcentury, though, the Society was no longer just a tract publisher for the British working classes. It had a wide range of foreign language tracts for overseas missionary work and, more importantly for our story, it had begun to issue nontract publications, thus beginning its transformation into a general Christian publisher. The reasons for the transformation were twofold. First, when the Society had begun producing tracts there had been little or no cheap reading material available, and tracts had only a few competitors. By the 1820s, a wider range of cheap reading material was beginning to appear, in response to which the RTS launched its first periodicals: the *Child's Companion* (1824), the *Tract Magazine* (1824), and the *Domestic Visitor* (1828). Similarly, in the 1840s, when cheap books became more widely available, the Society responded to that development by producing its own, Christian, series of cheap books.

The second reason for the transformation of the RTS publishing programme was a recognition of the existence of a wider and more heterogeneous audience for its publications.[52] It no longer published solely for the working classes deemed to be in need of conversion. It began to publish for members of the working or lower-middle classes who were already converted and for people like the members of the Society—in other words, middle-class evangelicals and their families. For this audience, the Society produced works of Christian devotion, such as its first range of bound books, a series of reprints of theological commentaries and treatises that appeared in the late 1820s. Most of these new publications were much more expensive than tracts, because they were aimed at a more affluent audience. By midcentury, therefore,

---

50. Circulation figures to 1849 are given in William Jones, *Jubilee Memorial,* app. V.

51. RTS membership estimate from lists printed in RTS Report (1850): appendix; SPCK figures in Clarke, *History of the SPCK,* 148.

52. Sheila Haines has argued that tract societies in general developed a more sympathetic understanding of the working classes (and their variety of positions in life) after midcentury, see Haines, "Am I My Brother's Keeper?"

the RTS was publishing a range of books and monthly periodicals—for children and adults, for heathen and Christian—in addition to its enormous catalogue of tracts.

The expansion of the Society's activities in the 1840s and 1850s extended to subject matter as well as format and audience. Up until this point, the Society's works (whether tract, book, or periodical) were all explicitly religious—intended either to convert, or to aid devotions. With the launch of a series of cheap nonfiction books in 1845 (the "Monthly Series") and a new weekly periodical in 1852 (the *Leisure Hour*), this changed. The Society was now publishing general nonfiction, including geography, history, biography, and the natural sciences. These works were pervaded with a distinctly Christian tone, but their subject matter was almost as wide-ranging as that of any commercial publisher. The Society's great success in the second half of the nineteenth century, and the fact that it could realistically entertain its global ambitions of evangelisation, depended on its successful publishing programme in Britain. The expanded range of publications for various audiences that was developed in the 1840s made this possible, both by providing the funds and by enlisting the working classes to work alongside their social superiors in the name of Christ. By the end of the century, the Society had reformulated itself as a British society bringing Christianity to the world, rather than a middle-class society evangelising the lower classes.

The 1840s was thus a decade of important change for the Society. The most public changes were those involving the publications programme, and in the final section of this chapter we will see how those changes were intimately related to developments in the contemporary book trade. Behind the scenes, however, there were also crucial changes in the organisation and functioning of the Society. We have already seen that the Society had moved into new, purpose-built premises in 1844, and its organisational structure had also adapted to changed circumstances. In particular, the Society's operations now involved large amounts of money, and it was competing directly with commercial members of the book trade, something it had not done when it issued only tracts. The sale of tracts at cost price yielded no profits to the Society, and for its first two decades it collected donations and subscriptions (the Benevolent Income) in order to pay the running costs. The arrival of the periodicals and books for middle-class readers changed the balance of the finances. The books did not need to be subsidised, and actually began to produce a surplus (to the committee's surprise) that was eventually able to cover the running costs of the Society. The success of the book sales enabled tracts to be sold at cost as before, but now the Benevolent Income could be used for other purposes. The Society developed a Charitable Fund, which made grants, occasionally of money, sometimes of printing paper. Most often, it "bought" Society tracts from the Trade Fund, which were then given to various missionary societies or philanthropic individuals.

In 1824, the Society had formally separated the two aspects of its operations, charity and trade. The ideal (which was not achieved until around 1835) was that all the subscriptions, donations, benefactions, and legacies received by the Society went into the Charitable Fund and were spent on grants. None of these funds were to support the activities of the Trade Fund, which was to be a completely self-sufficient publishing house. By the late 1830s, the publishing house was sufficiently successful that it could actually add to the Charitable Fund each year, thus allowing the Society to increase its benevolent activities. In the financial year 1849–50 (see table 1.1), the Society received £6,000 in benevolent income and almost £53,000 from sales of publications, indicating just how important the publishing operations had become. The grants scheme accounted for every penny of the Benevolent Income, and was supplemented by a half share (around £2,500) in the surplus from the Trade Fund. The finances continued to work in this manner until the 1890s.[53]

The Society's operations were often misunderstood by contemporaries, and we find the secretary insisting to aggrieved booksellers "that no part of our Subscriptions and Donations are applied to the production of our publications, but all such free Contributions are entirely given away, so that our books must be published on the fair principles of the Trade."[54] To convince the trade that its publications did not have an unfair advantage from subsidies, the RTS continually emphasised that it functioned just like any other publishing house. Admittedly, the Society did occasionally try to make the most of its unusual dual character—for example, by trying to use its charitable status to secure tax exemption. But in general, from the late 1830s onward, its publishing house did operate on entirely commercial grounds.[55]

---

53. In the 1890s, a fall in publishing income meant that it became impossible to cover operating costs and also sustain the (by then) massive grants programme without drawing on capital reserves.

54. USCL/RTS Corr., Jones to E. Thompson, 1 September 1849. See also Jones to J. V. Hall & Co., 30 August 1845.

55. On the attempts to secure tax exemption (which ultimately failed), see USCL/RTS ECM, 9 September 1844; FCM, 11 December 1844 and 17 December 1845. The right to exemption from local rates came from 5 Victoria 36. The RTS was granted a certificate of exemption in 1844, but it was contested, and within a year the Society had lost its certificate.

Table 1.1. Balance sheet for the Religious Tract Society, 1849–50 (as published in the annual report)

Income	£	Expenditure (*continued*)	£
Collection at annual meeting	41	Cost of publications: paper, printing, stereotype plates, drawing and engraving, binding, folding and stitching, translating, editing, etc.	41088
Auxiliary contributions	1440		
Donations and life subscriptions	622		
Annual subscriptions	2786		
Congregational collections	4	Foreign freight, shipping charges, packing cases	372
Christmas cards	46		
Dividends on gas shares	54	Marine insurance	64
Dividends on stock invested by desire of donors	52	Fire insurance	145
		Travelling expenses, visiting auxiliaries	187
Ground rents	49	Rent and Taxes	812
Special Fund for China	121	Expenses of annual meeting	37
Subtotal	**5215**	Repairs and fittings	62
Legacies	847	Advertisements	363
Subtotal	**847**	Society's library: repairing books	35
Interest on temporary investments	51	Salaries and allowances; and wages of warehousemen, clerks, shop-men, porters etc.	2700
Sale of stock: China Fund	185		
Drawback of duty on publications and paper exported, including grants	371		
		Books purchased	77
		Stationery and packing paper	348
Amount received for sales of publications	42394	Cartage, wharfage and carriage	189
		Coals and gas	98
Transferred from Benevolent Fund for grants of publications	7193	Postage and stamps	283
Balance from last year	2649	Disbursements of various incidentals, petty cash, packing cord and boxes, and sundry other charges	646
Subtotal	**52843**		
Total	**58905**	**Subtotal**	**47506**

Expenditure	£		£
		Total	56205
		Balance in cash	1217
Money grants to foreign societies	958	Bills receivable	1086
Grants of printing paper to foreign societies	1371	East India bonds	396
		"Cash in hand"	2699
Grants of tracts, handbills etc. at home and overseas	4608	**[Total]**	**58904**
Grants in aid of libraries for ministers and teachers	555		
Grants in aid of libraries for school libraries	633		
Grants in aid of Union House libraries	25		
Special Fund for China	410		
Collector's Poundage	139		
Subtotal	**8699**		

While this might reassure members of the book trade, the insistence on commercialism worried some subscribers. There were those who believed that an evangelical charity ought not to be engaged in making profit—and particularly not as successfully as the RTS. One subscriber, the Manchester merchant James Dilworth, believed that the Society's prices could be reduced by as much as 25 percent, which would then greatly enhance their circulation.[56] The committee disagreed with Dilworth's claim, and not just because they would have heard from friends in the Bible Society that Dilworth was "more the slave of Personal Vanity than any *Christian*" ought to be.[57] For the committee, reducing prices was not be the best way of increasing circulations, since it would reduce the effectiveness of the Charitable Fund. It would also bring the Society's operations much closer to the break-even point, and endanger the Society's role as steward of the Lord's wealth.[58]

As one of the RTS publications explained, all wealth came originally from God, and it was the Christian's duty to look after it, increase it, and do God's work with it. "Man is but the . . . steward of his bounty."[59] Profit for profit's sake was unacceptable, but reasonable profit to do God's work was extremely acceptable. The pious Christian should be grateful to receive wealth with God's blessing, for with it "he knows that he may make war against ignorance, intemperance, ungodliness, and the monster evils that infest society. At home there is disease to heal, modest merit to reward, struggling industry to foster, and, above all, the glorious gospel to diffuse."[60] The RTS committee members tried to exemplify the concept of stewardship in their careful management of the Society's finances, by making investments to preserve and augment its capital, by carefully examining and assessing the risks of potential new projects, and, of course, in the extensive scheme of international grants to spread the truth of the "glorious gospel." As stewards, they believed that it was possible to combine the commercial interests of the publisher with the benevolent interests of evangelicalism. Reducing prices might have increased circulations, but it would have severely curtailed the Society's grant

---

56. Dilworth's letter to the RTS does not survive, but his arguments can be deduced from the reply, USCL/RTS Corr., Jones to Dilworth, 6 November 1846.

57. The remark of the BFBS traveling secretary, quoted in Howsam, *Cheap Bibles*, 165.

58. Haines's discussion of the RTS is in terms of stewards of the Lord's wealth, Haines, "Am I My Brother's Keeper?" 29. On the problems of Christian businessmen, see Jeremy, *Business and Religion*, especially the introductory chapter. See also Garnett, "Evangelicalism and Business."

59. [Dunckley], *Money*, 166.

60. Ibid., 161–62.

programme. It was far better to create wealth and use it for good purposes than to risk squandering the Lord's bounty through ill-advised or overambitious publishing programmes.

Nevertheless, some people still believed that running a commercial publishing business was at odds with the Society's charitable aims and with the religious convictions of its members and employees. In 1847, an anonymous Congregationalist from Paddington, London, wrote a pamphlet called *The Power of the Press; is it rightly employed?*, which created quite a stir in evangelical circles.[61] Among other things, it argued that "With printing, publishing, correcting, or editing; with large investments in stock, stereotype plates, or copyrights, the author conceives the Religious Tract Society has nothing whatever to do."[62] The writer claimed the society should return to its professed aim of "*circulation*, leaving *production* to individuals."[63] Fortunately for the future of the RTS, most evangelicals appreciated that the point of having a publishing house was to produce the sorts of publications that commercial publishers would not undertake, such as tracts and certain devotional works whose publication was considered a Christian duty. A charitable publishing house ought also to be able to produce its works more cheaply, as there was no need to include a profit margin.

By the 1840s, the RTS was both a large charitable organisation with global ambitions and an important and respected member of the London book trade. Contemporaries could see either aspect, depending where they stood. In general, the Society wanted its subscribers, and the evangelical community at large, to see the charitable side, for its reputation rested on its credentials as an evangelical organisation. Nevertheless, its ability to assist the missionary effort, either by producing suitable publications or by making money grants, was utterly dependent on its success as a commercial publisher. When the Society was founded in 1799, the technologies of printing had not changed significantly since Gutenberg. By 1850, mechanised, steam-powered printing had arrived (fig. 1.8). Furthermore, the organisation of the book trade had been

---

61. The pamphlet was generously excerpted in the *Christian's Penny Magazine* (1847), and in the prospectus for the *British Banner* (1847), according to the *British Banner*, 7 January 1848, 15. The stir was recalled by the Reverend J. Weir, at the 1852 RTS annual meeting, see *Christian Spectator* (May 1852): 723. The pamphleteer's identity is partially revealed in his letter to the (Congregational) *British Banner* on "Religious Literature and the Christian Instruction Society," *British Banner*, 7 January 1848, 15.

62. *Power of the Press*, 39.

63. Ibid., 22.

Figure 1.8. "The contrast between the ancient scriptorium and the modern printing machine," "L.N.R," *The Book and Its Story,* 207. This image exaggerates the transformation in the production and dissemination of print in the mid-nineteenth century by comparing the steam-powered printing machine, not merely with the hand-press, but with the monastic scriptorium.

transformed by changes in copyright legislation and the emergence of a mass market for print. To be a success, the RTS needed to react to these changes.

TRANSFORMATIONS IN PUBLISHING

In the 1790s, new books were expensive. A standard volume would cost at least ten shillings, or more if it was extensively illustrated, and it was common for books to require two or three volumes. These prices were high enough to enable the publisher to break even on a run of just 500 or 750 copies, for only the most successful books went into multiple editions. Ten shillings was an enormous sum of money for a rural labourer, who might earn only twelve or fourteen shillings a week. It was even a large sum for a young curate, whose salary would be somewhere between £ 50 and £ 100 (in other words, between 20*s.* and 40*s.* a week). The combination of high prices and low print runs meant that most books were read by very few people. Since those few people were likely to be from the wealthier and more educated classes, it was a fair enough assumption that books that contained radical politics, dubious religion, or speculative philosophy would have little impact on the nation as a whole. Their readers were likely to be able to judge and dismiss dangerous opinions, and even if they did not, the number of people affected remained small. In the 1840s, however, books became available at a quarter of their previous price, and print runs in the tens of thousands became increasingly common.[64] In 1800, about a half of all books published cost over 10*s.*, with only a fifth below 3*s.6d.* Even the latter cost was not cheap by the standards of a labourer. By 1850, however, around half of the works published would have cost less than 3*s.6d.*, and increasing numbers of them were priced at only one or two shillings.[65] Publishing at such low prices involved much higher break-even points, so these books were being published in runs of several thousand copies at a time. There were, therefore, more books around, and the effect was exaggerated by the increased number of titles being published each year. This was why Thomas Pearson and others became so worried about cheap print.

The origins of these changes in the book trade lay in a decision made in the House of Lords in 1774, which changed the nature of copyright. The consequence was that all works that were more than twenty-eight years old came into the public domain, rather than being owned by a restricted group of London publishers.[66] This transformed publishers' attitudes to new books (which were now the only ones to be protected by copyright), and it opened up the trade in reprints, particularly in the provinces. The ensuing competition among reprint publishers produced some of the earliest "cheap" libraries of standard works, mostly in poetry and drama, but extending to

---

64. See Feather, *History of British Publishing;* on fiction in particular, see Sutherland, *Victorian Novelists and Publishers;* this transformation is described in detail in Weedon, *Victorian Publishing.*

65. Eliot, "British Book Production," 39, fig. 2.6.

66. Feather, "Publishers and Pirates"; Feather, *Publishing, Piracy and Politics;* Amory, "De Facto Copyright."

almost all genres by the 1820s.[67] These works were cheap only in comparison to the gentlemanly octavo volume, for they cost around five or six shillings. Such midpriced works found a market among the middle classes, for whom books had previously been expensive luxuries, but failed to affect either the lower-middle or the working classes.

The expense of printed matter, even after the 1774 decision, meant that few people could afford to have large libraries, and few working-class families owned any books other than the Bible and perhaps *Pilgrim's Progress* (fig. 1.9). Printed matter would have to be available at the cost of a penny or so before it could be afforded by the working classes, and only chapbooks and ballad sheets were that cheap. This was why tract societies had been founded, and why the British and Foreign Bible Society helped poor families buy their own Bibles through a system of penny-a-week subscriptions.[68] In addition to these religious publishing societies, there were also philanthropic organisations that wished to produce cheap publications on other matters. The Society for the Diffusion of Useful Knowledge (SDUK, 1826) was set up by a group of liberals led by Henry, Lord Brougham. Pointing out that there were already "numerous Societies" for disseminating religious instruction, the founders of the SDUK took it as their goal "to aid the progress of those branches of general knowledge which can be diffused among all classes of the community" and to avoid religious topics entirely. Although laying claim to "all classes of the community," the SDUK was particularly concerned with those who "are unable to avail themselves of experienced teachers, or may prefer learning by themselves."[69] Its goal was to provide publications that were inexpensive enough to be purchased by working classes, particularly those of the artisanal class who were expected to be the users of the recently founded Mechanics' Institutes.

The SDUK's first series of publications, the "Library of Useful Knowledge," was sold in fortnightly parts of thirty-two closely printed pages, at one and a half pennies each, although its subsequent "Library of Entertaining Knowledge" appeared in the more expensive format of half-volumes at 2*s.* each. Unlike the RTS, it was not a publisher in its own right, but lent its imprimatur to approved works of other publishers. After a brief association

---

67. Altick, "From Aldine to Everyman." Compare Erickson, *Economy of Literary Form,* on the popularity of different genres according to the economic situation.

68. Howsam, *Cheap Bibles,* chap. 2.

69. "Objects of the Society for the Diffusion of Useful Knowledge" (c.1827), appended to Smith, *Society for the Diffusion of Useful Knowledge.*

Figure 1.9. Books were scarce in working-class houses, so this man bringing home a book (a Bible given to him after a lecture) was a surprise. From [Sargent], *Story of a Pocket Bible*, 320.

with Charles Baldwin, the SDUK quickly became connected with Charles Knight. Fortunately, Knight was as much a supporter of cheap instructive print as were the SDUK members, and he was willing to absorb substantial financial losses to enable the society to continue its work until 1846, when it closed.[70] The existence of those losses, however, and the fact of the SDUK's demise, indicates that it was more difficult than had been anticipated to make a commercial success of cheap instructive print.

The various philanthropic societies, whether religious or secular, had a virtual monopoly on cheap print in the first three decades of the nineteenth century. Or, at least, on legal cheap print. In the decades immediately after the French Revolution, the provision of education to the working classes was perceived as liable to encourage them to imitate their French peers. Purely religious education could be presented as a valuable countermeasure to stem potential unrest, but most other publications for the working classes were potentially politically dangerous.[71] In an attempt to restrict access to knowledge, the government of the day introduced and increased various taxes on printed matter, and encouraged a strict adherence to the blasphemy and sedition laws. Thus, those radicals who printed political tracts inciting revolution, attacking the Church, or even carrying political news could be (and were) prosecuted.

Although the so-called taxes on knowledge were intended to constrain the dangerous sectors of the press, they applied to the entire publishing trade.[72] There was a tax on paper for all publications except Bibles.[73] There was a tax on political content, which meant that newspapers had to be printed on stamped paper to demonstrate that they had paid the tax. Religious tracts and SDUK educational tracts did not need to do this, as they did not carry news, but producing a news sheet on unstamped paper, as radicals frequently did, would lead to prosecution. A third tax was on advertisements, making the marketing of publications more difficult. All of these taxes hit the cheapest publications hardest, since an extra penny or two in tax made little difference to the cost of a ten-shilling volume, but could easily double the price of a cheap print. *The Times* newspaper, for instance, cost 6*d*. per issue, limiting its purchasers to the professional middle classes and institutions such as libraries and coffee houses. These legal restraints made it very difficult for a cheap

---

70. Bennett, "Revolutions in Thought."

71. Vincent, *Literacy and Popular Culture;* Vincent, *Rise of Mass Literacy.*

72. On the taxes, see Twyman, *Printing,* 52.

73. USCL/RTS Corr., Jones to Dilworth, 6 November 1846. See also Charles Knight, *Passages of a Working Life,* ii, endnote.

publication to be successful, and is a major reason why commercial publishers did not show a great interest in publishing for the masses before the mid-1820s. Cheap publishing was legally risky and economically difficult.

Things began to change as political tensions gradually died down and education for the workers came to be seen as a means of preventing, rather than inciting, rebellion.[74] The Mechanics' Institutes and the SDUK had been set up by liberals with reformist attitudes to education, but by the 1830s their views were more widely shared.[75] The earliest commercial publishers to get involved in cheap print were those who shared the societies' commitment to using the press to spread information and instruction among a wider reading audience. Such was the interest that one participant referred to there being a "perfect deluge" of such projects.[76] Some publishers tried to produce series of cheap books, while others launched cheap weekly periodicals.

Archibald Constable and John Murray are two of the commercial publishers who saw the potential of a wider audience in the mid-1820s. They knew of the success of the midpriced reprint publishers, and they were aware of the spread of literacy thanks to Sunday schools and their more recent siblings, day schools (fig. 1.10). Constable and Murray wished to produce original (that is, new) works at the same five- or six-shilling price that had been successful with reprints. The problem they faced was that producing original works entailed extra costs, and necessitated a higher break-even point. There certainly was a market for books at five or six shillings, but it was not clear that it was a big enough market to make either Constable's "Miscellany" or Murray's "Family Library" a success.[77] When Constable went bankrupt in 1826, the "Miscellany" was continued with limited success by George Whittaker, but Murray ended up remaindering over 140,000 volumes of his "Family Library" in the mid-1830s.[78] The price tag was certainly part of the problem, but it did not help that these publishers were used to targeting a relatively small, known group of regular book buyers and had not yet developed the skills to reach readers with different circumstances and habits.[79]

The Religious Tract Society began its own book publications at the same time as Constable and Murray were launching their series. For the RTS,

---

74. Vincent, *Bread, Knowledge and Freedom,* esp. sec. 3.
75. Cardwell, *Organisation of Science,* chap. 3.
76. William Chambers, *Memoir of Robert Chambers,* 207.
77. For the economics of the "Family Library," see Bennett, "John Murray's Family Library."
78. Ibid., 166.
79. Chapman, "Commerce of Literature," 519.

Figure 1.10. Arthur Pendennis is impressed with Blanche Amory when he discovers her helping with reading lessons at the local school. From Thackeray, *Pendennis*, ii, opp. 255.

book publishing was initially seen as a short-term experiment.[80] The justification for the Society's involvement was that it was re-issuing valuable works that were not otherwise available, ranging from sermons through theological treatises and scriptural commentaries to the Bible itself.[81] In later years, the Society's secretary admitted that not all of these works were profitable, but they were nevertheless "books we must keep."[82] Despite the existing success of reprint publishers, the Society initially doubted such a scheme could be self-funding, and appealed for generous individuals to subsidise particular

80. "The Bound Publications of the RTS, II," *Christian Spectator* (March 1841): 26.
81. See William Jones, *Jubilee Memorial*, 128, 129–30, 132.
82. USCL/RTS Corr., Jones to Dilworth, 6 November 1846.

books.[83] The decision to use reprints made the experiment more likely to succeed than the Constable and Murray schemes, and the first books appeared in 1825, priced in the 5*s*. or 6*s*. bracket. Somewhat to the committee's surprise, they sold very well, and the call for subsidies was quietly dropped.[84]

The experiences of Constable, Murray, and the RTS in the late 1820s indicate the uncertainty that publishers faced about both the size of the potential market and the price tag that the market could take. A few years later, the success of the penny weekly magazines demonstrated to the entire book trade that an enormous reading audience definitely did exist—if the price was pennies rather than shillings. The SDUK was one of the pioneers in this field, although the first of the new periodicals was actually *Chambers's Edinburgh Journal*. This was launched in February 1832 by Edinburgh publishers William and Robert Chambers. In the opening number, William Chambers announced: "The principle by which I have been actuated, is to take advantage of the universal appetite for instruction which at present exists; to supply to that appetite food of the best kind, in such form and at such price as must suit the convenience of every man in the British dominions."[85] Chambers had estimated that one and a half pennies weekly was a suitable price, but one penny quickly became the standard for this sort of publication. The SDUK launched its own *Penny Magazine* just a month after *Chambers's Journal*, apparently independently. The Chambers brothers shared the liberal reformist politics of the founders of the SDUK and believed that publications were needed to aid those who desired instruction. They also believed that the prevalence of religious interests in previous attempts to diffuse knowledge had been prejudicial, and declared that *Chambers's Journal* would be free from the personal politics or religion of its founders.[86] Unlike the SDUK, however, W. & R. Chambers was a commercial publishing operation, and the brothers proved that it was possible to combine commerce with philanthropy.[87]

These two pioneers were swiftly followed by the SPCK's *Saturday Magazine* (1832, 1*d*.) and the RTS's *Weekly Visitor* (1833, ½*d*.), as well as numerous other short-lived imitators. The *Weekly Visitor* was a relaunch of the Society's existing *Domestic Visitor*, but it lasted only three years.[88] The *Penny Magazine* and *Saturday Magazine*, on the other hand, survived until

---

83. RTS Report (1848): 83.
84. [Stokes], "Bound Publications of the RTS," 34.
85. Quoted in William Chambers, *Memoir of Robert Chambers*, 210.
86. Ibid., chaps. 9–10; Cooney, "Publishers for the People."
87. Cooney, "Publishers for the People."
88. The *Domestic Visitor* began as a quarterly in 1828.

the mid-1840s, while *Chambers's* closed only in 1956. As a group, these magazines are often referred to as the "first generation" of penny periodicals. They all avoided stamp duty by eschewing any mention of current political discussion. Their remit was to be "instructive and amusing," and this meant a mixture of articles on history, biography, and the natural sciences. Their educational ambitions meant that they did not (except *Chambers's*) admit fiction into their pages, but they did (except *Chambers's*) make extensive use of wood engravings to make their pages more attractive.

Initially, the *Penny Magazine* was the most successful of the group, with early sales reaching two hundred thousand a week, while *Chambers's Journal* could only manage twenty-five thousand.[89] This compares with sales of barely three thousand for the *North British Review* and around ten thousand for the *Quarterly Review,* both of which were heavyweight literary quarterlies.[90] The periodicals of the day with the largest circulations were probably some of the denominational monthly magazines, such as the *Evangelical Magazine* and *Methodist Magazine,* which sold around twenty thousand copies a month.[91] The *Penny Magazine's* early advantage may have been due to its local auxiliary societies, which formed a distribution network that Chambers could not initially match.[92] Nevertheless, the *Penny Magazine* sales declined to around forty thousand, while *Chambers's Journal* increased its circulation to over seventy thousand by 1839, perhaps aided by its more relaxed attitude to fiction.[93] The great success of these periodicals lay in demonstrating beyond doubt that there was an audience for print that could be counted in the tens of thousands.

Statistical work suggests that the decade 1845–55 saw the book trade's most rapid growth of the nineteenth century, as measured by titles published.[94] This was the growth that particularly alarmed Pearson and his friends. There were more publications, they were cheaper, and most of them were not Christian in tone, or even instructive. Periodical publishers realised that, if instruction sold well, unmitigated amusement might sell even better. The "second generation"

---

89. Cooney, "Publishers for the People," 96–97, 101–2.

90. Circulation details are given in the *Waterloo Directory to English Newspapers and Periodicals,* and the *Wellesley Index to Victorian Periodicals.*

91. Topham, "The *Wesleyan Methodist Magazine.*"

92. Cooney, "Publishers for the People," 101–2.

93. Bennett, "Revolutions in Thought"; Anderson, *Printed Image,* chap. 2; Cooney, "Publishers for the People," 98.

94. Eliot, *Patterns and Trends in British Publishing;* Eliot, "*NSTC,* Part I"; Eliot, "*NSTC,* Part II."

of penny periodicals introduced new features such as sensational serialised fiction, current affairs, and letters to correspondents. With such contents, the *Family Herald* (1843), the *London Journal* (1846), and *Reynolds's Miscellany* (1846) were able to sell over 250,000 copies a week by the mid-1850s.[95] By 1855, the *London Journal* had reached an incredible 450,000 a week.[96] The amazing circulations of these periodicals made life difficult for the older "instructive and amusing" periodicals. The *Penny Magazine* and the *Saturday Magazine* both closed in the mid-1840s. It was in this context, with penny periodicals becoming dominated by frivolous and perhaps scurrilous fiction, that the RTS saw the need for an instructive weekly periodical that could compete with the new arrivals, and that would do so in a Christian tone. The *Leisure Hour* was launched in 1852.

Meanwhile, the book publishers had been watching the success of the penny periodicals, and by the mid-1840s some had decided that it was time for another attempt at producing really cheap books. There was a resurgence of interest in midpriced reprints and renewed attempts at cheap reprints. These schemes almost always involved presenting a group of books together, as a "library" or a "series," and several of the earliest and best-known involved fiction. Chapman & Hall's "Monthly Series" and Richard Bentley's "Standard Novels and Romances" offered novels in one volume (rather than the usual three) for around five or six shillings, while in 1848, newcomer George Routledge launched his "Railway Library," offering volumes for just one shilling.[97] From then on, books routinely appeared at a whole range of prices, with some publishers continuing to specialise in new, expensive literature, others aiming at the new mass market, and yet others focusing on the midprice bracket.

Although the spread of licentious and immoral fiction was clearly a concern for evangelicals, nonfiction also posed problems of its own. It, too, was becoming more available, and that raised questions about the way in which scientific or other knowledge ought to be presented for the new audiences. Between 1844–47, there was a flurry of series of nonfiction books, as can be seen from the list in exhibit 1.1. As with fiction, some publishers focused on the five- or six-shilling price range, such as John Murray's "Home and Colonial Library," David Bogue's "European Library," and H. G. Bohn's "Standard Library." Although Bohn was involved in a legal kerfuffle with

95. Anderson, *Printed Image*, intro. and chap. 3.
96. Ibid., 90.
97. Sutherland, *Victorian Novelists and Publishers*, chaps. 1–2; Barnes, *Authors, Publishers and Politicians;* Nowell-Smith, *International Copyright Law*.

Exhibit 1.1. Nonfiction book series launched in the 1840s

"Home and Colonial Library"
    John Murray, 1843–49
    49 titles, in 37 volumes, 6s. per volume
"Miscellany of Useful and Entertaining Tracts"
    W. & R. Chambers, 1844–47
    177 tracts in 20 volumes, 1s. per volume
"Weekly Volumes" (later "Shilling Volumes")
    Charles Knight, 1844–49
    67 titles, in 186 volumes, 1s. per volume
"European Library"
    David Bogue, 1845–47 (taken over by Bohn after lawsuit)
    9 titles, in 15 volumes, 3s.6d. per volume
"Monthly Series"
    Religious Tract Society, 1845–55
    100 titles, in 100 volumes, 6d. per volume
"Standard Library"
    H. G. Bohn, 1846–62
    77 titles, in 150 volumes, 3s.6d. per volume (later 5s.)
"Cheap Series"
    William Collins, 1846–51
    57 titles in 57 volumes, 1s.6d. per volume (later 2s.)
"Scientific Library"
    H. G. Bohn, 1847–62
    48 titles, in 63 volumes, 5s. per volume
"Instructive and Entertaining Library"
    W. & R. Chambers, 1848–52
    17 titles, in 17 volumes, 2s.6d. per volume

Bogue in early 1846, as each accused the other of piracy (fig. 1.11), he emerged as one of the leading reprint publishers, with no fewer than fourteen different "libraries" on offer when he retired in 1863.[98] Unlike Murray and Constable, publishers in this price bracket in the 1840s were using reprints. There were also publishers who aimed at an even wider audience, also by using reprints. W. & R. Chambers may again have been the first with their "People's Editions" of the late 1830s, and they also launched new nonfiction series in the mid-1840s. Charles Knight, now publishing on his own account after the closure of the SDUK, produced a series of "Weekly Volumes" at a shilling each, some volumes of which sold around five thousand copies.[99] Such figures

---

98. A brief outline of the legal affair is given in the entries in DLB 106 for "Bohn" and "Bogue."

99. On sales of Knight's weekly volumes, see entry for "Knight" in DLB 106.

HENRY BOHN'S STANDARD LIBRARY.

On the First of February, or before, will be published,

IN ONE VOLUME, CROWN OCTAVO,

(Containing upwards of 500 Pages, beautifully printed,)

With a fine Portrait,

Price only 3s. 6d.

THE MISCELLANEOUS WORKS AND REMAINS

OF

THE REV. ROBERT HALL;

Containing all the principal Works which are out of Copyright, and several others:

WITH A SHORT MEMOIR, BY DR. GREGORY;

AND

OBSERVATIONS BY JOHN FOSTER.

This Volume will form the First of a Series to be called HENRY BOHN'S STANDARD LIBRARY; of which further particulars will shortly be given in a Prospectus.

The undertaking has been forced upon the Advertiser by the prospect of having some of his best Copyrights infringed by a cheap Serial Publication. Holding, as he does, many of the most valuable Literary Properties, he sees the propriety of taking into his own hands the republication of them in a popular and attractive form. The best German, French, and Italian Authors, by Translators of undoubted talent, will be included; and the whole produced at a price which nothing but the extraordinary march of printing, and the present very extensive demand for cheap books, would render possible.

HENRY G. BOHN looks with confidence to his numerous Correspondents for support in this undertaking; and pledges himself, in return, to afford them more than usual facilities and advantages.

Figure 1.11. Part of H. G. Bohn's accusation of piracy against David Bogue's "European Library." From *Publishers' Circular*, 15 January 1846, 24.

are impressive compared to traditional book print runs, but are significantly smaller than the periodical circulations mentioned earlier. The RTS appears to have been unique in this period in launching a cheap series of *original* works, and in pricing its volumes at less than a shilling.

The book series of the 1840s were successful in a way that their predecessors in the 1820s simply had not been. By using reprints, it was possible to break even at a price of five or six shillings, and publishers like Chambers, Knight, and Routledge showed that it could be done at even lower prices. There are several reasons why this had become possible. One was that the "taxes on knowledge" had begun to be repealed in 1833, although the process was not complete until 1861.[100] Attitudes toward cheap publishing were also changing. Particularly after 1848, there was much less fear of working-class unrest and potential revolt than there had been in the years before the 1832 Reform Act. Despite being the year of European revolutions, the British Parliament's rejection (for the third time) of the People's Charter, a petition demanding extensive electoral reforms, had passed off quietly in April 1848. The reduction of tension enabled an RTS writer to assert that "at the present day it seems to be a settled judgement, that man *should* be educated."[101]

Important as the political changes were, the most obvious cause of the transformation in cheap publishing was the introduction of mechanisation and steam power.[102] Most of the new industrial technologies were developed in the early nineteenth century, but had not at that time seemed relevant to book publishers. Newspaper and penny periodical publishers, on the other hand, were much quicker to see the advantages of faster production, since their product was one that had to be produced in large numbers, quickly, and on time. Investing in steam-printing machinery was an expensive business, and a publisher needed to be able to see a benefit, whether in speed or in eventual cost reductions, to undertake such a step. *The Times* was famously the first to use steam printing in 1814, while W. & R. Chambers installed their first machines in 1833, having found it difficult to print all the copies of *Chambers's Journal* by hand.[103] By 1842, they had four printing machines that were powered by a four-h.p. steam engine.[104] Most book publishers were

---

100. Twyman, *Printing,* 52.

101. Newnham, *Man,* iv.

102. A detailed explanation of printing technologies can be found in Gaskell, *Introduction to Bibliography;* an overview is presented in Twyman, *Printing.*

103. On Chambers, see Cooney, "Publishers for the People," 82–86.

104. "Printing," *Chambers's Information for the People,* no. 90 (revised 1842), 637.

issuing only a thousand copies of products that were not time-limited, and they found hand-press technology perfectly adequate.

The steam-printing machine was certainly the most obvious symbol of the changes, and even in 1851 visitors to the Great Exhibition were still marveling at the speed and size of the latest models. Steam's great advantage was speed, but it also reduced the unit price if there were more than about two thousand copies being printed. Chambers's first machines could print up to 900 sheets per hour, double-sided, whereas an experienced team on a hand press could only print 250 single-sided sheets per hour.[105] The steam-powered printing machine could be fed with enormous sheets of paper (and, later, continuous rolls of paper), which were manufactured by another new invention, the Fourdrinier brothers' paper-making machine. Developed in 1807, the machine continued to use linen and cotton rags as raw materials, but it could produce much larger sheets, more quickly. This did not actually reduce the price of paper, both because of the government tax on paper and because demand outstripped supply throughout the century. The ever-growing demand ultimately led to the development of wood-pulp paper (in the 1870s) to reduce the reliance on the limited number of available rags.

The Chambers brothers claimed that another key component helping to keep their prices down was the technology of stereotyping, which enabled printing to be done not from type, as usual, but from a replica plate. Conventional printing involved taking an impression from thousands of tiny pieces of lead, each with a raised letter, that had been arranged in order by a highly skilled compositor. Acquiring a set of type was a major investment for a printer, and only the very largest houses owned enough to set up more than one or two projects at a time, so there was enormous pressure to free-up type as quickly as possible. This had to be balanced against the likelihood of the work needing to be reprinted, since composition was such expensive labour. Stereotyping involved casting a single lead plate that was an exact replica of the printing surface created by composed type. It did not replace the original composition costs, but it allowed type to be dispersed immediately, even if reprints were to be made at a later date, and, since multiple replica plates could be made, allowed the same work to be printed on several machines simultaneously, perhaps even in several countries. The process of stereotyping had been invented in the 1790s, but its early incarnations were difficult to use reliably. Chambers began to use it in 1832, although it was not until the

---

105. Cooney, "Publishers for the People," 82–86.

late 1840s, following a further technical improvement, that it became more widespread.[106]

Machine-made paper, steam-powered printing, and stereotyping changed the nature of the printing process, but for most of the first half of the nineteenth century they were only of relevance to high-circulation publishers. It was not until the 1840s that some book publishers decided to try to reach the audience of the penny periodicals, and began to adopt some of their technologies. The Chambers brothers, with their experience in periodical printing, were well-placed to move into steam-powered printing of books, while the Religious Tract Society had vast experience from its tract publishing. Its printers regularly steam-printed tracts, and it had been using stereotyping for at least some of its projects since the late 1820s. Once these publishers began to produce cheap steam-printed books, they adopted another innovation—the ready-bound, cloth-covered book. Late-eighteenth-century books were supplied in temporary, plain board covers, and were later bound by their purchasers. Binding in leather, and perhaps decorating in gold, was an expensive process, one that added to the expense of buying the book. Industrial books were bound in cotton cloth, which was cheaper and was also amenable to prefabrication and mechanisation.

————

IN THE 1840s, therefore, when Thomas Pearson saw cheap print everywhere, he was noticing the expansion of the penny periodicals and the development of cheap books. In contrast to the 1820s, cheap print was no longer completely in the hands of such organisations as the Religious Tract Society, and some of the new arrivals on the scene cared more for profit than for literary merit, let alone instructional content or spiritual value. The sciences were certainly not the only subjects to be disseminated more widely by the cheap press, but they had particular features that made their wider accessibility potentially problematic. For the RTS to respond fully and effectively to the new threat of cheap science publishing, it had to grapple not only with the range of industrial technologies, but it also had to make sure that the contents of its publications could achieve their goals. The RTS was not simply selling publications to the nearest paying customer, but rather was trying to get publications to specific audiences, where they would have a specific effect on their

---

106. Ibid., 86–88.

readers. Because its readers had little general education and only basic literacy skills, RTS publications had to be simple to understand, which applied both to the scientific content and to the theological framework that was the point of the exercise. The Society shared with Chambers a strong awareness of the difficulty of (as the *British Quarterly Review* put it) "conveying useful information through a medium of an essentially popular character, without risking its popularity."[107] In this context, "popular" was not a description of the reception of a work (for example, a book was popular because everyone read it and liked it), but a statement about the intended audience envisaged by writers and publishers. This was the common usage.

A "popular" work was one that was intended for "the people," which by the middle of the nineteenth century increasingly included the working classes. Publishers such as the RTS and Chambers were early to realise that economic accessibility (that is, cheapness) was not enough. In the 1820s and 1830s, midpriced reprints were often labeled "popular" because their price was making them more accessible than before. By the 1840s, however, publishers who were committed to reaching the working classes were also focusing on literary accessibility, making sure that the language used was as clear and simple as possible. These changes are reflected in the changing meanings of the verb "to popularize," which came to mean "to make abstruse and technical subjects generally accessible" rather than simply "to make available to the populace."[108] This commitment to effective popularisation was why William Chambers was critical of the SDUK for publishing treatises that "were on the whole too technical and abstruse for the mass of operatives," and why the RTS insisted on having original works, specially written, in its "Monthly Series."[109]

Yet, although there are many similarities in the activities of the RTS and Chambers, their attitudes to Christianity were completely different, which means that the RTS saw itself as battling *against* Chambers. This sense of a battle in the arena of the cheap press was well expressed in that anonymous pamphlet from 1847, *The Power of the Press: is it rightly employed?* Its writer saw a battle between Good (religious publications) and Evil (the apparently numberless infidel publications), and attempted to quantify it. By including

---

107. "Cheap Literature," *British Quarterly Review* 29 (1859): 331.
108. OED, entry for "popularize" (1833). These new meanings of "popularize" coincide with new meanings of "the people," as discussed by Klancher, *English Reading Audiences*, chap. 3.
109. William Chambers, *Memoir of Robert Chambers*, 213.

the output of all the Bible societies, the RTS, and the religious periodical press, he arrived at a "religious" total of around 24.5 million publications a year.[110] Meanwhile, he calculated the total for the atheistic and corrupting presses at around 28.5 million a year, and that included only the main representatives of the stamped periodical press.[111] He estimated that there were another half million illegal publications of a sort "so awfully polluting" that the writer wished not to investigate too closely.[112] Infidelity appeared to be winning.

And the situation was even worse than it seemed. There was another category of works whose numbers the pamphleteer felt unable to estimate, but which had to be added to the opponents of religion. These were the works whose neutrality on issues of religion and morality "must be construed into virtual hostility."[113] By not mentioning Christianity when they could and should, such works were sinning by omission, and should be counted as agents of the "enemy cruising under a neutral flag."[114] Secular works could actually be more dangerous than those that were obviously infidel, for as Pearson later explained, "many a domestic circle ... would justly repel the organ of an atheistic secularism, or the grossly immoral trash of the Reynolds school, because their irreligion is too palpable," but they might admit a secular publication "for its 'recreation and harmless pastime,' while they receive along with it (knowingly or unknowingly) the teachings of an infidel theology."[115] That attitude to secular knowledge meant that all the publications of the Chambers brothers, as well as those of the SDUK and Charles Knight, had to be regarded as opposed to true religion. Those publishers were all advocates of large print run, cheap publications, so their annual output added to that of the infidel press would leave religious publishers even further behind. Although the pamphleteer did not point it out, those publishers were also known for issuing instructive works on the sciences. The situation looked bad for religion.

After setting the scene, the anonymous pamphleteer went on to accuse the Christian churches of failing in their duty toward the working classes they had helped make literate. "The writer conceives that, neither in respect to quantity or quality has the Church ever met the requirements of the strong

---

110. *Power of the Press*, 17.

111. Ibid., 15.

112. He claimed that pornography was easily obtainable beside cheap periodicals and newspapers, ibid., 14.

113. Pearson, *Infidelity*, 505.

114. [Patmore], "Popular Serial Literature," 117. See also Pearson, *Infidelity*, 505.

115. Pearson, *Infidelity*, 503.

appetite she was bound in justice to satisfy."[116] The numbers involved on the corrupting side appeared so enormous, yet, demanded the pamphleteer, "Where is the aggressive and defensive literature of the united Church of Christ?"[117] He called for the churches and the religious publishers to do more—and he focused specifically on the RTS. This choice was no doubt determined in part by his own evangelicalism, but it was also a logical choice. He was concerned primarily with philanthropic publishers, assuming that it was the quest for profit that encouraged publishers to stray into secular and infidel publishing, so his focus was on the large religious societies. The RTS did not have the same resources or support as the BFBS or the various overseas missionary societies, but those societies had very restricted publishing programmes. It also lacked the support of the SPCK, but nevertheless it was circulating at least six times as many publications a year as that society. [118] The RTS was thus by far the most significant player in cheap religious publishing in Britain. And in fact, by the time that the pamphleteer wrote, it had already recognised the problem of the infidel and secular press, and had launched a response.

Its Monthly Series had been one of the first of the cheap non-fiction series of the mid-1840s, and in launching it and later the weekly *Leisure Hour* magazine, the RTS chose a particular method of responding to the threat. Some evangelical groups wanted to reply directly to particular publications and refute them. The Edinburgh-based Society for the Opposition of Popular Errors had been founded in 1846 specifically to attack *Constitution of Man* and *Vestiges of the Natural History of Creation*.[119] The RTS did not adopt this mode of action. Rather than respond to specific publications, it produced works that could be promoted as a positive contribution to Christian general knowledge and not merely an attack on infidel works. It specifically rejected an offer from the Edinburgh society of the right to reprint tracts written against *Constitution of Man*.[120]

The RTS had a more subtle aim than simply defeating big-name infidels. Very few of its works took issue with explicitly controversial subjects or named

---

116. *Power of the Press*, 4.
117. Ibid., 18.
118. SPCK circulations are given in Clarke, *History of the SPCK, passim.*
119. This is surely the same society as that mentioned in James A. Secord, *Victorian Sensation*, 188–89 (where it is referred to as the society opposing "Prevalent Errors").
120. USCL/RTS ECM, 28 May 1850.

specific targets—for why draw them to people's attention?[121] It wished to demonstrate that all forms of knowledge, and particularly the sciences, were still part of a Christian framework. They were not to be abandoned to the infidel and secular publishers. If people could be persuaded to assuage their curiosity about the sciences with RTS publications, then they need never encounter the dangers of reading alternative works on the sciences. More realistically, the works could act as an antidote. Readers who might have thought that there was no other option than viewing the sciences in a secular manner could be shown that there was an alternative. It was always assumed that, in a fair battle, Good would vanquish Evil. The RTS publications had to walk a fine line between being religious enough to perform their function but not so religious that potential readers were repelled. The answer to this was Christian tone.

---

121. William Whewell shared this view, and therefore refused to review *Vestiges*, nor did his response to it (*Indications of the Creator*, 1846) name its target. See James A. Secord, *Victorian Sensation*, 227–9.

II

Christian Knowledge

AS corresponding secretary to the Religious Tract Society in the 1820s and 1830s, one of William Jones's tasks had been to travel around Britain meeting local representatives of the Society, speaking at gatherings, encouraging the formation of new auxiliary societies, and generally drumming up support and subscriptions for the Society. These duties took up eight or nine months of the year, and Jones apparently came to be a noted public speaker.[1] His family supported his RTS activities—indeed, in later life, his eldest son wrote for the Society and his middle son became its business manager—but they must have been relieved when he became general secretary in the mid-1840s, and was based in London. He did not give up traveling altogether, however, and in August 1844 he told the Society's executive committee about a conversation he had had with "an intelligent friend of the Society in a large town in the north of England." This friend suggested that the Society should begin to produce cheap books "to meet 'the new development and growing intelligence of the times,' and to 'supply a large number of people who could only spare time enough for the perusal of a small volume, and whose means would not allow of a large purchase' with works of acknowledged merit and worth on literary or scientific subjects."[2]

This was still three years before the call to arms by the anonymous pamphleteer whom we met in chapter 1, and nine years before Thomas Pearson's condemnation of the press as an agent of infidelity, but the RTS was already well aware of the threat posed by "the rapid extension of secular information and the unexampled activity of the sceptical and licentious press."[3] It accepted

---

1. William Henry Jones, *Memorials of William Jones*, chaps. 2–3.
2. Ibid., 124. Notice that the phrases quoted by Jones in this passage are those that appeared in the promotional material for the "Monthly Series" (see fig. 2.1). It seems highly probable that the account of what the "friend" said has been shaped by the advertisements, rather than vice versa.
3. RTS Report (1850): 141.

that these threats called "loudly on Christians to abound in the work of the Lord," and that this necessitated extra support for "the constant dispersion of decidedly religious books, adapted to the times in which we live."[4] The Society was thus adopting the relatively liberal position of maintaining the value of a free, uncensored press in the face of the threat posed by the cheap press, but it had to make sure that its own publications could convey Christian faith as a vaccination or antidote for readers. The effectiveness of such a plan depended on two different issues. One was the Society's ability to produce a publication that could reach the same audience as the competition, and we shall see in later chapters how this was achieved. The second concern related to the impact the publications would have, assuming they reached their intended readers.

In setting out to create a new sort of Christian publication, the Society had to decide which subjects should be included and how they should be presented. To learn what would be successful with the intended audience, the RTS could examine the contemporary activities of other publishers. The key to the whole project was the manner in which the subjects were linked to Christianity. The Society was hardly the first to combine faith with informative nonfiction, but its criticisms of the way this was managed by existing possible models meant that it had to develop its own style of presentation. If the Christian motive was too obvious, it would prevent the publications from reaching their targets. But if the Christian message was too subtle, it could not perform its function. Out of the efforts to resolve this conundrum came the RTS's concept of "Christian tone."

When William Jones told the committee about the suggestion to produce a series of cheap books on "literary and scientific subjects," it approved immediately. This became the "Monthly Series" of sixpenny volumes that ran from 1845 to 1855. In August 1844, oversight for the series was delegated to the copyright subcommittee, and the editor, William Lloyd, began recruiting possible writers.[5] The first volume appeared sixteen months later on December 1, 1845. The Society created a standard paragraph of manifesto for the series, which appeared time and again in the advertisements (fig. 2.1). This paragraph served as the Society's formal description of the content, format, purpose, and intended audiences of the series. Unlike most of its previous publications, these new works were not specifically about religious subjects, but they would nevertheless be Christian and "SCRIPTURAL" in tone.

---

4. Ibid.
5. USCL/RTS CCM, 14 August 1844.

They were to be specially written for the series ("Original"), and would be small and cheap ("Portable" and "Economical"). And they were to be "Popular," which implied a large, if not mass, audience. The conversion of sixpence monthly into "less than three half-pence per week" explicitly placed the series in the same price bracket as *Chambers's Edinburgh Journal* and the penny magazines, suggesting that it was aimed at the working classes. Yet, the final sentence is striking for the range of audiences and uses that were intended to be met by a single product. The same work was expected to suit

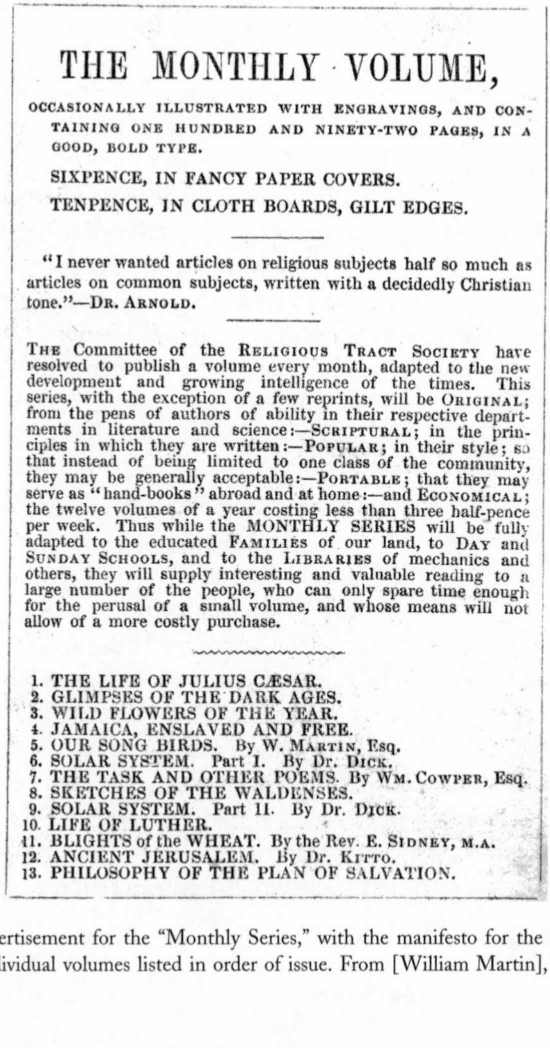

THE MONTHLY VOLUME,

OCCASIONALLY ILLUSTRATED WITH ENGRAVINGS, AND CONTAINING ONE HUNDRED AND NINETY-TWO PAGES, IN A GOOD, BOLD TYPE.

SIXPENCE, IN FANCY PAPER COVERS.

TENPENCE, IN CLOTH BOARDS, GILT EDGES.

"I never wanted articles on religious subjects half so much as articles on common subjects, written with a decidedly Christian tone."—Dr. Arnold.

The Committee of the Religious Tract Society have resolved to publish a volume every month, adapted to the new development and growing intelligence of the times. This series, with the exception of a few reprints, will be Original; from the pens of authors of ability in their respective departments in literature and science:—Scriptural; in the principles in which they are written:—Popular; in their style; so that instead of being limited to one class of the community, they may be generally acceptable:—Portable; that they may serve as "hand-books" abroad and at home:—and Economical; the twelve volumes of a year costing less than three half-pence per week. Thus while the MONTHLY SERIES will be fully adapted to the educated Families of our land, to Day and Sunday Schools, and to the Libraries of mechanics and others, they will supply interesting and valuable reading to a large number of the people, who can only spare time enough for the perusal of a small volume, and whose means will not allow of a more costly purchase.

1. THE LIFE OF JULIUS CÆSAR.
2. GLIMPSES OF THE DARK AGES.
3. WILD FLOWERS OF THE YEAR.
4. JAMAICA, ENSLAVED AND FREE.
5. OUR SONG BIRDS. By W. Martin, Esq.
6. SOLAR SYSTEM. Part I. By Dr. Dick.
7. THE TASK AND OTHER POEMS. By Wm. Cowper, Esq.
8. SKETCHES OF THE WALDENSES.
9. SOLAR SYSTEM. Part II. By Dr. Dick.
10. LIFE OF LUTHER.
11. BLIGHTS of the WHEAT. By the Rev. E. Sidney, M.A.
12. ANCIENT JERUSALEM. By Dr. Kitto.
13. PHILOSOPHY OF THE PLAN OF SALVATION.

Figure 2.1. Advertisement for the "Monthly Series," with the manifesto for the series across the top, and the individual volumes listed in order of issue. From [William Martin], *British Fish and Fisheries,* 1.

the children of middle-class families as well as their poorer peers at the Sunday schools, and to fit equally in the library of an educated family or an artisan.

What was not made explicit in the manifesto paragraph was the purpose of the series, or the effect these works should have on their various readers. When the "Monthly Series" was announced in the *Christian Spectator,* the Society's bimonthly newsletter for its subscribers, readers were reminded that "it becomes an imperative duty to make new and enlarged exertions, as the great mass of the community is more capable of profiting from instruction" than had been the case when the Society was founded.[6] This comment implies that the series was intended to provide instruction. Yet there were plenty of publishers other than the RTS who had experience with nonfiction publishing, and might have been thought better able to fill a gap in the market for instructive works. This was, of course, the problem. The RTS was not responding to a craving for information as much as reacting to other publishers' responses to it. As the Society's 1850 annual report noted, "that craving is met by much literature of a most debasing and pernicious character," which is "infidel and most demoralizing."[7] The Society borrowed a quotation from Dr. Thomas Arnold of Rugby as a slogan for the series: "I never wanted articles on religious subjects half so much as articles on common subjects written with a decidedly Christian tone."[8] The new series would fill this need.

Although its first response was a cheap book series, the RTS was not unaware that it was the penny periodicals that were reaching the largest audiences in the 1840s and exercising the greatest potential influence. In February 1848, the committee began to discuss whether it should launch a weekly magazine. Its earlier attempt, the *Weekly Visitor* (1833), had survived only three years. The SPCK's *Saturday Magazine* (1832) had done better, but it had closed in 1844. The amazing growth of the new generation of penny magazines showed that there was a need for a new Christian competitor, but the committee was not convinced that the time was right to undertake a project "requiring so large an outlay and involving so much risk."[9] The idea was discussed again in May and September of the same year, but the copyright committee still insisted that the Society should not undertake it because of "the large outlay" and "the Weekly loss that would take place."[10] Part of the reason for the committee's fears was that 1848–49 was a time of

---

6. "Announcement of the Monthly Volume," *Christian Spectator* (Sept. 1845): 65.
7. RTS Report (1850): 123.
8. "Announcement of the Monthly Volume," *Christian Spectator* (Sept. 1845): 65.
9. USCL/RTS CCM, 23 February 1848.
10. USCL/RTS CCM, 20 September 1848.

relative depression in the book trade. But the committee was also concerned about the performance of its existing periodicals. After its brief incarnation as a weekly, the *Visitor* had become a three-penny monthly magazine, but it was suffering from falling sales. Until the situation with the *Visitor* was resolved, the committee felt unable to embark on an experimental periodical.

In July 1851, the longtime editor of the *Visitor*, Esther Copley, died and the resulting necessity for change stimulated the committee into action. It decided that it was at last a suitable time to launch a weekly penny periodical. The *Visitor* would be closed at the end of 1851, to be replaced by the new journal. Early suggestions for the title of the new publication were firmly linked to the Society's past. The initial favourite, *Old Humphrey's Journal; or Christian Visitor,* had an explicitly Christian mission, retained the link to the older periodical, and played off the success of Copley's contemporary, George Mogridge. Mogridge specialised in pseudonymous authorship, writing for the RTS as "Old Humphrey" as well as being one of several British writers to assume the identity of children's writer "Peter Parley."[11] In the end, after a brief flirtation with the title *Friend of the People,* the periodical appeared in January 1852 with a completely new name: the *Leisure Hour; a family journal of instruction and recreation.*[12]

The title was a reference to the campaigns to reduce working hours, in which evangelicals were active. Lord Ashley (later Earl of Shaftesbury) is well known for his efforts to reduce the hours worked by women and children in factories, which culminated in the Ten Hours Act of 1847.[13] The related Early Closing Movement tried to reduce working hours for men, and not just for factory workers, by persuading employers to close their businesses earlier in the evening. Its supporters believed that "every man should have a leisure hour," a slogan borrowed by the RTS to promote its new periodi-cal.[14] This leisure hour was supposed to be used for healthy recreation and self-improvement. George Cruikshank ridiculed the movement in his *Comick Almanack,* suggesting that all private homes should close at 8 PM, since "after cooking our dinners, and washing up our tea-things, the female servant has

---

11. Darton, *Children's Books in England,* 221–28; Jackson, *Engines of Instruction,* 189–90; James A. Secord, Introduction to *Peter Parley.*

12. USCL/RTS ECM, 23 September 1851 and 28 October 1851. On the *Leisure Hour* in comparison with the competition, see Anderson, *Printed Image,* 167.

13. Battiscombe, *Shaftesbury,* chap. 14.

14. "Periodical Literature: a new weekly magazine," *Christian Spectator* (Nov. 1851): 665; *Publishers' Circular,* 4 December 1851, advert 989.

a right to go and get her mind cultivated, and her tastes elevated."[15] Where Cruikshank pointed to the chaos this would produce, the RTS believed that the benefits to shop workers, clerks, and others in the service industries would be enormous. It had itself received a petition from its employees in 1845, and had agreed to close its depository an hour earlier, at 7 PM, on the condition that the extra hour of leisure would be devoted "to healthful recreation, mental improvement and the duties and enjoyments of domestic life." Unsurprisingly, it added the hope that "a regular attendance on the means of religious improvement will never be overlooked."[16] The Society promoted the *Leisure Hour* as the ideal blend of mental and religious improvement for those newly acquired hours of freedom. Together, the "Monthly Series" and the *Leisure Hour* were the Society's response to the threat of the popular press, and its first ventures into secular publishing.

THE CLASSIFICATION OF KNOWLEDGE

When the "Monthly Series" was completed, in August 1855, it contained one hundred volumes, all of which were 192 pages long and issued in uniform green paper covers at sixpence, or cloth-covered boards with gilt edging at tenpence (fig. 2.2). (The whole series is listed in order of issue, and with the names of the mostly anonymous writers, in appendix B.) There was no apparent order to the issue of the volumes. The series began with a *Life of Julius Caesar*, which was followed by *Glimpses of the Dark Ages* and *Wild Flowers of the Year*. It ended with *The Field and the Fold, Paris: ancient and modern* and a *Life of Calvin*. Almost all of these short volumes were complete in themselves, with a few exceptions such as the two volumes of *The Solar System* and the four volumes on the *Lives of the Popes*. Overall, there were around twenty titles each in biography, history, and the natural sciences, with ten in geography. The remainder included contributions on industry, philosophy, and social science, as well as two volumes of William Cowper's poems. Although the series is clearly part of the general phenomenon of cheap nonfiction series, it does have some notable differences. As well as the low price and short length, which will be discussed later, the series had a strong emphasis on true knowledge, and contained an unusually high proportion of works on the sciences.

---

15. Cruikshank, *Comick Almanack*, ii, 213.
16. USCL/RTS FCM, 9 July 1845.

Figure 2.2. The Monthly Volumes in their tenpenny binding of dark green cloth-covered boards, with blind embossing and gilt edges. The volumes were 14.5 cm by 9.5 cm, and just over a centimetre thick.

Knowledge was a topic of much debate in the 1840s, particularly in the sciences. Claims to expertise were grounded in claims about knowledge, and although the gentlemen of science who ran the British Association for the Advancement of Science liked to think that they had the right to decide such matters, their claims were still contested by some writers of popular science, as well as by biblical literalists. The British Association created the concept of a unified field of knowledge called "science," even if William Whewell's neologism for its practitioners ("scientists") was slow to catch on, but the association also carved up that field into sections. The designation of "Mathematical and Physical Science" as Section A, and the relegation of "Zoology and Botany" to Section D, made a statement about the association's vision of the classification and hierarchy of knowledge.[17] Yet issues about what counted as knowledge and how it should be classified also had practical consequences for the editors and publishers who wished to present knowledge to the masses.

One of the threats of the cheap press came from the prevalence of licentious and corrupting works of fiction, so one possible response for the RTS would have been to produce fiction with a better standard of writing and more suitable morals. Some of the other publishers of cheap nonfiction series did include works of "literature" alongside the other volumes. Charles Knight, for instance, included five works of "Original Fiction," six by the "Great Writers" and nine on "General Literature" among his sixty-nine "Shilling Volumes." There was already a genre of evangelical moral fiction that the RTS could have used but it chose otherwise.[18] To be effective, its publications had to be convincing, and only truth had the power to convince. The Society agreed with the *British Quarterly Review* that attempts to convey instruction or morals through fictive narratives were "absurd or illogical," since authors clearly had the power to come to any conclusion they wished.[19] It was for this reason that the Society was so keen on checking the veracity of the stories that it used in tracts, believing that their power to convert readers would be undermined if the narratives were fictional.[20] As the *Christian Spectator* explained in 1845, "Truth, in the highest sense of the term, is the only means for counteracting human depravity, and producing what is morally

---

17. On the British Association, see Morrell and Thackray, *Gentlemen of Science;* Morrell, "Brewster and the Early British Association."

18. Rosman, *Evangelicals and Culture,* 189–93.

19. "Cheap Literature," *British Quarterly Review* 29 (1859): 313–45, at 332.

20. Samuel G. Green, *Story of the Religious Tract Society,* 10. See also USCL/RTS CCM, 20 February 1850.

excellent."[21] The RTS response to the threat of the cheap press had to be based on knowledge.

Since knowledge comes in many forms, the Society then had to decide what sort of knowledge was suitable for educating the working classes of Britain and convincing them of the continuing relevance of Christ to their lives. It referred to the sort of material that appeared in the "Monthly Series" and the *Leisure Hour* as "general" or "secular" knowledge.[22] Before this point, the Society had published only on "sacred" knowledge, in the form of tracts for conversion, or scriptural commentaries and sermons for devotional reading. The development of its secular publishing programme therefore appears to be a shift in emphasis. Yet the line between sacred and secular could be a matter of judgement. In the 1830s, the Society had no trouble including such subjects as natural history as part of sacred knowledge. In 1833, it had published a *Popular Introduction to the Study of Quadrupeds; with a particular notice of those mentioned in Scripture.* Most of this work was natural history, but it was presented as an aid to the understanding of the Scriptures, and thus perfectly in keeping with the Society's other devotional works. A companion volume on birds followed in 1835, but by the early 1840s, the category of the sacred appeared to have expanded even further. Apart from the infamous serpent, the *Popular History of Reptiles, or introduction to the study of class Reptilia, on scientific principles* (1842) had few opportunities for describing the reptiles mentioned in Scripture. Nevertheless, in the curiosities of the anatomical arrangements of reptiles, the writer claimed that "the atheist is at once confounded, while the man of science and piety recognizes with pure delight the power and superintending care of Him."[23] Even though the reptiles book was not as directly a guide to the reading of Scripture as its predecessors, it was written in a strongly devotional tone and could be presented as part of the Society's publishing programme on sacred knowledge. Indeed, given evangelicals' emphasis on the all-pervading nature of faith, we might ask whether any subjects were *not* sacred. In 1841, the *Christian Spectator* claimed that all "subjects that describe God's works, and illustrate his word, or refer to his dealings with the children of men through successive generations" could not be truly secular.[24] On this reading, the natural sciences, history, and biography

---

21. "Announcement of the Monthly Volume," *Christian Spectator* (Sept. 1845): 65.
22. For the RTS on "secular knowledge," see RTS Report (1847): 116–17; RTS Report (1851): 115.
23. [William Martin], *Popular History of Reptiles,* 7 and *passim.*
24. "Notice of objections," *Christian Spectator* (July 1841): 67.

could all be claimed as sacred, and the *Christian Spectator* could suggest only "trade, statistics, or politics" as secular subjects.[25]

This definition was based on the medieval distinction between the sacred and secular (or profane) realms. In this context, "secular" meant "belonging to the world and its affairs as distinguished from the church and religion."[26] It refers to those things in the world that are not directly concerned with or devoted to the service of religion. By arguing that virtually all subjects were sacred, the RTS in the early 1840s was reiterating the evangelical perception that everything in the world was part of the Creation and God's Providence. By the mid-1840s, however, the boundaries had moved. Geography could now be described as "a branch of secular knowledge," as could history and the natural sciences.[27] This description was a recognition that some sorts of knowledge were more directly linked to religion and theology than others. Secular knowledge had a less direct connection with salvation and was not under the control of the church, but it was nevertheless useful, and could aid the Christian in his daily life and in his understanding of some aspects of sacred knowledge.

There is no implication in this usage of "secular" that the religious was to be actively excluded from geography or the sciences. That usage (which is now the common one) became more prevalent only after the development of George Holyoake's "secularism" in the 1850s and the campaign for secular education in the later nineteenth century.[28] When the RTS wished to refer to publications that neglected to mention religion while discussing history or science, it only rarely used the adjective "secular." It was more likely to describe the works directly as those that omitted or neglected Christianity. As Pearson put it, these were works that "pass by Christianity in silent contempt, falsely exalt human nature, and endeavour to keep it independent of divine spiritual aids. This class of cheap literature sins in the way of defect rather than in positive statements."[29] Some commentators called these works "neutral" with regard to religion, yet evangelicals felt this to be misleading, since they were really enemies in disguise.[30]

The RTS regarded secular knowledge as important, and a series of articles in the *Christian Spectator* in 1844–45 argued that Christians had a duty to

25. Ibid.
26. OED, "secular," meaning A.I.2.a. See also A.I.2.c and A.I.2.d.
27. RTS Report (1853): 115.
28. OED, "secular," meaning A.I.4.
29. Pearson, *Infidelity*, 504.
30. For example, [Patmore], "Popular Serial Literature," 126; Pearson, *Infidelity*, 505.

study natural history, history, and geography to better understand the world, and God's relationship to it and mankind.[31] As one of the "Monthly Series" writers expressed it, "Far from condemning with narrow bigotry the general pursuit of knowledge, the Christian sees how valuable every new acquirement may become, and how greatly it may subserve the cause of truth."[32] The Society was thus not opposed to the increased dissemination of secular knowledge, but it faced the problem that many of the other publishers who were issuing cheap publications on history, geography, and the sciences were presenting those subjects without religion. The Society for the Diffusion of Useful Knowledge and W. & R. Chambers were prime examples of this tendency. When the RTS declared its opposition, in 1850, to the "rapid extension of secular information" it made a rare conflation between the two meanings of "secular" to refer not only to nonsacred knowledge but also to the absence of religion.[33] It also described its own programme of new publications as "secular," but added a rider to make clear which definition of "secular" was meant. Thus, the "Monthly Series" was described in 1847 as a series "of works on secular subjects treated in an evangelical manner."[34] On other occasions, the Society avoided the word entirely, and used the term "general" or "common" in its place, as with the slogan it used in advertisements for the "Monthly Series": "common subjects, written in a decidedly religious tone."[35]

When addressing members of the Society through the *Christian Spectator,* the new "secular" works of the 1840s could be presented as part of the same tradition as the histories of quadrupeds, birds, and reptiles—that is, as useful information to aid Christians in their understanding of God's Works and Word. Yet the principal purpose of the new works was that they were to be marketed much more widely; indeed, their primary audience was to be readers in need of conversion, rather than those already saved. For such readers, there was no utility in arguing that it was a Christian duty to study history or the sciences. These intended readers already sought information on such subjects, as the sales of other publishers' works testified. The problem was to ensure

---

31. "On the union of general and scriptural knowledge," *Christian Spectator* (Oct. 1844): 89–90; "The society's works on natural history," *Christian Spectator* (March 1845): 26–27; "The Tract Society's publications on history," *Christian Spectator* (July 1845): 50–51; "The union of general and scientific instruction with scriptural knowledge," *Christian Spectator* (Sept. 1845): 69–70.

32. [Charles Tomlinson], *British Nation,* 62.

33. RTS Report (1850): 141.

34. RTS Report (1847): 116.

35. RTS Report (1846): 106.

that they were not led further away from salvation by reading the works of "the followers of evil, or . . . those who at best studiously exclude all references to Him."[36] "Must the Christian be content to leave the whole extensive field of historical and scientific literature to the devil?" asked the *Christian Spectator*.[37] The obviously negative answer presented the Society with an enormous task: "All branches of knowledge must be imbued with evangelical sentiment."[38]

At first glance, all the cheap series of the mid-1840s that were listed in exhibit 1.1 covered a similar range of subjects: biography, geography, history, natural sciences, industry, and philosophy. The presence or absence of literature was one of the more obvious differences. Yet a closer look at the numbers of titles in each category reveals that the RTS series was markedly different from most of its competitors in its balance between the categories.[39] Many series were dominated by one particular category. With John Murray's "Home and Colonial Library," this was geography and books of travels, while with William Collins's "Cheap Series" it was philosophical and theological works. One of the consequences of the balance between the various categories of knowledge in the RTS series is that there was a substantial number of titles on the sciences—indeed, as many as there were on history or biography. This was not true of the series of Murray or Collins, or of H. G. Bohn's "Standard Library," all of which had only small numbers on the natural sciences, and nothing at all on the applied sciences or industry. This absence in Bohn's "Standard Library" might be attributable to the separate existence of his "Scientific Library" were it not that his series dedicated to history and to philology and philosophy did not prevent the appearance of those subjects in the "Standard Library."[40] The only other series that did contain a substantial proportion of science books were Charles Knight's "Shilling Volumes" and, to a slightly lesser degree, W. & R. Chambers's "Miscellany of Tracts." It is presumably no coincidence that these were the publishers who shared with the RTS a philanthropic commitment to educating the working classes.[41] All three publishers recognised a role for the sciences in such a programme of improvement.

---

36. "The society's works on natural history," *Christian Spectator* (March 1845): 26.

37. "Notice of objections," *Christian Spectator* (Oct. 1841): 91.

38. RTS Report (1850): 141.

39. A more detailed version of this analysis can be found in Fyfe, "Industrialised Conversion," 88–90, esp. figures 2.7–2.13.

40. If numbers of titles is any measure, however, the "Scientific Library" was far more successful than the other two.

41. Temperance campaigner John Cassell would also fit this pattern, since he did include the sciences in Cassell's Library (1850–). Further investigation of this phenomenon would be extremely interesting.

Since Knight and Chambers were the two best-known publishers of cheap books, and were also known for omitting religion, it would not be surprising to learn that the RTS was responding to their series when launching its own. This would also fit with the fact that the series of Knight and Chambers were two of the few that preceded the "Monthly Series" into the world. The similarity between the subjects represented in the "Monthly Series" and those of Chambers and Knight helped the RTS to target the same audiences as the secular publishers, from whom it hoped to woo readers. Furthermore, when the Society was challenged about its place in the competitive literary marketplace, its officers frequently replied by comparing its publications with those of Chambers—arguing, for instance, that readers got more words for their penny with the RTS than with Chambers.[42] The *Christian Spectator* had also been known to quote approvingly from *Chambers's Journal* on the difficulty of getting publications to the working classes.[43] This strongly suggests that the RTS positioned itself very close to Chambers in the marketplace, and was entirely aware that they were both using the same sorts of techniques to reach the same audience. The difference, of course, was in the matter of religious spirit.

The relatively high proportion of works on the sciences in the "Monthly Series" is only obvious with the benefit of hindsight. While the series was issuing, the advertisements and listings printed in each volume arranged the titles in order of issue, as in figure 2.1. This was typical publisher's practice at the time. It meant that readers could glance down the list of titles and ascertain that, for example, John Murray was being truthful when he claimed that his "Home and Colonial Library" included works on "Geography, Voyages and Travels, Biography, Natural History, Manners and Customs."[44] What these listings did not do, however, was encourage the reader to consider the constitution of the series as a whole, since the relative extent of the various categories was not emphasised. It would take the curious reader several minutes to work out that the five categories named were not equally represented in the "Home and Colonial Library."

It was usually not until a series had ceased issue that publishers began to pay more attention to the balance of the categories in their series and, therefore, to the classification of their series. Although the "Monthly Series"

---

42. "Letter from a correspondent," *Christian Spectator* (July 1845): 49–50, at 50; USL/RTS Corr., Jones to Hall, 30 August 1845; Jones to Dilworth, 6 November 1846.

43. "Cheap publications," *Christian Spectator* (March 1847): 209–10.

44. *Publishers' Circular*, 15 October 1846, advert 1022; 1 December 1849, advert 1216.

ceased issuing in 1855, it remained on the Society's catalogue until 1883. A finished series needed a different marketing approach, and this often involved some claims to be a complete library of knowledge. Some publishers' series never did finish, of course. Bohn's numerous series were still running when he retired in 1864, and were continued under the management of his successors, Bell & Daldy.[45] Yet, although most publishers hoped to be able to continue their series as long and successfully as Bohn, circumstances were not always favourable. The financial crisis of 1849 forced both Knight and Murray to bring their series to unexpectedly sudden conclusions. Although there were henceforth no further issues, both publishers wished to continue to sell the existing volumes. Murray put a positive gloss on the situation by claiming that he had been "anxious to guard against the objection of overloading the subscribers with too large and cumbrous a series of books of one size," and had therefore decided to close his series at thirty-seven volumes. He argued this was just right for "the compass of a single shelf, or of one trunk" for the emigrant.[46] Knight, too, presented his abruptly terminated series as a library complete within itself, in need of no further expansion, claiming that it "comprehends something like that range of literature which well-educated persons desire to have at their command."[47]

In contrast to Murray's thirty-seven volumes, the RTS "Monthly Series" ended at a round one hundred volumes, giving it the appearance of planned completion. Yet it is clear from the Society's minute books that this "plan" appeared only late in the day. It was not until November 1853, virtually eight years into the series, that the committee suggested one hundred volumes as a desirable end point.[48] There had been an earlier suggestion of sixty volumes, but the series was going so well that it was allowed to run on.[49] Even though the new decision involved dropping some planned volumes and delaying the appearance of the final volume by over a year, the committee did stick to its

---

45. See appendix B to *English Catalogue of Books,* and DLB 106, "H. G. Bohn." The figures given in exhibit 1.1 referred to the period under Bohn's control.

46. *Publishers' Circular,* 1 December 1849, advert 1216.

47. *Publishers' Circular,* 1 May 1849, advert 485.

48. Mention of the closure of the Series was first made in RTS Report (1851): 120; USCL/RTS CCM, 18 June 1851. A hundred volumes was the accepted end point in USCL/RTS CCM, 16 November 1853.

49. USCL/RTS CCM, 19 April 1848, 20 February 1850, and 18 September 1850. The committee had access to sales figures, which allowed them to reach an informed decision about the progress of the Series. USCL/RTS CCM, 17 December 1851, mentions a letter of support for the series from George King of Aberdeen.

goal of a hundred volumes. The RTS also adopted one of Knight's strategies for making his a finished series look like a planned and complete library. In contrast to the earlier advertisements that listed the volumes in order of issue, the new advertisements listed the volumes by category, to suggest that all heads of knowledge were included in the series. These advertisements, such as that issued in 1859 (fig. 2.3), implied that the purchaser of the set would

Figure 2.3. Classified advertisement for the "Monthly Series" from the 1859 RTS catalogue. Congregational Year Book 1859, by permission of the Syndics of Cambridge University Library (L139.c.16.14).

be supplied with all the information needed for a basic education in all the important areas of human knowledge.

Classifications of knowledge are always arbitrary, and we have already seen how the RTS could move the boundary between sacred and secular.[50] The fact that the classification schemes for the series of Knight and the RTS were going to be used in advertisements should alert us to the fact that they cannot be regarded as simply descriptive. One of the consequences of the RTS's choice of classification was that the high proportion of works on the sciences was disguised, and pride of place was given to biography and geography.[51] The RTS and Knight systems are represented in table 2.1, and were roughly similar. Both placed biography and geography at the head, followed by history and the natural sciences (and literature, in Knight's case).

Despite the broad similarities, the RTS classification system tended to divide categories into smaller groupings, separating "Geography" from "Topography" and "Biography" from "Ecclesiastical Biography." The use of finer detail was most obvious in the case of the natural and social sciences. In Knight's system, there were only two scientific categories: "Natural History" and "Arts and Sciences—Commerce, Political Philosophy." The RTS also used "Natural History," but subdivided Knight's second category into five different classes. These six classes, covering natural, social, and applied sciences, accounted for an enormous one-third of the titles in the series. Biography and geography/topography had only a fifth of the titles each, despite appearing above the sciences in the classification scheme, and history had slightly fewer again. The overall effect of the classification scheme was to emphasise the role of biography, geography, and history, and to disguise the prominence of the sciences, broadly defined.

The downplaying of the scientific nature of the series in the later advertisements suggests that the RTS did not intend to create a heavily scientific series. What the Society did set out to create is not much clearer, however. Its classification scheme was imposed after the series had been completed, and therefore had to describe an already-existing entity. The best example of such an after-the-fact scheme is the annual classified index of the trade journal, the *Publishers' Circular*, which had to organise all of the books advertised in the journal in the previous year. It used an extremely detailed classification

50. On classifying knowledge, see Yeo, *Encyclopaedic Visions*, esp. introduction and chap. 3.
51. For other classification schemes that hide things (in particular, Diderot and D'Alembert's *Encyclopédie*), see Darnton, "Tree of Knowledge."

Table 2.1. Comparison of classification systems of the RTS and Charles Knight

RTS's "Monthly Series"		Knight's "Shilling Volumes"	
Biography	13	Biography	9
Ecclesiastical Biography	7		
Geography	12	Geography, Travels, and Topography	15
Topography	9		
		Original Fiction	5
		The Great Writers: English and Foreign	6
Church History	14		
Natural History	9	Natural History, profusely illustrated	7
		General Literature	9
		Fine Arts, Antiquities, etc.	4
		History	3
Sciences etc	5	Arts and Sciences—Commerce, Political Philosophy	6
Agriculture	2		
Commercial and Political Economy	5		
Natural Phenomena	5		
Physical and Social Phenomena, Moral Economy, etc.	6		
The Bible, Evidences of Christianity, etc.	4	Natural Theology and Philosophy	5
Poetry	2		

Source: From advertisements in the appendix of the Congregational Year Book 1859, and in the Publishers' Circular, 1 May 1849, advert 485.

Note: Headings are given in the order originally used by the publishers. Numbers refer to the number of titles under each heading.

scheme, with thirty divisions.[52] Since it reflected the actual output of publishers, fiction and theology were easily the largest classes. As an attempt to bring order to categories that were becoming increasingly large, the index for 1845 used some very specific divisions, such as those for the professions (for example, law, medicine, military affairs, and naval affairs) and the various natural sciences (for example, arithmetic, botany, chemistry, geology, mechanics, natural history, and natural philosophy). This level of classification would have been ridiculous if used for a single publisher's series, which could

---

52. See classified annual index to Publishers' Circular 8 (1845).

Table 2.2. Classification of knowledge according to the SDUK
(as set out in the Society's prospectus)

Philosophy		History	
Natural Philosophy	65	History of Science	9
Intellectual Philosophy	6	History of Art	6
Ethical Philosophy	4	History of Nations	22
Political Philosophy	8	History of Individuals	57
		Of which : Patriots	9
		Warriors	12
		Discoverers	12
		Self-Exalted Men	6
		Moral Philosophers	6
		Navigators	6
		Statesmen	6

Source: "Objects of the Society for the Diffusion of Useful Knowledge" (ca.1827), reprinted in Smith, *Society for the Diffusion of Useful Knowledge,* app. C (i).

Note: Numbers refer to the number of titles under each heading.

only have one or two titles per category, but for describing the state of the expanding book trade, it was essential.

The classes used by the *Publishers' Circular* are clearly a reflection of the reality of the British publishing trade in the 1840s, rather than an ideal scheme of all knowledge. Most publishers' schemes were similarly after-the-fact, but there is an exception: the Society for the Diffusion of Useful Knowledge. Its "Library of Useful Knowledge" was launched in 1827 with a prospectus containing a classification scheme outlining the contents to be included in the new series (table 2.2). This ideal system formed a manifesto for the fledgling society and illustrates again the power that classification systems have to portray knowledge in particular ways. Like the RTS, the SDUK dealt solely with knowledge, and had no category for fiction. It had also decided to avoid the potentially contentious areas of politics and religion, so there were no headings for "Church History" or "Ecclesiastical Biography," as did appear in the RTS scheme. The SDUK scheme appeared to be entirely composed of "Philosophy" and "History."

Depending on one's interpretation of philosophy, it might be read as a very humanistic collection or as a collection balanced between humanities and sciences (natural philosophy), yet neither of these readings would be quite right. The list of proposed titles of the individual volumes revealed that the series was to be very strongly scientific and technical, far more so than the "Monthly Series." "Philosophy" was not just natural philosophy, but included a large component of practical, applied science (dyeing, bleaching, cattle breeding, and hop planting). Meanwhile, the apparently humanistic "History" included not only the "history of science" but also the "history of art," which turned out to involve the arts of navigation and war as well as the fine and useful arts. "History" also included biographies, of which all of the "Discoverers" were men of science, from Galileo through Newton to Lavoisier, and the "Self-exalted Men" included the inventors Franklin, Watt, and Arkwright. The SDUK's avowed object of "useful knowledge" explains its focus on nonfiction, but the classification system implied that all useful knowledge was either philosophy or history, thus making the library appear balanced between the humanities and sciences, and focused on intellectual rather than practical knowledge. Since the prospectus in which the system appeared would have been intended to raise support among the philanthropic middle classes, this impression was surely carefully constructed.

In contrast to the "Library of Useful Knowledge," but like most series, the RTS "Monthly Series" was never planned in such detail. The editor was to find writers to produce short, cheap volumes on literary and scientific subjects, but the question of which subjects would be acceptable, and in what proportions, was never explicitly discussed. Unlike most series, however, the selection of topics for the "Monthly Series" can be followed in detail thanks to the Society's surviving copyright committee minute books. These record the titles of all the topics suggested, along with the committee's decisions as to their perceived suitability at the planning stage, and often a later record regarding the suitability (or not) of the finished manuscript. As well as revealing which proposed topics were rejected, these records demonstrate that the series as published was not identical to that approved by the committee. There was a substantial number of topics that were provisionally accepted, but were either never completed or never completed to the committee's satisfaction. But the key revelation to be gleaned from the minute books is how very dependent the committee was on the suggestions of its writers. It rarely set out to commission a work on a specific subject, but selected its topics from those proposed by writers. The contents of the published series are at least as illustrative of the interests and abilities of the writers, as of any idealised plan by the committee.

Some of the topics that appeared in the "Monthly Series" can be linked to contemporary events in politics or in literature, and their inclusion in the series can be seen as an attempt to benefit from an existing success. *Remarkable Delusions; or illustrations of popular errors* (vol. 72, 1851), for instance, bears a clear resemblance to Charles Mackay's *Popular Delusions* (1841), while *Nineveh and the Tigris* (vol. 63, 1851) would have been inspired by the success of Austen Layard's account of his excavations of *Nineveh and its Remains* (1849). Both Mackay's and Layard's books were bestsellers.[53] Although William Roscoe's *Life of Leo the Tenth* (1805) was less recent, it had been the focus of a tussle between cheap reprinters H. G. Bohn and David Bogue just five years before the RTS included a *Life of Leo X* (vol. 54, 1850) in its series.[54] Histories of the 1789 French Revolution, including that issued by the RTS (vol. 23, 1847), were all given fresh topicality by the French Revolution of 1848. The early 1850s was the time of "Papal Aggression," as Anglicans and Nonconformists alike reacted furiously to Pope Pius IX's reestablishment in 1850 of a Roman Catholic hierarchy of bishops in England. Evangelicals had a long-standing objection to what they saw as the superstitious and corrupt practices of the Roman Catholic Church, and this was exacerbated by the perceived aggression from Rome. The "Monthly Series" included several anti-Catholic works between 1851 and 1853. *Lives of the Popes* (vols. 64, 73, 81, and 85, 1851–52) and *The Jesuits* (vol. 68, 1851), in particular, were promoted in the *Christian Spectator* as "formidable exposure[s] of the arrogance and wickedness of the Romish system."[55] Evangelicals hoped that if Roman Catholics were encouraged to read the Bible, they would, like the dying merchant in an RTS story of 1859 (fig. 2.4) see the error of their ways and renounce their priests, relics, and Virgin worship.

A surprising number of topics that were considered but did not appear in the published series were rather similar to titles in Chambers's "Miscellany of Tracts." They included the "Life of Oberlin," "The Norman Conquest," "Gustavus Adolphus and the Thirty Years War," "Spectral Illusions," "Life of Peter the Great," "British India," and "Hindoo superstitions." Whether this means that such topics were of great current interest, or that some of the RTS writers sought inspiration for new topics in the publications of a competitor, is an open question. Most of these titles were in fact initially approved by the RTS committee, but were not finished satisfactorily. Identifying why a proposed topic was rejected is virtually impossible. Sometimes it was the writer who was being rejected, not the topic, and sometimes the topic was rejected due to lack of space or overlap with recent volumes, rather than for its own (de)merits. Lives of Augustus Caesar and Galileo were rejected, while

---

53. Altick, "Nineteenth-Century Bestsellers."
54. See *Publishers' Circular*, 2 February 1846, advert 114 and 16 February 1846, advert 207.
55. "Lives of the Popes," *Christian Spectator* (Jan. 1852): 691.

Figure 2.4. A dying Roman Catholic merchant refuses all invitations to kiss saintly relics or confess his sins and brandishes his Bible at the cowering priests. He has already removed his painting of the Virgin Mary. From [Sargent], *Story of a Pocket Bible*, 193.

those of Julius Caesar and Newton were accepted. Spanish America and Iceland were rejected, but Switzerland and Canada accepted. It is difficult to find any pattern in the rejections or acceptances.

At the level of the broader categories discussed earlier, however, some patterns can be seen. Strikingly, the minute books reveal that the rejection rate for suggested historical topics was far lower than in the other three main categories. In biography, geography, and the sciences, about two-thirds of suggested topics were accepted, while in history the acceptance rate was over 90 percent.[56] History had been particularly recommended by the *Christian Spectator* as a suitable subject for Christian study, for its illustrations of God's relations with his people, and the high acceptance rate suggests that the committee would have been happy to have more histories than biographies or science works in the series. The only reason the history category did not end up significantly larger than the others in the published series was that, over the series as a whole, around 14 percent of approved topics never metamorphosed into completed manuscripts, and a further 8 percent were completed but did not meet with approval. For some reason, this attrition affected history more than other categories. A partial explanation is that George Stokes, former co-editor of the Society, had offered to write half a dozen works, all historical, in his retirement, but died before completing the majority.[57]

The committee's apparent enthusiasm for history in the "Monthly Series" may also indicate a desire to broaden the Society's publication list. The RTS already had experience with publishing original works on the natural sciences, such as the works on quadrupeds, birds, and reptiles. Hence, having science publications in the "Monthly Series" involved a change of emphasis but not a complete innovation. History was slightly different. Prior to the "Monthly Series," the Society's histories were almost all reprints and adaptations. Ancient history was based on the early eighteenth-century works of Charles Rollin, church history was reprinted from Joseph Milner's *History of the Church of Christ* (1794–97), and that of the Reformation was translated by agreement from Jean Henri Merle d'Aubigné's *History of the Reformation* (1835–53).[58] The desire to create a comprehensive list of original historical works may account for history's prominence in the committee's discussions,

---

56. For more details of this analysis, see Fyfe, "Industrialised Conversion," 90–91, esp. figure 2.14.

57. USCL/RTS CCM, 16 September 1846. He died 31 May 1847; see RTS Report (1848): 81–95.

58. Milner's work was reissued by the RTS in thirty-two parts from 1842.

even though, in the end, most of the volumes were on relatively familiar Church and religious topics. The Society's new ambition to provide up-to-date, accurate, and Christian histories—not just of Scriptural events but of all the ancient nations, of Britain, and of other European nations—found fuller release in its "Educational Series" launched in 1849, which did include original histories of Greece, Rome, and England, as well as "books of travels, and good geographical maps."[59]

The RTS's launch of a separate "Educational Series" should also alert us to another aspect of its intentions. That series contained books intended as textbooks, for formal or informal education. The "Monthly Series" was certainly providing information, but its contents were supposed to be read for interest and pleasure rather than used in the school room. Knowledge provided for didactic purposes would have been classified differently, as the educational series issued by both the RTS and Chambers reveal. Chambers's "Educational Course" had been running since the mid-1830s, and, at the time of the 1854 Society of Arts Educational Exhibition, was rather more developed than its RTS competitor. Chambers's advertisement in the exhibition's advertising supplement classified the volumes according to pedagogical practice.[60] It began with English and the teaching of reading, proceeded from there to writing, and then passed through the other subjects until eventually reaching Latin and German. Reading came before writing, and before all other education, just as English preceded other languages, and arithmetic was a prerequisite for science. This sort of classification scheme, which embodies the formal disciplines of the education system, as well as assumptions about the order in which they should come, is part of a tradition going back at least to medieval classifications of knowledge.[61]

The RTS also had an advertisement in the exhibition catalogue, but since its "Educational Series" was at an early stage, many of the books listed were actually those of the "Monthly Series," in an attempt to make the list appear more impressive.[62] In that advertisement, the publications were arranged with reading books at the start, followed by geography and history, and then by natural history and the sciences, and culminating with the religious and moral categories. Although it began in the same way as Chambers's series, the later categories were unusual, for there was no arithmetic, despite the

---

59. "The Tract Society's publications on history," *Christian Spectator* (July 1845): 50–51.
60. "Educational Exhibition Advertiser," p. 14, appended to Yapp, *Official Catalogue.*
61. Yeo, *Encyclopaedic Visions*, introduction.
62. Yapp, *Official Catalogue*, entry 31.

presence of so many works on the sciences, and no languages. On the other hand, agriculture did appear, yet was not a usual part of a school education. That the RTS could not construct an entirely convincing pedagogic classification system out of the "Monthly Series" confirms the different expected context of that series—as general self-improvement rather than formal education.

The RTS committee never sat down with a plan for its series, so neither the list of published volumes nor the classified version of that list can stand as exemplars of an ideal, comprehensive, evangelical education in secular knowledge. The contents of the series do indicate which subject areas evangelicals thought were appropriate and necessary for Christians, and conversely, which subjects were in need of being saved from the hands of the secular and infidel publishers. Although the archival record reveals that the committee did not set out to create a series that had as many scientific/technical/industrial volumes as the final series turned out to have, it is also clear that the evangelicals of the RTS were far from averse to scientific topics. Indeed, they were in a minority of publishers, alongside Charles Knight and W. & R. Chambers, in paying serious attention to the sciences and including works on the sciences in general nonfiction series.

POTENTIAL MODELS

All publications, even when specially commissioned, carry debts to previous works. These may be reference works consulted by the writer, but they could also be works whose mode of arrangement, narrative style, or manner of combining religious sentiment with instruction acted as an inspiration, either positive or negative, for the writer. As is already apparent, the publications of Knight and Chambers had much in common with the RTS, yet they were certainly not the only potential models. Given the expansion of the publishing trade in the 1840s, it would be nigh impossible to survey all potential models, but we can get a good idea of their range by examining samples from periodicals and books, including some intended as school texts, others for pleasurable reading; some intended for knowledgeable readers, others for those with no prior knowledge; and some including religion, others not. Important as Christian tone was, the RTS also had to ensure that its works were suitable in terms of purpose and assumed educational background for their intended readers. Since the "Monthly Series" was intended for a very broad readership, from artisans to educated families, these questions had to be just as carefully managed as those of religion. Works from atheistic or secular publishers might be inappropriate from the religious point of view, but they might suggest useful ways of condensing, simplifying, and narrating information. Even the existing works from Christian publishers were not completely suitable, which was, after all, why the RTS was getting involved in the first place. In the end, the Society's writers and editors had to create their own style, and their own version of Christian tone.

In order to focus the discussion, my examples here and in the next chapter come from a single area of natural history, one that is peculiarly appropriate for an analysis of the Christian tone in popular science works. Fish have been highly symbolic in Christianity throughout its history, beginning with the miraculous fishing expeditions on the Sea of Galilee and the close associations between Jesus and fishermen, of whom there were four among his disciples. The link endured in the symbolism of the ιχθυς. In Greek, the initial letters of the phrase "Jesus Christ, son of God, Saviour" spell out the word "fish," or ιχθυς. St. Augustine expanded on the potency of this Christ–fish connection by explaining that Christ "had power to exist alive, that is, without sin, in the bottomless pit of our mortal life, as in the depths of the sea."[63]

Focusing on an aspect of zoology also redresses the imbalance created by the existing emphasis on botany in studies of popular science.[64] This emphasis contrasts with the centrality of zoology for nineteenth-century experts, including George Cuvier, Charles Darwin, and Richard Owen. One of the advantages of fish for this purpose is that there are many species native to Britain, which could be found and caught relatively easily in lakes, rivers, and by the coast, whether by the sportsman angler, the North Sea fishing fleets, or a child playing with a net. Thus, many readers could have had some personal experience with fish, in contrast to rarely encountered reptiles (fig. 2.5) and difficult-to-get-close-to birds. Even those without easy access to living fish might be able to gain an acquaintance with a range of species from visits to a fish market, or maybe even from their dinner plates. Certain classes of families had long had goldfish bowls, and the development of the aquarium in the early 1850s sparked a new interest in the habits of fish and their relations to other species of fauna and flora.[65] For experts, the position of fish among the other vertebrate phyla was an important question for the relationships between species. The *Histoire des Poissons* (1826) by Cuvier and Valenciennes

---

63. Augustine, *City of God*, bk.18, chap. 23, 447.

64. For instance, much of Allen, *Naturalist in Britain*. Also Anne Secord, "Corresponding Interests"; Anne Secord, "Science in the Pub"; Anne Secord, *Artisan Naturalists*.

65. Allen, "Tastes and Crazes."

Figure 2.5. A visit to the reptile room at the Zoological Gardens, London, one of the few places where it was possible to see a range of living reptiles up close. [E.V.], "A visit to the Reptile Room," *Visitor* (1850): 361.

was still the standard work of fish taxonomy, but by the late 1840s it was being challenged by discoveries of completely new species of fossil fish.

In 1836, William Yarrell, one of the vice-presidents of the Zoological Society of London, completed *A History of British Fishes,* a two-volume work describing the species of fish to be found in Britain. After two supplements, a second edition appeared in 1841. At sixty shillings for the two volumes, it was an expensive work. Nevertheless, information about fish, much of it derived from Yarrell, was widely available through periodical articles and cheap books, as can be seen from the list of publications in exhibit 2.1. Two of the main instructive penny periodicals, the SDUK's *Penny Magazine* and the SPCK's *Saturday Magazine,* ran series of articles on fish in 1841–42. The RTS issued *British Fish and Fisheries* (vol. 49, 1849) in its "Monthly Series," and the SPCK included a volume on *Fishes* (1851) in its *Natural History.* The works were not confined to British fish. Monographs for experts, such as Leonard Jenyns's 1842 volume of Charles Darwin's *Zoology of the Voyage of HMS Beagle,* introduced readers to 137 species of fish collected by Darwin on his voyage to South America. A different approach could be found in William Carpenter's *Scriptural Natural History* (1828), still in print until at

Exhibit 2.1. Publications on fish, available in the 1840s

William Paley, *Natural Theology; or evidences of the existence and attributes of the deity, collected from nature* (London: R. Faulder, 1802), ca. 9s. but subsequently reprinted many times and in cheaper editions.

William Carpenter, *Scripture Natural History; or, a descriptive account of the zoology, botany and geology of the Bible, illustrated by Engravings*, 6th ed. (London: Thomas Tegg, 1836 [1828]), octavo, price unknown.

William Yarrell, *A History of British Fishes, illustrated by 500 wood-engravings*, 2d. ed., 2 vols. (London: John van Voorst, 1841), octavo, 60s.

[William Chilton], "Fishes," *Oracle of Reason* (1842), article twenty-one of a series of articles on "The theory of regular gradation," magazine was 1d. weekly.

Leonard Jenyns, *Fish*, vol. 4 of Charles Darwin, ed., *The Zoology of the Voyage of HMS* Beagle *under the command of Captain Fitzroy, RN, during the years 1832 to 1836. Published with the approval of the Lords Commissioners of her Majesty's Treasury* (London: Smith, Elder, 1842), quarto, 34s.

William B. Carpenter, *Zoology; a systematic account of the general structure, habits, instincts and uses of the principal families of the animal kingdom, as well as of the chief forms of fossil remains*, 2 vols. (Edinburgh: W. & R. Chambers, 1842), octavo, 4s.

[Charles Williams], *The Fish*, part of [Charles Williams], *Wonders of the Waters* (London: RTS, [1842]), 16mo, 2s. for the book, 4d. for the thirty-two-page part.

"Freshwater Fish," *Saturday Magazine* (London: SPCK), series of fourteen articles in 1841–42, magazine was 1d. weekly.

"Freshwater Fish," *The Penny Magazine* (London: SDUK), series of nine articles in 1841–42, magazine was 1d. weekly.

[Robert Chambers], *Vestiges of the Natural History of Creation* (London: John Churchill, 1844), 12mo, 7s.6d.

[William Martin], *British Fish and Fisheries* (London: RTS, [1849]), 16mo, 6d.

Philip H. Gosse, *Natural History: Fishes* (London: SPCK, 1851), 16mo, 3s.4d.

---

least the late 1830s, which discussed only the fish mentioned in the Bible. Fish also appeared in works that were not explicitly dedicated to them, such as the volume in Chambers's "Educational Series" on *Zoology* (1842), the RTS work *Wonders of the Waters* (1842), or, indeed, Paley's oft-reprinted *Natural Theology* (1802). In broader zoological works, fish were often presented as part of a sequence of species, from primitive to complex. For some writers, this sequence was divinely ordained and culminated in man, but others, such as the contributors to the *Oracle of Reason* and the author of *Vestiges of the Natural History of Creation* (1844), disagreed. For them, the continuous sequence should be presented as evidence of the progressive development of species—in our terms, evolution.

These works on fish ranged in price from the articles in the penny periodicals, through the cheap and midpriced popular works at around four shillings, up to the seriously expensive illustrated volumes at thirty shillings each. The variation in price was accompanied by differences in physical format and intended audience. The chapter on "The Fish" in *Wonders of the Waters* was originally issued as a small square four-penny pamphlet intended for children.[66] It was later reissued, with others in the series, bound in a brown cloth cover, with a single wood engraving and a small amount of gilt on the cover as its sole decorative embellishments. At the opposite end of the scale, *Fish of the Beagle* made a major contribution to zoology. It is a large quarto volume, bound in leather, with thick paper, large print, large margins, and twenty-nine metal-engraved plates. The different audiences and purposes of these works are visible from their appearance and price. Yet, if we were to take a less extreme comparison, and look at the cheap books and the penny periodicals, the relationship between price and audience is less straightforward. Price tells us who could afford to purchase a work, but not who actually did, let alone who actually read it. Books priced at three or four shillings could not have been routinely bought by artisans, but they might have been picked up second-hand, read in a library, or bought by a group of friends. And in reverse, articles in the penny periodicals could be afforded by a much wider audience than any of the books, and were generally written for the working-class section of that audience. Nevertheless, readers who could afford more expensive works also bought penny periodicals. The Darwin family are an obvious case in point, as Susan Darwin's letters to her brother Charles about learning geology from the *Penny Magazine* make clear.[67] Which work a reader chose would be determined not just by price, but also by local availability (for example, shops or libraries) and by the reader's level of interest and existing knowledge in the subject.

The periodicals were suited for those interested in learning a little about a range of subjects, and with no great knowledge of any of them. Readers did not choose the *Penny Magazine* or its competitors specifically for their articles on fish, but for a mixture of introductory-level articles on varied topics. Their articles on natural history tended to concentrate on British species— or on particularly unusual species—and did not attempt to be exhaustive. The aim of a periodical series was usually to present the highlights rather than the minutiae, as the readers of the periodical could not be assumed to have any existing interest in the subject at hand, but had to have their

---

66. Fyfe, Introduction to *Wonders of the Waters.*

67. See letters from Susan Darwin to Charles Darwin, 12 November 1832 and 3 February 1833, in Burkhardt and Smith, *Correspondence of Charles Darwin,* i, 284, 299.

attention grabbed before they passed on to the next article. The illustrated journals might use pictures as part of the attraction; other possible tactics included using interesting quotations or exciting opening sentences. The *Saturday Magazine*'s article on the char (fig. 2.6) illustrates the combination of an illustration and an opening quotation. Although the *Saturday Magazine* and *Penny Magazine* came from rather different publishers, their articles on freshwater fish were very similar. Usually, each article dealt with one species of fish, recounting its habitat, general appearance, breeding and feeding habits, and a selection of "curious antiquarian and anecdotal information"—methods of catching or cooking it, unusual specimens, or its encounters with famous

THE CHAR, (*Salmo savelinus.*)

THE CHAR, (*Salmo savelinus.*)

BUT, scholar, there is a fish, that they in Lancashire boast very much of, called a char; taken there (and I think there only) in a mere called Winander Mere; a mere, says Camden, that is the largest in this nation, being ten miles in length, and (some say) as smooth in the bottom as if it were paved with polished marble. This fish never exceeds fifteen or sixteen inches in length, and is spotted like a trout; and has scarce a bone, but on the back. But this, though I do not know whether it make the angler sport, yet I would have you take notice of it, because it is a rarity, and of so high esteem with persons of great note.

Figure 2.6. The char, as presented in the *Saturday Magazine*, 5 November 1842, 181. The opening to the article included several elements: the picture of the fish (in realist mode, rather than as a technical diagram); the common and systematic names of the fish, which were used both as title to the article, and as caption to the picture; and a quotation from the great angler, Isaac Walton. The text of the article begins just below the quotation.

people.[68] The *Penny Magazine* included occasional references to God as Creator, and the *Saturday Magazine* did little more, so that, out of context, it would not necessarily be obvious in which journal a fish article had been published.

In most cases, the editors of the *Saturday Magazine* did not attempt to introduce a Christian tone to their natural history articles, but filled the spare column inches at the end of articles with excerpts, which were sometimes religious. The article on the tench was followed by excerpts on the "Commerce of Leeches" and "The Alps after Sunset," but that on the char was followed by nine short quotations on the value of the Sabbath and missionaries, on Christianity as truth, the dangers of sin and temptation, and the importance of religion to morality.[69] This method of juxtaposing natural history with explicitly Christian excerpts was also used by the RTS in the *Visitor.* Regular readers of the *Saturday Magazine* might also have remembered that the introductory article to the series on fish had justified the focus in theological terms. As well as a general account of fish anatomy and physiology, the introduction included the reminder that the adaptation of fish to their environment illustrated the foresight of the Creator. Such adaptation is "a principal charm of natural history," but it also reminds the naturalist of "the gentle monition of the Saviour, that God, who forgetteth not the sparrows, who feedeth the ravens and clotheth the grass of the field, will not discontinue His watchful care over those whom He has declared to be far better than they."[70] Although the *Saturday Magazine*'s article on the char was very similar to that which appeared a month later in the *Penny Magazine,* the memory of the introductory article, combined with the juxtaposed religious excerpts, meant that readers of the *Saturday Magazine* would have been encouraged to think about the char in a Christian framework.[71]

Readers who already had some knowledge or interest, perhaps from periodical articles, might decide to acquire an introductory book on the subject. What sort of book they chose would depend on their reasons for wanting to know more about fish. Some books catered more to the "armchair" naturalist who wished to know about the general characteristics of fish, but who did not (yet) feel the desire to actively pursue natural history. Children's books,

---

68. "Freshwater fish: introduction," *Saturday Magazine,* 27 March 1841, 119.

69. "Freshwater fish: the tench," *Saturday Magazine,* 2 October 1841, 132–33; "Freshwater fish: the char," *Saturday Magazine,* 5 November 1842, 181.

70. "Freshwater fish: introduction," *Saturday Magazine,* 27 March 1841, 119.

71. "Freshwater fish: the char," *Penny Magazine,* 3 December 1842, 476–77.

as well as the RTS *British Fish* and SPCK *Fishes,* would fit in this category. They were more detailed than the periodical articles, but still presented their subject as a passive activity. Unlike reference works, they were written in continuous prose and were intended to be read from cover to cover. This discursive format implicitly provided the reader with ways to converse about fish, as well as actual information, and presented natural history as a form of rational recreation.

In contrast, the *Zoology* in Chambers's "Educational Course" was a text-book of anatomy, physiology, and the basics of taxonomy, intended for formal study. It lacked the rhetorical touches to the narrative with which the introductory books enticed the reader to continue, and used a much starker, matter-of-fact presentation. As with other Chambers works, religion did not appear in the body of the text. The narrator of the *Zoology* played the role of the authoritative schoolteacher, and this impression was enhanced by the division of the text into numbered paragraphs, each containing a point to be learned. There were more illustrations in *Zoology* than in the rational recreation works, and many of them were diagrams, emphasising the pedagogical purpose of the book. The contrast can be seen between the realistic representation of a fish against background scenery in figure 2.6 and the line diagrams of *Zoology* in figure 2.7. The narrator of the *Zoology* contrasted his "scientific" presentation of natural history with the "taxonomical" presentation of other works that made zoology appear "a Science of names and of *intricate classification.*" According to the *Zoology,* names "are *not* the objects of the Science, but merely furnish the mechanism (so to speak), by which its true ends are to be attained."[72]

Despite this critique of names, the correct identification of specimens was essential for communicating with other naturalists and for determining whether "new" observations were indeed new. To identify species, the would-be naturalist needed yet another sort of book, such as Yarrell's *History of British Fishes.* This provided detailed descriptions of all British fish, along with details of where they were to be found, their breeding habits, food sources, and assorted other information relating to their origins, the etymology of their name, or their economic importance. At sixty shillings, however, the *History* was only for those who were both seriously interested and sufficiently well-off. Other readers with an interest in fish identification might be able to consult the *History* in a library, but would generally have to

---

72. William B. Carpenter, *Zoology,* 1.

make do with the descriptions provided in the cheaper books, which tended to be detailed enough only for the most common fish.

And for those few who really wished to become ichthyological experts, even Yarrell's *History* would not be enough, for it dealt only with British fish and was being superseded by new discoveries almost as soon as it was published. Trainee experts would start with the encyclopaedic works of Cuvier, but, as new species were discovered, would need to watch for papers in learned journals like the *Transactions of the Zoological Society*, while being alert as well to the publication of such monographs as the *Fish of the Beagle*. The quarto format of many of these works, not to mention their thick paper, enormous margins, and pages of engraved plates, testified to the expense involved in being an expert, while the technical vocabulary of fish anatomy and the use of Latin for standard descriptions points to the amount of prior knowledge needed.

The narrators of the SPCK *Fishes* and the Chambers *Zoology* made some brief theological references in their introductions, mostly to the Creator and his awe-inspiring works, but wrote the remainder of their works in

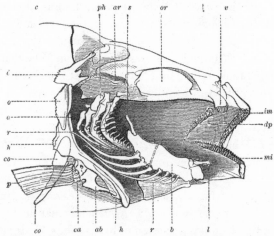

FIG. 248.—Bones of the head of the Perch, after the removal of the jaws, lateral partition, and operculum, on one side, to show the interior of the mouth, and the hyoid apparatus; *c*, cranium ; *or*, orbit ; *v*, vomer (armed with teeth) ; *im*, superior maxillary ; *dp*, teeth implanted on the palatine arch ; *mi*, lower jaw ; *l*, lingual bone ; *b*, lateral branches of the hyoid apparatus ; *s*, process for the attachment of these to the lateral partition ; *r, r*, branchio-stegal rays ; *a*, branchial arches ; *ph*, superior pharyngeal bones ; *ar*, articular surface by which the lateral partition is attached ; *o* to *h*, bony framework supporting the pectoral fin, *p ; o* and *o'*, scapula divided into two pieces ; *h*, humerus ; *ab*, bone of the fore-arm ; *ca*, bone of the carpus ; *co*, coracoid bone.

Figure 2.7. Chambers's *Zoology* contained many more illustrations than the RTS Monthly Volumes, but they were mostly technical line diagrams, such as this image of the bones of the head of a perch. From Carpenter, *Zoology*, ii, 5.

an essentially secular tone. Yarrell's *History* and *Fish of the Beagle* made no theological references at all, signaling the supposed independence of expert natural history from theology, notwithstanding the fact that *Fish of the Beagle* was written by a clergyman. Even worse, from the evangelical point of view, than these omissions of religion were the writers who used natural history to undermine religion. Fish could have a particularly key role in such an argument for, in a scheme of continuous development, such as those proposed in the articles on regular gradation in the *Oracle of Reason* and in *Vestiges,* fish were the first of the higher animals. The relationship between their anatomy and that of reptiles, birds, and mammals could be used to suggest a developmental link between classes.[73] The similarities could also be traced in the embryonic development of the higher mammals, which impressed the *Vestiges* author so much that he proposed a mechanism for evolutionary development based on embryology.[74] Although he claimed to believe this was "in the first place arranged in the counsels of Divine Wisdom . . . , and as being carried on, from first to last . . . under the immediate favour of the creative will or energy," many readers saw this mechanism as a way of taking God out of the picture.[75]

Contributors to the *Oracle of Reason* were much more explicit. They were, after all, writing in a periodical that made no effort to hide its atheism, proudly claiming to be "the only exclusively ATHEISTICAL print that has appeared in any age or country."[76] In the long series of articles on "The theory of regular gradation," which took readers from animalcules, through trilobites, worms, and molluscs to reptiles, birds, and mammals, fish appeared midway through the sequence, as the first of the vertebrates.[77] In this context, however, there was no mention of a superintending divine wisdom, but the claim, "My principal object . . . has been to prove the capabilities of unassisted, unacted upon, uncontrolled, undirected matter for the production of all the varied, complicated, and beautiful phenomena of the universe."[78] Matter alone was enough to explain the history of life on earth, leaving no space for God. Fortunately for Christians, the *Oracle of Reason* only managed to sell as many as four thousand copies for its first few numbers, so the spread of its appallingly

---

73. Robert Chambers, *Vestiges*, 193.

74. Ibid., 198–202, 212–13.

75. Ibid., 203–4.

76. Preface to first volume, *Oracle of Reason* 1 (1842): ii.

77. [William Chilton], "Theory of regular gradation, article 21," *Oracle of Reason* 1 (1842): 277–78.

78. [William Chilton], "Theory of regular gradation, article 15," *Oracle of Reason* 1 (1842): 191.

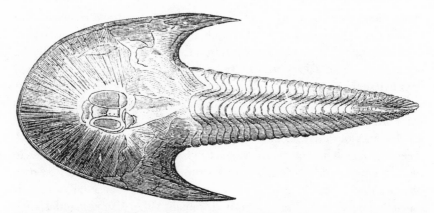

Figure 2.8. The *Cephalaspis,* one of the fossil fish from the Old Red Sandstone deposits. From Miller, *Old Red Sandstone,* plate IX. According to the *Vestiges* author, it was similar to a trilobite. According to Sedgwick, these fish have not "the most remote affinity to Crustaceans, or any other Articulata. On the contrary, they in many respects make an approach to the higher class of Reptiles" ([Sedgwick], "Natural History of Creation," *Edinburgh Review* 82 (1845): 35).

infidel sentiments, while undoubtedly greater than would be desirable, was not huge.[79]

Both the *Oracle of Reason* and the *Vestiges* author engaged with the contemporary debate over the significance of fossil fish.[80] The fish of the Old Red Sandstone had been only recently discovered and were used by the *Vestiges* author as examples of fish that were little more than crustaceans, thus helping to fill the gaps in the continuous sequence of progressive life forms.[81] Cambridge geology professor Adam Sedgwick referred to these passages in his lengthy *Edinburgh Review* article as being "more worthless and untrue to nature" than anything he had ever met.[82] The *Vestiges* author defended his interpretation of the fossil fish in *Explanations: a sequel* (1845).[83] The episode provides a vivid illustration of how the interpretation of fish mattered. Where the *Vestiges* author saw the fossil fish as more primitive forms, Sedgwick insisted that even the earliest fossils, such as the *Cephalaspis* (fig. 2.8), were highly complex forms resembling reptiles more than

79. Preface to volume 2, *Oracle of Reason* 2 (1843): iii.

80. [William Chilton], "Theory of regular gradation, article 12," *Oracle of Reason* 1 (1842): 157–59.

81. Robert Chambers, *Vestiges,* 69.

82. [Sedgwick], "Natural History of Creation," 39.

83. *Explanations* is reprinted in Robert Chambers, *Vestiges.* See 46–52, esp. 51.

crustaceans. If Sedgwick was correct, then the *Vestiges* author's claims of continual gradual progression from higher to lower forms were undermined.

If fish could be interpreted either way, it should not be surprising that they were used by Christian writers as well as deists and atheists. They regularly appeared in the two main Christian genres of natural history: natural theology and scriptural natural history. The classic *Natural Theology* (1802) of William Paley was still frequently being reprinted in the 1830s and 1840s, and used the evidence of design in nature to prove the existence of a designer God. Paley was able to find plenty of evidence of God's benevolent contrivances in the adaptation of fish to their watery environments.[84] For instance, he wrote, "we find that the eye of a fish, in that part of it called the crystalline lens, is much rounder than the eye of terrestrial animals. What plainer manifestation of design can there be than this difference?"[85] He also found, in the cunning mechanism of the air bladder, an argument against the theory of the transmutation of species by characters acquired from the environment, which was to be linked with the name of French zoologist Jean-Baptiste Lamarck. Paley pointed out that "a life in the water has no natural tendency to produce a bag of air. Nothing can be further from an acquired organization than this is."[86]

Although natural theologies like Paley's could use fish to make a Christian point, the style of writing was problematic for the evangelical RTS, due to the lack of emphasis on Christ and the Atonement. The *Christian Spectator* described it as being "the device of Satan, to speak of the wonders of creation without notice of those of redemption."[87] The RTS's *Popular History of Reptiles* had used many of the tropes of devotional natural theologies, but its writer was careful to make plain, in both introduction and conclusion, that

> the study of nature, though it enlarges our ideas of the power and wisdom of God, and tends to humble us, shows to us his glory as manifested only in creation; it gives us no information as to our condition before God, as to our hopes for eternity, as to our need of salvation, and the way of our obtaining it.[88]

Even if the inadequacies of natural theology could be remedied, the style would still have been wrong for the "Monthly Series" and its successors, for it was quite obviously devotional in tone, aimed at an audience of Christians.

---

84. Fyfe, "Publishing and the Classics."
85. Paley, *Natural Theology*, 19.
86. Ibid., 246.
87. "On the union of general and scientific instruction with Scriptural knowledge," *Christian Spectator* (Sept. 1845): 69.
88. [William Martin], *Popular History of Reptiles*, 13.

It would not have endeared itself to the intended audience of the new secular publishing programme.

The other Christian genre that might have served as a potential model had the same problem. Scriptural natural history involved the description of the natural history of the Bible and the biblical lands. The RTS had occasionally published articles in this style in the *Visitor*, such as that describing the mustard tree of the New Testament, and it had issued a translation of Christian Gottlob Barth's *Scripture Natural History* in 1843.[89] A successful example of this genre was William Carpenter's *Scripture Natural History* (1828), which was reprinted several times in the 1830s. In certain respects, this work is very similar to *Fish of the Beagle*. Both were aimed at relatively expert audiences, as is clear from their use of a technical vocabulary, including non-English words without explanations, and their frequent references to the works of other authorities to support their cases. Where they differ is in the purpose of their natural history. *Fish of the Beagle* presented its descriptions of new species of fish with the aim of "render[ing] all species, whether rightly named or not, easily recognizable; and, however little the science may be advanced by what is brought forward, to make that advance, so far as it goes, sure."[90] Rather than advancing natural science, *Scripture Natural History* sought to advance biblical understanding, for, "destitute of a tolerable acquaintance with the natural history of the East, the import of many passages in the Sacred Writings will inevitably elude our search."[91] *Scripture Natural History* did not attempt to put taxonomic names to species nor to describe their appearance, habits, or physiology, but rather aimed to explain which animals and plants were indicated by the Hebrew and Greek terms, and why they had deserved particular mention. The authorities to which it referred were theologians and Bible translators, rather than the naturalists who filled the pages of *Fish of the Beagle*. *Scripture Natural History* was, then, more an exercise in translation and interpretation than in natural science.

Scripture Natural History differed from most other natural history works in its choice of classification system. All the other writers who used any classification at all chose a taxonomic system based on that of Cuvier.[92] The

---

89. "Mustard tree of the New Testament," *Weekly Visitor*, 5 February 1833, 44.

90. Jenyns, *Zoology of the Voyage of HMS Beagle*, x.

91. William Carpenter, *Scripture Natural History*, 2.

92. The periodical series on fish, which chose a few of the most well-known British species, and the children's book *Wonders of the Waters*, which selected particularly unusual species, made no attempt to classify their species. SPCK *Fishes* used an updated version of Cuvier. *Zoology* supplemented Cuvier with Agassiz for fossil fish.

narrator of *Scripture Natural History*, in contrast, contended that he could not use systems like those of Linnaeus or Cuvier, since his aim was to discuss the species mentioned in the Bible, and the systematic identity of many species intended by the inspired writers remained uncertain. Therefore, *Scripture Natural History* followed another system based on "the three-fold arrangement of Moses, in his strictly philosophical, and sublimely beautiful narrative of the creation."[93] The narrator also promoted Solomon as the first natural historian, in opposition to the pagan Aristotle.[94] In this system, the early phases seem familiar. The members of the three classes of geology, botany, and zoography take their place on a chain of creation leading up to man. The animal group was then divided into man, beasts, birds, fishes, reptiles, and insects. The difference becomes clear when the beasts are divided into "Domestic Animals," "Ferocious Wild Beasts," "Wild Inoffensive Animals," and "Dubious Animals" (the behemoth, leviathan, and unicorn). Within any one of these subgroupings, the animals were ordered according to their importance to the patriarchs, and the length of the discussion depended on how often the animal was referred to in the Bible, and how straightforward the identification of its modern counterpart was.

The section on fish, therefore, was much shorter than in the other natural histories, because the biblical writers mentioned no species of fish by name, and only occasionally referred to fish at all, since, "the Jews being an agricultural people, fish formed no considerable part of their food."[95] *Scripture Natural History* needed little more than three pages to discuss the main references to fish and fishing in the Bible. Of this, over a page and a half was devoted to the meaning of the word "κητος," used to describe the creature that saved Jonah. The RTS edition of Barth's *Scripture Natural History* had experienced a similar problem with the lack of scriptural fish, and used it as an opportunity to discuss the characteristics of fish in general, the species of fish that are now to be found in places mentioned in the Bible, and the metaphorical uses of fish and fishermen in the gospel stories.[96] This emphasis on the story of Jesus can be seen as an evangelical approach to the traditional genre of scriptural natural history.

---

93. William Carpenter, *Scripture Natural History*, 3.

94. Ibid., 10–11.

95. William Carpenter, *Scripture Natural History*, 285. Opinions clearly differed on this. As we shall see, *British Fish* claimed that the Jews did eat fish.

96. [Barth], *Scripture Natural History*.

When announcing the new series in 1845, the *Christian Spectator* had explained, "most desirable is it, therefore, that it [gospel truth] should pervade all our literature; not appearing, indeed, abruptly and offensively, but in accordance with sound judgment and good taste, as well as with the principles of vital godliness."[97] Thomas Pearson would note, eight years later, that attempts to supply the masses with "acceptable and yet wholesome and elevating reading" by providing "purely religious publications, in the form of tracts or biographies" had largely failed.[98] It was awareness of this that convinced the RTS that scriptural natural histories, such as Carpenter's or the ones it already published, would not suit the aims of the "Monthly Series."[99] The "Christian tone" that was developed by the RTS writers and editors was supposed to combine faith with knowledge without being tasteless or too obvious.

Christian Tone

The existence of natural theologies, scriptural natural histories, and the articles and books by the SPCK shows that the RTS was not the only Christian publisher interested in issuing natural history works. Even Charles Knight, usually linked with secular publishing due to his long association with the SDUK, admitted afterwards that he wished the SDUK publications had involved more Christianity. He claimed that his "Shilling Volumes" would fulfill that ambition. The series did include some religious works, such as a revised edition of Paley's *Natural Theology* which the SDUK had refused to publish, yet the RTS was not alone in failing to find Knight's own publications any great improvement on those of the SDUK.[100] The evangelical *Churchman's Monthly Review* complained of Knight's reprint of a work by the SDUK founder Henry, Lord Brougham, stating that "there is not a line of Christianity in them. His Lordship, too, has almost well-nigh forgotten that there is a 'God in History'; and therefore, in our view, his Sketches are

---

97. "Announcement of the Monthly Volume," *Christian Spectator* (Sept. 1845): 65.

98. Pearson, *Infidelity*, 509.

99. One work of scriptural natural history, *Plants and Trees of the Bible*, did appear in the Series.

100. For Knight on Christian tone, see Charles Knight, *Passages of a Working Life*, ii, 189–92. For the SDUK's refusal to publish Paley, see Brougham, *Discourse of Natural Theology*, i, 8.

not reading for the people."[101] The reviewer was writing in 1846, comparing the recent volumes of Knight's series, the RTS "Monthly Series," and James Burns's "Fireside Library." Of these, the reviewer believed that only the RTS series was suitable and genuinely "useful" for "the people," notwithstanding the cheapness of the other volumes.[102]

James Burns, the other publisher compared with Knight and the RTS, shared the widespread concern about the effect of unsuitable reading on morality. He was particularly worried by "the not unfrequent occurrence of passages of an objectionable kind" in even the standard works of English literature. In February 1846, he launched his "Select Library," aimed at young people though with the added claim that it would "be suitable to a large number of older Readers, especially in the middle and lower classes." The series was to be conducted under the auspices of "the Rev Alexander James Howell, BA (afternoon lecturer at St. Andrew's, Enfield; and domestic chaplain to his grace the duke of Cumberland)" with the aid of "several literary gentlemen, well qualified for such an undertaking." Burns and Howell intended to adapt and revise standard works to remove any objectionable passages and at the same time to tidy up faults of "prolixity and occasional heaviness" that might deter youthful readers.[103] Some longer works would also be abridged. The ambition was to create editions of the *Spectator*, the *Tatler*, Boswell's *Life of Johnson*, *Gulliver's Travels*, Froissart's *Chronicles*, and various ancient classic authors that could safely be given to young people without the exercise of parental censorship.

The concern underlying this series was similar to that inspiring the RTS "Monthly Series": how can you make sure that readers are able to gain instruction and amusement without being laid open to objectionable moral and religious sentiments? For Burns and Howell, the answer was to take the acknowledged standard works on the various subjects and adapt them as necessary to make them suitable. The RTS, however, was already under criticism for some of its adaptations of standard theological works, where references to such controversial issues as the effect of baptism and the legitimacy of state-established churches had been invisibly edited out.[104] As a consequence of

101. The review was of Brougham's *Sketches of Statesmen of George III*, in *Churchman's Monthly Review* 6 (1846): 156.

102. "Short Notices," *Churchman's Monthly Review* 6 (1846): 153–56.

103. *Publishers' Circular*, 2 February 1846, advert 143.

104. William Jones, *Jubilee Memorial*, 625; for the criticisms, see *Christian Observer* 45 (1846): 579. See also 464–66, 512, 577–86, 595–603, 814.

the criticisms, particularly from the evangelical Anglican monthly *Christian Observer*, the Society became much more careful about making changes to respected writers. Moreover, simply removing objectionable passages would not be enough, since the Society's aim was a positively Christian tone throughout the work. If Christian sentiments had to be grafted on, they were likely to show it, and to look unconvincing and artificial.

Thus, when the RTS had to decide what form its new works on secular subjects were going to take, commissioning new works seemed the best way of ensuring an appropriately Christian tone. This decision increased the editorial expense and effort involved, compared with reprints, but at least it guaranteed that all the publications would contain a clear statement of the Atonement, be written in a manner consistent with evangelical Christianity, and contain no support for one sect or denomination over another. Using original works also allowed the RTS to control the length of the works, and to keep them short enough for production costs to be kept low. When the "Monthly Series" was launched, therefore, it was the originality of the works, not any claim to classic status, that was promoted as a selling point.[105]

Although the sheer amount of contemporary authorship, according to the Nonconformist *British Quarterly Review*, "bewilders all sober contemplation," it was still (just) possible to distinguish the few writers of "true, or high literature" from all the rest. "Originality" was one of the distinguishing features of this sort of writing.[106] Some reviewers believed that this was the sort of originality that ought to be provided in cheap form for the masses, with a reviewer in the weekly *Athenaeum* welcoming the launch of Bogue's "European Library" in 1845 with the hope that "learning and genius unemasculated" would "take the place of the insipid compilations and useless abridgements." The *Athenaeum* reviewer also criticised those publishers that he regarded as being but "pseudo-benefactors of the people," because they "have found them ignorant, and left them so," by publishing watered-down compilations, with too many facts "compressed in one small volume."[107] In this context, compilations and derivative works, which surely included the "Monthly Series," did not merit the appellation "original." Indeed, with regard to societies, the anonymous writer of *The Power of the Press* pamphlet claimed that "the works

105. The Series did contain six abridgements, two of which (from William Scoresby's work) had certainly been approved by the committee.

106. [Masson], "Present Aspects and Tendencies," 157, 159–65.

107. "The European Library," *Athenaeum*, 13 December 1845, 1192.

of a society will seldom bear the stamp of originality, [for] they will usually be copies of some successful individual speculation or idea."[108]

Whether originality in the literary sense really was crucial for popular publications depended on what one was trying to achieve. The *British Quarterly* reviewer who praised "high" literature also recognised two other categories of literature: "wholesome popular literature" and "trash."[109] "Trash" was certainly a problem, and embodied all the reasons why compilations were to be looked down upon. He described these works as frequently the result of a secondhand or thirdhand "dilution" from a "substantial book," generally lacking any "certificate in the name of their author."[110] But while that sort of literature was certainly to be condemned, the wholesome sort of authorship was "greatly in request," and its "workman" (note, not "author") might pursue it "respectably and honourably."[111] Wholesome popular literature was felt to be necessary to inform and instruct the perceived growing intelligence of the times. The religious periodicals generally concurred in counting the RTS "Monthly Series" a good example of this genre, and the *British Quarterly* itself variously recommended the volumes as "intrinsically good," giving an "intelligent account," and being "interesting and trustworthy."[112] The *Christian Lady's Magazine* commended the series as "admirably calculated, to supersede some of the trash that inundates the country at a merely nominal price."[113] This "admirable calculation" was only possible because the works were specially commissioned, but it did not require their writers to display the creativity of geniuses.

The RTS borrowed the term "Christian tone" from Dr. Thomas Arnold (1795–1842). The reforming headmaster of Rugby, subsequently immortalised in Thomas Hughes's *Tom Brown's School Days* (1857), had been deeply interested in the SDUK's projects, and had tried to convince the committee that its publications ought to have not just a "plain and sensible tone" but "a decidedly Christian tone."[114] Arnold had praised one article in the *Penny Magazine,* saying, "That article is exactly a specimen of what I wished to

---

108. *Power of the Press,* 38.
109. [Masson], "Present Aspects and Tendencies": wholesome literature is discussed at 165–69, trash at 170–76.
110. Ibid., 170.
111. Ibid., 166.
112. "Glimpses of the Dark Ages," *British Quarterly Review* 3 (1846): 548; "Life of Cyrus," *British Quarterly Review* 5 (1847): 561.
113. "Jamaica," *Christian Lady's Magazine* 25 (1846): 371.
114. Arnold to Tooke, 18 June 1831, quoted in Stanley, *Life of Arnold,* i, 271; Arnold to a member of the SDUK, ibid., i, 253.

see, but done far better than I could do it. I never wanted articles on religious subjects half so much as articles on common subjects written with a decidedly Christian tone."[115] "Tone" refers to a literary style, which reveals the writer's sentiments, and to the mood it creates. It is particularly linked to issues relating to morality and manners, wherein "tone" is a measure of the moral health or fitness of a community. This is related to its usage in "muscle tone."[116] "Christian tone" would therefore be a literary style intended to create a mood of sound morality and Christian faith. For Arnold, a work that had Christian tone had "something of the religious spirit."[117] Spirit was an important concept for him, as inspiration of the writers—although not dictation by the Holy Spirit of every word—was a way for liberal Anglicans, including Arnold, to preserve the unitary meaning of Revelation while coming to grips with the arguments of recent German historical scholarship on the Bible.[118] Although Arnold did not expect the writers of the SDUK or RTS to be inspired in the same sense as the biblical writers, their faith would prevent them from making errors, and was essential in ensuring that they presented their secular subjects in accordance with God's intentions.

The RTS adopted Arnold as the figurehead of the "Monthly Series," using as the slogan on all its advertisements his comment, "I never wanted articles on religious subjects. . . ."[119] Evangelicals were not usually admirers of German biblical criticism, while Arnold had referred to evangelicals (particularly those radical Anglicans who ran the *Record* newspaper in the 1830s) as having "infinitely little minds" and no "Christian wisdom," so the choice of figurehead initially seems a little odd.[120] The RTS was united with Arnold in their disappointment with the SDUK and in their opposition to the Tractarians. Arnold had written of the Oxford Tracts that, "as to Christianity, there is more of it in any one of Mrs Sherwood's or Mrs Cameron's, or indeed of any of the [Religious] Tract Society's, than in all the two Oxford octavos."[121] As an evangelical writer put it in 1845, given the choice of a companion for eternity, Thomas Arnold was far preferable to John Henry Newman.[122]

---

115. Arnold to Tooke, *ca.*1832, quoted in Stanley, *Life of Arnold,* i, 272 n.

116. See "tone" in the OED, meanings 5, 7, and 9.

117. Arnold, quoted in Stanley, *Life of Arnold,* i, 252.

118. Harding, *Coleridge,* 98–104; Brent, *Liberal Anglican Politics.*

119. For example, see "The Monthly Volume," *Christian Spectator* (Jan. 1846): 98.

120. Arnold to Susannah Arnold, November 1830, quoted in Stanley, *Life of Arnold,* i, 260–61.

121. Sherwood and Cameron were evangelical children's writers. Arnold to Stanley, 24 September 1836, quoted in Stanley, *Life of Arnold,* ii, 43.

122. *Brief Observations on the Late Rev Dr Arnold,* 4–5.

Arnold's inclusive views on Christianity could also be presented as in tune with moves towards pan-evangelical unity in the 1840s, though Arnold's vision was far broader than that of the evangelicals.

The choice of Arnold was, in fact, a carefully chosen advertising ploy by the RTS. It was quite common for publishing projects to include a quotation from a well-known literary source as an epigraph, to establish a certain tone for the work to follow. The *Visitor,* for instance, carried biblical verses on its front page, which produced a rather different impression from the slogan used to advertise the *Movement* (the successor to the *Oracle of Reason*): Jeremy Bentham's "Maximize morals, minimize religion!"[123] Thomas Arnold, three years dead by 1845, was well on his way to becoming an iconic figure in British intellectual life. He was not only the headmaster whose reforms would be copied in public schools across the land, he had also been a respected Regius Professor of History at Oxford and one of the foremost liberal Anglicans of his day. The widespread popularity of Arthur Penrhyn Stanley's *Life and Correspondence of Thomas Arnold* (1844) fed the enthusiasm for Arnold, and the RTS's use of him the following year was a shrewd publicity move.[124]

As Arnold's comment on the SDUK article made clear, "Christian tone" did not mean that only religious subjects should be addressed. Arnold himself particularly recommended history and biography as subjects that would do more good than "any direct comments on Scripture, or essays on Evidences."[125] Influenced by German scholarship, he believed even more strongly than evangelicals that sound historical understanding was essential for the interpretation of the Scriptures.[126] His attitude to the sciences was rather more ambivalent. He wrote that he did wish "that my children might be well versed in physical science, but in due subordination to the fullness and freshness of their knowledge on moral subjects." Yet, he believed that the sciences had to be studied in their entirety, if at all, and that this would tend to exclude the moral and Christian study he believed to be essential. Thus, he continued, "rather than have it the principle thing in my son's mind, I would gladly have him think that the sun went round the earth, and that the stars were so many spangles set in the bright blue firmament."[127] The RTS shared

---

123. Advertisement for *Movement, Oracle of Reason* 2 (1843): 398.

124. For RTS writer John Stoughton's admiration of Arnold and his biographer, see Stoughton, *Recollections*, 78–79.

125. Arnold to Tooke, *ca.*1832, quoted in Stanley, *Life of Arnold*, i, 272 n.

126. Harding, *Coleridge*, 102–3.

127. Arnold to Greenhill, 9 May 1836, quoted in Stanley, *Life of Arnold*, ii, 37.

Arnold's desire to include Christian elements with secular knowledge, but unlike him, its staff believed it was possible to do so with the sciences.

The issue of incorporating Christian spirit had been addressed by the RTS in 1841, when the editor of the *Christian Spectator* responded to criticisms of some of the Society's children's books, particularly the manner in which "religious instruction should be blended with topics of popular interest."[128] Although this article was concerned with explicit religious instruction, much of the advice would apply equally to the more implicit Christian tone. The verb of choice seems to be "blended." Certainly, Christian sentiments "should not be 'lugged in,' 'intersected,' or 'patched on.'"[129] They must be made to appear integral to the main subject matter, rather than artificially added. Quoting from a sermon by the late Bishop of Chichester, William Otter, the *Christian Spectator* argued that such sentiments are to be "burnt in, not pasted on."[130] Pearson agreed, adding, "We do not want the literature . . . sermonized, nor to be taken up with theological controversies; but we want in it a distinct recognition of the fact that distinctively Christian elements are alone efficacious in radically regenerating the world."[131]

A few references to sacred history or the works of the Creator were not enough for Christian tone, especially if those references were made without "religious feeling." Hence, the fish works of the SPCK were unsuitable, for they had but few religious references, and those merely to God the Creator. Nonetheless, the *Christian Spectator* writer also warned against the opposite tendency, which he believed had become more prevalent, in which popular works of instruction had become too much like sermons or religious tracts. He argued that there was no need to draw out the moral every time. After all, in the Bible, "the application is very much left to each man's understanding and conscience." If narratives were carefully constructed, then readers could be left to draw the conclusion on their own, so that "there is no need for a recurrence to them [that is, doctrines] on every page." Writing several years before the Society adopted the term "Christian tone," and before Arnold's views on "religious spirit" were published, the writer nevertheless urged an

---

128. "Notice of objections," *Christian Spectator* (July 1841): 65–68. Much of the section discussing Christian tone is quoted from a recent article in another periodical by "an author who is entitled to be heard as one of the oldest and most experienced Christian writers of the present day" (66). The article appears to have been a review of a work on Egypt (68), but I have been unable to identify it or its writer.

129. "Notice of objections," *Christian Spectator* (July 1841): 68.

130. Ibid.

131. Pearson, *Infidelity*, 505.

attention to "the general tendency, and the main impression conveyed by the whole book"—rather than working out "the precise proportion of religious remark in every ten pages."[132]

Arnold had sometimes used the term "Christianize" for the manner in which religious sentiment should be blended into a work on secular subjects.[133] But because of denominational differences, it was impossible for this term to be straightforward. Arnold believed there was common ground between all Christians, including Unitarians and Roman Catholics. When some of his letters on the subject were published in Stanley's *Life*, the *Record* newspaper issued a savage critique of Arnold's religious views, clearly demonstrating that such an inclusive definition of "Christian" would not be shared by all evangelicals.[134] The same issue arose in one of the few extended contemporary analyses of the "Monthly Series" as a whole. In March 1848, the *Biblical Review and Congregational Magazine* announced:

> The *Monthly Volume* proceeds, on the whole, satisfactorily. . . . While some of its volumes realize perfectly the idea of the series, there are others which show that the Society cannot guard too much against the dangers of inaccuracy in the use of authorities, the forcible introduction of religious reflections, instead of the natural and graceful religious spirit in which it is their intention that each subject should be treated, and, above all, the least approach to that species of religious fraud, by which the best ascertained results of human inquiry are treated lightly or unfairly in order to force them into harmony with the writer's own views on the teaching of revelation on the same subject. As a whole, however, we give our warm and earnest commendation to the series.[135]

The range of denominations represented in the RTS, both as members and writers, meant that all its publications were supposed to be nondenominational. As the *Biblical* reviewer pointed out, however, sometimes "the writer's own views on the teaching of revelation" appeared too obviously. To a certain extent, this had to be the case, as the RTS did not want merely Christian tone, but evangelical tone. History should reveal the workings of Providence, and show "a clear recognition of God's moral administration;" the subjects of biography should be assessed by "the true test of commendation and censure," which will be applied at the Day of Judgement; and the sciences should

---

132. "Notice of objections," *Christian Spectator* (July 1841), all quotations from 68.
133. See Stanley, *Life of Arnold*, i, 252, 285.
134. *Brief Observations on the Late Rev Dr Arnold*, esp. 13–18.
135. "The Tract Society's works," *Biblical Review* 4 (1848): 436.

demonstrate the "perfections of the Almighty." But all these subjects also had to present the Deity "not only as the Creator, but Redeemer."[136] The Word of God had to be at least as prominent as his Works, and, as in all other RTS publications, there had to be explicit mention of the doctrine of salvation through faith in Christ crucified. Yet, these views were shared by all evangelicals, so it could not have been personal views of this sort that upset the *Biblical* reviewer.[137]

The *Biblical* reviewer also noted that the "religious spirit" was not always introduced as naturally and gracefully as could be wished.[138] The forcible introduction of religious reflections could come close to "sermonizing," and the Society was aware that exhibiting religion "in a repulsive or a puerile form" could "occasion levity, or ... deter from perusal."[139] A year after its initial criticism, the *Biblical Review* reported that the Series had now been "regularly sustained ... with great general excellence," and Pearson was able to commend it as "a step in the right direction," away from sermonizing.[140] This suggests that the RTS managed to sort out early problems so that the "Monthly Series" acquired a relatively consistent Christian tone. Given the number of writers involved, the tone was unlikely to be uniform, but the committee took care in selecting writers, and had no qualms about rejecting manuscripts that failed to measure up. One such manuscript was described thus: "The style is much too feeble and quite unsuitable in other respects for this subject. It scarcely comes up to the Society's standard for the most ordinary publications."[141]

THE RTS had very specific requirements for its ideal Christian tone. It had to be a balance between the requirement for Christian content and the equally strong need to avoid scaring off potential readers. The problem was

136. "Announcement of the Monthly Volume," *Christian Spectator* (Sept. 1845): 65.

137. The critical review of March 1848 coincided with the Society's disciplining of editor Charles Williams. By May 1849, he had been replaced. This is discussed further in chapter 4.

138. See also Stanley, *Life of Arnold*, i, 252.

139. "On the union of general and scientific instruction with Scriptural knowledge," *Christian Spectator* (Sept. 1845): 70.

140. "The Tract Society's publications," *Biblical Review* 6 (1849): 429; Pearson, *Infidelity*, 509.

141. RTS Corr., Jones to Copley, 12 December 1846, regarding George E. Sargent's rejected draft of "The Crusades."

how to present the sciences so that they were similar enough to secular presentations to reach the same readers, but different enough to be efficacious in conveying the importance of a Christian framework. The model of the *Saturday Magazine* could have been adapted to evangelical purposes, but the juxtaposition of articles was only possible in the context of a periodical. The *Leisure Hour* would include this as one of its ways of creating Christian tone, but the "Monthly Series" needed something suited to continuous narrative. The model provided by the SPCK *Fishes* was no more suitable, due to its lack of evangelical emphasis and restriction of theological references to the introduction. The existing Christian genres of the natural theology and the scriptural natural history were both unsuitable because too obviously Christian. A scriptural natural history was explicitly a work of theological interpretation, where it was legitimate and desirable to have religious references on every page. It was highly unlikely that a reader who was accustomed to the secular natural history of the *Penny Magazine* would be tempted to read a scriptural natural history. The "Monthly Series" needed something rather more subtle, which would enable its publications to carry out their mission among the working classes of Britain.

III

Reading Fish

EVANGELICALS attributed immense power to the printed word. Reading could lead a man to salvation or it could lead him astray. This power was regularly demonstrated in the accounts of successful conversion that were published in missionary society reports and other evangelical periodicals. In July 1843, for instance, the Religious Tract Society's own *Christian Spectator* told the story of two evangelicals who were trying to enlist more subscribers to the Bible Society. One man they met was adamantly opposed, and the language in which he described the Bible shocked his listeners. The source of this infidelity was soon discovered to lie in his choice of reading material: "On inquiry they found he was a reader and admirer of the works of Paine, and that he had them in his house." Thomas Paine was a noted radical and unbeliever. The evangelicals met print with print, and left the man a tract "written in defence of Divine revelation." On returning to the house some time later, all was changed.

> As soon as the man whom they had formerly conversed with came forward, he addressed them, "Gentlemen, the tract which you left me I read, and am obliged to you for it. By the blessing of God, it has gained a complete triumph in my mind over the writings of Paine. You shall witness the destruction of his trash." He then, with much earnestness, took the books, and cast them into the fire. "So," said he, "may all blasphemous publications burn!"[1]

He then told them of his intention to read his father's old Bible, and teach his own children to read it.

This story is typical of the conversions in which evangelicals delighted. The simple reading of a religious tract was enough to overcome infidelity, no matter how strongly entrenched that infidelity had previously been. This was why

---

1. Quoted (source not stated), in *Christian Spectator* (July 1843): 65.

evangelicals placed so much faith in the utility of religious tracts and similar publications, and made so many efforts to distribute them wherever they might potentially be "a word in season." What these stories neglect, however, is the complexity of the reading process itself. Although evangelicals often wrote as though simply delivering a tract into a reader's hands was enough for reading and conversion to follow, neither of these steps was inevitable. Doubtless, many thousands of the tracts that were so energetically distributed on omnibuses, at race meetings and at executions languished unread, or had their paper appropriated for less spiritual purposes. In an attempt to engage the reader's attention, tracts were given attention-grabbing titles and curious opening paragraphs, and often carried a picture of some striking scene on the front page. The RTS committee was well aware of the importance of "good and striking pictorial embellishments" when trying to reach "a lower class than the papers of the Society are at present doing."[2] Penny magazines used the same technique, and the first article in each number of a periodical was carefully chosen. The *Leisure Hour* frequently opened with its current serial, which gave the artists plenty of opportunity for creating striking images (fig. 3.1). In its book publications, the Society was among the earliest users of colour printing, again noting that "the use of Coloured Pictures would greatly increase the attractiveness" of its publications.[3]

The publications had to be read, but they also had to convert their readers, and every publication by the Society included a statement of Christ's sacrifice, "so that, if a person were to see but one, and never had an opportunity of seeing another book, he might plainly perceive [his path to salvation]."[4] But, however much evangelicals hoped to the contrary, there was no guarantee that reading the words that explained the atonement Christ made for the sins of mankind would lead to conversion. For all the occasions where missionary journals reported a person converted by a tract, there must have been at least as many more cases where a tract was read and its contents ignored or ridiculed. This was why the instructions to RTS writers also recommended that works should be plain, striking, entertaining, full of ideas, and adapted to a specific person or situation, rather than aimed at a general, and necessarily impersonal, audience. If carried out successfully, these features should ensure not only that a work was read, but that it made a personal connection with each of its readers and convinced them of the importance of spiritual faith.

---

2. USCL/RTS CCM, 15 November 1854.
3. Ibid.
4. [Bogue], Tract No. 1, quoted in Samuel G. Green, *Story of the Religious Tract Society*, 6.

Figure 3.1. Serialised fiction often took the front page, because of its opportunities for dramatic illustrations, such as this escape from a flood in the *Leisure Hour*, 13 April 1854.

Ideally, reading an RTS publication was an educational experience similar to conversing with a trusted and learned friend, someone who could explain complicated things and whose opinion would be taken seriously. The *Leisure Hour* made the evangelical attitude to reading explicit when a contributor wrote, "If you do not grow wiser, in some way, by what you read—that is, if you are *only* amused and not instructed by what you read—you are throwing away the greater part of the time spent in reading."[5] The reader was assumed to be someone who was struggling to improve himself through reading and education. The authors of the books he read were superior in intellect and knowledge, but willing to share their wisdom.

---

5. *Leisure Hour* 4 (1855): 543. The RTS approach to reading is also discussed in James A. Secord, *Victorian Sensation*, 323–25.

In the secular expository works published by the RTS following the 1840s, the writer had to act as learned interlocutor with regard to the explicit contents of his work and the Christian message it conveyed. This was a particularly interesting challenge in those areas where religious sentiment was not so closely or easily linked to the subject matter. Of course, the RTS maintained that "all branches of knowledge must be imbued with evangelical sentiment."[6] Nevertheless, works on the history of the Holy Land or the river Jordan obviously lent themselves to a discussion of Christian history in a way that works on whaling or the steam engine did not. This difficulty was exacerbated by the increasing number of secular publications on the sciences, which demonstrated that it was perfectly possible to write on these subjects without mentioning religion. The RTS science writers had first to convince their readers that the sciences were interesting. Then they had to convince them that the sciences remained part of a Christian worldview, and that a discussion of the Atonement was by no means out of place in a work on fish or geology. This chapter considers how "Christian tone" was made to work in the science books in the "Monthly Series," beginning with a general analysis of the range of approaches and culminating with a detailed reading of the volume on *British Fish*, which follows the way in which Christian tone was constructed during the narrative.[7] This is not intended as a means of uncovering individual writers' attitudes to evangelicalism and the sciences, but as a means of examining how the writers tried to ensure that readers took away the "correct message" by closing down the number of possible interpretations open to a reader.[8]

DEALING WITH GOD AND NATURE

Apart from its general instructions to all writers (regarding the inclusion of the Atonement, writing in a striking and clear style, and so forth), the RTS imposed no specific rules on its "Monthly Series" writers. This is why at least one periodical could express concern about the Society's ability to produce a uniform series when working with so many writers. Even after the

---

6. RTS Report (1850): 141.

7. For the approach used in this chapter, I am indebted to Myers, "Science for Women and Children"; Myers, *Writing Biology;* Beer, *Darwin's Plots;* Jordan and Patten, *Literature in the Market Place,* chaps. 8–9. For surveys of this literature, see Suleiman and Crosman, *Reader in the Text,* introduction; Rose, "Rereading the English Common Reader"; Topham, "Scientific Publishing and the Reading of Science"; Griffin, "Anonymity and Authorship."

8. Fish, *Is There a Text in This Class?*

Series found its stride, there continued to be variation among the works that appeared. Their writers were all evangelicals, but they came from different traditions of worship and authority, and had their individual writing styles. In practice, Christian tone was never a single set of rules about how to combine secular material with the Christian message, but was a range of suitable styles. That variety of style is well illustrated by the books of the "Monthly Series." Their Christian tones were all approved, but some volumes were presented as Christian from the start, while others incorporated Christianity later, and they all differed significantly in the number of religious references they contained.

The "Monthly Series" books were not intended to be devotional treatises, containing explicit discussions about the proper relationship between the Word of God and his Works, as visible in nature and society. Hence it is rare that such issues were addressed in the Series. On the few occasions where narrators did pause to expound the relationship between Revelation and Creation, they expressed the typical evangelical position that Revelation was the key to all spiritual knowledge. As the writer of *The Senses and the Mind* (vol. 51, 1850) expressed it:

> Who by searching can find out God? Unless God graciously reveals himself to us, a true knowledge of him in our fallen state is impossible; the capabilities of our minds are, after all, but limited; and though, through our reflection on the evidences of our senses, we may come to the conclusion that there is an omnipotent Power, we remain in ignorance as to what that Power is, and as to our relationship thereunto.[9]

Thus, a study of nature might lead to conclusions about the existence of a Deity, but that was not enough for the evangelical Christian, who needed to know what sort of Deity existed and how that Deity interacted with mankind. Evangelicals did not believe that the study of nature could lead to any significant conclusions about the personality of God, let alone to the details of Christ's sacrifice and Atonement. Such teachings could come only from the volume of Revelation itself. This is in clear contrast to the stance found in William Paley's work, according to whom, "Were there no example in the world, of contrivance, except that of the eye, it would be alone sufficient to support the conclusion which we draw from it, as to the necessity of an intelligent Creator."[10] Paley had gone on to deduce the attributes of the Creator,

9. [William Martin], *Senses and the Mind*, 143–44.
10. Paley, *Natural Theology*, 75.

111

and was criticised for doing so by evangelical reviewers who were not convinced of his reasoning, nor impressed that so few of the important attributes relating to salvation had been deduced.[11]

This was not to say that it was pointless to study nature. Knowledge of the natural world could be useful in this life, even though it would reveal little about the future life. And if interpreted correctly, it could confirm some of the teachings of Revelation, thus acting as an aid to faith. The narrator of *The Blights of the Wheat, and their Remedies* (vol. 11, 1846) admitted that he had a "higher calling as a minister of the word of life," and he was using skills gained as a sermon writer when he explained:

> The wisdom and goodness of God which shone in weaker rays in the morning dawn of nature, break forth with stronger beams in the scheme of redemption, now that the Sun of righteousness has risen with healing in his wings, and the day hath appeared. We, then, should live as children of the day; and we should remember that we see the things of creation, as the key of knowledge opens them to our view, not in the light of early morn, before the mists had begun to melt, but with the advantages of those on whom the true light shineth.[12]

Light had long been used as a metaphor for the grace of God or for Jesus. The image of the "Sun of righteousness" came from Malachi 4:2, and was also familiar from the third verse of Wesley's hymn "Hark, the herald angel." The narrator of *Blights of the Wheat* followed the common evangelical analogy between light and the gospel to compare two ways of seeing the Creation. The weak and feeble vision possible in mankind's early history, in the days before the coming of Christ, was contrasted with the clearer and more acute vision of those who live in the daylight of the gospel message brought by the Sun/Son of God. This contrast held for individuals as well as mankind, so that those individuals who had yet to accept the Christian message were effectively living in prehistory. The readers of *Blights of the Wheat* were reminded that the objects of nature, as unlocked by "the key of knowledge," cannot stand alone but must be viewed through the light of the gospel.

In both these passages, the point was made that a revelation was needed for men to understand the nature of God. Studying the sciences was not a way of acquiring belief. It was something that those who *have* belief should do, and this could be supported by Bible quotation, such as Job 37:14: "Stand

---

11. For example, "Review of Dr. Paley's Natural Theology," *Edinburgh Review* 1 (1802): 287–305.

12. [Sidney], *Blights of the Wheat,* 191.

still, and consider the wondrous works of God," as cited in *The Atmosphere and Atmospheric Phenomena* (vol. 31, 1848).[13] This sort of justification was all very well for evangelical readers, who would read nature through Revelation and be confirmed in their faith, but the "Monthly Series" was not originally intended for readers who were already converted. This is presumably why explicit discussions of the relationship between nature and Revelation, such as the two just quoted, were so rare. The works were primarily intended for those readers who did not have a strong (or any) evangelical faith and might thus be tempted astray by the works of secular and infidel publishers. Any evangelical reader ought to have strong enough defences against such works to be in no need of the antidote of the "Monthly Series." The natural world had to be presented in the Series as of interest in its own right. The skill of the writer had then to show that the sciences were not opposed to faith, and that they were more complete if prosecuted in the light of Revelation than otherwise. Thus, the works would play a pre-evangelical role by making readers think about the claims of Revelation and Christianity, and spurring them on to further investigation and thought, which it was hoped would culminate in their conversion. The inclusion of an explicit statement of the Atonement might even catch a few readers who were already on the cusp of a conversion experience.

As will become clear, it seems certain that many of the actual readers of the RTS publications, including the "Monthly Series," were in fact already evangelicals or the children of evangelicals. Thus, although the works were written for an intended audience of the unconverted, they were also read by a converted audience. It may be that some of the writers, particularly toward the later stages of the Series, were aware of this double audience. It is also likely that some of them were so used to writing for the converted that they had trouble adapting their style to the unconverted. These ambiguities about intended and actual audiences help to explain the range of approaches to Christian tone that are to be found in the hundred volumes of the Series. Some writers made Christianity and Revelation far more prominent in their works than did others, with some of them even beginning their works with an obvious theological framework. The volume on *British Fish and Fisheries*, which is the focus of this chapter, fell somewhere in the middle of the spectrum.

Works that emphasised the theological framework tended to open and close with explicitly theological material, and to infuse appropriate references

---

13. [Dick], *The Atmosphere*, 7–8.

or morals into the body of the work. *Caves of the Earth: their natural history, features and incidents* (vol. 24, 1847) began as follows:

> The "earth, given to the children of men" by the Divine Author of all being, according to revealed announcement, is a lofty and beneficent grant, viewed in itself, and in connexion with the purposes for which the donation has been bestowed.... It is in harmony with these views to study the constitution and mark the aspects of the material world.[14]

God was introduced immediately, and the reader was left in no doubt that the narrator is taking a theological position. Geology was presented as part of a theological way of viewing the world: Revelation tells us that God gave the earth to mankind, and geology will tell us what sort of gift this was.

As an example of the other extreme, where the secular material was more prominent, take the opening paragraph of *James Watt and the Steam Engine* (vol. 75, 1852):

> For the last two hundred years there has been a large class of industrious and intelligent men who have employed themselves in scientific investigations. By them the earth has been explored; they have ascended to the summits of its mountains, and descended into the depths of its cavities.... But of all they have done nothing is more strange, nor more important to the human race, than their investigation of steam, which, by an ingenious mechanical contrivance, they have, in THE STEAM ENGINE, employed as a motive force.[15]

The steam engine was presented in the context of scientific endeavour, and the reader was to be awed by the ingenuity of man. In works stressing the theological framework, it was more usual for the ingenuity of God to be emphasised. The stress on man's abilities was not a slur on God as the divine artificer, however, because the invention of the steam engine is presented as a gift in which "we may clearly trace the benevolence of God; while in its provision at a fitting period of the world's history, his providential care is no less apparent."[16] This transformation of a narrative that seems secular into part of a theological framework illustrates a different method of setting up Christian tone.

In addition to the introduction, Christian tone could be created by inserting passing references in the body of the work. These usually came in three varieties: references to God the Creator; references to God the hand

---

14. [Milner], *Caves of the Earth,* 7–9.   16. Ibid., 9.
15. [Higgins], *James Watt,* 5–6.

of Providence; and the drawing of morals. For instance, the beginning of the "May" chapter in *Garden Flowers of the Year* (vol. 17, 1847) referred to God as Creator and Sustainer: "How has the Almighty's word been working ... in bringing forth the bright verdure and radiant flowers from their wintry darkness."[17] God's Providence could be seen in the relative ease with which useful animals were domesticated, or in the rescue of a whaling ship from arctic ice.[18] The morals were rarely about theological doctrine, but referred more to living a Christian life: not being covetous, avoiding sin, and not being Roman Catholic.[19] The narrator of *Caves of the Earth*, for instance, noted the ancient use of caves as places of refuge, but added that it was impossible to hide sin or crime from God, even in the darkest of caves.[20] Generally, writers included only a few such references, usually one or two per work, occasionally one or two per chapter.[21]

Very few of these passing references were specifically evangelical, rather than Christian. A rare exception occurred in the case of the domestication of fowls, where Genesis was explicitly presented as "the only history of man in his primeval condition ... (irrespective of the claim, which its internal evidence justifies, to the pen of inspiration)."[22] After introducing the Bible as history book, the narrator placed the domestication of animals in a larger narrative centred on the consequences of the Fall. The swiftness with which man managed to domesticate useful animals indicates that even after the Fall, man was not in a savage state, despite being "doomed to 'the toil and work of his hands, because of the ground which the Lord had cursed.'"[23] There was nothing in this about salvation, but the reader was made fully aware of the sinful state of mankind, on which an appeal to make reconciliation with God could later be grounded.

Occasionally, the subject matter encouraged references to biblical stories, as with fish (fishers of men) and wheat (the good steward harvesting souls for his master). The lack of parables about telescopes or printing presses, though, meant that this strategy had limited application.[24] Another option was for the

---

17. [Pratt], *Garden Flowers*, 63.

18. [William Martin], *Our Domestic Fowls*, 18; Scoresby, *Northern Whale-Fishery*, 189.

19. On covetousness, see Scoresby, *Northern Whale-Fishery*, 17. On Roman Catholics, see [Pratt], *Wild Flowers*, 161, and [Milner], *Caves of the Earth*, 92.

20. [Milner], *Caves of the Earth*, 152.

21. The exception to this rule was Thomas Dick.

22. [William Martin], *Our Domestic Fowls*, 5.

23. Ibid., 7.

24. [William Martin], *British Fish and Fisheries*, 17–18 (fishers of men); [Sidney], *Blights of the Wheat*, 190–91 (harvesting).

writer to create new parables. As an admitted cleric, the narrator of *Blights of the Wheat* was perhaps better trained than most to use such techniques, and he developed several complex analogies, one of which concerned a New Zealand caterpillar. This caterpillar could become infected by a fungus, whereupon it buried itself in the earth. The fungus would grow inside the caterpillar, finally emerging as a tapering filament from its neck. Metamorphoses in nature were often used as analogies to the rebirth of the soul, as in *The Geography of Plants* (vol. 52, 1850), where the narrator exclaimed, "how beautifully does the approach of spring illustrate the doctrine of the resurrection!"[25] But rather than becoming a butterfly, this particular caterpillar regressed to a more corrupt state. The narrator continued:

> Can we see no analogy here, comparing things small with great, and things natural with things revealed, of the going down of the ungodly into a state of degradation, and of their coming forth into a state of life far below that in which they now are? ... [This] forcibly implies the possibility of those who are to the last under an uncured and unpardoned taint of sin, rising to shame and contempt.[26]

The natural world had to be regarded as a book filled with lessons for the reader, and these lessons were not just about the benevolence and wisdom of God, as so often presented in natural theologies, but about the typically evangelical concern with the corruption and degradation of the world, and the risk of hell. The use of analogy to interweave the scientific and religious aims of the "Monthly Series" was also a carefully constructed attempt to follow the *Christian Spectator*'s call for revealed religion to mix with the subject matter "in accordance with sound judgment and good taste," for the narrator hoped that his remarks "will be regarded as natural inferences from the subjects before the reader."[27]

The transition from natural history to salvation could potentially be somewhat abrupt, so its success might depend on the extent to which the reader trusted the narrator. Since most of the writers were anonymous, they had to develop this relationship with the reader through careful management of their narrative voices. The narrator of *Northern Whale-Fishery* (vol. 41, 1849) was an exception, for he was identified with the whaler captain and minister,

---

25. [Notcutt], *Geography of Plants*, 190.   27. Ibid., 191.
26. [Sidney], *Blights of the Wheat*, 28.

William Scoresby.[28] This narrator was much more highly personalised than the others in the Series, as he recounted his dangerous and exciting voyages in search of whales, and interspersed his history of whaling with tales of derring-do in the arctic seas. Through these tales, and especially in the last chapter (the story of a voyage that came close to disaster), the Scoresby-narrator was able to build a close relationship with the reader. He was the knowledgeable and experienced captain and man of action, someone the reader should trust when he says that "to the rude and courageous mariner, as well as to the inhabitants of refined and luxurious homes, God's message is one and the same...."[29] The anonymous narrators of other volumes did not have such well-developed identities, and were further disadvantaged by not having stories of exciting and adventurous voyages to tell. Most of the works made extensive use of anecdotes, which helped to hold the reader's attention, and gave the narrator a chance to narrate. For instance, the narrator of *Caves of the Earth* loses his dry tone when explaining that Bauman's Höhle, a cavern in Brunswick, was named after "a miner, who, in 1670, ventured into it alone, to search for ore, lost his way, wandered about for three days and nights in solitude and darkness, and at length found the entrance, only to die of utter exhaustion from hunger and fatigue, upon extricating himself."[30]

Another way of constructing a narratorial identity was by introducing the personality of the writer. The narrator of *Blights of the Wheat* revealed, "The author has more than once shown these corn diseases to the members of a farmers' club, who viewed them with extreme interest."[31] The same effect comes from remarks in the introductory material about the writer's aims for the work, for example, "A concise, but clear description of the causes and...action of the steam engine is all that can be attempted by the author."[32] The reader is reminded that there is such a person as the writer, who sat down and wrote the words the reader is about to encounter. Even these tiny personal elements give the reader something to pin onto their impression of the narrator, making him less abstract and thus hopefully more credible.

All the works had to include a statement of the Atonement, which almost always appeared at the end of the book, where it did not obstruct the flow of the narrative, and had greatest impact as the "take-home message" of the

28. It was actually an invisibly edited version of Scoresby's work.
29. Scoresby, *Northern Whale-Fishery*, 189.
30. [Milner], *Caves of the Earth*, 109–10.
31. [Sidney], *Blights of the Wheat*, 46.
32. [Higgins], *James Watt*, 10.

book.[33] Despite the claim that these works should be able to convert the unsaved reader, the narrator of *James Watt* was unusual in providing some details of the way to salvation:

> To have a saving interest in the Lord Jesus Christ; to be born again by the Holy Spirit; to have a true repentance for sin; to be reconciled to God through faith in the blood of his dear Son; and to yield up the heart and life to be sanctified by his grace, and to be conformed to his will.[34]

More typical were oblique references, such as "that which the Holy Scriptures reveal," "that benign arrangement," or "repent, believe and live," none of which would be much help to a reader who did not know how to be saved.[35] The narrator of *Blights of the Wheat* provides an extreme example. When he moved from a discussion of the natural antagonists of wheat pests to the following passage, he was clearly writing for readers who already knew what the point was:

> These considerations lead us, by analogy, to look for some such provision against the disease of the heart. We find it in the revelation of mercy God has made to man. There is only this difference, that while the antidotes to the pests which injure the fruit of our labours in the soil are as numerous as the pests themselves, the great remedy for all our moral miseries is but one, but that one is capable of every conceivable modification to suit the necessities of every case, and the wants of every age of the world.[36]

The passage relies on the reader following the analogy between natural and moral diseases, and then upon a preexisting knowledge of what "the great remedy for all our moral miseries," otherwise known as "the revelation of mercy," actually was, as well as what one should do with it. The lack of detail about salvation is further evidence of the ambiguous audience that writers

---

33. An exception was *Garden Flowers of the Year* (vol. 17, 1847), where the only mention of the Atonement appeared in an entry on the knot-flowered fig-marigold, in the chapter for April: "As it is in our day, so it was then, man could not atone for past pollution or present sin, and the only means of purification and forgiveness was that which the Holy scriptures reveal" (59). Not only does this sentence not make clear *what* the "Holy scriptures reveal," but its burial deep in the book deprives it of effect.

34. [Higgins], *James Watt*, 192. Equivalent statements were given in *Geography of Plants* and *Domestic Fowls*.

35. [Pratt], *Garden Flowers*, 59; [William Martin], *British Fish and Fisheries*, 192; Scoresby, *Northern Whale-Fishery*, 189.

36. [Sidney], *Blights of the Wheat*, 187.

thought they were addressing. Some writers seemed to be aiming more at the "educated families of our land" than at the unfortunate unsaved.

How the Readers of *British Fish* Were Caught

Christian tone was created in a variety of ways by the different writers, commensurate with their writing styles and subject matters. *British Fish and Fisheries* falls somewhere in the middle of the range. It did have a theological framework, but it was not brought to the reader's attention quite as early as the example from *Caves of the Earth*. It also had fewer passing references to religion than *Caves of the Earth*, yet it had one of the most explicit calls to salvation of any of the volumes. The success of that summons depended significantly on the degree of trust that had been built up between reader and narrator over the course of the book. This is something that is best demonstrated by following the reader through the book and noting the cumulative effect of the narrative techniques.

On picking up and opening the forty-ninth volume of the "Monthly Series," the reader would have been struck by the lack of decorative arts and by the anonymity of the writer. Both the paperback and hardbound versions were plain on the outside, the title page was undecorated (fig. 3.2), and there were only three diagrams (and two tables) in the entire book. It contained far fewer illustrations than any of the other works on fish discussed in the previous chapter, particularly compared with the periodicals. The absence of a writer's name on the title page was compensated for by the strong presence of the RTS imprint. The first four pages of the volume contained advertisements for RTS publications and, on most copies, the printer's mark at the foot of the final page was also that of the RTS. Rather than a publication date, the only date was that of the Society's founding, which gave the work a timeless quality, implying that the knowledge it contained would endure.

Its first two chapters focused on the domestic and industrial importance of fish, primarily as foodstuffs. While an interest in British species was assumed from the book's publication in Britain, the narrator defended his focus on fish. One possible motivation was the economic importance of the fisheries to modern Britain. This had been stressed by William Yarrell in his *History of British Fishes* (1841), to which the narrator of *British Fish* acknowledged his debt, and was also the *raison d'être* of several articles on fisheries in the *Leisure Hour* in the 1850s. In *British Fish*, the second chapter began with the comment that "there are few nations, it may be observed, which do not make use of fishes as food. . . . So important to a nation, indeed, are its fisheries, that they are made the subjects of legislation" (24). The narrator went on to explain the extent, location, and value of the British fisheries.

Yet, the very fact that this happened in the second chapter suggests that the principal motivation for studying fish was something else. This had been made clear in the opening paragraph of the first chapter:

> The use of fish as an article of food is of remote antiquity. The Israelites, in their journey through the wilderness, when pressed by scarcity of provisions, exclaimed, "We remember the fish which we did eat in Egypt freely, the cucumbers and the melons, and the leeks, and the onions, and the garlic;" and it is recorded, that among the plagues brought upon the Egyptians by Moses and Aaron, at the command of God, one was the turning of the water of the river Nile into blood, and the consequent destruction of the fish, Exod. vii. 19–21. (7)

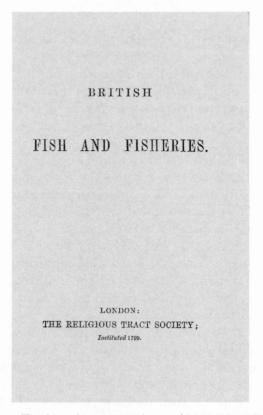

Figure 3.2. The plain and anonymous title page of *British Fish and Fisheries.*

The opening sentence immediately set out the antiquity of man's relations with fish, implying that fish were worthy of study for having been a major food source for so long. The rest of the paragraph presented evidence for this claim: two Old Testament passages, from Numbers (11:5) and Exodus, confirm that fish were eaten in ancient Egypt. Later paragraphs provided more biblical and classical evidence to this effect, citing paintings, "the mosaic pavement of Praeneste," Herodotus, the Arabic writer Abdallatif, and several pagan sources quoted in the *Pictorial Bible* (1838), as well as more Biblical passages (7–11). The narrator was presented as someone with knowledge of a wide range of sources, both sacred and secular. Thus, the Bible was presented as one source among many for information about early human history, but no comment was made respecting the Bible's claim to divine inspiration.

On pages eleven through twenty-one, the Bible was given far more prominence, as the narrator recounted most of the notable episodes involving fish. This started with a discussion of the Levitical laws respecting the foods that may or may not be eaten: "fishes with scales were decidedly allowed, and evidently constituted a considerable portion of the food of the Israelites" (12). Piscine edibility was central to the book's motivation, and this discussion of Israelite attitudes prefigured the later accounts of British fish, which regularly included comments on whether particular species are edible, how tasty they are, and (occasionally) recommended methods of cooking. Most of this section of the work, however, concerned the Gospel accounts of the occasions on which "our Saviour condescended to exercise his miraculous powers upon these creatures, thereby demonstrating that the laws of matter were subject to his control" (15). These included the feeding of the five thousand, the finding of the tribute money in the mouth of a fish, and two episodes of bountiful fishing on the Sea of Galilee. These accounts played a different role from those of the Old Testament, for they directly involved theology rather than history or natural history. The Gospels should not be considered only as history books, for they presented the life and actions of the Son of God. That such matters were presented in *British Fish*, without any sense of narrative incongruity, indicates that the work was being narrated in a firmly Christian framework. That Jesus was referred to as "our Saviour" suggests that the narrator and his reader shared, or ought to share, this framework, while the choice of "Saviour" and later of "Redeemer" (17, *passim*) in preference to "Jesus," "Lord," or "Christ" brought the issue of the Atonement subtly before the reader's consciousness.

Not only did Jesus perform miracles with fish, but four of his disciples were fishermen, which, the narrator suggested, meant that fish and fishermen might be particularly important to Christians. Unlike scribes or money changers, fishermen had an honourable employment, and "the hearts of such men, by nature, were fitted for quietness and contemplation—men of mild, and sweet, and peaceable spirits" (20). Thus, perhaps, those who studied or caught fish might be peculiarly able to grasp the "new way to everlasting life" offered by Jesus.[37] The narrator also used the metaphor of fishing for the souls of men, remembering Jesus's charge to his disciples that "from henceforth thou shalt catch men" (Luke 5:10). The narrator continued:

> These humble fishers were hereafter to throw the net of the gospel, which must ever be the work of their faithful successors; and thus are they enjoined to draw men from the depths of sin and destruction to the glorious light of that revelation, sent in mercy to beam upon the path which leadeth to the kingdom of heaven, where He who bore our sins in his own body on the cross ever liveth to intercede in behalf of all who come unto God through him. (17–18)

The fishing metaphor was used to illustrate how men could be brought out of "the depths of sin and destruction," and by reading the Gospels, "the glorious light of that revelation," they could start on the path to salvation. This pathway was belief in the doctrine of the Atonement, that Jesus bore the sins of mankind "in his own body on the cross," and that those who believe in him and his sacrifice will find heaven, for they "come unto God through him." The narrator thus introduced the Atonement, as he would do again at the conclusion of the work.[38] Its introduction through a fishing metaphor was a way to avoid being abrupt or in poor taste.

The introduction and motivation for the work on *Fishes* (1851), published by the Society for Promoting Christian Knowledge (SPCK), bore some similarity to that of *British Fish*. It began differently, with an introduction to fish anatomy and physiology, but the second half of the introduction discussed the economic importance of and methods for catching fish. The transition from physiology to foodstuffs was made with the following remark:

> We have briefly alluded to the value of Fishes as human food, a value which was appreciated in very early times. . . . Still earlier than this, the paintings which so copiously illustrate the manners of the ancient Egyptians, combine with the

---

37. There is evidence of evangelical revivals being particularly successful among fisherman and their families. See Bebbington, *Evangelicalism in Modern Britain*, 117.

38. *British Fish* is unusual for explicitly mentioning the Atonement twice.

Figure 3.3. Egyptian paintings, such as this one reproduced in the SPCK *Fishes,* could provide evidence of ancient methods of catching fish. Here, fish are being caught with spears (and birds with nets). From Philip H. Gosse, *Fishes,* 34.

> Holy Scriptures, to prove the fact that fish, both in a fresh and salted state, formed a large part of [the diet of] that industrious people [the Israelites]. (30–31)

Like his RTS counterpart, the SPCK narrator recounted the evidence for the ancient use of fish, citing the same mixture of biblical passages, Egyptian paintings, and classical sources, although with a different emphasis. *British Fish* included the New Testament miracles involving fish alongside the Old Testament examples of eating fish. In the SPCK *Fishes,* the main thread of the discussion was the methods of catching fish, and the biblical passages, especially those from the Old Testament, were presented as evidence of the long history of the use of nets or of hooks and lines. Greater prominence was given to the evidence of Egyptian paintings, several of which were re-produced to illustrate ancient methods of catching fish (fig. 3.3). The SPCK narrator shared with his RTS counterpart the belief that the Bible could and should be used as a source of history, but he was less concerned to tell the story of Jesus alongside that of fish. The SPCK shared the RTS's belief in the value of a Christian tone for publications on secular subjects, but not the evangelical drive that emphasised the New Testament. The SPCK volume had no discussion of the Atonement at all, and tended to refer to God the Creator, rather than to Christ the Redeemer.

The first chapter of *British Fish* ended with a brief account of Greek and Roman attitudes to fish. These civilisations were dealt with in a mere three pages, and the last paragraph noted that "we need not extend our review to

Figure 3.4. The herring fishery employed a great many people, and the return of the boats was a local event. This illustration accompanied an article on the Yarmouth herring fishery in *Leisure Hour* 2 (1853): 665, which was probably written by the same writer as *British Fish and Fisheries.*

other nations of antiquity, among whom, as in the present day, fishes were of more or less importance as an article of food" (23), an assessment that called attention to the comparatively vast amount of space devoted to the Israelite nation. Their importance was commensurate with their status as the Chosen People. The next chapter continued the concern with fish as food, but moved to modern Britain. The account of the fisheries of Great Britain began with those in "more distant places," such as Newfoundland and Labrador, before moving on to those on "our own shores." The local group were dealt with according to species, such as cod, pilchard, sole, mackerel, and eel, with one of the longest accounts being allocated to herring (fig. 3.4). This included a history of the fishery, the government's attempts to encourage herring fishing by paying bounty, the locations where herring are caught, and the number of ships and people involved in catching and curing almost four hundred thousand barrels of herrings a year (27–36). The chapter ended with the observation that the fisheries were almost all concerned with sea fish. This was not to say that river fish are not caught or eaten, but that "with regard to the consumption of these fishes we have no statistical data; it is far larger in proportion in the rural districts of our islands than in London, or in the chief towns" (51). The lack of statistical data was a problem for the narrator, because the accounts of the sea fisheries contained a lot of numerical data. The narrator, it seems, had a certain conception of what was needed in order to properly describe a fishery—and we shall see that the same was true of descriptions of species.

The remainder of the work described the fish of the British isles, or at least "such as are most likely to come under the observation of the general reader, or have more than ordinary interest" (52). The writer, after all, had fewer than two hundred small pages to deal with British fish, in contrast to the thousand larger pages of Yarrell's *History*. The fish were divided into five chapters according to "a scientific arrangement," following Cuvier though with English translations for the Latin taxonomic terms. *British Fish* was unusual for having preceded the taxonomic chapters with the two chapters on the importance of fish. In both Yarrell's *History* and the SPCK *Fishes*, the introductory remarks on the economic importance of fish and general fish anatomy were made distinct from the main texts by being placed in a section titled "Introduction." Their main texts began immediately with the first order, *Acanthopterygii*, and the perch family.

The beginning of the first of *British Fish*'s taxonomic chapters contained some of the material that Yarrell's *History* and the SPCK *Fishes* put in their introductions, but in more compact form. The narrator apologised for this material, but announced his intention to "forbear from entering into details which are rather more proper for purely scientific works than popular treatises." Nonetheless, "it is necessary that the reader should know the names of the fins," since it is by their "structure, position and number" that the orders and families of fish can be determined (52–53). The first diagram of the book was introduced at this point to illustrate the positions of the fins, along with the formula for expressing the number of fins. This explanation was important, for throughout the rest of the book, the fin formula would be part of the full description of a fish. The introductory section also described the so-called lateral line, the structure of the gills, and gave a brief account of the variety of teeth arrangements. These features were all used later to distinguish similar fish from one another.

Although the brief description of anatomy seems to fit well as an introduction to the taxonomic chapters, it did not deal with the physiological functioning of fish in general. This was a particular strength of the section

125

on fish in the Chamber's textbook on *Zoology* (1842), but there were brief discussions in Yarrell's *History,* the SPCK *Fishes,* and the introductory article in the *Saturday Magazine* of the circulatory and respiratory systems, the method of propulsion, the effectiveness of the senses, and the state of development of the neural system. The absence of any physiological discussion in *British Fish* suggests that the main aim of the work was to describe fish, not to explain how they function. It was a work of natural history, rather than a work in the relatively new sciences of comparative anatomy or physiology.

After the preliminary remarks on anatomy for identification purposes, the narrator of *British Fish* moved from the general to the specific:

> Fish are divided into two great primary sections, namely, the *osseous* and the *cartilaginous.* . . . These two sections are resolved into several orders. . . . The first order of the osseous series is termed the acanthopterygious, (*Acanthopterygii*) which, in plain English, means "fishes with the fin-rays of their dorsal fin spinous, or at least, mostly spinous." Of this order the perch family (*Percidae*) is very conspicuous. (55–56)

The choice of the *Acanthopterygii* as the first order was standard among all the books that followed Cuvier's classification of fish. What came next varied. The SPCK *Fishes* and Chambers's *Zoology* both aimed to give a general overview of the class Pisces. The SPCK narrator introduced every order, described the families within that order, and gave full descriptions of one typical genus per family, usually with one typical species per genus. The *Zoology* had less detailed descriptions, and named several representative species per genus. As is clear from their titles, *British Fish* and Yarrell's *History* had a different aim, to describe those fish commonly found in Britain (though not only native species). Thus some families were more numerously represented than others, and the reader got a more specific and localised overview of the class Pisces. It so happens that Cuvier's first fish, the perch, *is* found in Britain, so all the books began with the same fish.

After announcing the perch, *British Fish* gave two pages of description to this species, followed by similar descriptions of its close relatives, and then of members of other families in the same order. These were written in continuous prose, with one following from the other with nothing more than a paragraph break, as can be seen with the descriptions of the barbel, gudgeon, and tench in figure 3.5. This contrasted with the style more commonly used in reference works. Yarrell's *History,* for instance, started the entry for each fish on a new page (fig. 3.6), with its name in capitals, an illustration, and details of those

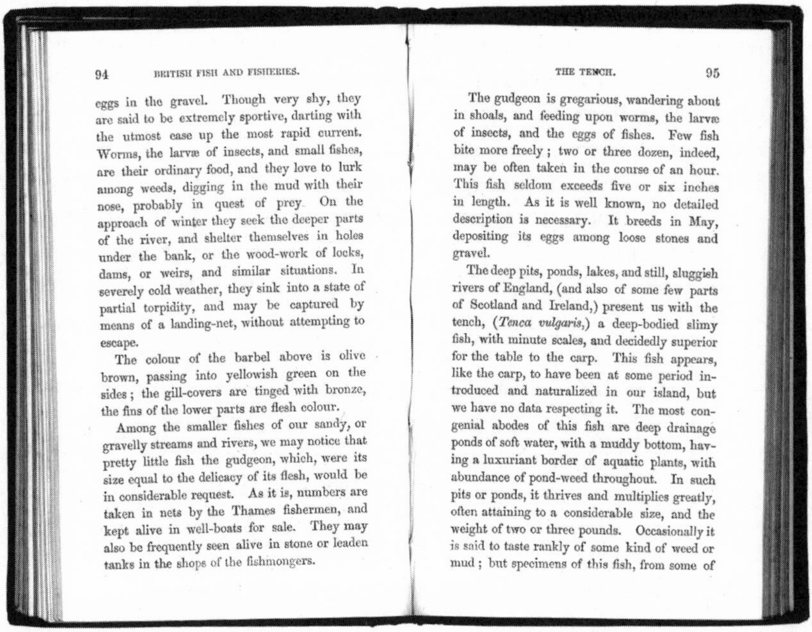

94 BRITISH FISH AND FISHERIES.

eggs in the gravel. Though very shy, they are said to be extremely sportive, darting with the utmost ease up the most rapid current. Worms, the larvæ of insects, and small fishes, are their ordinary food, and they love to lurk among weeds, digging in the mud with their nose, probably in quest of prey. On the approach of winter they seek the deeper parts of the river, and shelter themselves in holes under the bank, or the wood-work of locks, dams, or weirs, and similar situations. In severely cold weather, they sink into a state of partial torpidity, and may be captured by means of a landing-net, without attempting to escape.

The colour of the barbel above is olive brown, passing into yellowish green on the sides; the gill-covers are tinged with bronze, the fins of the lower parts are flesh colour.

Among the smaller fishes of our sandy, or gravelly streams and rivers, we may notice that pretty little fish the gudgeon, which, were its size equal to the delicacy of its flesh, would be in considerable request. As it is, numbers are taken in nets by the Thames fishermen, and kept alive in well-boats for sale. They may also be frequently seen alive in stone or leaden tanks in the shops of the fishmongers.

THE TENCH. 95

The gudgeon is gregarious, wandering about in shoals, and feeding upon worms, the larvæ of insects, and the eggs of fishes. Few fish bite more freely; two or three dozen, indeed, may be often taken in the course of an hour. This fish seldom exceeds five or six inches in length. As it is well known, no detailed description is necessary. It breeds in May, depositing its eggs among loose stones and gravel.

The deep pits, ponds, lakes, and still, sluggish rivers of England, (and also of some few parts of Scotland and Ireland,) present us with the tench, (*Tenca vulgaris,*) a deep-bodied slimy fish, with minute scales, and decidedly superior for the table to the carp. This fish appears, like the carp, to have been at some period introduced and naturalized in our island, but we have no data respecting it. The most congenial abodes of this fish are deep drainage ponds of soft water, with a muddy bottom, having a luxuriant border of aquatic plants, with abundance of pond-weed throughout. In such pits or ponds, it thrives and multiplies greatly, often attaining to a considerable size, and the weight of two or three pounds. Occasionally it is said to taste rankly of some kind of weed or mud; but specimens of this fish, from some of

Figure 3.5. British Fish and Fisheries was written in continuous prose, so it is not easy to spot where one fish stops and the next begins. The transition from gudgeon to tench is in the middle of the right-hand page. From [William Martin], *British Fish and Fisheries,* 94–95.

naturalists who had previously described it. There was also an index of general and systematic names to help the reader find entries for specific fish, but the clear demarcation of each entry made it easy to skim through the book to identify an unknown fish. Such a task would be difficult in *British Fish,* which had no index and where the only easy way to skim through the continuous text was to use the running heads at the top of each page, or to look for the use of italics when the systematic name of a species was mentioned, usually near the beginning of its description. The use of continuous prose also contrasted with comparable cheap books from secular publishers, such as those in series from Knight and Chambers (one of which is illustrated in fig. 6.6). These natural history works adapted the reference style used in Yarrell's *History,* keeping the picture and some distinctive typography (numbering, or the practice of putting the name at the beginning in capitals), but starting new entries wherever on the page they came in order to save paper. *British Fish,* in contrast, belonged to a discursive genre.

The end of the first taxonomic chapter had no concluding passage. It stopped at the end of the section on the last fish and the next chapter began, "The second order of osseous fishes is termed *Malacopterygii*...." (89). In each of the later chapters, another order of fish was described. To examine the treatment of a typical species, let's take the tench. Like the carp, it is a member of the *Cyprinidae* family and belongs to the order *Malacopterygii*, or fish with soft fin rays. The account of the tench took up three pages, ending with the comment, "The tench is too well-known to require a particular description" (98). Whatever it was, then, the contents of those three pages were not deemed to be a "description." The narrator was using "description" in a strict zoological sense to mean a definition that ties a specimen to its systematic name in the taxonomic system. These were the descriptions published in learned journals and in monographs like Jenyns's *Fish of the Beagle*

TENCH.   375

ABDOMINAL
MALACOPTERYGII.   CYPRINIDÆ.

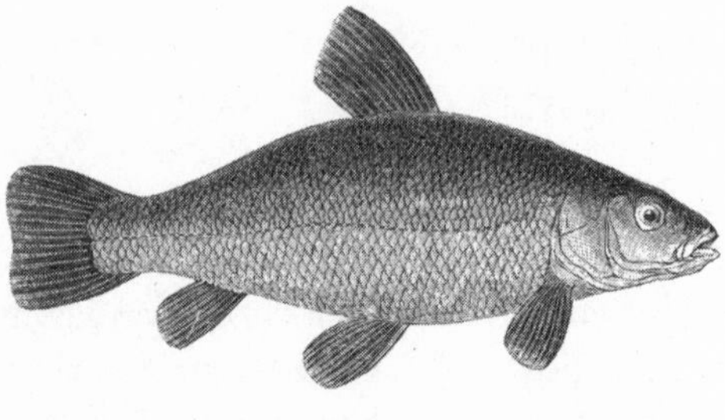

THE TENCH.

Tinca vulgaris, Cuvier, Règne An. t. ii. p. 273.
    ,,   ,,   *Tench*, Flem. Brit. An. p. 186, sp. 61.
    ,,   ,,   *Tinca*, Willughby, p. 251, Q. 5, fig. 1.
Cyprinus tinca, Bloch, pt. i. pl. 14.
    ,,   ,,   *Tench*, Penn. Brit. Zool. vol. iii. p. 474.
    ,,   ,,   ,,   Don. Brit. Fish. pl. 113.
    ,,   ,,   ,,   Jenyns, Brit. Vert. p. 405.

    Tinca. *Generic Characters.*—To those common to the Gudgeons (*Gobio*),
    may be added, that the scales are very small, the mucous secretion on the sur-
    face of the body abundant, the barbules or cirri very small.

Figure 3.6. In the formal description of a species, there are certain things that have to be included, and a particular technical language that should be used. From Yarrell, *History of British Fishes*, i, 375.

(1842). Such a description included details of order, family, class, and genus, a list of defining characteristics by which this species differed from other members of its genus, and a fin formula. This section was usually in Latin, which, combined with the abstract nature of the fin formula, conveyed the impression of remote, technical knowledge. The description then continued in the vernacular, with a standardised description of the creature's appearance, usually accompanied by a detailed illustration and a note of its geographical location. It might end with a discussion of the origin of the specimen and the naturalist's reasons for identifying it as a new species.

The "descriptions" that were then used by other writers drew on these definition-descriptions, generally using the vernacular throughout and giving as many or as few details as needed for their purpose. The narrator of Yarrell's *History* gave very detailed descriptions that were close enough to the definitions for his readers to positively identify specimens, while the narrator of Chambers's *Zoology* barely described the fish at all, merely citing them in illustration of the sorts of fish in each family. *British Fish* and the articles in the *Saturday Magazine* and the *Penny Magazine* fell between these extremes, partly because their readers were unlikely to be trying to identify specimens, but also because their focus on British fish meant that some species, such as the salmon or perch, could be assumed to be well known. Such a claim might be backed up by a reference to the waters in which it is found, but equally by its common appearance in the fish market in Billingsgate (fig. 3.7) or on the dinner plate. The gudgeon, for instance, was reported in *British Fish* to be "taken in nets by the Thames fishermen, and kept alive in well-boats for sale. They may also be frequently seen alive in stone or leaden tanks in the shops of the fishmongers" (94). Those fish that were given fuller descriptions, including fin formulae, in *British Fish* were those that the reader might not know and for which a "particular description" might be necessary. Although this might suggest that the accounts of fish were presented to help the reader identify unknown fish, the layout of the book, as already discussed, suggests otherwise, as does the variation between the accounts. Rather, they were intended to add to the reader's stock of general knowledge.

The readers of *British Fish* were told a little about the appearance of each fish, but also about its habitat, habits, food, breeding season, and suitability for eating. The longer descriptions contained anecdotes, often quoted directly from other writers, about particularly large fish, fish that were difficult to catch, the introduction of the species into Britain, or proverbs and historical

Figure 3.7. The fish market at Billingsgate, London. From *Leisure Hour* 1 (1852): 321.

incidents involving fish. This range of information was apparent in the very first sentence on the tench:

> The deep pits, ponds, lakes and still, sluggish rivers of England, (and also some few parts of Scotland and Ireland,) present us with the tench (*Tenca vulgaris,*) a deep-bodied slimy fish, with minute scales, and decidedly superior for the table to the carp. (95)

In this one sentence, the reader was informed of the geographical distributions and preferred habitats of the tench, given a brief physical description, and told that it is better eating than the carp (which was dismissed a few pages earlier as "in our opinion, anything but agreeable" [90]). The narrator continued by noting that the tench was not indigenous to the British isles, before giving a fuller description of its favourite habitat:

> Deep drainage ponds of soft water, with a muddy bottom, having a luxuriant border of aquatic plants, with abundance of pond-weed throughout. In such pits or ponds, it thrives and multiplies greatly, often attaining to a considerable size, and the weight of two or three pounds. Occasionally it is said to taste

rankly of some kind of weed or mud; but specimens of this fish, from some of the muddiest ponds in Essex, which a few months since were placed before the writer at table, were of very superior flavour, and finely grown. Their colour, for he saw them when alive, was very dark, with a pink tinge about and under the pectoral fins. (95–96)

Just as the opening sentence contained a variety of different pieces of information, so in this later passage the reader was taken to and fro between different aspects of the tench: from habitat to size, to edibility, to colour. Later sentences described the breeding season, tench's superiority over carp as food, how to stock a pond with tench, what tench themselves eat ("worms, larvae, and various vegetable matters" [96]), and their method of surviving the winter. This mixture of information, and the movement back and forth, was a way of providing variety between the account of one fish and that of the next. A reference work with a standard format for its descriptions becomes a tedious read after a few entries, but *British Fish* was supposed to be read from cover to cover, and had to guard against being dull.

The introduction of the character of the writer toward the end of the passage just quoted was another way of keeping the reader's attention—by bringing in a personal element. The majority of the work was written in the third person, with a narrator who was almost invisible except for a few remarks made in the first person plural. Although the discreet narrator was typical of natural history reference books, creating a narrator–reader relationship was an important way for *British Fish* to encourage the reader to read the whole book. The third-person mention of the writer at his dinner table reminded the reader that the narrative voice was connected to an actual writer, who needed to eat just like other men. The personality of the narrator was otherwise only to be deduced from his comments ("in our opinion") on the taste of certain fish, so the glimpse of his daily routine made him seem more human.

The regular inclusion of textual or footnote references to authorities, especially Yarrell's *History*, did help to bolster the credibility of the work, but the personal authority of the narrator was just as important. The most usual way for demonstrating such authority was to place the writer's name and credentials on the book's title page, as in Yarrell's *History* (fig. 3.8). But the only avowed "author" of *British Fish* was the Religious Tract Society, not a widely known ichthyological authority. The fact that the narrator informed his reader that he saw the fish when they were alive, and could testify personally to their colour, helped create the narrator's authority as fish expert. Similarly, at other places in the work, the narrator stressed that "we have had the opportunity of seeing" (123) and "we have ourselves seen" (120) certain characteristics of trout. Some of these observations were made in the fish markets of London and thus had a similar status to the dinner-table observation above, but others were made by rivers and at the coast, where fish were observed in their natural habitat. Such "field" observations were even more effective at creating the authority of the narrator than domesticated observations could be.

The use of the first person plural in *British Fish* contrasted with the occasional use of the first person singular in Yarrell's *History*. In Yarrell's account of the tench we learn: "So engrossed are they at this time ... , that I have

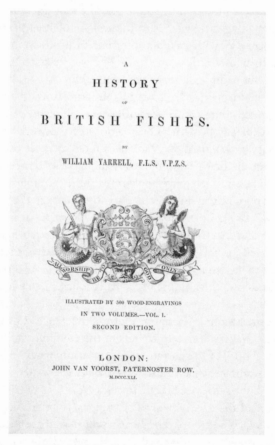

Figure 3.8. The title page of Yarrell's *History of British Fishes* makes the most of his credentials as vice-president of the Zoological Society and Fellow of the Linnean Society. It also carries the coat of arms of the Fishmongers Company.

frequently dipped out all three fish by a sudden plunge of a landing net."[39] This particular passage had a stronger narrative authority than *British Fish,* partly through the use of "I" and partly because of the activity involved in catching, rather than passively seeing, the fish. Yet, the authority was gained by excluding the reader from the narrative. In the opening sentence of the account of the tench, for instance, the narrator wrote that "the rivers of England . . . present *us* with the tench" (95, my italics); and later, "of its fecundity *we* may form some estimate, when *we* learn from Bloch that . . ." (96, my italics). In these instances, the narrator invited the reader to join him, to explore the rivers of England, and to make deductions together. The use of the plural was not uncommon in anonymous writing, especially in periodicals where the lack of an explicit author to whom the singular pronoun could be linked meant that authority came from the editorial staff and the publisher. It served a similar function in *British Fish,* but also helped to create a narrator–reader relationship that was both closer and more equal than that suggested by the authoritative "I" in Yarrell's *History.*

The inclusion of anecdotes was another method of keeping the reader's interest, and also of forging the narrator–reader relationship. In the case of the tench, the narrator of *British Fish* moved from a discussion of the fish's winter habits, when they "retire to holes and snug recesses," to their ability to survive even when "blocked up in their retreats . . . as long as they are bedewed with water and their gills kept wet" (96–97). This was followed by a page-long anecdote about men who, clearing out a pond, discovered a trapped tench "of most singular form, having literally assumed the shape of the hole in which . . . he had been for many years confined" (97). Such anecdotes enlivened the narrative. However, not all of the events recounted in *British Fish* had been directly witnessed by the narrator. The story of the strange-shaped tench occurred in no fewer than four of the contemporary works on fish. *British Fish* attributed it to "Daniel, in his Rural Sports . . . , quoted by Mr. Yarrell" (97). In Yarrell's *History* and the *Saturday Magazine,* the episode was attributed directly to William Daniel's *Rural Sports* (1801).[40] The story appeared again, paraphrased, in the *Penny Magazine,* where it was used as a filler after an article on "Domestic economy: boiling food."[41] This time, the excerpt was

39. Yarrell, *History of British Fishes,* i, 380.

40. Ibid., i, 377; "Freshwater Fish: the tench," *Saturday Magazine,* 2 October 1841, 132–33, at 133.

41. "Tenacity of Life in a Tench," *Penny Magazine,* 29 January 1842, 36.

attributed to Yarrell's *History,* and it is clear that Yarrell's repetition of the episode gave Daniel's account additional authority.

Anecdotes could also allow an alternative narrative voice to speak to the reader, as when the tench episode was recounted in *British Fish* as a direct quotation.[42] This gave the reader some variety, and perhaps a brief respite from the main narration, while the primary narrator took the credit for introducing the reader to the subnarrator. Assuming the anecdote was relevant and amusing, the primary narrator might be able to increase the reader's trust in his selection of facts and sources, thus improving the narrator–reader relationship. Most of the anecdotes were not direct quotations, but were narrated by the primary narrator in the third person—unlike some of the first person comments testifying to having seen fish of an unusual size or colour. They nevertheless contributed to the reader's image of the narrator as a knowledgeable man who commanded a range of interesting information. These anecdotes included accounts of how fish are caught—by line or net, from ship or shore—as well as the origins of their names. The John Dory came in for special attention. The French call it *jaune dorée* (gilded yellow), while its Italian name is *il janitore* (gatekeeper), and John Dory could be a corruption of either. The Italian choice of name occasioned a footnote from the narrator:

> This name is an allusion to St. Peter, who took the tribute money from the fish at the command of our Lord, and who, in Roman Catholic countries, is supposed to bear the keys of heaven; a black spot on each side the fish is superstitiously imagined to indicate the pressure of the apostle's thumb and finger—but the haddock may on this account put in a claim. (79)

We have already seen how the Scriptures were given prominence in the first chapter of *British Fish,* and we shall see the Atonement brought in again as the climax to the work, but this episode with the John Dory is one of only a few theological allusions in the body of the work. Although most of the text was very similar to that found in secular works, the occasional use of a judicious anecdote reiterates the Christian tone that is intended to pervade the whole work. Accusing Roman Catholics of superstition was a common device among evangelicals, and the remark about the haddock's claim to St. Peter's touch was intended to ridicule the belief. In addition, the simple reference to Jesus as "our Lord" brought the Redeemer back to the reader's attention.

---

42. In the *Saturday Magazine,* the same words are used, but they are not acknowledged as a quotation.

The final chapter of *British Fish* addressed the cartilaginous family, which included the sturgeon, dogfish, sharks, rays, and lampreys. The chapter was much like the preceding ones until three pages before the end of the book. The last fish to be discussed was the myxine. Linnaeus had classed it as a worm, but it was to be given a place among the British fish, albeit as "one of the lowest in structural organization" (189). Its underdeveloped appearance and curious habits provided one last gruesome anecdote. Cuvier claimed that it attacked and ate into other fish, for it was often found deep inside the bodies of those fish. The narrator ended his description with the observation:

... on some parts of our eastern coast it is called the borer.

Here terminates our sketch of the fish and fisheries of our British islands—a sketch, indeed, for our limited space will allow no more. Yet we trust that the reader, desirous of some general information on the subject, will not be altogether disappointed. To those who wish to make this portion of zoology a study, Mr Yarrell's work on British Fishes is indispensable. (190)

Although this recommendation, almost encouragement, for further study may seem an appropriate ending, it was unusual. Yarrell's *History*, the SPCK *Fishes*, and the Chambers *Zoology* all stopped abruptly at the end of the last entry. Such a sudden termination fitted the format of a reference work with discrete entries, as there was no continued narrative that needed to be wound up. The main text of Yarrell's *History*, for instance, had no progressive narrative structure—no beginning, middle, or end of the narration—and no climax. Nor would a reader expect this from a work of reference, which was unlikely to be read as a whole. *British Fish*, however, did have narrative movement from the history of fish, to modern fisheries, to the description of species. In completing this movement with concluding remarks, the narrator closed his work, indicating yet again that he was working in a different genre to that of the reference work or textbook. The SPCK writer had combined aspects of the continuous prose of the RTS narrator with the model of the reference work to produce a work with narration around its descriptions. Yet there was no conclusion to the SPCK *Fishes*, which ended with the sentence: "There are one or two other species of the genus [lampreys] found in our waters, but they are small, and of no importance."[43] The lack of conclusion was potentially unsettling for the reader, who had followed the narrator through the book for, it seems, no greater purpose than the accumulation of facts. The reader

---

43. Philip H. Gosse, *Fishes*, 324.

of the RTS work, on the other hand, was given a conclusion and a sense of fulfilled achievement.

Having a conclusion was rare enough in natural history works, but it was even more unusual for a writer to continue for a further two pages after announcing the conclusion. The recommendation of Yarrell's *History* was not, it transpired, the end of the work, for the narrator followed it with a new page and a new paragraph: "We ought not to conclude, however, without a thankful recognition of that adorable Being who made 'the seas and all that is therein.' How true it is that 'God is love!'" (191). The last two pages of the work completed the framing that was begun in the first chapter by bringing the reader back to the subject of religion. But where in the first chapter the narrator set up his theological framework and mentioned the Atonement, but made no attempt at conversion, he was far more explicit in the final pages. This was the "moral" to the rest of the work, and the narrator took on quite a different tone, becoming more dogmatic and awestruck ("How true ...!" "How wonderful ...!"), and ultimately appealing directly to the reader to save his soul. Despite the claim in the preceding paragraph that the sketch "here terminates," the acknowledgement of God's love, and the call to salvation which followed it, was a crucial part of the work for the RTS—as it was not for the SPCK. But having announced the end of the work on p. 190 with a suitable closing paragraph, the writer had to ensure that his reader kept reading until p. 192. To do this, the writer had to rely on the relationship he had created between narrator and reader over the course of the preceding chapters of the book. Given a sufficiently strong relationship, in which the reader had grown to trust the narrator as a reliable, interesting, and authoritative voice, the reader should be willing to treat the last two pages as integral to the work simply because the narrator said they were: "We *ought not* to conclude ... without ..." (my italics). This transition might seem rather abrupt, but throughout the work the reader had become accustomed to the narrator introducing anecdotes and moving from one subject to another and back again. If the final transition was any more abrupt, it was because evangelical conversion was supposed to be a life-changing moment, often precipitated by a surprise or a forced change of viewpoint.[44]

The narrative that led to the call to salvation was predicated on the evidences that "God is love" provided by the natural world. "Every examination of his works, as the Creator, furnishes illustrations of this fact, and may

---

44. Bebbington, *Evangelicalism in Modern Britain,* 7–8.

prepare us to acknowledge with gratitude that pre-eminent exhibition of his kindness, which he made in the gift of an Almighty Saviour" (191). Nature was not called on to prove the existence of God, but to prove his benevolence, which the reader had to accept to be able to understand how Christ's death could atone for the sins of mankind. The nature of the "gift" was explained in a direct quote from I John 4:9–10 ("God sent his only begotten Son that we might live through him"), and the narrator added parenthetically that the gift had been "rendered necessary" by "the apostasy of our race." This comment prefigured the emphasis on man's rebellion that would be the motive force behind the call for salvation on the final page.

Before moving on, however, the narrator again emphasised God's concern for "man's earthly happiness," as demonstrated in the variety of "nutritious food" to be found among "the roaming tenants of the waters" (191). In contrast to many works in the natural theology genre, where every example of the benevolence of God mentioned in the main text would have been flagged and emphasised, *British Fish* left this all to the end. The edibility and taste of fish, as well as their uses to man, had been mentioned throughout the work, but not until this point was the reader asked to regard them as evidences of divine benevolence. In this way, the point was not overstressed, but came as a logical conclusion. And on this rested the final paragraph of the book:

> Alas, that we should have rebelled against so much goodness! Alas, that any should be inattentive to the message of reconciliation! Is the reader one who has hitherto preferred distance from God to that communion with him which is to be enjoyed through the mediation of his Son? Let him hearken to the invitations of mercy, and in the spirit of the repentant prodigal say, "I will arise and go to my father." Let him avail himself without delay of that benign arrangement, by which the renewing influences of the Holy Ghost are imparted to every believer, and guilty outcasts are accepted, through the righteousness of our Lord and Saviour, in a way consistent with the integrity of the Divine character and the supremacy of the Divine law. (192)

This was the climax of the work. For the first time, the narrator appealed directly to the reader in a series of imperative statements, urging him "without delay" to renew his soul in the mercy of God. At the beginning of this passage, the narrator continued the use of the first person plural, and put himself in the same group—mankind—as the reader, deploring that "*we* should have rebelled" (my italics). However, as the next sentence implies, mankind was in fact divided into two groups: the saved and the unsaved. The narrator was clearly placed in the first group, but where was the reader? Here, the writer had to tread a thin line. The books of the "Monthly Series" were, like all RTS publications, to contain the message of conversion for those who needed it. But unlike tracts, they were also to be suitable for "the educated families of our land," who could be assumed to be already converted. The reader, therefore, might be in either the saved or unsaved group of men, and the conclusion to *British Fish* must be read in (at least) two ways.

The narrator asked the question "Is the reader one who has hitherto preferred distance from God ... ?" and the rest of the conclusion appeared to be addressed to the reader who had answered positively to this question, in other words, the reader who was not an evangelical Christian. The narrator urged this reader to take note of the "invitations of mercy" and to return to God as the prodigal finally returned to his father's welcome. And lest he prevaricate, he was reminded that this welcome was assured to "every believer," even the "guilty outcasts," for God had said that Jesus died for *all* men's sins, and God is "righteous" and "consistent." The repetition of the imperative "Let him ... " emphasised the urgency with which this reconciliation should be effected, for although it was never too late in life to return to the fold, the risk of dying without God's grace should be avoided. This shift from the objective narrative tone used to discuss species of fish to a direct and impassioned plea to the reader to save himself gained in impact from its placement at the very end of the book, as the message the reader took away.

Although the final paragraph referred to "the mediation of his Son," "the invitations of mercy," and "that benign arrangement," it did not actually indicate *what* the reader should do to be saved. There was no set of instructions for action. This suggests that the writer was perhaps thinking more of his second group of readers, those who were already close to God. Such readers had already accepted the mediation of Christ, and might be thought not to need the reminder contained in this passage. Assurance of salvation was presumed to accompany faith and one of the characteristics of justification through faith, rather than through works, was that evangelicals had no expectation of proof of their saved state.[45] Hence, a reminder that God had promised to save all who believed in him, even the extreme cases of guilty outcasts, could come as a timely reassurance for the reader whose faith was wavering, and would not be taken amiss by those of strong faith.

The concluding three pages of *British Fish* thus completed the framing that began with the Israelites eating fish in Egypt. The bulk of the work contained

---

45. On the power of the doctrine of assurance, see ibid., 42–50.

material very similar to that found in contemporary secular works, such as those published by Chambers and in the *Penny Magazine,* and was also similar to the Christian but non-evangelical SPCK works. The RTS volume differed by having a Christian tone throughout, created by the framing passages at start and finish, and maintained by occasional passing references in the main text. The theology was thus clearly present, but not so overpowering as to discourage the casual reader. Where many of its competitors were praised for being "instructive and entertaining," the "Monthly Series" was praised by its reviewers for containing "an almost inexhaustible store of entertaining, instructive, and, above all, *Christian* literature."[46] The strong climax was a sudden transition, but it was hoped that the reader–narrator relationship was strong enough for the narrator to convince the reader of the necessity of considering the conclusion as an integral part of a book on fish. The double readings of the conclusion were indicative of a problem that suffused the Series as a whole, relating to the uncertainty about whether the actual readers would be the converted or the unconverted.

By putting the hundred separate works into a series and marketing them together, the Religious Tract Society was trying to create a uniform identity for them. This ought to encourage someone who had read one to read another, while as a whole, the respectable Christian reputation would recommend the Series to families, schools, and parish libraries. But packaging and marketing would not have sold the Series if the contents did not meet expectations. As one reviewer acknowledged, the interdenominational membership of the Society and the wide audience at which its works were aimed made it "absolutely impossible that it should be conducted to please them all."[47] Despite this difficulty, and the variation among its writers' personal styles, the Society did succeed in creating a regular, dependable, and trustworthy style, such that reviewers were willing to remark of a new volume in the Series, "It might be a sufficient recommendation of this publication to say, that it is one of the excellent series of Monthly Volumes published by the Religious Tract Society."[48]

I have used the example of *British Fish* to show how its writer created a narrative voice that led the reader through natural history, God the Creator, his Revelation, and the Atonement. The RTS committee asked the writer of *British Fish* to write six of the works in the Series, which suggests that his

---

46. "People of Persia," *Englishwoman's Magazine* 5 (1850): 253.
47. "The Leisure Hour," *Baptist Magazine* 44 (1852): 229.
48. "Idumaea," *Englishwoman's Magazine* 6 (1851): 383.

version of Christian tone met with their approval. The Christian tone of the narrative voice was intended to control readers, to encourage them to read on, and to consider the theological framework as integral to the subject matter of the volume. By the end of *British Fish*, readers would have learned general information about fish species in Britain, as would be suitable for use in conversation, been told where to go to find out more, and had the relevance and importance of Christian faith brought to their attention. The non-Christian reader should have grown to trust the narrator during their exploration together of the habits and haunts of British fish, and would be forcibly struck by the message of the Atonement. Ideally, such a "word in season" would lead to the reader's conversion, but failing that, to the beginnings of some serious spiritual enquiry. Meanwhile, the Christian reader would understand how fish should be fitted with faith, and would henceforth be able to judge secular works as wanting and infidel works as corrupt.

IV

The Techniques of Evangelical Publishing

IN 1846, the *British Quarterly Review* discussed the plethora of new cheap books, commenting in particular on H. G. Bohn's "Standard Library":

> Each volume is beautifully printed, handsomely bound in cloth, embellished with a portrait, extended to more than five hundred pages, and is sold for three shillings and sixpence! Mr. Bohn no doubt knows what he is doing, but how he is to manage so as to perpetuate such a combination of quantity, quality, and cheapness, is to us something of a mystery.[1]

Achieving a suitable combination of "quantity, quality, and cheapness" was the central problem for all publishers of cheap books. For the Religious Tract Society (RTS), cheapness and quality were paramount. Books had to be substantially cheaper than 3*s*.6*d*. if they were to reach the working-class readers about whom the Society was particularly concerned. And their quality had to be impeccable, containing accurate wholesome knowledge conveyed in a suitably Christian tone. The quantity, in the sense intended by the reviewer, was less important—indeed, the Society was able to publish its books so much more cheaply partly because they were much shorter than Bohn's. For the Society, the important aspect of "quantity" was the circulation figures, not the length of the work, as it was only by achieving high circulations that its publications could hope to be effective against the onslaught of the corrupting and secular press. This was made possible by the economies of scale generated by the new printing technologies.

Producing popular science works involved acquiring suitable manuscripts, turning them into printed works as cheaply as possible, and arranging for them to be marketed and distributed as effectively as possible. These were processes that every publisher had to consider, but the RTS differed in one

---

1. "Bohn's Standard Library," *British Quarterly Review* 3 (1846): 547.

major way. It was dedicated to reaching its target audience, rather than simply selling its wares to any paying customer. This was why the Society produced the cheapest nonfiction series of the late 1840s. It was also why the Society was not content with the usual trade channels of distribution, but experimented with innovative methods of distribution that might be more likely to reach people who did not generally visit booksellers' shops or read literary reviews. This determination extended to a concern about whether the publications would be comprehensible to their intended readers, and whether the Christian tone would be effective, and this shaped the way in which the Society approached the problem of obtaining manuscripts. Managing writers and their productions involved a range of techniques and technologies, from editing through production to distribution.

EDITORIAL

For reprint publishers, acquiring manuscripts for publication was a relatively straightforward matter of investigating which works were out of copyright, choosing the desirable ones, and sending copies to be typeset. By deciding to publish original works, the RTS made things more difficult for itself. It first had to find writers to produce specially written manuscripts, and then had to work with them to make sure those manuscripts arrived on time and were the right length and in the right style. These tasks fell to the Society's editorial department, which had grown from a one-man show in the 1820s to become a sizeable operation by the 1840s. In 1846, William Lloyd, assisted by George Stokes, was in charge of a department with four editorial assistants and one reader. A year later, Stokes retired due to ill health and Lloyd decided to follow suit, although he continued to act as an advisor until his death in 1853. This meant that the Society's new programme of secular publishing was being developed during a time of substantial reorganisation within the editorial department. Between 1847 and 1853, three new staff members were hired, but the biggest shake-up concerned the editor-in-charge.

On Lloyd's retirement, the senior editorial assistant, Charles Williams, took over. Williams was a bookseller's assistant who later became ordained in the Congregational ministry. This combination of talents must have seemed ideal when he joined the RTS editorial staff in 1838, but his stint as editor was brief. After two disciplinary hearings, he was dismissed with six months notice in October 1849. There were "many painful meetings" over the next year, as Williams protested against his treatment by the Society. Throughout, the committee maintained that they "cannot admit the correctness of Mr

Williams's views," and emphasised "the dissatisfaction, on various grounds, that existed through a considerable period of time."[2] Williams eventually gave up, and, perhaps as a consequence of the "dissatisfaction," his tenure as editor was written out of the official history.

The committee then hoped that one of the Society's regular writers, William Haig Miller, would become the new editor. Miller held a job at the National and Provincial Bank, but was persuaded to join the editorial department for three hours a day. A year later, he was asked to become full-time, as editor, and agreed.[3] A few months later, he changed his mind.[4] He did continue his part-time work at the Society, however, and was the first editor of the *Leisure Hour*. The editorial situation was finally resolved in 1853, when William Lloyd died. Throughout these years of transition, the department had been kept in a functioning state by the two senior assistants, John Henry Cross and James Whitehorne. Cross had joined the department in 1833, when he was in his late twenties. He initially read manuscripts, but had gradually taken over responsibility for the children's works. In 1853, he became the children's editor. Whitehorne was a committee member who had become Lloyd's full-time assistant in 1845.[5] In 1853, he became the general editor.

Given all the changes taking place in the editorial department in the late 1840s, it is almost incredible that the "Monthly Series" did actually appear at its regular monthly intervals, and that the *Leisure Hour* was launched so successfully. Something of the care and attention that the Society believed the "Monthly Series" deserved can be seen in the proceedings against Charles Williams, for the (mis)management of the Series was one of the issues specifically mentioned at his first disciplinary meeting in February 1848. He was accused of having "inefficiently and negligently attended to the duties entrusted to him," with the consequence that the committee believed "that the Society has been materially injured."[6] The minutes do not record exactly what was wrong with Williams's handling of the "Monthly Series." The meeting came five months after an arbitrator had fined the Society for (inadvertently) breaching another author's copyright, with its publication of *Jamaica: enslaved and free* (vol. 4, 1846).[7] The meeting also coincided closely with the anomaly

---

2. USCL/RTS ECM, 12 November 1850 and 26 November 1850. See also USCL/RTS CCM, *passim*, January to May 1851.
3. USCL/RTS CCM, 14 November 1849 and 18 December 1850.
4. USCL/RTS CCM, 16 April 1851.
5. USCL/RTS FCM, 29 October 1845.
6. USCL/RTS CCM, 2 February 1848.
7. USCL/RTS CCM, 19 May 1847 and 15 September 1847.

of an abridgement appearing in a series of original works (*Self Improvement*, vol. 27, 1848) and with the critical review in the Congregational monthly *Biblical Review.* The reviewer claimed, "While some of its volumes realize perfectly the idea of the series, there are others [that do not]."[8] Several of his concerns related to editorial oversight, such as inaccuracies and the "forcible introduction" of religious reflections.[9] He also felt that the works were too varied, and not uniformly up to standard. It had been Williams's job as editor to smooth over the differences between the many writers and ensure more uniform suitability. The regulations for Williams's future duties, drawn up by the disciplinary meeting, were intended to ensure that he spent more time attending to the periodical and serial works, and took more care in preparing manuscripts for the press and proofreading them afterward. The new regulations also requested detailed plans of the future volumes intended for the "Monthly" and "Educational" series.[10] The *Biblical Review*'s more positive report a year later may indicate the success of these regulations.[11]

The editor was ultimately responsible for the Society's publications, but he was assisted by a group of editorial assistants, inhouse readers, and external expert readers. It is presumably because these people did their jobs effectively that the "Monthly Series" carried on, despite Williams's inattention. The editorial department was the liaison between the writers and the Society, and it was responsible for all aspects of processing completed manuscripts, from assessing their suitability for publication to checking the proofs before the final printing. When completed manuscripts arrived, they were sent for inspection to the readers. The first was an internal reader, who had to decide whether the work was written in a suitable style and with a suitably Christian tone for the Society to publish at all. William Lloyd referred to this sort of reading as being done with "my *tract-eye*."[12] Manuscripts were also sent to an external reader who was "*up to the subject*" and could assess the content.[13] The names of these external readers suggest that they were the same mixture of evangelical ministers and laymen as the Society's writers. The Reverend Thomas Milner wrote ten volumes for the "Monthly Series," and acted as

---

8. "The Tract Society's works," *Biblical Review* 4 (March 1848), 436.

9. Ibid.

10. USCL/RTS CCM, 9 February 1848, "Regulations for the Management of the Editorial Department."

11. "The Tract Society's publications," *Biblical Review* 6 (May 1849), 429.

12. USCL/RTS Add. (23), Lloyd to Jones, 15 September 1847.

13. Ibid.

reader for the *Life of Alfred the Great* (vol. 46, 1849).[14] The editor of the *Baptist Magazine*, the Reverend W. Groser, was reader for *Iona* (vol. 57, 1850) and for the prize-essays on the state of the working classes. He was also the author of several tracts.[15] The Reverend Thomas Birks completed an *Astronomy* (not for the "Monthly Series") in the same month as he examined the *Bible Handbook* for the "Educational Series."[16] One writer was reassured that the readers of his manuscript were "thoroughly talented men. One of them has been accustomed to literary pursuits for the last thirty years and is an eminent Classic.—I only mention this that you may feel satisfied that we did not refer your paper to incompetent persons."[17]

The readers' reports were sent to the editor, who would usually also read the work himself. If both readers reported unfavourably on a work, and the editor saw no reason to disagree, it would be rejected outright; if the readers disagreed over a work's merit, a third opinion was sought. Very few readers' reports survive, and the minute books tend to record only that the reports were "quite unfavourable to its adoption" or that the work "did not appear . . . adapted for publication by the Society."[18] The editorial staff generally exercised their control over writers by means of outright acceptance or rejection, and were far more likely to reject an unsuitable manuscript than to request major revisions. The extent of desirable revisions is indicated by James Whitehorne's remarks on a prize-essay, in one of the few surviving reader's reports. Whitehorne reported that "a few isolated statements would have to be omitted or modified for publication by this Society and this may easily be done."[19] This is suggestive of minor tweaking, rather than major restructuring. Major changes would, of course, be extremely time consuming with manuscripts written in longhand. *Geography of Plants* (vol. 52, 1850) and *Jordan and the Dead Sea* (vol. 55, 1850) were rare in being recommended for revisions, so presumably needed only minor changes.[20] Since the specific titles that ended up in the Series did not matter all that much, the committee might have preferred to cut its losses on an unsuitable manuscript and concentrate on getting a

---

14. USCL/RTS CCM, 16 May 1849.

15. USCL/RTS CCM, 21 August 1850; USCL/RTS ECM, 11 March 1851.

16. USCL/RTS CCM, 21 June 1854.

17. USCL/RTS Corr., Jones to Smith, 12 December 1846. Another reader (or perhaps the same one?) was described as "a celebrated Classical Man who is altogether unacquainted with the writer," USCL/RTS Corr., Jones to Copley, 12 December 1846.

18. USCL/RTS CCM, 23 February 1848.

19. USCL/RTS ECM, 11 March 1851.

20. USCL/RTS CCM, 14 November 1849 and 20 March 1850.

replacement, rather than committing itself to waiting a year and a half for a revised manuscript that had no guarantee of being significantly improved.

The difficulty of making revisions meant that the writers' role in creating Christian tone was crucial. In fact, it was so important that the Society selected writers rather than subject matter. The first thing the copyright committee did upon being given responsibility for the new "Monthly Series" was to tell Lloyd to canvass for writers. Eleven of the sixteen writers he contacted agreed immediately to contribute.[21] The topics of the first volumes were not selected *de novo* by the RTS committee but were those suggested by this first batch of writers. Since all knowledge could and should be presented in a Christian tone, there was a sense in which the provision of that tone was more important than the actual subject matter it illuminated.

Lloyd's first batch all had credentials as suitable evangelical writers. They were either already members of the Society's "stable" of writers or were well-known evangelical writers whom the Society wished to attract.[22] Once the "Monthly Series" was underway and well received, Lloyd began to receive unsolicited offers of manuscripts. Some of these came from known writers, but most did not. This new group had to be carefully vetted for evangelical credentials and writing skills before their specific offers could be considered. One of the first unsolicited offers came from the Reverend Henry Christo-pherson (*fl.* 1846–1876), of Newcastle-upon-Tyne, who wished to write on the evidences of Christianity. The committee decided that "a specimen of the work [should] be obtained from Mr. Christopherson with an outline of the whole."[23] While his ministerial vocation gave some evidence of his faith, the specimen of written work and the outline sketch would provide an indication of both his writing style and his grasp of the subject matter. Christopherson complied, and was asked to proceed with the work.[24] The committee decided to adopt this procedure as a rule, "that in future such specimens + outline be required of Authors not previously known to the Society."[25] In addition, the committee began to ask for personal character references for unknown writers. The Reverend Charles Elton of Sidney Sussex College, Cambridge,

---

21. USCL/RTS CCM, 14 August 1844 and 13 November 1844.

22. On Lloyd's idea of a stable, see USCL/RTS Add., Lloyd to Jones, 15 September 1847.

23. USCL/RTS CCM, 18 November 1846.

24. Christopherson discovered a few months later that he was not as able to write on the subject as he had thought, and informed the committee that he "had found it necessary to abandon his plan." He offered to write on something else, but his work on missionaries also failed to materialise. USCL/RTS CCM, 17 February 1847 and 19 May 1847.

25. USCL/RTS CCM, 18 November 1846.

wished to write on Iceland, and, although it turned out that his plan was "quite unsuitable," a Mr. Scott had reported satisfactorily on his personal qualities.[26] Some of these introductions proved extremely successful, such as that of the Reverend Samuel Manning of Frome. John Sheppard, a devotional writer published by the RTS, and a Mr. Gotch gave reports "quite favourable to Mr. Manning's ability," and his *Life and Times of Charlemagne* (vol. 78, 1852) subsequently appeared in the "Monthly Series."[27] Manning went on to write many more works, eventually becoming book editor and general secretary of the Society.

The spate of unsolicited offers enabled the committee to broaden the range of subjects in the Series. Most of the Society's existing stable of writers had originally been tract and devotional writers, so it is debatable whether the Series could have reached a hundred volumes without some new writers with new areas of knowledge. It also allowed the committee to be more selective about accepting suggestions for suitable topics. Initially, from a feeling of obligation and the need to get enough works together as quickly as possible, the Society accepted virtually every suggestion made by its writers. No suggestions were rejected until May 1847, when "Light in Dark Places" and "Terrestrial and Meteoric Chemistry" had that dubious honour.[28] The rejection rate increased toward the end of the Series, as the offers continued to come in but the number of possible acceptances decreased. Although this method of choosing topics may not seem the most efficient, the few occasions when the committee actively sought writers for specific topics were fraught with difficulty. The volume on the Inquisition was begun and abandoned by three writers before the Reverend James G. Miall of Bradford eventually completed it seven years later.[29] British India, on the other hand, was entrusted to three writers, yet never appeared.[30]

---

26. USCL/RTS CCM, 15 January 1851 and 19 February 1851.

27. USCL/RTS CCM, 18 December 1850 and 15 January 1851. On the RTS link with Sheppard, see USCL/RTS Corr., Jones to Sheppard, 28 October 1843.

28. USCL/RTS CCM, 19 May 1847.

29. It was originally written by Henry Christmas, but it was not approved by the committee. Thereafter, it was begun and abandoned by S. Massey Heathfield and by William Alexander. The progress of the volume can be traced at USCL/RTS CCM, 16 September 1846, 14 July 1847, 17 November 1847, 15 November 1848, 17 October 1849, 19 June 1850, 21 August 1850, 18 February 1852, 16 June 1852, and 16 March 1853. Miall's version was finally published in April 1853. The volume on *Good Health* also went through three writers before being published.

30. It was initially undertaken by the Reverend W. Campbell, then by William Arthur, and finally by the Reverend W. Lechmann. Only Arthur's apologies for being unable to fulfill his obligations are recorded. See USCL/RTS CCM, 12 March 1845, 16 September 1846, 21 May 1851, 19 November 1851, 16 March 1853, and 18 May 1853.

Once a writer and a topic had been approved by the committee, there was very little by way of formal contract between the two agents.[31] Legal contracts between writer and publisher were only starting to become common in the 1840s and, like most publishers, the Society preferred to treat its arrangements as gentlemen's agreements.[32] Usually, the committee minutes recorded simply that a writer's suggestion to produce a Monthly Volume on a specific topic had been approved. If details such as payment, expected completion date, or length were discussed, this must have happened in informal correspondence with the writer; but in the first few years, it seems probable that little was discussed.

As the first batch of completed manuscripts began to arrive at the depository in Paternoster Row, and were examined by the editor and his readers, it became clear that they were not all suitable. The Society seems to have felt morally obliged to accept these manuscripts and paid for them as if they had been accepted. A few of these were later published by the Society in other formats, but most languished unpublished. The rejects cost the Society £80 in 1845 alone.[33] Beginning in 1847, therefore, the committee adopted the practice of informing writers that their payment was conditional on approval of the final manuscript by the executive committee. Miall appears to have been the first to be told, with respect to his proposed work on "Remarkable Death-beds" (published as *Life's Last Hours; or, the final testimony*, vol. 44, 1849) that, "if on examination it be approved, the sum of £35 be paid him; but if not approved then half that sum, and the Manuscript be returned."[34] A similar phrase appeared regularly in subsequent minutes. This change of procedure coincided with the increased precautions about obtaining writing samples, character references, and outline plans. The combined result was that fewer completed manuscripts were rejected, and the cost of those rejections (sixteen over the whole Series) was far less.

Although Miall's agreement had stated a payment of £35 on approval, this amount was not fixed. At the Society's standard rate, based on the number of printer's sheets of text, the Monthly Volume writers could have expected to receive £30. The RTS rates were similar to those of *Chambers's Journal*

---

31. Thomas Dick did receive a formal agreement, perhaps because, as an experienced writer, he requested one. See USCL/RTS CCM, 13 November 1844.

32. On the development of contracts in this period, see Sutherland, *Victorian Novelists and Publishers*, 53–62, and chap. 4.

33. USCL/RTS CCM, 8 January 1845, 12 March 1845, and 21 May 1845.

34. USCL/RTS CCM, 17 February 1847.

and the *Penny Magazine,* but, as with most publishing enterprises, the "set rate" was frequently varied to suit the editor's appraisal of the standard of the text or the reputation of its writer.[35] Although many of the Monthly Volumes were indeed paid for at £30, more were paid £35. Female writers typically received £25, while a few well-known, full-time writers, such as John Kitto and Thomas Dick, were paid £40. For those struggling to keep up a slipping middle-class station in life, these amounts were significant. For instance, young ministers could be surviving on little more than twice that amount per year. John Kennedy received just £80 per year from his first congregation in Aberdeen, although by the time he was writing for the Society in the 1840s, he had moved to London, where his stipend was around £400.[36] Even for those who were established in their professions, the money from a Monthly Volume was a useful addition, though no longer an essential resource, and the payments probably reflect the committee's awareness of different writers' circumstances. The reasons behind the variation were not usually made explicit, but when Miall became the first writer to successfully complete the *Inquisition,* the committee noted that "the preparation of the Manuscript had been attended with extraordinary labor," and paid him in guineas rather than pounds as thanks.[37]

In their printed forms, all the volumes fitted onto 192 pages, but the compositors' craft masked an underlying variety of length. Some volumes were set in different sizes of type, varying from twenty-seven to thirty-seven lines per page. These changes represent a substantial difference in the lengths of the works, from about forty thousand to almost seventy thousand words. The majority of the works in the Series were between forty and fifty thousand words, which suggests that the editorial team must have given the writers a fairly specific idea of the desirable length of a Monthly Volume. The obvious exception to the rule was *Self Improvement,* with its thirty-seven lines per page. Surprisingly, this is one work that ought to have been firmly under the control of the editorial department, as one of the team must have been responsible for abridging it from the successful guide written by Massachusetts minister John Todd, *The Student's Manual: designed, by specific directions, to aid in forming the intellectual and moral character and habits of the student* (1835).

---

35. On *Chambers's Journal,* see Cooney, "Publishers for the People," 94–95. On *Penny Magazine,* see Ryland, *Memoirs of John Kitto,* 528.

36. Kennedy, *Old Highland Days,* 114–15, 180, 146.

37. USCL/RTS CCM, 16 March 1853.

Although the committee knew how many manuscripts it had ordered, it did not know when, or, indeed if, they would arrive. In November 1847, Charles Williams, then newly appointed as editor, discovered that some works had been "in progress" for two and a half years. He was directed to make enquiries and, if the volumes were not forthcoming, "to strike them off the list."[38] This seems to be the only time when the Society made an attempt to chase its writers, and it was not particularly successful. When the Series closed, eighteen works were allegedly still "in progress." A range of factors from overwork to illness could delay or prevent the completion of a promised work. George Stokes planned to write a long list of works in his retirement, but died after completing only "The Scottish Covenanters" (which was judged unsuitable for the Series).[39] The Reverend Henry Woodward of Bungay, Suffolk had agreed to produce a geological volume in September 1846, and confirmed that he was working on it in 1849 and 1851.[40] But by 1852, he had written to the Society, saying he was "prevented by circumstances from accomplishing the work."[41] Woodward's "circumstances" explain why the only geological volumes in the series were those on *Caves of the Earth, Mines and Mining* (vol. 66, 1851) and *Volcanoes: their history, phenomena and causes* (vol. 74, 1852).

Other works arrived after enormous delays. *Alfred the Great,* for instance, was being written by the Reverend William H. Jones, the son of RTS secretary William Jones, and took over four years to arrive. Jones was probably distracted by his move from Shoreditch, London to Bradford-on-Avon, Wiltshire.[42] Fortunately for the RTS, he was an extreme case. Almost two-thirds of manuscripts arrived at Paternoster Row within a year of their topics being approved, and 90 percent within eighteen months.[43] Nevertheless, the variation between the three months it took for *Jamaica* to arrive and the twenty-three for *The Crusades* (vol. 42, 1849) made planning difficult.

The finance committee had originally recommended that completed manuscripts should be ready twelve months in advance of publication.[44] This

---

38. USCL/RTS CCM, 17 November 1847.
39. USCL/RTS CCM, 17 February 1847.
40. USCL/RTS CCM, 16 September 1846. I have been unable to discover any connection between this Woodward and the geologist father and son, Samuel (1790–1838) and Henry Woodward (1832–1921), both of Norfolk.
41. USCL/RTS CCM, 18 August 1852.
42. Crockford's Clergy Lists (1850) and (1852).
43. Fyfe, "Industrialised Conversion," 113–14.
44. USCL/RTS FCM, 17 December 1845.

would ensure that there were plenty of works in hand, and would allow printing to be done at least seven weeks before the publication date. If this ideal had been met, at least twelve completed manuscripts would have been constantly in hand. So far as the actual progress of the Series can be reconstructed, it appears that the committee usually had from ten to fifteen works in progress at any one time, but only had a couple of completed publishable works in hand.[45] This is consistent with planning a year ahead, but it also indicates that the committee started publishing the Series so quickly that it never built up the reserves of completed works that its finance committee had recommended.

This is borne out by occasional evidence from the minutes. In February 1848, editor Charles Williams was reprimanded for various reasons, including the fact that he had not yet sent April's volume to the printers, when it "should have been ready two months since." The *History of Protestantism in France, to the reign of Charles IX* (vol. 29, 1848) was hurriedly sent to the printers, although it had been completed only a month earlier.[46] After this close shave, the committee gave up the ideal of having twelve volumes always in hand, and recommended instead that there should always be at least three volumes ready. It was hoped this would be sufficient "to prevent any disappointment in the regular appearance of the Series and to secure the careful printing and getting up of the Books."[47] Yet even this more modest requirement was not always attainable, and in December 1852 the new editor, William Haig Miller, found himself without an available volume for February 1853. He decided to turn a manuscript on the Greek Church, which had only just been approved by its readers, into a Monthly Volume (*The Greek and Eastern Churches,* vol. 87, 1853). The committee approved his action retrospectively.[48]

Despite these problems, the only times when the promised monthly issue failed to appear was with the final two volumes, *Paris, ancient and modern* (vol. 99, 1854) and *Life of Calvin* (vol. 100, 1855), which were one month and seventeen months late, respectively. In these cases, the problem of the irregular supply of manuscripts was compounded by the implications of the decision to finally close the Series at one hundred volumes. At the point when that decision was taken, in late 1853, the committee did have just enough volumes in hand to complete the series. However, one of them was part of a set of four volumes on Christian martyrs, and there was no longer space

---

45. Fyfe, "Industrialised Conversion," 113.
46. USCL/RTS CCM, 2 February 1848 and 19 January 1848.
47. USCL/RTS CCM, 9 February 1848.
48. USCL/RTS CCM, 15 December 1852.

for all four volumes in the "Monthly Series." The first martyr volume had already been printed in early 1854, but it was pulled from the Series so that it could appear with its sister volumes at a later date.[49] This meant that all the remaining volumes were moved forward a month, which created the problems at the end. Quite why the final volume was a stunning seventeen months late is a bit of a mystery. The Society had several completed works in hand that had not been explicitly noted as unsuitable, including ones on "Domestic Surgery" and "Canada." The *Life of Calvin* that finally appeared had actually been ordered as part of a trilogy on church history, and was diverted to the "Monthly Series."[50] Perhaps neither "Canada" nor "Domestic Surgery" was felt to be a fitting climax to the series, whereas a *Life of Calvin* would complement the *Life of Luther* (vol. 10, 1846), which had already appeared. The main reason for adding a hundredth volume to the Series, when it had effectively been closed for a year and a half, was to give the finished library the appearance of planned completeness.

Fortunately, these delays came at the end of the Series rather than the beginning, and were unlikely to seriously damage its reputation. In selecting the name of the Series, the RTS committed itself to a specific periodicity, something that most publishers avoided doing. When advertising his "Home and Colonial Library" (fig. 4.1), John Murray did mention the frequency of the issues on the top line, but it was in small print and was not a major feature. This meant that he avoided the fate of Charles Knight's series, which had changed its name from "Weekly" to "Monthly" and finally to "Shilling."[51] If periodicity was not a prominent part of the marketing strategy, then a drop in issues, such as that experienced by Bohn's "Standard Library" during the trade depression of 1849, was merely unfortunate rather than disastrous.[52] That the RTS succeeded in maintaining monthly issues for ninety-eight months, and, in particular, doing so with freshly commissioned works rather than reprints, is a testament to the hard work of the Society's writers and editorial team.

PRODUCTION

Once the editorial process was completed, the next task was to transform manuscripts into cheap printed books. The other publishers who produced

---

49. USCL/RTS CCM, 18 January 1854 and 19 April 1854.

50. USCL/RTS CCM, 16 November 1853, 15 February 1854, and 21 June 1854.

51. See Appendix B to *English Catalogue of Books*, and DLB 106, "Charles Knight."

52. The series of both Murray and Bohn also suffered drops in issue in 1849. See annual indexes to *Publishers' Circular*, 1846–49.

Publishing Monthly, price 2s. 6d.; or alternate Months, in cloth, price 6s.

MURRAY'S
HOME AND COLONIAL LIBRARY.

Printed in good readable type, on superfine paper, and designed to furnish the highest Literature of the day; consisting partly of *original Works*, and partly of New Editions of *popular Publications*, at the lowest possible price.

The popularity and variety of this Series,—comprising Geography, Voyages and Travels, Biography, Natural History, Manners and Customs,—and the utmost care being exercised in the selection of works, that they contain nothing offensive to morals or good taste, together with the moderation of price (*an annual outlay of only Thirty Shillings*), recommend it to all classes.

To the Clergy—As fitted for Parochial and Lending Libraries.

School Inspectors, Schoolmasters, &c.—As Prizes for the Young, or for School Libraries.

The Student and Lover of Literature at Home, who has hitherto been content with the loan of a book, may now become possessed of the work itself, at the moment of its publication, at a much less cost than before.

The following have already appeared, and form Sixteen Volumes:—

1.
PHILIP MUSGRAVE: or, MEMOIRS of a MISSIONARY in CANADA. By the Rev. J. Abbott.

2.
TYPEE; or, a PEEP at POLYNESIAN LIFE. By Herman Melville.

3.
A JOURNEY through INDIA. By the late Bishop Heber.

4.
NOTES and SKETCHES of NEW SOUTH WALES. By Mrs. Meredith.

5.
HISTORY of the FALL of the JESUITS in the Eighteenth Century.

6.
THE BIBLE in SPAIN; or, an Attempt to Circulate the SCRIPTURES in the PENINSULA. By George Borrow.

7.
TRAVELS in EGYPT, NUBIA, SYRIA, and the HOLY LAND. By Captains Irby and Mangles.

8.
LIVES of JOHN BUNYAN and OLIVER CROMWELL. By Robert Southey.

9.
MEMOIRS of FATHER RIPA during Thirteen Year's Residence at the Court of China.

10.
NEGRO LIFE and MANNERS in the WEST INDIES. By M. G. Lewis.

11.
LETTERS from the SHORES of the BALTIC. By a Lady.

12.
HISTORY of the SIEGE of GIBRALTAR. By John Drinkwater.

13.
THE FRENCH in ALGIERS, and ABD-EL-KADER. By Lady Duff Gordon.

14.
LIFE of the GREAT CONDE. By Lord Mahon.

15.
LIVONIAN TALES. By Author of "Letters from the Baltic."

16.
MARY SCHWEIDLER, the AMBER-WITCH: a Trial for Witchcraft. Translated by Lady Duff Gordon.

17.
THE GYPSIES of SPAIN; their MANNERS, CUSTOMS, and RELIGIOUS CEREMONIES. By George Borrow.

18.
MOROCCO and the MOORS; or, TRAVELS in WESTERN BARBARY. By Drummond Hay.

19.
LIFE of SIR FRANCIS DRAKE. By John Barrow.

20.
SKETCHES of PERSIA. By Sir John Malcolm.

21.
VOYAGE of a NATURALIST round the WORLD. By Charles Darwin.

22.
BRACEBRIDGE HALL. By Washington Irving.

23.
WILD SPORTS of the HIGHLANDS. By Charles St. John, Esq.

24.
LETTERS from MADRAS. By a Lady.

No. 25 will contain—

SIR FRANCIS HEAD'S ROUGH NOTES during rapid Journies across the PAMPAS.

JOHN MURRAY, ALBEMARLE STREET;
And to be had of all Booksellers.　　　　(1022)

Figure 4.1. Most publishers avoided a definite commitment to a specific periodicity. This advertisement for Murray's "Home and Colonial Library" does mention the frequency of issue, but only in small print. This was a full-page display advertisement. *Publishers' Circular*, 15 October 1846, 310.

cheap book series around the same time priced their volumes at between one and six shillings, as was shown in exhibit 1.1. The cost of a completed work from Bohn, Bogue, or Murray was around six shillings, while from Knight, Chambers, or Collins it was around two or three shillings. Although the six-shilling works were "cheap" in comparison to the usual cost of new literary works, they were far from cheap enough to be bought on a regular basis by the mechanics and members of the lower-middle classes targeted by the RTS. Even works priced around the two-shilling mark were not really cheap enough for the readers who were just able to pay a penny a week for a periodical. When the RTS decided to sell its volumes at sixpence monthly, it was clearly aiming at that periodical audience, rather than the more affluent audience of Murray and Bohn. The significantly lower price was achieved not simply by the absence of a requirement for profit, but through careful management of costs and the use of the latest printing technology. The Society's experience in tract publishing stood it in good stead here, for it was familiar with the economies of scale that made it possible to sell short tracts very cheaply by printing in tens or hundreds of thousands. As a slightly higher-priced product, the "Monthly Series" did not need to be sold in quite such numbers, but its first print run was still far larger than was typical for book publishers.

Writing to Esther Copley, editor of the *Visitor* and a regular tract writer, William Jones revealed that publishing each Monthly Volume had the potential to "lose several hundred pounds" if the work was a failure.[53] We do not have a detailed breakdown of costs for any RTS publication from this period, but table 4.1 gives a general idea of the costs involved for a volume of the "Monthly Series." The figures are based on contemporary rates charged to the publishers Longman and Routledge.[54] The costs for copyright, editorial labour, composing the type, and making stereotype plates were all fixed costs per volume, regardless of the number of copies printed. The cost of paper, printing, folding, and stitching the sheets (plus any binding) increased with the size of the print run. To break even, the selling price had to be balanced with the size of the first print run such that the sales income would cover all the costs. Subsequent print runs would be sold at the same price, but if they were printed from stereotype plates, the only costs were those of the actual printing and binding. The first print run for the "Monthly Series" was initially planned to be ten thousand copies. Due to the discounts allowed to

---

53. USCL/RTS Corr., Jones to Copley, 12 December 1846.
54. Rates from Longman and Routledge archives between 1846–58, as cited in Fyfe, "Copyrights and Competition," 49.

Table 4.1. Estimated costs of production for a Monthly Volume

Item	Rate	10,000 copies	15,000 copies
Copyright	£30	£30	£30
Editorial	unknown	unknown	unknown
Type composition	£2.6.0 per sheet	£6.18.0	£6.18.0
Making stereotype plates	£1.10.0 per sheet	£4.10.0	£4.10.0
Paper	15/- per ream	£45	£67.10.0
Printing	10/- per ream	£30	£45
Folding, stitching	unknown, per ream	unknown	unknown
Total Costs		£116.8.0 + X	£153.18.0 + Y
Income on 6*d.* volumes at trade prices		£187.10.0	£281.5.0

Note: Apart from copyright, none of the actual costs are available. These are based on the costs charged to Longman and Routledge in the same period. One Monthly Volume used three sheets of paper, and there are five hundred sheets to a ream.

members of the RTS (20 percent) and to the book trade (25–33 percent), the Society would receive only 4½*d.* or less on any copies sold outside its own depositories. The sale of ten thousand copies would thus bring in around £187, which we can assume would be enough to break even, but probably not by much. After the high sales of the first volumes, the first print run was increased to fifteen thousand copies. All the fixed costs had already been paid by the first ten thousand copies, so the extra five thousand had to cover only the 2*d.* per copy that was the cost of paper and printing.[55] Most of the income generated by the extra copies was clear surplus.

The main reason that most of the competing "cheap" series were more expensive than the "Monthly Series" was that they used more paper. The price of paper accounted for a large proportion of a publisher's costs: in the first quarter of 1850, the RTS paid almost £5,500 for printing paper to its main suppliers, John Dickinson & Co. of Norwich and Spicer Brothers of London. In contrast, its printing bill for the same period was just over £3,000.[56] Even after mechanised methods of paper manufacture had been introduced in the first decades of the nineteenth century, the enormous demand kept the price of paper high, as did the tax on paper. Paper was so expensive that enterprising publishers were "virtually paralyzed" in their efforts to produce cheap books.

---

55. Cost of paper plus working, per ream: 25*s*. Each copy = 3/500 of a ream.

56. USCL/RTS ECM, 1850 *passim*. Although some of the paper was probably for grants, and was not printed in Britain.

As publisher John Chapman put it, the paper tax "presses so injuriously upon the people as to forbid them that instruction which would otherwise be within their reach." In contrast, "Publishers like Mr. Murray, and the readers of his costly books, are scarcely conscious of the restriction."[57]

As the *British Quarterly* reviewer had noted, Bohn's volumes were over five hundred pages long, and this required a lot of paper. This sort of length was typical of his works and those from Murray, Knight, and occasionally even Chambers, because they were reprinting works originally published for the mainstream middle-class market. The use of reprints did avoid copyright and editorial costs, however, and helped make the series of the 1840s more successful than their 1820s predecessors. The RTS decided to use original works because of the difficulty of finding works with a suitably Christian tone, but it had the additional advantage that the Society was not constrained by the length of existing books, and could publish books with fewer than two hundred pages. The Society also claimed that such works were more suited to the education, experience, and domestic habits of their potential readers. Readers who had only a limited experience of reading might lack the stamina to follow an argument for five hundred or more pages, so the short book with clear and concise arguments could be an attractive option. Finding the time, space, and peace to read was also a significant challenge for working-class readers, so the RTS's short books could legitimately be seen as responding to those needs in a way that two fat volumes from Knight did not.[58] The Society's advertisement targeted these readers by pointing out that the "Monthly Series" was intended for those "who could only spare time enough for the perusal of a small volume," as well as for those "whose means would not allow of a large purchase."[59]

Another way to keep costs down was to use a cheap form of binding, or no binding at all. Tracts, for example, were simply folded and stitched through the spine. Weekly periodicals were also sold in this way, which is why the first page of each number of the *Penny Magazine* and the *Leisure Hour* always had a large picture on it, since it functioned as the front cover. Bulkier periodicals, such as the monthlies and quarterlies, usually came with paper wrappers. These temporary covers carried advertisements, and were removed by purchasers who wished to bind their periodicals in annual volumes. When

---

57. Chapman, "Commerce of Literature," 514.
58. Vincent, *Bread, Knowledge and Freedom*, pt. I.
59. William Henry Jones, *Memorials of William Jones*, 124, and advertisements in each volume.

a weekly periodical was also issued in monthly parts (as was the case with *Chambers's Journal* and the *Leisure Hour*), these monthly parts usually had a paper wrapper. Even short books, however, were longer than periodicals, and needed a more substantial form of binding to keep all their folded sheets together. There was a long tradition of issuing books in uncovered boards with spine labels made of paper; these served as a temporary binding until the book could be bound properly in leather (by its purchaser), but they were too fragile to be viable as a cheap permanent binding. Boards bound in coloured cloth were more durable, and from its introduction in the late 1820s, this became the standard binding for cheap books.[60] It was thus possible for inexpensive books to be issued ready-bound, and for publishers to develop "edition bindings." In this format, all the copies of an edition looked the same, although wealthy purchasers could still choose to replace the binding with something more suited to their own libraries.

The RTS routinely issued its books in several different bindings, which allowed it to market the same work to different classes of readers. Cloth on boards was standard for the cheapest version, but there might also be sheep, calf, and morocco leather, with varying amounts of gilt detail and illustration. The "Monthly Series" volumes were available for 10*d*. in dark green, cloth-covered boards, with blind embossing and gilt edges (as shown in fig. 2.2).[61] The binding was done by one of the Society's regular binders, James Davison of Jewin Crescent, London.[62] This would usually be the cheapest form of binding for a book, but the Society was so determined to make the Series even more available, that it took the rare step of issuing the volumes in a six-penny form, in stiff green paper wrappers, printed in black ink (fig. 4.2). These were probably done by James Key of Oxford Arms Passage, Warwick Lane, who was the Society's stitcher and was responsible for most of the works that were not being fully bound, such as tracts, periodicals, and some of the children's books.[63]

The six-penny covers were described in the RTS catalogue as "fancy paper covers," but contemporary reviewers were not convinced. The monthly *Baptist Magazine* liked the contents of the first volume, but bemoaned the fact that "it should have no covers corresponding better with the character of the interior,

---

60. Gaskell, *Introduction to Bibliography*, 245–47.

61. Most of the surviving volumes are dark green, although there are some copies in dark blue and mid-brown in the same style. These may be from later reprintings.

62. Several extant copies bear binder's tickets with Davison's name. He did so much work for the Society that his bills for the "Monthly Series" cannot be identified.

63. Key is described at USCL/RTS ECM, 3 February 1852.

Figure 4.2. In their six-penny forms, the Monthly Volumes were bound in green paper covers, printed in black ink. The volumes were 14.5 cm by 9.5 cm, and just over a centimetre thick. By permission of the Syndics of Cambridge University Library (1852.6.243).

than thin glazed paper."[64] This indicates just how unusual paper covers were on anything other than a tract or periodical. Paperbacks as we know them did not become common until the 1930s, although an alternative cheap form of binding did appear within a few years of the "Monthly Series." Boards could be covered in paper, which was cheaper than covering them with cloth, yet stronger than the unboarded Monthly Volumes. It also had the advantage that the paper could be printed with colourful illustrations, and this style of binding became widespread on the railway novels, which had to be cheap but also attractive to passersby on the station platform.[65]

The Society was aware that some potential readers might be repelled by the unusual plain and flimsy green paper covers, which is why it also issued the

---

64. "Life of Julius Caesar," *Baptist Magazine* 38 (1846): 28.
65. Gaskell, *Introduction to Bibliography,* 248; Schmoller, "Paperback Revolution."

ten-penny version. Unlike their paper-covered siblings, the bound volumes looked like miniature books that were respectable enough to appear in family or institutional libraries. On reviewing a later volume in its ten-penny binding, the *Baptist Magazine* was pleased that now "he appears in clothing which will facilitate his reception into good company, and conduce to his preservation from the casualties of the way."[66] Helping the series into "good company" was the main purpose of the ten-penny binding, clearly indicating that that it was not intended only for mechanics and skilled artisans. But while the *Baptist Magazine* also praised the protection offered by hard covers, the *Christian Spectator* was more ambivalent, suggesting that this was perhaps detrimental to the purpose of the books. If the ten-penny volumes now looked like fine books, which had to be treated with care by children and library users, then perhaps they would be less read than their cheaper counterparts. The *Christian Spectator* claimed that "we are rather inclined to dislike the finer book bound at tenpence," and commended the six-penny paper versions for being "so cheap that we need not care if they are destroyed!"[67]

Despite calling for books to be "used, worn out, and worn to pieces," the Society actually made further concessions to the desire for good-looking books.[68] Once the Series had been underway for a year, a double-volume format was introduced, where the sheets of two volumes were bound together with a frontispiece.[69] These were sold at 1*s*.6*d*. in cloth boards, or 2*s*. in extra boards with gilt edges. Small, thin books were often associated with children, who, as small people were expected to read small books. In double volumes, the "Monthly Series" became more substantial and suitable for an adult library.

If one were to judge a book by its covers, the small size, paper- or cloth-covered boards, and small typeface marked the "Monthly Series" as a product of industrialised, cheap, large-scale publishing. Those features would have been obvious to most contemporary observers, but a tiny shred of archival evidence relating to the printing allows us to confirm that first impression. The sheets of paper used by printers were much larger than the pages of a book. During the printing process, groups of two, four, eight, twelve, or sixteen pages were printed together onto a single sheet, and the same again on the reverse. The pages were carefully oriented so that when the sheet was folded

---

66. "Glimpses of the Dark Ages," *Baptist Magazine* 38 (1846): 98.

67. "Cheap books," *Christian Spectator* (July 1846): 146, 145.

68. Ibid., 146.

69. The double volumes first appear in USCL/RTS Publ., Dec. 1846. By March 1854, there were thirty-six double volumes on offer.

in half, and in half again (and again . . .), the result was a pamphlet with all the pages the right way up, in the right order. A tract might be just one folded sheet, but books would contain many sheets, stitched and bound together. Books that were printed with only two or four pages per sheet (known as folios and quartos) were large format, being half or a quarter the size of the original sheet of paper. The standard size for books in the nineteenth-century was the octavo (8vo), but cheaper books used the smaller duodecimo (12mo) or hexadecimo (16mo) formats, which allowed more pages (set in smaller type) to be squeezed onto the same-sized sheet of paper.

All the surviving copies of the "Monthly Series" are folded in groups of thirty-two pages, that is, sixteen pages per side of the original printer's sheet. They therefore appear to be hexadecimos, which is unsurprising given their size and price. The curious thing is that hexadecimo format requires six sheets for a 192-page book, yet surviving records relating to the "Monthly Series" printing refer to just three printers' sheets.[70] This anomaly confirms the industrial production of the volumes. Sheets of handmade paper had been limited in size to approximately the span of a man's arms. This was also as big as the two men working a hand-operated printing press would be able to handle. Machine-made paper could be much larger, easily twice the size and sometimes more. Only steam-printing machines could print such large sheets. With these extra large sheets, it was possible to fit twice the usual number of pages on each sheet. To keep folding simple, the pages would be arranged in groups as if for standard sheets, but printed two groups at a time, with the printed sheet being cut in half before folding as usual.[71] The result of printing three double sheets hexadecimo would frequently be indistinguishable from six sheets hexadecimo, as is the case with the finished Monthly Volumes.

The use of extra large sheets was one of the ways in which new technologies speeded up the printing process. Steam printing was itself about four times faster than an experienced pair of hand-press operators, producing around a thousand impressions per hour (continuously, without getting tired). If the Monthly Volumes had been set as six ordinary sheets, it would have taken at least 720 hours on a hand-press to produce the fifteen thousand copies—but only 180 hours on a machine. With double-sized sheets, the machine was printing twice as many pages each cycle, reducing the time taken to about 90 hours. A single printing machine would thus be able to produce a run

---

70. USCL/RTS FCM, 23 March 1846.
71. Gaskell, *Introduction to Bibliography*, 258–60.

of Monthly Volumes in just over a week. It would have taken well over ten weeks on a single hand-press, making monthly issues extremely difficult. The scale of the "Monthly Series" print runs was only possible thanks to industrial printing.

Unlike W. & R. Chambers, the RTS did not have its own printing house (though it did have a bindery). New projects were put out to tender among several of the Society's usual printers. The first volumes of the "Monthly Series" were printed by Tyler & Reed, of Bolt Court, off Fleet Street. This firm had been formed in 1842 by the partnership of regular RTS printer William Tyler with Charles Reed. They printed the *Evangelical Magazine* and the evangelical newspapers the *Patriot* and the *British Banner*.[72] As newspaper printers in the 1840s, they would have been steam printers, possibly with more than one machine, making them a sensible choice for the "Monthly Series." Tyler & Reed printed the series until 1849, when their partnership was dissolved. After the breakup, Tyler continued to print for the RTS on his own account, while Reed petitioned successfully for a share of the business and of future work.[73] He took his share into the new concern of Reed & Pardon. There is no archival evidence of who printed the "Monthly Series" after 1849, but surviving imprints suggest that, for at least some of the period 1850–55, it was printed by Blackburn & Burt, of Holborn Hill.[74] It so happens that Stephen Blackburn's father, John, had been an RTS printer who was in business until 1848 with one Benjamin Pardon.[75] The connection raises the intriguing question of whether Stephen Blackburn might have been, briefly, in business with Pardon and Reed between 1849–50. Such a partnership could explain how Blackburn & Burt ultimately became involved with the "Monthly Series."

---

72. For details of printers' addresses and partnerships, see P. A. H. Brown, *London Publishers and Printers*.

73. USCL/RTS FCM, 19 September 1849.

74. Although RTS works usually bore the mark of the RTS as their printer, there are many extant copies of Monthly Volumes bearing the mark of Blackburn & Burt on their last page. According to P. A. H. Brown, *London Publishers and Printers*, this partnership existed only between 1850–55, suggesting that they were printers to the original Series, rather than to the (presumably many) reprinted impressions.

75. The breakup of the partnership of John Blackburn and Benjamin Pardon is recorded in USCL/RTS CCM, 9 February 1848, where it is also noted that Blackburn had been with the RTS before joining with Pardon. The precise relationship between John and Stephen Blackburn is not clear—I am guessing that they were father and son. P. A. H. Brown , *London Publishers and Printers,* records the name of Blackburn as "John" before the partnership with Pardon, and "Stephen" afterward.

During Blackburn & Burt's period as "Monthly Series" printers, they were paid around £50 for each volume, figures of the same order of magnitude as the estimates in table 4.1. This had to cover the costs of composing the type, making stereotypes, and printing for the fifteen thousand print run. Although the volumes were all three double sheets, the actual cost varied from £40.12s.6d. to £54.12s.[76] This was because of the different lengths of the volumes (in terms of words to be typeset) and because some volumes had a few illustrations. The printing costs of Chambers's "Educational Course," which made frequent use of diagrams, could vary by as much as £20 or £30.[77]

The Society appears to have been an early exponent of stereotyping, using it for book projects as early as the mid-1820s. By 1850, it was in use for almost all RTS publishing projects.[78] Tyler & Reed's original quotation for the "Monthly Series" had been based on the assumption that they would be able to introduce a new method of stereotyping. In fact, they were unable to do so, and had to apply for permission to increase their charges by £4.10s. per volume.[79] The new method may have been the use of flexible paper moulds, which replaced plaster of Paris around midcentury and made making moulds (prior to casting) much easier and more reliable.[80] Stereotyping allowed type to be rapidly released for other projects, but it was especially useful to the Society for the ease and cheapness with which subsequent reprinting was made possible. With tracts such as "The Swearer's Prayer" having sold 1.7 million copies by 1850, and still selling, being able to reprint without paying compositor's charges was useful.[81] The alternative had been to print large runs and store the extra copies until needed, so the use of stereotyping also reduced warehouse costs. In 1850, a report on the state of the RTS warehouse and stock strongly recommended "the importance of Stereotyping all the Society's publications in order to avoid future accommodation of Stock, and

---

76. The bill payments appear in the Executive Committee Minutes, but the minute book for 1844–50 is unfortunately missing. Payments to Blackburn & Burt appear regularly from 1850, and include quarterly payments and smaller monthly payments. I assume the monthly payments to be the ones for the "Monthly Series."

77. Cooney, "Publishers for the People," 195.

78. The use of stereotyping appears to date from the beginning of the bound publications of the Society, ca.1825. The *British Reformers* printed from 1832 was certainly stereotyped. See William Jones, *Jubilee Memorial*, 130–33; Samuel G. Green, *Story of the Religious Tract Society*, 35, 51.

79. USCL/RTS FCM, 23 March 1846.

80. Gaskell, *Introduction to Bibliography*, 203–4.

81. William Jones, *Jubilee Memorial*, app. V.

that only in special cases Type [alone] should be used and then by previous approval of the Committee."[82] Stereotyping was also essential for the higher-circulation periodicals, such as the *Leisure Hour*, as it allowed multiple presses to work simultaneously on the same project, thus producing copies more quickly.

This speed was amply demonstrated in late January 1852. The first four numbers of the new weekly *Leisure Hour* had appeared, and the first monthly part was due to be ready on Thursday, January 29, for a nominal publication date of the following Saturday. On the night of Wednesday, January 28, there was a fire at the premises of James Key, where the parts were being folded and stitched into wrappers. Most of the new tracts and monthly publications due for the start of February had already been moved off the premises, but a substantial number of reprinted tracts and children's books were destroyed. So too were the monthly parts of the *Leisure Hour*. Key and the RTS were adequately insured, but a payout from the insurers could not compensate for the damage to the prospects of the young *Leisure Hour* if its first monthly part failed to appear. The entire batch of monthly parts had to be reprinted. The steam-printing machines of two printing houses ran all through Thursday night, producing perhaps thirty thousand copies. On Friday, the loose sheets were folded and stitched into wrappers by Key's staff, working in temporary premises found by the RTS. By Saturday, everything was ready, and the launch could go ahead.[83]

Stereotype plates were equally useful for planned reprintings. The Monthly Volumes were reprinted as needed for thirty years, although there are unfortunately no records of these reprintings. The plates could also be shipped to North America for reprinting there. The RTS made an arrangement with the American Sunday School Union (ASSU) to send copies of the plates of the volumes that the RTS thought likely to be suitable for American circulation. The ASSU agreed to pay £17.10s. per volume, and the RTS promised to ship the plates seven weeks ahead of publication to allow the ASSU to be first to reprint them in the United States.[84] This arrangement was an attempt to get round the absence of an Anglo-American copyright treaty. British works had no copyright protection in the United States, and were

---

82. USCL/RTS FCM, 19 June 1850.
83. USCL/RTS ECM, 3 February 1852. Total sales of the first four numbers varied from sixty-four thousand to eighty-three thousand copies, but the proportion of monthly/weekly sales is not recorded.
84. USCL/RTS FCM, 13 August 1845 and 17 December 1845.

widely reprinted with no benefit to their original publishers or writers.[85] By paying the RTS for advance plates, the ASSU would be first in the field with American Monthly Volumes. Quite how effectively the RTS/ASSU arrangement worked in practice is unclear, but the RTS's inability to have its volumes ready as far in advance as originally intended must have strained the relationship.

The existence of the arrangement with the RTS did not guarantee that the ASSU would be the only reprinter of the "Monthly Series." We know that several U.S. publishers reprinted the volumes by Thomas Dick, thanks to his popularity as a Christian philosopher among American evangelicals. Messrs. Biddle of Philadelphia reprinted *The Atmosphere* within two years of its first publication, and paid £20 directly to Dick in thanks, despite the fact that the RTS had bought the British copyright for £35.[86] The (American) Methodist Sunday School Union (MSSU) also reprinted several of Dick's volumes in revised versions, including *The Atmosphere, The Telescope and Microscope* (vol. 67, 1851), and the second *Solar System* volume.[87] Having bought the plates, the ASSU could do little to alter the text beyond adding a preface.[88] In the case of the MSSU, however, which had to reset all the type anyway, making the revisions suggested by its secretary was not difficult.

The problem of making revisions in subsequent impressions of stereo-typed works affected the RTS's own reprints. Suggestions for revisions were generally ignored. When it was recommended that the *Solar System* should be brought up to date with recent discoveries in astronomy, the copyright committee did investigate how extensive the changes would have to be, pre-sumably to take account of all the new "planets" (asteroids) discovered in the late 1840s. Making numerous small changes throughout a stereotype plate was very difficult, and if alterations affected the line arrangement or pagina-tion, the work would need to be recast. In the case of the *Solar System,* the committee ultimately declared itself of the opinion that "it need not be recast at present."[89] Removing entire passages was theoretically easier, as they could simply be cut out of the plate—but unless they were at the end of a chapter, large gaps would be left. A change of this sort was indeed made to the first volume of the *Solar System* at some point after its first printing. A paragraph,

---

85. Barnes, *Authors, Publishers,* and Nowell-Smith, *International Copyright Law.*
86. Astore, "Observing God," 240; USCL/RTS CCM, 21 June 1848.
87. Astore, "Observing God," 241.
88. Ibid.
89. USCL/RTS CCM, 19 May 1852.

which fortunately fell at the end of a chapter and which the editorial team had inserted without Dick's permission, was removed.[90]

Without an international copyright treaty, the RTS could not have protested about the reprintings of its publications by Biddle in Philadelphia and the MSSU, but in any case, it was probably more pleased than distressed by their eagerness.[91] It was willing to help evangelical societies in other countries reprint the volumes, making a gift of copies of the illustrations for *The Atmosphere* to the Toulouse Book Society for use in the French translation of the work.[92] It also helped with the translation of the *Life of Mohammed* (vol. 22, 1847) into Maráthí and Gujuráti by the Bombay Tract and Book Society.[93] Assisting with such projects was a way of increasing distribution for the Society's publications, and giving them more opportunities to aid the Christian mission. Such overseas circulation was a pleasant addition, however, as the "Monthly Series" and *Leisure Hour* were primarily intended for the British market. Nevertheless, getting publications to the British working classes required an equally serious attention to distribution.

DISTRIBUTION

Producing cheap publications on secular subjects was not of any use unless those works were somehow made available to their target: working- and lower-middle-class readers. The main way of getting publications to readers in mid-nineteenth-century Britain was through the wholesale and retail book trade. The RTS claimed to do over half of its business through the trade, and if tracts were excluded, the proportion would have been much larger. The problem with distributing through the trade was that its target audience was the book-buying middle classes. As Chambers pointed out "at present, few of the . . . [working classes] enter booksellers shops; and unless a person frequent these establishments, he cannot, according to established

90. Astore ("Observing God," 179) refers to Dick's disapproval of this paragraph. A comparison of extant copies has revealed that some copies do not contain this paragraph, suggesting that it was removed at some point after the initial printing. My thanks to Bill Astore for investigating this with me.

91. It would be interesting to know whether the MSSU had consulted with the ASSU. In Britain, evangelical societies were frequently on sufficiently good terms to assist each other in such ventures.

92. USCL/RTS ECM, 24 December 1850.

93. USCL/RTS ECM, 9 December 1851. "Life of Mohammed," *Christian Spectator* (March 1854): 25–26.

usage, become a buyer of books."[94] Giving tracts away—at fairs, on omnibuses, and in the street—was one solution to this problem, but was only
viable for very cheap publications. Tracts were sold for a shilling or two per
hundred, which allowed distributors of even modest means to reach hundreds, even thousands, of people. Books and periodicals were in a different
class. They might be given as a gift to a particular recipient, but they could
not be used in blanket distribution. The "Monthly Series" was distributed
mostly through the RTS's existing book trade connections, but the Society
came to recognise the limitations of that network. It began to experiment
with alternative methods of reaching the working classes, and by the time it
launched the *Leisure Hour,* there was a far more aggressive marketing campaign, particularly at the local rather than national level.[95]

In marketing to the trade, the Society drew on its established contacts with
individual booksellers. Each month, a flyer announced its new publications
to all the booksellers who had accounts with the Society. These accounts had
been set up through personal visits to booksellers, either by the corresponding
secretary or, later, by the Society's commercial traveler.[96] With the "Monthly
Series," some members of the trade were also sent advance specimens, while
for the new periodicals of the early 1850s, the Society sent out a prospectus
and provided "show cards" for display in booksellers' shops and in schools.[97]
Maintaining personal connections with booksellers was important for distributing the Society's usual books and periodicals, but it was not as helpful
with the attempt to reach out on a much wider scale. The journal for the book
trade at that time was the fortnightly *Publishers' Circular.* It carried advance
advertisements from all the major publishers, and was essential reading for
booksellers. The RTS placed a small advertisement every month.

In the 1840s, the style of advertising was beginning to change. Advertisements ceased to be simple announcements of new titles and began to
try to sell their products, using display fonts, pictures, and enticing slogans
and promises.[98] The advertisement in the *Publishers' Circular* of December 1,
1845, which merely announced the launch of the "Monthly Series" in small

---

94. "Booksellers," *Chambers's Edinburgh Journal,* 6 February 1847, 88.

95. For a more detailed comparison between the "Monthly Series" and the *Leisure Hour,*
see Fyfe, "Periodicals and Book Series."

96. USCL/RTS FCM, 10 April 1844 and 20 June 1849.

97. USCL/RTS CCM, 17 September 1845. An announcement on USCL/RTS Publ.,
June 1854 detailed the promotional material available for the *Sunday at Home.*

98. Hindley and Hindley, *Advertising in Victorian Britain,* is a well-illustrated introduction
to the history of advertising.

print (fig. 4.3), seems plain and unattractive, particularly compared with the Bohn advertisement from the following month (shown earlier in fig. 1.11).[99] The Bohn notice was visually more striking, but it also attempted to persuade readers of the virtues of its product, assuring them that the series would be "popular and attractive" and by authors and translators of "undoubted talent."

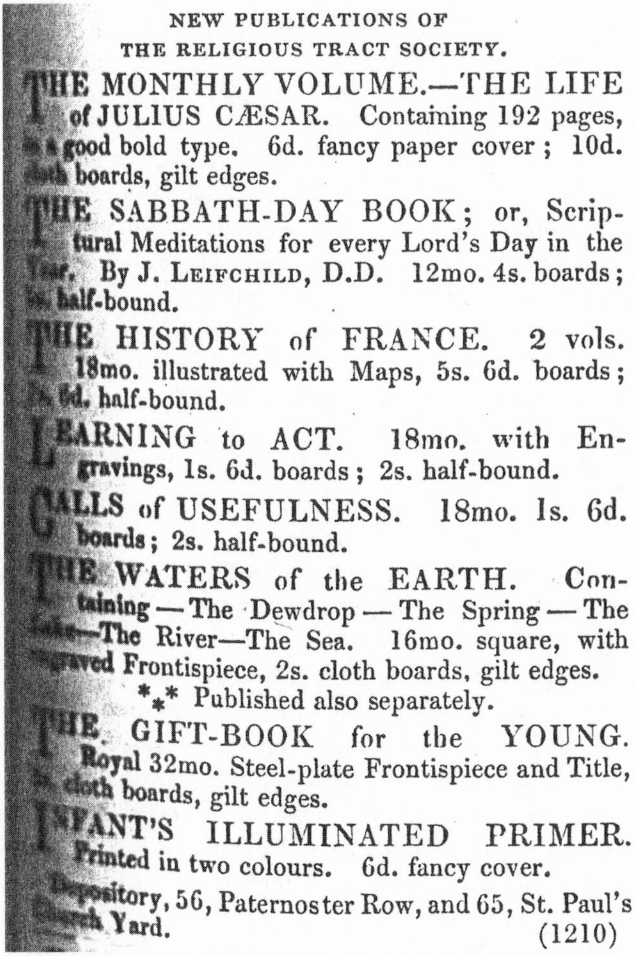

NEW PUBLICATIONS OF
THE RELIGIOUS TRACT SOCIETY.

THE MONTHLY VOLUME.—THE LIFE of JULIUS CÆSAR. Containing 192 pages, a good bold type. 6d. fancy paper cover ; 10d. with boards, gilt edges.

THE SABBATH-DAY BOOK ; or, Scriptural Meditations for every Lord's Day in the Year. By J. Leifchild, D.D. 12mo. 4s. boards ; half-bound.

THE HISTORY of FRANCE. 2 vols. 18mo. illustrated with Maps, 5s. 6d. boards ; 6d. half-bound.

LEARNING to ACT. 18mo. with Engravings, 1s. 6d. boards ; 2s. half-bound.

CALLS of USEFULNESS. 18mo. 1s. 6d. boards ; 2s. half-bound.

THE WATERS of the EARTH. Containing — The Dewdrop — The Spring — The Lake—The River—The Sea. 16mo. square, with engraved Frontispiece, 2s. cloth boards, gilt edges.
₊ Published also separately.

THE GIFT-BOOK for the YOUNG. Royal 32mo. Steel-plate Frontispiece and Title, cloth boards, gilt edges.

INFANT'S ILLUMINATED PRIMER. Printed in two colours. 6d. fancy cover.

Depository, 56, Paternoster Row, and 65, St. Paul's Church Yard.
(1210)

Figure 4.3. Announcement of the launch of the "Monthly Series." This was a small advertisement, placed toward the foot of the left column in the *Publishers' Circular,* 1 November 1845, 841.

---

99. *Publishers' Circular,* 1 December 1845, advert 1210.

Yet, in the winter of 1845–46, the Bohn advertisment was still unusual, while the plain RTS announcement was utterly typical.

By the time the *Leisure Hour* was launched in January 1852, the RTS had taken stock of the situation and realised that old-style announcements would make no impact among the ever-increasing number of display advertisements. The problem for the Society was the expense of the new-style advertisements, which required large amounts of space on the page. The Society could not afford to use display advertisements every month, but when it mattered—as with the launch of a new periodical—it knew what to do. The launch of the *Leisure Hour* in the *Publishers' Circular* of December 1, 1851 (fig. 4.4) was as elaborate in its use of various typefaces and sizes as that of any other publisher. The basic details of price, publisher, and available date were far outnumbered by the number of words describing the aim of the periodical in a way that might persuade the reader to buy it. The copy described the "eminent artists" and "able contributors" on whom "no expense will be spared," and emphasised that the work was sold at "so low a price."[100] But this advertising approach was reserved for those special occasions when it was essential to make an impact. In the *Christian Guardian,* for instance, where the *Leisure Hour* advertisement sat alone on the inside front cover of a periodical with a sympathetic evangelical (Anglican) readership, a plain and simple advertisement was striking enough.[101]

Although the "Monthly Series" had been merely announced in the *Publishers' Circular,* it was more actively promoted in the *Christian Spectator* and on the monthly list of new publications sent out to individual booksellers. On the list of new publications, the manifesto was printed in a banner across the top of the page, while on the front page of the *Christian Spectator* it was prefaced by an explanation of the committee's reasons for deciding to launch a project that was so different from anything else it had previously published. The committee emphasised the "progress of mind," that education had become much more "widely extended . . . [and] of a higher character" than when the Society began, and that knowledge and instruction "must have for its basis the inspired word of God."[102] The committee made careful efforts to justify its project, remembering the last time it launched a new nontract product. As George Stokes recalled, "It is, however, rather painful to have to reflect

---

100. *Publishers' Circular,* 4 December 1851, advert 989.

101. *Christian Guardian* 44 (1852), January, inside front cover. The Cambridge University Library copy retains the covers for this issue.

102. "Announcement of the Monthly Volume," *Christian Spectator* (Sept. 1845): 65.

In a few days, in 1 vol. square crown 8vo. with Illustrations, price 10s. 6d. the THIRD EDITION of

The Knights-Templars.

BY C. G. ADDISON, ESQ. OF THE INNER TEMPLE;
BARRISTER-AT-LAW.

London: Longman, Brown, Green, and Longmans, Paternoster Row.   (988)

NEW WEEKLY PERIODICAL.

On the 1st of January, 1852, will be issued, price ONE PENNY, *No. I. of*

THE LEISURE HOUR:

A FAMILY JOURNAL of INSTRUCTION and ENTERTAINMENT:

Illustrated with Engravings by Eminent Artists.

THE rapid growth of periodical literature is one of the characteristic features of the present day. The weekly journal is adapted to answer ends which are not attained by books. Materials elsewhere provided are, by this agency, presented in such quantities, and with such a regard to adaptation and variety, that the short and broken intervals of daily toil may be turned to profit; and the humblest artisan, though denied access to larger stores of knowledge, may treasure up during his leisure hours abundant facilities of usefulness and pleasure.

It is impossible for the Christian Church to be faithful to its duties, and yet leave this powerful agency unemployed. The various sections of the religious world have been actively engaged in the cultivation of a periodical literature suited to their own wants, and efforts have from time to time been made, not unsuccessfully, to gain the eye of the masses. Yet still, in surveying the prodigious volume of thought which hastens weekly to meet the intellectual wants of the people, it is startling to observe how small a portion of it has been consecrated by religion to her own uses. It would not be easy to analyze the enormous mass. Of much the larger part we need not speak. Silence is fittest for it.

The Religious Tract Society having had its attention called to the subject by many of its supporters, has determined, as far as practicable, to supply this deficiency. The projected serial is intended to meet the requirements of all classes. Its aim will be to make every vacant moment the means of enriching the memory with instructive and pleasant thoughts. In this respect, it will be adapted to meet a common and growing want. The recent efforts in our cities and large towns to abridge the hours of business by means of the Early Closing movement—the tendency of the Legislature in the same direction, as evinced by its Act for shortening the period of factory labour—these, and many other equally significant social phenomena, seem to indicate, as one of the recognised principles of the day, that

EVERY PERSON SHOULD HAVE A LEISURE HOUR.

To assist in garnering this fragment of precious time, and to supply the fire-side circle with a copious fund of entertaining information, will be the design of the proposed journal. Avoiding the pernicious principle of creating a distinctli terature for each of the different sections of society, there will be no ostentatious parade of condescension in the choice of topics or the mode of treating them; but animated by feelings of pure catholicity, "THE LEISURE HOUR" will seek to utter sentiments which shall meet an equally quick response in the parlour and the workshop, the hall and the cottage. While the work will be imbued with a religious spirit, it will comprise papers on every subject which can elevate, gratify, or instruct. Articles on the more prominent topics of the day will be mingled with interesting narratives, instructive sketches from history, visits to places of celebrity in distant parts of the world, popular dissertations on scientific questions, and the choicest effusions of poetry : the whole forming a miscellany aiming to be highly attractive in itself, and one which the Christian parent and employer may safely place in the hands of those who are under his influence.

In carrying out this object, no expense will be spared. The services of able contributors have been secured, and every thing will be done to render "THE LEISURE HOUR" fully commensurate with the wants of the times. The Committee are aware that in fixing so low a price, nothing short of a very extensive sale will avert pecuniary loss. For this they trust to the intrinsic merit of the publication, and to the warm cooperation of their friends and supporters; while they would earnestly supplicate upon the whole undertaking the effectual blessing of Almighty God.

The publication will consist of Sixteen large Pages, printed with new and clear type, on good paper, and illustrated with Engravings.

WEEKLY NUMBERS, price **One Penny**; or, MONTHLY PARTS, in a neat wrapper, **Five-pence.**

May be had of Booksellers, Stationers, and other Vendors in Town and Country.

RELIGIOUS TRACT SOCIETY :—56, Paternoster Row; 65, St. Paul's Churchyard; and 164, Piccadilly. (989)

Figure 4.4. This advertisement of the launch of the *Leisure Hour* took up almost a full page in the *Publishers' Circular,* 4 December 1851, 399.

that for many a long month, even for years," after the launch of the first periodicals in the 1820s, "the Committee were assailed by statements that they were injuring the cause, which they knew they were benefiting by these efforts."[103] Stokes's comments appeared in a *Christian Spectator* article while the "Monthly Series" was still at the planning stage, and may have been intended to smooth its path. He argued that the success of the periodicals "may now be referred to as presenting strong reasons for confidence in other measures which the conductors may think it their duty to adopt."[104] Nevertheless, when the Series was launched, the committee received a letter from a well-known evangelical, the Reverend William Carus Wilson, who berated it for losing sight of its primary mission of tract circulation. There were probably more such correspondences that were not minuted.[105]

After the launch of the Series, each subsequent volume was announced in the monthly list to booksellers and in the *Publishers' Circular*, and was given a brief review in the *Christian Spectator*. The *Christian Spectator* entries were usually solely descriptive, as this example (for *Blights of the Wheat*) illustrates:

> This work treats of the different fungi which attack the straw, leaves, chaff-scales, flower and grain of the wheat; also, of the ergot, wheat-midge, fly, and infusorial insects—gives the results of various experiments and suggests antidotes. Its contents are not only of great importance to the agriculturalist, but to the public at large; the author connects the advancement of popular science with its highest and best end—the manifestation of the Divine glory. The author is the Rev E. Sidney, of Acle.[106]

The attribution of authorship is unsurprising, since *Blights of the Wheat* had a signed preface, but the *Christian Spectator* did sometimes reveal the identity of the anonymous writers. For instance, it referred to *Ancient Jerusalem* (vol. 12, 1846) as "written by Dr Kitto."[107] Later impressions of both Sidney's and Kitto's works acknowledged their writers openly. The same is true of the few other well-known writers in the Series, suggesting that the committee changed its mind about the relative importance of the Society's tradition of anonymity in light of the advertising advantage to be gained from named writers.

---

103. [Stokes], "General and Scriptural Knowledge," 90.
104. Ibid.
105. USCL/RTS FCM, 20 January 1847.
106. "Blights of the Wheat," *Christian Spectator* (Nov. 1846): 187.
107. "Ancient Jerusalem," *Christian Spectator* (Nov. 1846): 187.

The RTS appears to have done relatively little advertising in the 1840s, and it was mostly targeted at the readers of religious periodicals.[108] The "Monthly Series" was advertised in the biweekly evangelical newspaper, the *Patriot*, and probably in some of the denominational monthlies, but, unlike competitors such as Bogue's "European Library," it was not announced in *The Times*.[109] By the early 1850s, the committee's increasing awareness of the importance of advertising can be seen in the wider range of publications it targeted. These now included weekly evangelical newspapers, such as the *British Banner*, the *Patriot*, the *Record*, and the *Nonconformist*, as well as such monthly reviews as the *Evangelical Magazine* and the *Eclectic Review*. There were even advertisements in the *Manchester Examiner* newspaper.[110] The archival evidence suggests that most of these periodicals probably carried advertisements for the *Leisure Hour*, confirming that it was more heavily advertised than the "Monthly Series" had been. Weekly newspapers were undoubtedly more widely read than the monthlies, but most of the ones used by the RTS were still aimed at the religious part of the population.

The RTS in the 1840s and 1850s was certainly learning how to use advertisements better, but, like all the traditional book trade marketing methods, advertisements were most effective at reaching the book-buying middle classes. They could do very little to promote publications like the "Monthly Series" and the *Leisure Hour* among their intended working-class readers, since such people rarely visited bookshops and rarely had access to the sorts of periodicals that carried advertisements or reviews.

All publishers of improving material for the working classes faced the same problem, which was why the RTS quoted with approval Chambers's assertion that, "the only sure way to reach the masses is to act aggressively—take the booksellers' shop to their doors and firesides, and let them see and handle what is going on in the department of literature specially addressed to them."[111] The Chambers brothers cited examples of unemployed individuals

---

108. In 1844–45, the RTS spent £100 on newspaper advertisements, £118 on magazine advertisements, and £72 on those in the *Patriot* and *Record*. See USCL/RTS FCM, 9 July 1845. By the late 1840s, it spent around £350 a year on advertisements. See USCL/RTS FCM, 16 June 1847 and 21 August 1850.

109. *Patriot*, 4 December 1845, 809, col. d. The "Monthly Series" was certainly not announced in *The Times* during the month around its launch date. Advertisements for Bogue's library appear at *The Times*, 27 November 1845, 11, col. f and 5 December 1845, 12, col. b.

110. USCL/RTS ECM, for example, 20 January 1852 and 27 January 1852.

111. "Booksellers," *Chambers's Edinburgh Journal*, 6 February 1847, 88, quoted in *Christian Spectator* (March 1847): 210.

Figure 4.5. Hawkers carried their publications with them, and could take them directly to the working classes. In this case, the hawker and his wares have penetrated deep into the heart of the home. From Fison, *Colportage,* opp. 28.

who made a living as book and tract hawkers, and suggested that publishers should be more willing to supply such individuals with publications.[112] Such itinerant vendors sought out working-class readers directly, at their homes or meeting places (fig. 4.5), and made their living on the difference between the trade and retail prices of their publications. They could "frequently gain access to places far removed from all other agencies."[113] The RTS had been aware of the possibilities of hawkers since the 1810s, and it had devoted strenuous efforts toward supplanting the hawkers' usual wares of chapbooks, ballads, and other unsavoury publications with religious tracts. The Society strongly supported the individuals and societies that supplied hawkers with RTS publications. In 1849, its annual report included details of the sales successes of five hawkers employed by the Town Missionary and Scripture Readers Society, who had sold no fewer than sixty thousand RTS publications and twenty-four thousand Bibles in the past year.[114]

---

112. "Booksellers," *Chambers's Edinburgh Journal,* 6 February 1847, 88–89.
113. RTS Report (1845): 87.
114. RTS Report (1849), app. III, item 8.

The RTS's interest in the possibilities of reaching the working classes with hawkers climaxed in 1850, when Joseph Gurney, one of the trustees, suggested that the RTS ought to employ its own hawkers to increase sales in London.[115] Two men were employed early in 1851, and by the summer were each selling around £2 of publications per month.[116] They were therefore having similar levels of success as the tract and pamphlet sellers interviewed by journalist Henry Mayhew, who claimed to sell about a shilling's worth of publications per day.[117] Although the sales almost covered the wages the RTS men were being paid, they did not cover the four-pound-a-year hawkers' licences.[118] There was also a problem finding suitable men, as the Reverend William Urwick of Dublin discovered when the RTS asked him to find ten hawkers to work in Ireland. A hawker had to possess "strong bodily vigour, so that he may endure the fatigue of constant journeys," and also be a model of evangelical piety.[119] Even if he failed to sell a publication, he could still, by his character, present a valuable lesson. One of the Society's London hawkers had been recommended by a minister, while the other, a Leicestershire framework knitter, had won the Society's prize-essay "On the Temporal Advantages of the Sabbath to the Labouring Classes" in 1849.[120] In Ireland, however, only three men applied for the positions, and after a year Urwick gave up, citing a lack of suitable men, the small wages that could be offered, the poverty of the population, and the lack of a taste for reading.[121]

Despite the limited success of these efforts in London and Ireland, the committee's belief in hawkers was eventually justified. It was impractical for a central society (or publisher) to organise hawkers all over the country, but unlike Chambers, the RTS had a network of representatives at the local level. Through articles in the annual reports, it encouraged subscribers and auxiliaries to employ hawkers, and offered grants on RTS publications for

---

115. USCL/RTS ECM, 10 December 1850.

116. Sales after ten weeks, USCL/RTS FCM, 16 April 1851; after almost six months, USCL/RTS ECM, 29 July 1851.

117. Mayhew, *London Labour*, i, 308.

118. They were being paid 10*s*. a week on top of the difference between trade and retail prices. See USCL/RTS CCM, 18 December 1850.

119. RTS Report (1850), "Colportage," unnumbered appendix before catalogue.

120. USCL/RTS FCM, 19 March 1851; manuscript note on archive copy of USCL/RTS Publ., March 1849.

121. USCL/RTS FCM, 6 September 1848, 16 January 1850; ECM, 25 June 1850 and 29 July 1851.

such enterprises.[122] By the late 1850s, specialist societies, such as the Church of England Book-Hawking Association, were set up specifically to manage this aspect of book distribution.[123]

Although it was generally asserted that the working classes did not frequent bookshops, the reports of city missionaries and investigative journalists were revealing the existence of alternative bookselling outlets. New, remaindered, and secondhand books were sold from barrows and stalls (fig. 4.6), and even from small shops in the working-class districts. Henry Mayhew reported that there were around a thousand individuals employed in sale of stationery and literature on the streets of London. Of these, he found forty selling tracts and pamphlets, twenty with book stalls, and fifty running book barrows.[124] The barrow and stall keepers were able to earn about 15*s*. per week.[125] RTS publications would usually appear in such outlets only in secondhand condition, although the Society was particularly delighted to hear that the *Leisure Hour* was selling well in an infidel bookshop in Southampton.[126]

In 1850, the committee was informed by a correspondent that "great efforts were being made in Manchester and other large Manufacturing Towns, to open small Shops in Poor districts for the sale of cheap and irreligious publications." Even worse, "these shops are kept open on the Lord's Day."[127] A year later, the annual report carried a worrying description of the spread of such shops: a Manchester clergyman estimated that "in his small parish he has at least one [irreligious] shop to each 500 of the population"; and in London, a city missionary reported that "there are *thirty-eight* shops wholly or partially supported by the sale of such trash, in the parishes of St John's and St Margaret's, Westminster."[128] Since the customers of these shops were highly unlikely to enter the regular bookshops that stocked Christian literature, the RTS annual report concluded that the only solution was "the establishment of similar shops conducted by pious persons."[129]

---

122. For example, RTS Report (1850), "Colportage," unnumbered appendix before catalogue. Compare RTS Report (1891): 245–46.

123. The activities of one such society are described in Haines, "Am I My Brother's Keeper?" chap. 5.

124. Mayhew, *London Labour*, i, 308–9.

125. Ibid., i, 296.

126. USCL/RTS ECM, 13 July 1852 and "The Leisure Hour," *Christian Spectator* (July 1852): 733. The correspondent was the Reverend Wigram, Archdeacon of Winchester.

127. USCL/RTS ECM, 29 October 1850.

128. RTS Report (1851): 123.

129. Ibid.

Figure 4.6. A bookstall in a working-class district. From [Sargent], *Story of a Pocket Bible,* 40.

The committee tried to help its auxiliary societies to set up such shops, particularly in Manchester.[130] In London, it was more directly involved. Between 1843 and 1856, it acquired the use of a stand in the Soho Bazaar, and it may also have had one in the Baker Street Bazaar.[131] The Soho stand was run by a Mrs. Stratford, who had "passed though much affliction and therefore calls for kindness and sympathy."[132] For the first few years, the stall sold around £200 of books a year, rather better than the stalls surveyed by Mayhew, but with less profit, for the RTS stall made only £3 a year.[133] The Society was certain the works sold there went "into Channels which would not have been otherwise reached."[134] Unfortunately, the Society had not allowed for Mrs. Stratford's inexperience in keeping accounts, and there were several occasions on which they did not add up, to the Society's loss. In 1855, after the third such discrepancy, sales had fallen from their original high, and the Society decided to discontinue the experiment.[135]

Hawkers and market stalls were distribution channels that could actually place publications in the hands of the working classes, and although they rarely brought in much financial profit, there was a strong moral imperative for the Society to run them, as long as they did not make too much of a loss. Here, the Society's relative uninterest in profit allowed it to experiment in ways that commercial publishers could not. Hawkers and market stalls were too difficult and time-consuming to organise on anything other than a small and local scale, and again, the RTS had an advantage over Chambers through its network of subscribers and auxiliary societies. Although the auxiliaries were not organised for the selling of books or periodicals, they (and individual subscribers) could be mobilised to promote the works on a local level, and to organise book stalls or hawkers much more effectively than the London committee could hope to do.

The pages of the *Christian Spectator* were the way for the RTS committee and officers to encourage such work. At the beginning of the "Monthly

---

130. On Manchester, see USCL/RTS ECM, 13 May 1851.

131. On Baker Street, see USCL/RTS FCM, 20 January 1847 and 2 February 1847. This project disappeared from the minute books after its plans appeared to have been finalised.

132. USCL/RTS Corr., Jones to Capt. Trotter, 29 April 1847.

133. USCL/RTS FCM, 19 December 1855 and 12 February 1845. Mrs. Stratford was paid 12s. a week and 10 percent commission on all sales over £4 per fortnight, and after expenses. Mayhew, *London Labour*, i, 309, estimated average weekly sales of around £1.11s.

134. USCL/RTS FCM, 13 March 1844 and 20 May 1846; USCL/RTS Corr., Jones to Capt. Trotter, 29 April 1847.

135. USCL/RTS Corr., Jones to Capt. Trotter, 5 May 1847; USCL/RTS FCM, 19 May 1847, 18 December 1850, 19 December 1855, and 16 January 1856.

Series," articles in the *Christian Spectator* announced and justified the new project, reported on the great success of the first volume (its ten thousand copies had sold out almost immediately), and reprinted laudatory reviews from the press. The coverage kept subscribers informed of the progress of the new venture, and tried to persuade them to recommend it to their servants and local schools. Two years later, the *Christian Spectator* asked, "Do you know the Monthly Volume?" and commented pessimistically, "Were this question proposed to individuals in families and social circles, we are persuaded the answer would most commonly be in the negative." It then printed a letter from a subscriber who wrote, "I never travel without a number in my pocket; and many have thanked me for bringing it to their knowledge, and have at once ordered the whole series."[136] His example was presented to other subscribers for emulation.

The Society also used the *Christian Spectator* to promote the *Leisure Hour*, again urging subscribers to actively promote it in their neighbourhoods, and printing successful examples for imitation and inspiration.[137] The Edinburgh auxiliary society and a bookseller in Manchester both printed circular letters promoting the *Leisure Hour*, which they sent to local booksellers, ministers and schoolteachers. The Edinburgh society even enclosed specimen copies of the first number with its letter. Meanwhile, in Birmingham and Liverpool, the auxiliary societies employed agents to make "a thorough canvass of the small shops, dining-rooms, coffee-houses, factories etc.," distributing advertisements among the customers and employees. A Derbyshire clergyman requested specimen copies of the first numbers, which he intended to take round to the "three public-houses in this district, which I am informed take in newspapers . . . and endeavour to persuade them to take in the work for the entertainment of their customers." Itinerant hawkers sold periodicals as well as books, and one employed by the Liverpool Tract Society in late 1852 managed to sell each month around 2,000 weekly numbers and 270 monthly parts of the *Leisure Hour*.[138] If this represents regular sales to returning customers, it suggests that only slightly more than one-third of the hawker's customers were saving up for the five-penny monthly parts. The rest were presumably those working-class readers the Society was so keen to reach.

---

136. "Do you know the Monthly Volume?" *Christian Spectator* (Nov. 1847): 280.

137. The following examples come from "Periodical Literature and the People: Success of the Leisure Hour," *Christian Spectator* (March 1852): 697–98.

138. "Colportage," *Christian Spectator* (March 1853): 793.

Another way of reaching workers was to seek the help of their employers. The secretary of the Glasgow auxiliary society made "very great and generous efforts" to encourage the city's manufacturers to promote the *Leisure Hour* among their employees. Robert Johnston, the owner of the Oakbank Cotton Spinning and Power Loom Weaving Works, of Garscube Road, purchased four hundred copies of the first number to distribute among his workers.[139] Johnston also offered to subsidise subsequent issues by half for those of his workforce who wished to receive it. Those who signed up would have it "delivered to . . . [them] every Saturday afternoon, when the engine stops." Johnston shared the Society's desire to improve his workers, but he also wanted to protect his own interests. The Society published the *Leisure Hour* on a Thursday, rather than the more usual Saturday, in an attempt to prevent the Sabbath being occupied by nonsacred reading material. Johnston, however, delivered the periodical to his workers on Saturday to reduce the chances of them reading it during working hours. He ended his announcement by saying: "Mr Johnston trusts that no one will abuse this privilege, and defraud him, by bringing these or any other books into the mill to read during working hours."[140]

As an ongoing periodical, the *Leisure Hour* required continuous marketing after its launch. In contrast, the RTS made relatively little effort to promote the "Monthly Series" once it was underway, although announcements continued to appear in the *Publishers' Circular* and *Christian Spectator*. Once the Series closed, it remained on the Society's catalogue, still available, but not actively promoted.[141] With the *Leisure Hour*, there were several promotional efforts in its early years, attempting to boost its circulation among the working classes, in addition to the regular announcements that continued till its eventual closure in 1906. After the initial publicity, circulation figures stood at around sixty thousand a week, but, as with *Chambers's Journal*, too many of the sales were in monthly parts to (presumably) more affluent readers.[142] In late 1852, the committee began to advertise the *Leisure Hour* more widely, placing notices in "the periodicals most read by that [working] class" rather than the usual religious periodicals.[143] It also produced a new prospectus

---

139. My thanks to Morag and Alastair Fyfe for identifying "Mr Johnston, of Oakbank."

140. "Periodical Literature and the People: Success of the Leisure Hour," *Christian Spectator* (March 1852): 697–98.

141. The complete series remained available till 1876, and odd volumes were available until 1883. See RTS Reports (1877–83).

142. "Booksellers," *Chambers's Edinburgh Journal*, 6 December 1847, 87–89.

143. USCL/RTS ECM, 1 June 1852.

that included complimentary remarks from reviewers. Rather than selecting quotations from the relatively grand London-based reviews, most came from provincial newspapers, such as the *Brechin Advertiser,* the *Leeds Intelligencer,* and the *Nottingham Journal,* whose recommendations were presumed to be more meaningful to the target audience.[144]

The Society's commitment to securing a wide readership for the *Leisure Hour* was also indicated by the decision to publish it without the RTS imprint. Generally, all RTS publications, from tracts to books, carried "The Religious Tract Society, instituted 1799" on their title pages (see, for instance, figs. 1.7 and 3.2). Yet the Society was aware that its imprint would repel certain classes of readers, and had more than once discussed the possibility of removing it from specific works. In 1844, the finance committee noted that there were two works on the catalogue that did not carry the imprint, and recommended additionally removing it from the *Introduction to the Study of Birds* (1835) and its companion volumes on quadrupeds and reptiles, which were selling slowly.[145] The executive committee did not approve this suggestion. The works in question were described as "expensive and scientific" natural history books "and others of the same class," so were clearly not aimed at the working classes. Educated readers would expect to see some indication of authority and reliability. Like most RTS works, these books carried no writer's name, so removing the publisher's name as well would leave an utterly anonymous work. The RTS did not want its nonfiction works to carry such uncertain and suspicious connotations. The fact that the "Monthly Series" did carry the RTS imprint indicates that the committee was still thinking at least partly in terms of an extension of previous nonfiction publishing, and had yet to fully realise the challenges of publishing this sort of material for a much wider audience.

The *Leisure Hour* was a slightly different case. Periodical articles were usually anonymous, and this did not detract from their perceived authority, which depended instead on the reputation the editor and journal had established. Some periodicals tried to boost their reputation from the start by advertising the identity of the editor, as with *Reynolds's Miscellany* or Dickens's *Household*

---

144. Ibid. Jones had suggested using these reviews on the covers of the monthly parts but the committee suggested putting them into the *Christian Spectator,* where they appeared in March 1852, at 698. See USCL/RTS ECM, 2 March 1852. A similar tactic was used in the *Christian Spectator* (Jan. 1854): 15, where reviews from the *Eclectic Review, Baptist Magazine,* and *Evangelical Magazine* appeared after those from provincial papers.
145. USCL/RTS FCM, 26 June 1844, and ECM, 9 July 1844.

Words. It was traditional for the improving journals issued by societies to do the same, and the *Penny Magazine*'s full title had been the *Penny Magazine of the Society for the Diffusion of Useful Knowledge.* The *Visitor* had always displayed its affiliation. What the RTS realised in the early 1850s, though, was that for much of the working-class audience, the name "RTS" would be more likely to suggest patronising middle-class interference than trustworthy information. In these circumstances, the uncertainty of an invisible editor/publisher would be better than the certainty of a disliked editor/publisher. The *Leisure Hour,* therefore, did not carry the RTS imprint in its banner (see fig. 3.1), or even at the foot of the last page. By law, it did have to carry an identification of the printer and/or publisher, but the Society got around this by using the name of its secretary and the address of the depository. Thus, the imprint was "W. Jones, 56 Paternoster Row," which was technically correct, but gave no hint of the RTS.[146] Of course, evangelicals might well recognise the address, and it was a very open secret. The very first advertisement in the *Publishers' Circular* (fig. 4.4) and some of those in the religious press had announced the publisher as the RTS. The result was that evangelical readers—the sort of people to whom the RTS imprint was a sign of quality—would know that the *Leisure Hour* was an RTS product, while working-class readers would not. By the end of 1852, the committee had even altered the style of advertisements in the *Publishers' Circular,* so that the *Leisure Hour* no longer appeared in the RTS advertisement but had an advertisement of its own.[147] The RTS was essentially creating an alter ego for itself. It could publish as "the RTS" or as a separate, not obviously religious, entity. Three decades later, when the Society launched its most successful periodicals, the *Boy's Own Paper* (1879) and the *Girl's Own Paper* (1880), they were officially published by "The *Leisure Hour* Office."

The RTS was happy enough with the *Leisure Hour*'s sales to launch a sister periodical in May 1854. The *Sunday at Home* competed directly with the Sabbath-breaking papers, acknowledging (shockingly, for some) that people might wish to read something other than directly religious works on a Sunday, and offering a suitable alternative. By 1855, however, the committee was again concerned about the sales in weekly numbers. In March, it printed a new handbill advertising both periodicals, and distributed almost three hundred

---

146. The hiding of the link between the *Leisure Hour* and the RTS was so successful that a twentieth-century historian refused to accept the attribution on the grounds that there was no evidence in the journal itself. See Hinton, "Popular Science in England," 330.

147. *Publishers' Circular,* 3 December 1852, advert 1015.

thousand copies. It also employed an additional traveling agent for a year specifically to promote the periodicals in the north of England, Scotland, and Ireland.[148] A further appeal went out in November 1855 to five thousand clergy and ministers, four thousand boarding schools, and one thousand Sunday schools.[149] After this year of determined promotion, the annual report announced that there had been an increase of ten thousand in the circulation of the *Leisure Hour*.[150] The target now was to reach sales of one hundred thousand per week.

DESPITE its image as an evangelical charitable organisation, the Religious Tract Society was an efficient Victorian business enterprise. These evangelicals did not merely decry the expansion of the cheap press, they set out to do something about it. Their existing techniques for printing large numbers of publications cheaply stood them in good stead, but in other areas they were learning as they went along. The RTS had never had to deal with many living writers before, and it took the copyright committee several attempts before it worked out a viable method of selecting suitable writers. Nor was the editorial department used to the demands placed on it by having to have a complete book ready each month. Nor had the Society ever really had to try to sell its wares directly to the working classes.

Despite dilatory writers and delinquent editors, the "Monthly Series" was successfully maintained to one hundred volumes and was widely welcomed among reviewers for bringing a much-needed religious tone to secular information. Its launch was followed by Christian series on secular subjects from several other publishers, which was, perhaps, the sincerest form of flattery. In terms of sales, it was extremely successful for a book series in the 1840s. We have sales figures from three different points in the series, all of which suggest that, on average, the volumes sold their entire print runs within a year or two, and continued to sell, more slowly, thereafter.[151] Of course, the

---

148. USCL/RTS FCM, 18 April 1855.
149. USCL/RTS FCM, 21 November 1855.
150. USCL/RTS Report (1856): 6. Report (1855): app., xix, had claimed eighty thousand a year. These figures are almost certainly inflated, since in the cases where we have circulations recorded in the minute books (USCL/RTS ECM, 2 March 1852 and USCL/RTS FCM, 26 September 1855) they are around ten thousand lower than the ones publicly announced.
151. The figures are analysed in Fyfe, "Industrialised Conversion," 127–29.

volumes differed in popularity, as is very clear from the list of best-selling volumes published in the Society's fifty-year anniversary history, in 1850.[152] *Wild Flowers* (vol. 3) and *Solar System, part I* (vol. 6) had both sold just over thirty thousand copies since publication, and were closely followed by *Solar System, part II* (vol. 9) with twenty-seven thousand copies. On the other hand, *Jamaica* (vol. 4) and *The Task, and other poems* (vol. 7), alone of the early volumes, had yet to sell their break-even ten thousand copies. Unfortunately, *British Fish* appeared too late to make it into the list, which stopped in March 1849. Although three of the top four best-selling volumes were on the sciences, it is also significant that the number one spot went to *Philosophy of the Plan of Salvation* (vol. 13, 1846), which had sold 38,500 copies. This gives a hint that the Monthly Volumes were most appreciated by existing Christians of straitened means, as their unconverted cousins would be unlikely to buy the most obviously evangelical book in the entire series.

The attempt to reach multiple audiences was almost certainly too ambitious to succeed completely. Sales in the low tens of thousands were highly impressive for books, but they were tiny compared with the hundreds of thousands achieved by some of the penny periodicals. The "Monthly Series" demonstrated that there was a significant audience of readers among the lower-middle classes who were not yet being adequately supplied by publishers. The Society appears to have been satisfied with finding this audience, and decided not to make more efforts to promote the "Monthly Series" among the lower ranks of readers, as initially intended. The *Leisure Hour,* on the other hand, with sales approaching the one hundred thousand mark, clearly could reach some of the working classes, so the mission was to make sure it reached more and more of them. Hence, the *Leisure Hour* was supported by a publicity campaign that was far more aggressive than anything seen for the "Monthly Series."

The RTS had launched its new scheme of secular publishing with the aim of combating the effects of the secular and infidel presses on the mass readership. Price, marketing, and distribution were all essential to this enterprise, but it was the Christian tone that would ultimately determine its spiritual effectiveness. In contrast to the placing of advertisements, the quality of printing paper, or the style of binding, the range of acceptable solutions made Christian tone much more difficult for the committee to specify with precision. It could try to vet its writers and it could reject clearly unsuitable

---

152. William Jones, *Jubilee Memorial,* app. V.

manuscripts, but it could not define exactly what Christian tone was, nor how best it should be integrated with a particular subject matter. These were matters that had to be entrusted to the writers. Yet, just as the public charitable face of the RTS tended to obscure its underlying commercialism, by considering writers primarily as creators of Christian tone the RTS itself tended to overlook the physical strain and financial difficulties of being a writer.

V

The Ministry of the Press

WILLIAM Thackeray's novel *The History of Pendennis: his fortunes and misfortunes, his friends and his greatest enemy* (1848–50) contains a vivid description of mid-nineteenth-century authorship.[1] Arthur Pendennis regularly scribbles his reviews and articles in chop houses and taverns in the early hours of the morning, and staggers home to his lodgings as the dawn appears. Captain Shandon edits his journal from the debtors' prison, and, despite the presence of his wife and children, drinks his fee as soon as he receives it. George Warrington is the only moral and upright writer in the novel (fig. 5.1). Thackeray's unfavourable depiction of authorship distressed literary commentators, and in 1850 the *North British Review* printed a long article on "The literary profession," using *Pendennis* as a launching point.[2] The reviewer acknowledged that there was some truth to the image presented by Thackeray, but he claimed that, ultimately, writing was a far nobler enterprise than it was made out to be in the novel. That some of its practitioners gave it a bad name should not distract from the fact that writing was a moral and spiritual occupation of great responsibility. For the *North British* reviewer, "It is no small thing to influence public opinion—to guide men to light from darkness, to truth from error—to inform the ignorant, to solace the unhappy, to afford high intellectual enjoyment to the few, or healthy recreation to the many. Of all professions, worthily pursued, it is the least selfish."[3]

Just a few years later, in the world of fact rather than fiction, William Martin described his life as a professional writer to the committee of the Royal Literary Fund (RLF, 1788), an organisation that made grants to impoverished writers.[4] Martin had written many works on natural history for the Religious Tract Society (RTS) and other publishers. He acknowledged his role as mentor and instructor, and was willing to regard writing as part of

---

1. Thackeray, *Pendennis*, chaps. 31–36.   3. Ibid., 371.
2. [Kaye], "Pendennis."   4. Cross, *Royal Literary Fund.*

Figure 5.1. George Warrington reads a review of one of Arthur Pendennis's works, as Pendennis sits at his writing desk. Thackeray, *Pendennis*, i, opp. 352.

his Christian duty, but these roles did not provide bread or pay the rent. As Martin wrote:

> I would enter into a long train of events which have tried me sadly;—some connected with the failure of Publishers..., others with domestic transactions I would willingly forget were it possible. In addition to these, I could explain to you how, for months and months, I have received no order of any great importance from any publisher—how my days have been spent in restless anxiety, and my nights in mental agony.[5]

---

5. RLF 1315.3, Martin to RLF, 11 April 1853.

The *North British Review* had trouble untangling the truth from the fiction in Thackeray's account of authorship, but writers themselves also operated on two intertwined levels: the noble ideal of authorship and the underlying reality of trying to make a living from it. Thanks to the growth of the periodicals in the 1840s and 1850s, "writers were never so numerous" as at that time."[6] They included large numbers of poverty-stricken writers as well as a few great success stories such as Thackeray and Dickens. Like most of those who wrote for the RTS, Martin fell somewhere between the extremes. Most of the time, he managed to support himself and his wife by his writing, but it was always more unpredictable and fragile as a source of income than such an honourable occupation ought to be. In times of sickness, a death in the family, or unexpected financial problems, Martin had no resources to fall back on, and he was reduced to writing begging letters to the Royal Literary Fund.

All the efforts that the RTS put into editing, printing, and distributing its works would be for naught without the writers like Martin who created the Christian tone. In some respects, the RTS staff regarded writers as just another cog in the machine of the production process, but of all the cogs, the writers were the only ones whose creativity was recognised and appreciated. Printers were expected to do what they were told, but the instructions to writers were necessarily more vague and relied substantially on the individual writer's ability to understand what was needed and to produce it. This was why the Society took so much care to select suitable writers, and is also why its writers received a more public image than, for instance, its printers. Even so, the writers were shadowy figures. Most RTS works were anonymous, and discussions of authorship tended to focus on the idealised Christian vocation of the writers. The reality was far less exotic, and had far more to do with hard work and financial necessity. Christian writing had the advantage of being one of the few acceptable ways of making money from one's faith, but the balance between faith and finances was a tricky one.

IDEAL WRITERS AND ASPIRING NOODLES

There were around twenty thousand people in nineteenth-century Britain who could be regarded as persistent writers, having engaged in literary activity over a number of years.[7] The sheer number of writers and the variety

---

6. Saunders & Otley, *Advice to Authors,* [i].
7. Cross, *Common Writer,* 2.

of their circumstances illuminates why contemporaries found it so difficult to generalise about authorship. Some commentators celebrated the fact that "Literature has become a profession. It is a means of subsistence, almost as certain as the bar or the church."[8] Others countered that "It is much worse than nonsense for Mr. Thackeray to stand up at a Literary-Fund club dinner, and tell us that all authors might be comfortable and independent if they pleased."[9] Financial security was the main focus of such discussions, and commentators disagreed whether the precarious state of so many writers should be blamed on the book-buying public, the government, profit-seeking publishers, or the careless financial habits of the writers themselves.[10]

Although authorship was often referred to as a profession, its status as such was problematic.[11] Unlike other professions, as the *North British Review* acknowledged, there were no entrance requirements for literary work: "no articles to be subscribed—no probationary dinners to be eaten—no examinations to be undergone—no qualifications to be tested—no degrees to be taken—no diplomas to be granted."[12] In the absence of gate-keeping qualifications, the membership of the nascent "profession" could not be tightly defined. As *Fraser's Magazine* pointed out, in addition to those writers who hoped to make their entire living from literature, authorship was open to "barristers with scarce briefs, and physicians with few patients, clergymen on small livings, idle women, rich men, and a large crop of aspiring noodles."[13] This meant that there was little group identity among writers, and that, unlike the lawyer or the physician, the full-time writer was "surrounded with rivals, not only as hungry as himself, but willing and able to work for lower wages, because they are not, as he is, solely dependent upon literature."[14] Those arguing for professionalisation in other areas, including the sciences, wished to exclude part-time practitioners such as clergymen, physicians, and idle rich men.[15] But whereas in the sciences, it was becoming possible to insist on

---

8. [Lewes], "Condition of Authors," 285.

9. "Authors and Publishers," *New Quarterly Review* 3 (1854): 9–17, at 10.

10. "Authors and Publishers," ibid., blamed the publishers; [Lewes], "Condition of Authors," implicated the government; [Kaye], "Pendennis," blamed the writers' moral habits, but attributed some responsibility to the public for the poor remuneration of unknown authors.

11. Bonham-Carter, *Authors by Profession,* chaps. 3–4.

12. [Kaye], "Pendennis," 369–70.

13. [Lewes], "Condition of Authors," 285.

14. Ibid., 294–95.

15. Turner, "Victorian Conflict between Science and Religion"; Cardwell, *Organisation of Science.*

expertise as an entry requirement, which could be demonstrated by the new university courses, there was no obvious way to exclude literate people from authorship.

Despite these gate-keeping problems, the most common image for authorship in the mid-nineteenth century was as a learned profession, primarily because of the possibility it offered of earning a genteel living.[16] Other ways of making money had less highbrow connotations. *Chambers's Journal,* for instance, suggested the image of "authorcraft."[17] This gave authorship the status of a highly skilled but manual occupation. Although the combination of physical activity with skill was an accurate description of many writers' lives, authorcraft was not a commonly used image. Most writers were from the middle classes, and preferred to gloss over the physical aspect of their work. An alternative image for authorship was as a trade, such as publishing, which was, "like all other trades, undertaken with the one object of making money by it."[18] A trade was purely mercenary and involved no apparent creativity. Writers who were too closely involved with the trade produced "mere compilations . . . , hack-work, and are paid for as such."[19] Such writers were represented as "mere composing machines" (fig. 5.2), producing unoriginal works purely for money.[20] In contrast, the ideal writer had an "unmistakable vocation" to enlighten and provide recreation, and this sense of vocation made his work into a profession.[21] It was the sense of vocation that enabled true writers to be creative and original, and that placed their work on a higher plane than a mercenary trade. Representations of the hack writer often included references to the physical conditions of production, perhaps describing him in "the attic, the broken teacup as an inkstand, and the blanket for all covering."[22] While the hack toiled, the identification of authorship with the learned professions linked the true writer with mental, rather than physical, work.

These images of authorship were all secular, and, not surprisingly, the RTS had an alternative. The ideal Christian writer was closely related to the writer as learned professional, being someone who engaged in mental

---

16. For instance, [Lewes], "Condition of Authors," and [Kaye], "Pendennis," where the predominant, although not only, image for authorship is as a profession.

17. "The Authors of Calamities," *Chambers's Journal,* 27 February 1847, 129.

18. [Kaye], "Pendennis," 349.

19. [Lewes], "Condition of Authors," 290. On the eighteenth-century distinction between the true author and the Grub Street hack, see Brewer, *Pleasures of the Imagination,* 144–51.

20. [Kaye], "Pendennis," 335n.

21. [Lewes], "Condition of Authors," 285.

22. Ibid., 293.

rather than physical labour and had a sense of vocation. But for the Christian writer, that sense of vocation was strictly religious, and was so strong that it pushed financial issues even further into the background. Christian writers were routinely presented as writing specifically for Christ, rather than for general enlightenment, and certainly not for money.

Figure 5.2. "The new magazine machine." Hack writers produced such unoriginal work that they could be replaced by machines. From Cruikshank, *Comick Almanack,* ii, 120.

When the *North British* reviewer described writers leading their readers "to light from darkness, to truth from error," he was referring to enlightenment in both secular and sacred knowledge. Direct benefits to the writers themselves were dismissed as "mere worldly gains" of far less eternal importance.[23] The ideal Christian writer was thus like the minister in having a vocation for spreading the gospel, albeit through the medium of print rather than the pulpit or the personal visit. Writing was a "literary labour in the cause of Christian truth" or a "ministry of the press."[24] The son of Congregational minister and RTS writer John Kennedy expressed this sense of vocation in his account of his father's writing:

> Few, if any, of his books, as he clearly saw and said, are likely to be remembered long after he is forgotten; but they have served their purpose—they have been useful in their own day; they have strengthened many in weakness, enlightened many in darkness, comforted many in grief. With this he was content, as well he might be.[25]

Biographies and obituaries frequently emphasised the Christian vocation of their subjects. The *Visitor* editor Esther Copley was "early in life ... brought to a knowledge of Christ as the only and all-sufficient Saviour; and was constrained by love to him, to devote her talents to his service."[26] As a woman, she was unable to consider being ordained, so she played her part through her role as a minister's wife and through her writing.[27] Her contemporary, George Mogridge, better known to RTS readers as "Old Humphrey," was brought to his literary career "under the evident leadings of Divine Providence." He gave up an apprenticeship in business for a life of Christian writing, "for which the qualities of his heart and peculiar talents so eminently qualified him."[28]

For evangelical lay people, serving Christ through their lives was a serious issue. It could be done by giving money to the big evangelical organisations, by joining the committee of a local society for domestic mission work, by teaching in a Sunday school, or by visiting the poor and the sick.[29] Evangelicals were

---

23. [Kaye], "Pendennis," 371.

24. "The late Mrs. Esther Copley," *Christian Spectator* (Nov. 1851): 667; Davidoff and Hall, *Family Fortunes*, 67 (re children's writer Jane Taylor).

25. Kennedy, *Old Highland Days*, 246.

26. "The late Mrs. Esther Copley," *Christian Spectator* (Nov. 1851): 667.

27. Her first husband was an Anglican curate, her second a Baptist minister.

28. "The last hours of Old Humphrey," *Christian Spectator* (Nov. 1854): 82.

29. Bebbington, *Evangelicalism in Modern Britain*, 120–123; Donald M. Lewis, *Lighten Their Darkness*, esp. chaps. 2 and 7.

urged to work hard to serve Christ, and in the context of such activism the labour involved in writing might be recognised. One of the few references to the work involved in Christian authorship was made by the Reverend Thomas Binney, when he told the Young Man's Christian Association in 1854 that the writer must "work and toil—toil and work."[30] Nevertheless, the emphasis on devotion to faith and to serving others meant that this was a rare reference, as were comments on the financial dimension of Christian writing. Married women could devote significant proportions of their time to Christian works without worrying about remuneration, but activism in the name of Christ usually had to be combined with another occupation that earned money to support the Christian and his family during their earthly lives. Ministers, missionaries, and writers were among the very few who could combine Christian works with earning potential.

The dual function of Christian writing made it widely attractive to all sorts of people, only a small proportion of whom were solely dependent on it, but all of whom had a committed faith and the ability to express themselves well in writing. Starving curates could write for money while remaining true to their vocation and increasing their reputations as men of godly learning. Wealthy men could salve their consciences and fill their hours by writing for the cause. Although those arguing for turning authorship into a profession were dismissive of these part-time practitioners, for publishers such as the RTS they were invaluable. Looking back thirty years later, historian of the book trade Henry Curwen argued that no sooner were writers for cheap books in demand than "men thoroughly competent and thoroughly earnest, came forward to supply the want." These writers were "acted upon invisibly, insensibly, and inevitably, by the true, if word-worn, laws of supply and demand."[31] This may well be true for some areas of the trade, such as fiction, but the RTS was in the vanguard of Christian nonfiction. There were a few professional Christian writers, such as William Martin, Thomas Dick, and Thomas Milner, but there was barely enough demand for them to make their livings. Without clergymen, physicians, and women working part-time, the RTS would have had trouble recruiting enough writers to put its new publishing programme into action.

Personal faith alone did not make a successful Christian writer. Such a person had to be able to write well and develop a suitably Christian tone—one that was effective but not off-putting. The RTS committee had been used to

---

30. Binney, "Authorship," 14–15.
31. Curwen, *History of Booksellers,* 235.

working with a relatively small number of writers, who became known quantities and could be trusted to produce suitable work. The "Monthly Series" and *Leisure Hour* required more writers, with expertise on more subjects, and consequently involved assessing the standard of new writers. The committee was well aware that there were many possible writers who were not up to its standard, but this was graphically illustrated when a prize-essay competition in 1850, on the state of the working classes, received 176 submissions.[32] Of these, just forty were deemed worth reading in detail, and only ten were actually considered for the prizes.[33] No doubt a prize-essay competition attracted an even wider range of potential writers than the Society would normally have dealt with, but the episode nevertheless illustrates how demanding the Society was. Unusually, the judges' comments for that competition survive. Many of their concerns would have been common to any publisher. They wanted works that had been "put together in a comprehensive and orderly manner," with each topic in "its proper place, and . . . fully and satisfactorily discussed, nothing material . . . being omitted." The examples and facts introduced should be "beautiful and striking," yet "backed with sound reasoning."[34] Of course, the RTS additionally required that arguments should be made "on the sound basis of Christian principles," and that the works were entirely "free from anything that could be deemed objectionable by any class of the Society's friends."[35]

What publishers required of writers was not limited to the style of their prose, and numerous writers' manuals offered advice on even more mundane practical details. They particularly urged the importance of clear handwriting on good clean paper.[36] This was essential for those trying to catch the eye of an editor or publisher, since an illegible manuscript was hardly an attractive proposition for publication. If writers could not themselves write in a clear hand, they were urged to have their manuscript copied out before sending it to the publisher or editor.[37] This was even more necessary "whenever a manuscript [was] roughly written, and full of emendations or alterations, erasures and interlineations," or, in other words, whenever a work

---

32. RTS Report (1851): 90.
33. USCL/RTS ECM, 14 January 1851, 4 March 1851, and 13 May 1851.
34. USCL/RTS ECM, 11 March 1851.
35. Ibid.
36. For an analysis of such manuals, see Dooley, *Author and Printer,* chap. 1.
37. Ibid.; "Hints to our Contributors," *Leisure Hour* 3 (1854): 316–18, at 317; Saunders & Otley, *Advice to Authors,* 5.

was significantly revised.[38] Thus, even though another of the RTS writers, the Reverend William Stowell, was said to produce "beautifully-penned manuscript," each draft would be "blurred, blotted, interlined, supplemented, and patched, till it was absolutely necessary to have it written again." The copying was done by his eldest daughter.[39] Recycling paper was another habit to be avoided, as manuscripts written on old scraps of paper looked particularly unappealing. William Alexander cannot have done himself any favours if he wrote his works for publication as he did his sermons. In addition to displaying a "somewhat loose and careless penmanship," he wrote on paper "of all sizes, from a broad quarto page to one not larger than an ordinary envelope, and of all kinds—the back of a circular or blank page of a letter, or any scrap of paper that came readily to hand."[40]

Illegible manuscripts could carry financial risks for the writer beyond the obvious one of outright rejection. If the compositors could not read the manuscript easily, there were likely to be more mistakes in the typesetting, and the cost of corrections in proof might be charged to the writer. As one advice manual pointed out, "It would have been better economy in him to have laid out a little money upon decent writing-paper, instead of using dirty parings and savings."[41] For the Christian writer, these general injunctions regarding the personal benefits of legibility were turned into a specific duty to the compositor. An article in the *Leisure Hour* urged potential contributors to remember that the compositor was paid by piece work, and thus needed to be able to work rapidly. "He has, therefore, a *right* to legible copy, and those who set before him a scrawl of puzzling hieroglyphics, whatever they may intend, do virtually pick his pocket by diminishing his wages."[42] And those writers who tried to save money by using "torn and angular fragments of letters and notes, of covers of periodicals, grey, drab or green, written in thick round hand over the small print" were just as guilty of starving the compositor as those with poor handwriting.[43] The ideal Christian writer, therefore, was someone who was writing as a vocation, to be useful to society and to Christ. This was someone who had a strong personal faith, combined with a clear, plain writing style. The ideal Christian writer could not be a hack, and was perceived as far removed from the mercenary world of physical literary toil. Nevertheless,

38. Saunders & Otley, *Advice to Authors*, 5.
39. Stowell, *Life of William Hendry Stowell*, 214.
40. Ross, *W. Lindsay Alexander*, 290.
41. Saunders & Otley, *Advice to Authors*, 8–9.
42. "Hints to our contributors," *Leisure Hour* 4 (1854): 317.
43. Ibid., 317.

writing was a physical activity, and Christian writers were expected to carry out that part of their vocation with care and consideration for others.

It is no surprise that, in real life, money and labour played a far more prominent role than they did in an ideal world, as the lives of the RTS writers reveal. During publication of the "Monthly Series," the names of only seven of the writers were announced. Fortunately, the remaining names can be unearthed in the Society's archives. The articles of the very first number of the *Leisure Hour* carried the initials of their contributors, many of whom were also writers of Monthly Volumes, but from number two onwards, the *Leisure Hour* ceased to carry initials, making it virtually impossible to identify the writers. Among the forty writers whom we can identify, there are many ministers and some women, but no "aspiring noodles." Almost all were part-time writers. The bare prosopographical details can be found in table 5.1, and for some

Table 5.1. Prosopography of the RTS writers

Gender	
Male	35
Female	5
Average age*	
Female	52 years
Male	47 years
Ministers	44 years
Laymen	49 years
Marital status (women)	
Married	1
Unmarried	4
Occupational status (men)	
Physician	2
Banker	1
Writer**	5
Science lecturer	2
Of independent means	4
Minister/clergymen	23
Anglican	7
Baptist	5
Congregationalist	10
Unknown	1

* Average age includes only those known. For the women, the ages of two of the younger unmarried women are unknown, which skews the average significantly.

**Two of the full-time writers were also ordained, which is why there are 37 men listed under occupations, but only 35 actual people.

of the writers, this represents the sum total of known information. A few, mostly ministers, were made the subject of memoirs after their deaths; others, mostly professional writers, wrote letters of appeal to the Royal Literary Fund seeking help during illness or old age. The unevenness of the available information is such that some of the writers inevitably are more prominent than others in the following discussion, but all the writers are mentioned in the appendix A.

The RTS writers were mostly male, and mostly ministers.[44] The link with the ordained is even found among the women, who include two minister's daughters and one minister's wife. Among the entire group of writers, there were approximately equal numbers of Baptists, Congregationalists, and Anglicans (for those whose affiliations are known), so that Nonconformists outnumbered Church members by two to one. Among the subgroup of ordained writers, nonconformity again outnumbered Church membership by two to one, but in this case there were relatively fewer Baptists and more Congregationalists. Both of these proportions contrast with the rule for the executive committee, as the public face of the Society, that it comprise Church members and Nonconformists in equal numbers, but it is consistent with findings from the British and Foreign Bible Society that Nonconformists were more active behind the scenes.[45] The lack of Methodist writers, despite their participation in the RTS membership as a whole, may be due to the strong encouragement Methodist ministers received to publish under the auspices of the Wesleyan Bookroom.[46] We might expect that the ministers who took up writing would be those who were least well paid, in which case that the average age of forty-four years would disguise a mixture of young curates and retirees.[47] This is indeed the case with the Anglican and Baptist ministers. The Congregationalists, on the other hand, were mostly in their forties, established in their careers and hardly planning their retirements.

The composition of the group of writers, including the dominance of forty-something-year-old Congregational ministers, is a reflection of the manner in which the committee found its writers—or the manner in which writers

---

44. Despite the large printed output of nineteenth-century ministers and clergy, there has as yet been no detailed study of this group as writers.

45. Howsam, *Cheap Bibles*, 28.

46. My thanks to Jon Topham for discussing this with me.

47. More details of this analysis can be found in Fyfe, "Industrialised Conversion," 177–78, esp. fig. 4.2.

chose to join the RTS. In the early 1840s, the Society already had a stable of writers, but as most of its publications were devotional or conversional, most of its writers specialised in that sort of writing. The *Visitor* was no exception, because most of its mixture of scriptural history, biography, and the natural sciences was actually excerpted and reprinted matter. When William Lloyd began to recruit writers for the "Monthly Series" in August 1844, he started with a list of sixteen writers. Some of these were already RTS regulars, including Anne Pratt, William Martin, and John Kitto, all of whom wrote for the *Visitor*. Others, such as James Montgomery, John Harris, and Thomas Dick, do not appear to have had any previous RTS connection, but were well-known evangelical writers whose works and names were familiar to the Society and its audiences.[48] A further group were ministers, such as John Stoughton and William Stowell, who do not appear to have written for the RTS before, but were probably known to the committee members from their mutual involvement in pan-evangelical organisations. Once the Series was underway, writers who had already contributed to it were encouraged to write again; unsolicited offers were weeded out with help from character references and writing samples; and more friends and acquaintances were invited to write.

Personal connections were the most important factor in becoming an RTS writer. Apart from the few well-known evangelical writers, Lloyd wrote to people he knew, or people who had been suggested by other members of the committee. Even when unsolicited offers began to come in, those that came from someone known to the RTS committee or staff were clearly preferable to those submitted by complete unknowns. The personal connection might be with someone on the committee, a staff member, or someone who was already an RTS writer. There are several examples of family connections. Two of the women writers, Emily Stokes and Thalia Henderson, were the daughters of RTS committee members, while one of the young Anglican clergymen, William H. Jones, was the son of the general secretary. Selina Bunbury came from a family of Anglican evangelicals, and once she was established as an RTS writer, she encouraged her clergymen brother and cousin to write (occasionally) for the Society. The *Visitor* editor Esther Copley appears to have encouraged her young neighbour, George Etell Sargent, to

---

48. First batch of writers listed at USCL/RTS CCM, 13 November 1844.

write for the Society, which, after an initial rejection, he was to do for many years.[49]

Evangelicalism itself provided the other major networks of connections that brought writers to the RTS. These networks were especially strong in London, as so many of the denominational unions and interdenominational societies were run from London and needed committee members. Provincial evangelicals could tap into these networks, perhaps through introductions from friends, but especially if they came to London for the annual May meetings. Evangelicals who were active in their local denominational union or Bible Society auxiliary might also come into contact with the London-based evangelicals, and thence be invited to write for the RTS. The connections between Congregational ministers and laymen provide an excellent example of these networks. John Stoughton was a Congregational minister in Kensington, London, and was firm friends with one of his congregation, Thomas Coombs, who happened to be an RTS committee member.[50] Stoughton had met John Kennedy, an Aberdeen minister, through the Congregational Union.[51] When Kennedy moved to Stepney, London in the mid-1840s, he renewed the acquaintance. Stoughton and Kennedy were both active in the Bible Society, the London Missionary Society (LMS), and the Evangelical Alliance, and they were members of *Sub Rosa*, a monthly lunch-meeting for select London ministers.[52] George Smith, the Congregational minister of Poplar, London, was a friend and neighbour of Kennedy's, and was also on the LMS committee.[53] Yet another of Kennedy's friends was the Baptist minister Joseph Angus, who taught at the nearby Stepney College. Angus was the brother-in-law of another RTS committee member, Joseph Gurney.[54] Kennedy would presumably also have known John Cox, the Anglican curate at Stepney, who had been writing for the RTS for two years before Kennedy's arrival in London. Stoughton, Kennedy, Smith, Angus, and Cox all wrote for the "Monthly Series," and Stoughton, Kennedy, and Angus continued to write for the Society for the rest of their (long) lives.

---

49. Printed sources give Sargent's middle name as either "Etell" or "Eliel." Copley and Sargent lived in Eythorne, Kent. Copley's interest in Sargent is indicated by RTS Corr., Jones to Copley, 12 December 1846.
50. Stoughton, *Recollections*, 81.
51. Kennedy, *Old Highland Days*, 152.
52. See ibid.; Georgina K. Lewis, *John Stoughton.*
53. "George Smith," *Congregational Year Book* (1870): 346–49.
54. Kennedy, *Old Highland Days*, 249.

Despite the half-and-half rule for executive committee membership, copyright committee members appear to have been mostly Nonconformists,probably in midcareer. Since personal networks tended to form between people of roughly the same age and background, this helps to explain the predominance of Congregationalists in their forties among the writers. These were the sorts of people the copyright committee knew. The role of personal links also explains why, although the initial list of writers who were asked to contribute to the "Monthly Series" was roughly half Church and half Nonconformist, those writers who were asked at a later stage were predominantly Nonconformist. Not every RTS writer, of course, had personal connections. Of the Baptist ministers, the oldest, Angus, was related to a copyright subcommittee member, but two others were completely unknown to the RTS. Samuel Manning made the first contact when he wrote to offer a Monthly Volume, while Henry Dunckley entered a prize-essay competition. Not only were these two ministers a decade or more younger than the Stoughton-Kennedy group, they were not based in London. It was the name and reputation of the RTS that prompted them to submit works, and for Manning, at least, the RTS was his entry into national evangelical circles, rather than vice versa.

After the ministers, the other distinct subgroup of the Society's writers was those trying to make a living from full-time writing. Of these, Charles Williams, as salaried RTS editor, was removed from the vicissitudes of freelance writing. The others were Selina Bunbury, Thomas Dick, John Kitto, William Martin, and Thomas Milner. All five had strong evangelical sentiments, although the necessity of writing as much as possible meant that they could not afford to write only for the RTS. Dick was one of the well-known writers asked to contribute to the "Monthly Series," but we do not know how the others made first contact with the RTS. Martin had certainly been writing for the Society since the early 1830s. One of the curious things about this group is that it includes the only two writers who could not be described as being from the professional middle classes. Most of the writers, like the committee members, came from a background of the learned professions, or, occasionally, commerce. William Martin, however, was the son of an illustrator and was apprenticed to an apothecary. Deaf John Kitto had been trained as a shoemaker's apprentice in the workhouse and later became a printer with the Church Missionary Society. This pair did not have the resources to be part-time writers, and becoming a professional writer offered them the possibility of a rise in social status (fig. 5.3). Martin was certainly able to earn more as a writer than he had done as a museum assistant, even though there

Figure 5.3. John Kitto, D.D., FSA had come a long way from the Plymouth Workhouse. Frontispiece of Ryland, *Memoirs of John Kitto.*

were additional costs involved in living as one of the middle classes. He conceded to the Royal Literary Fund, "Hard indeed for some time has been the struggle to maintain that respectability of appearance which my position requires."[55] For many other professional writers, in contrast, becoming a writer was a last-ditch attempt to retain a middle-class status that was dangerously close to slipping away. Both Bunbury and Milner turned to writing when left without other sources of income. From their point of view, writing was barely enough to sustain a middle-class lifestyle, but at least it was still a genteel way of earning a living.

Ambitions and Rewards

There can be little doubt that a sense of spiritual vocation explains why writers chose to write particularly for the RTS, but for most of them it was only a minor part of their decision to write in the first place. When discussing their work, writers did acknowledge the spiritual aspect. Bunbury regarded her novels and travel stories "as helps to the cause of morals and religion," and

---

55. RLF 1315.2, Martin to RLF, 8 April 1853. His wife also noted the need, and the effort involved, "to keep our position," 1315.28, M. J. Martin to RLF, May 1860.

Martin aimed to engender "a healthy love of nature & of Nature's God, in the minds of "general readers."[56] Kitto's works dealt with the geography and history of biblical lands, and he described them as aiding "the diffusion of scriptural knowledge," adding that he felt this to be his "proper vocation."[57] Despite making a living from their literary work, these writers would all have agreed with Stoughton that "To lead men and women to Christ, is one of the highest honours God can bestow upon His children."[58] Sales figures could be seen in this light. The majority of popular writers generally sold their copyrights outright and had no financial interest in the sales, but greater sales meant the possibility of bringing more people to a knowledge of Christ. When Kitto discussed with an Edinburgh publisher whether to produce "*popular* (as distinguished from *scholastic*) books," he decided that popular would permit him "an extended measure of *usefulness.*"[59] Equally, when Bunbury welcomed the news that one of her works had sold a hundred thousand copies, she did so as good news for evangelicalism rather than her personal finances.[60]

Another intangible benefit from writing was a degree of personal fame. The anonymity of many popular works, including the "Monthly Series" volumes, did not necessarily prevent them contributing to their writer's reputation. Deep anonymity, such as that surrounding the *Vestiges of the Natural History of Creation* (1844) for almost forty years, was exceptionally rare.[61] The names of anonymous writers were usually known within the trade, and if the book gained any literary success the secret would be widely known within a few months. The *Pictorial Bible* had appeared anonymously in 1838, but Kitto's identity as editor was soon known to interested parties, particularly biblical scholars and other publishers of theological works.[62] Furthermore, anonymity was not necessarily a bar to building a reputation. Bunbury had begun writing anonymously in the 1820s when "an authoress was a curiosity," but her later books were identified as being by the "author of *A Visit to my Birthplace* etc." It was thus possible for her to build a reputation pseudonymously, and it was only once that reputation was secure that she began to put her name on her works.[63]

56. RLF 1089.18, Bunbury to RLF, 23 October 1848; RLF 1315.11, Martin to RLF, 16 April 1853.
57. Ryland, *Memoirs of John Kitto*, 603.
58. Georgina K. Lewis, *John Stoughton*, 217.
59. Ryland, *Memoirs of John Kitto*, 603.
60. RLF 1089.18, Bunbury to RLF, 23 October 1848.
61. James A. Secord, *Victorian Sensation*, chap. 11. See also Griffin, *Faces of Anonymity.*
62. Eadie, *Life of John Kitto*, 297–300.
63. RLF 1089.86, Bunbury to RLF, 1 July 1878.

Although intangible, a reputation could help to bring worldly rewards. For professional writers, it improved their chances of getting new commissions and being paid more for future works. Thus, Bunbury's *Rides in the Pyrenees* (1844) yielded her "more fame than pecuniary remuneration," but by doing so it had "done me service, having been so well received by the public press."[64] Similarly, Kitto counted his fame as a reason for optimism about the future, writing in 1845 that "my resources for such occupation [literature] are unexhausted, my publishing connections good, and my standing with the public much higher now than it has been at any former period of my career."[65] This was true for ministers as well, for a certain kind of reputation as a writer might help with a ministerial career. Promotion within the Nonconformist and Church ministries largely depended on becoming known to the people with control of wealthier parishes, whether that was the congregation itself or the patron with the gift of the living. Writing for publication, preferably in a scholarly manner on theological topics, could draw attention to a young minister, which was the first step toward preferment. William Stowell's son attributed his father's appointment as president of Rotherham theological college to the success of his first book, *The Ten Commandments Illustrated and Enforced on Christian Principles* (1824), which gained him "wide and lasting esteem among his brethren in various sections of the church."[66]

Reputation was about all that ordained writers could expect from most of their publications, for tracts, pamphlets, and even volumes of sermons were rarely snatched up by publishers unless the writer was particularly well known. Most of these publications were issued at "author's risk," which meant that the writer paid for production and took all the profits (if any) except for a commission to the publisher. This method of publication indicated that the publisher had little expectation of the work's making a profit, and he was frequently right.[67] Friends and members of the congregation often encouraged a minister to publish his sermons, presenting it as a duty to society that such an excellent sermon should not be restricted to the small group of its original listeners. More rarely, such friends recognised that ministers were not wealthy enough to sustain losses from publishing. Stoughton's first three publications,

---

64. RLF 1089.11, Bunbury to RLF, 5 March 1845. This is even although Bunbury herself was disappointed with the way in which the work was rushed through the press. See Bunbury, *My First Travels*, i–ii.

65. RLF 1115.2, Kitto to RLF, 27 October 1845.

66. Stowell, *Life of William Hendry Stowell*, 122.

67. On methods of publication, see "Authors and Publishers," *New Quarterly Review* 3 (1854): 9–17, 143–50.

for instance, were all based on sermons and lectures and were published at the insistence of others. In one of those cases, however, the encouraging friend indemnified him against the potential loss resulting from publication.[68]

Popular works, such as the Monthly Volumes and their equivalents, were at least more likely to make money, since they were by definition expected to reach a wide audience. However, the routine omission of these works from the published memoirs of ordained writers, including Stoughton, Stowell, and Kennedy, suggests that they did less for reputation than tracts and sermons. Ministers sought reputations not merely as writers but as theological scholars. A successful Monthly Volume might commend its writer to a publisher seeking a "popular" volume, but it was not equal commendation to the learned. A popular volume on volcanoes, for instance, added little to the reputation that Kennedy gradually built up in apologetics.

Non-ordained writers were equally aware of the low regard in which popular volumes were held in learned circles, even in those cases where the subject lay within the writer's area of expertise. Martin had been a curator at the Museum of the Zoological Society and had contributed to the Society's *Transactions*. After losing his job in 1839, he felt relegated to the fringes of natural history circles. His former associates included Richard Owen, the comparative anatomist, John Gould, the ornithologist, and George Waterhouse, later the British Museum keeper of minerals and fossils. All of these men held paid positions in the London natural history museums, and their expertise was recognised by Charles Darwin when he sought their help to classify specimens from his *Beagle* voyage.[69] They all wrote references for Martin to the Royal Literary Fund extolling his services to natural history.[70] Gould, for instance, explained that Martin's works were "duly estimated by Professor Owen, Dr. Gray, and indeed everyone in the same walk of science who may be considered competent judges of their merit."[71] Owen, himself an RLF committee member, wrote that Martin "has been most industriously and honorably occupied in diffusing sound scientific information, in Zoology."[72] Those solid adjectives were mirrored by Martin himself, when he referred to his works as "not brilliant," but having a "plain utility."[73]

---

68. Georgina K. Lewis, *John Stoughton*, 48–50.
69. Desmond and Moore, *Darwin*, for example, 203–9, 225, 309–12.
70. Cross, *Common Writer*, 58, discusses the men of science who were involved in the RLF.
71. RLF 1315.23, Gould to RLF, 2 February 1859.
72. RLF 1315.4, Owen to RLF, 11 April 1853.
73. RLF 1315.11, Martin to RLF, 16 April 1853.

Martin's publications were certainly seen as having merit, but it was solely as popular works, not as original contributions to natural history, such as the papers he had published in the *Transactions* and *Proceedings* of the Zoological Society in the 1830s. Martin admitted the introductory status of his works when he described his aim as being "to teach the principles of zoology *popularly* yet on a *truthful basis*, and, avoiding the 'clap-trap' style, to impart some degree of information relative to the laws of organic structure and the thence-deduced rules on which the system of Zoology as a science is founded."[74] But this sort of usefulness was not really what Martin desired. A decade after leaving the Zoological Museum, he was still hoping to find another museum-based job, or some other position where his "scientific knowledge would render my services advantageous."[75] Scientific jobs continued to elude him, and it was small comfort to discover "that my labours were not unappreciated, even by the learned."[76] A reputation as a popular writer could help pay the rent, but it was not equivalent to the reputation Martin had hoped to gain as a man of science.

The importance of money as a reason for writing was most obvious in the case of the writers who supported themselves by their literary work. It was, however, extremely helpful for ministers as well, who might find it difficult to live on the income from their profession at any stage of their careers. John Kaye, bishop of Lincoln in the 1830s and 1840s, believed that £200 a year was the absolute minimum for a clergyman to discharge his parish duties respectably, although historian Frances Knight suggests that £500 would have been a more realistic figure.[77] This estimate would presumably have held true for Nonconformist ministers as well, even though their careers followed a different structure.[78] Anglicans started out as curates, who were notoriously poorly paid, earning only £50 to £100 a year.[79] They might spend a decade waiting for vacant living to become available. The value of livings varied enormously, without any apparent relation to their location, size, or the seniority of the incumbent, but they certainly paid better than a curate's stipend. Just over half of all Church of England livings were valued below £300 a year, but 4 percent were worth over £1,000.[80] Of the RTS

---

74. Ibid.
75. Ibid.
76. Ibid. See also 1315.14, Martin to RLF, 1 June 1854, and thereafter.
77. Kaye cited in Frances Knight, *Nineteenth-Century Church*, 132.
78. Kenneth Brown, *Nonconformist Ministry*.
79. Curate incomes are analysed in Frances Knight, *Nineteenth-Century Church*, 127–29.
80. Ibid., 131–32.

Anglicans, Cox, Jones, and Sidney had all just gained their first livings when they began writing for the "Monthly Series." Cox had a small London parish worth £269 a year, whereas Sidney received £509 for his Suffolk parish, even though both men had the cure of fewer than seven hundred souls.[81] Jones seems to have been the most unfortunate for, although he received £400 a year, his busy London parish contained over ten thousand souls.[82] Within a few years, he managed to move to a smaller, better-paying living in Wiltshire.[83]

Moving to a living of one's own gave clergy a certain financial security, but the end result was not usually more spare cash. This was the time in a clergyman's life that he was likely to get married and start a family, both of which involved considerable expense. Furthermore, as public figures in their parishes, clergymen had additional drains on their income.[84] Their standing made it essential for their families to appear well-dressed and their homes tidy and respectable, and they were expected to respond willingly to appeals for charity, and perhaps even pay for the local school.[85] Nonconformist ministers faced a similar problem, and Kennedy was reported to give to all but the most "improbable stories" contained in the begging letters and personal applicants for relief. He commented that "no income conceivable to a dissenting minister would enable him to keep his family in luxury, not to speak of saving money."[86] Clergymen appeared to have the benefit of free accommodation, for church livings usually came with houses; but, by the mid-nineteenth century, decades of neglect had left many such properties in very poor condition, and it was the incumbent who was responsible for the expensive repairs.[87] Knight suggests that assistant clerks in the civil service, who earned similar annual salaries of around £350 to £600, were actually better off than their clerical equivalents, as they did not have these extra expenses.[88] It was unlikely that a clergyman

---

81. The value of livings is given in Crockford's Clergy Lists. Cox became vicar of St. Helen's Bishopsgate in 1849. Sidney became rector of Little Cornard, Suffolk, in 1847.

82. Jones became incumbent of St. James Curtain Road, Shoreditch, between 1845 and 1850.

83. As vicar of Bradford with Westwood, he received £590. The Bradford population was 3,259, and that of Westwood was 356. Crockford Clergy List (1852).

84. Urwick gave "at least *one-tenth* of his income to religious and philanthropic objects," through "subscriptions to religious societies and charitable institutions" (Urwick, *Life of William Urwick*, 370).

85. Frances Knight, *Nineteenth-Century Church*, 132.

86. Kennedy, *Old Highland Days*, 180.

87. Frances Knight, *Nineteenth-Century Church*, 136–38.

88. Ibid., 134.

would be able to save a significant amount toward his retirement or rainy days.

In most of the Nonconformist churches, a ministerial stipend depended on congregational numbers and wealth, not endowments.[89] As there were no curates or bishops, the range of stipends was smaller than that for clergymen, so although there were fewer very poor ministers, there were also fewer rich ones. Young ministers usually started with smaller congregations, often in poorer communities, and hoped to draw attention to themselves through writing, supply preaching, and public preaching. They might then be invited to a more wealthy congregation, and might be able to marry. Kennedy's first stipend of £80, and Alexander's (in Edinburgh) of £130, suggest that Congregational ministers were marginally better off at the beginning of their careers than their Church counterparts.[90] Again, it was often ten years before ministers were called to other congregations. Alexander, Kennedy, and Stoughton (who was initially at Windsor) were all offered churches in London as a consequence of their fame as preachers, and William Urwick was able to move from rural Sligo to Dublin for similar reasons.[91] Alexander's decision to decline the call to the Stepney meeting house enabled Kennedy to become its minister a few years later.[92] Kennedy had survived in Aberdeen because he had to support only his sister and a family servant. In Stepney, he had a wife, seven children, and a servant. Including his literary earnings, he now had an income of between £400 and £600 a year, but it was barely sufficient.[93]

The printed figures for stipends disguise another problem of ministerial life—the irregularity of their incomes. Kennedy's son commented, "Perhaps the worst of it is that the prosperous Church, loving him as it does, has a very unbusiness-like way of crystallising its affection. Not only is his ministerial stipend uncertain in amount, but it arrives at irregular intervals, and often in mere driblets."[94] Nonconformist ministers were paid when their congregation could afford it, which meant that Kennedy occasionally found himself having "to borrow from a friend when heavy school and college bills come in."[95]

---

89. Kenneth Brown, *Nonconformist Ministry*, 155–57.

90. Kennedy, *Old Highland Days*, 114–5; Ross, *W. Lindsay Alexander*, 63. Kenneth Brown (*Nonconformist Ministry*, at 156) suggests Congregationalists were better paid than other Nonconformists.

91. Urwick, *Life of William Urwick*, 73.

92. Ross, *W. Lindsay Alexander*, 124; Kennedy, *Old Highland Days*, 166–67.

93. Kennedy, *Old Highland Days*, 180, 146.

94. Ibid., 180–81. See also Georgina K. Lewis, *John Stoughton*, 213–14.

95. Kennedy, *Old Highland Days*, 180.

Since most livings derived their income from land rents, which were due at five- or seven-year intervals, clergymen had a similar problem.

Old age was yet another problem. Anglicans could keep their livings until they died, but this usually necessitated the expense of employing a curate once they became too feeble to work. Nonconformist ministers did not have this option, and many worked well into their seventies. They all, however, benefited from a large circle of well-wishers who might assist a frail, elderly, or impoverished minister.[96] Several of the Congregational ministers were able to retire thanks to the generosity of their congregations. Urwick and Stoughton were surely unusual, but they received purses containing £2,000 and £3,000 respectively amid the speeches at celebrations for their twenty-five years in the ministry.[97] Once invested, £2,000 would provide an annual income of around £150 for the years of retirement.

The meagre and unreliable income of ministers and clergy, combined with the particular demands on their purses, meant that the financial remuneration available from writing could be very useful at all stages of their careers, not just in the early years. But writing was always an optional extra for ministers: if they had time and opportunity, then the income was welcome, but if they did not, they would not starve, though they would have to budget very carefully. Full-time writers, on the other hand, were writing for subsistence. They usually had no other options left. Like ministers, they had to learn to live on small and irregular incomes, and found it very difficult to save for old age. They had fewer demands from charity cases, but they also lacked the support of a wide circle of well-wishers and thus found it much more difficult to get out of financial trouble.

In the early 1830s, before he had decided to make the ministry his profession, William Alexander had considered a literary career. He wrote to Adam Black, the Edinburgh publisher, mentioning that "a friend" was considering settling in Edinburgh to write for the periodicals, and he got the following discouraging reply:

> He must be a very young man indeed, and unacquainted with the difficulties in his way. Besides, I do not know any one who writes for the periodicals but who has something else to trust to, except Dr B., who is very clever, but who after all is starving. Any young man who thinks of such a thing would require

---

96. Frances Knight, *Nineteenth-Century Church*, 130.

97. Kennedy, *Old Highland Days*, 260–61; Urwick, *Life of William Urwick*, 340; Georgina K. Lewis, *John Stoughton*, 147. On more typical payments, see Kenneth Brown, *Nonconformist Ministry*, 195.

to bring with him a good purse, as he would get very little for any of his papers until he acquired a name, and even then he could not live by it. Advise your friend to think of something else.[98]

Black's response made clear both the value of a "name," or reputation, as a writer, and the need for an alternative source of income even once established. His reference to the starving "Dr B." may well be to David Brewster, and reminds us that despite eventually being knighted for his scientific work, Brewster struggled to make a living by editing and writing for the first three decades of his career.[99]

By the 1840s, the growth of the periodical press created salaried positions for literary men. A salaried writer would have less freedom to work on his own projects, but his day job protected him from the vagaries of the publishing trade and made it possible to live entirely by the pen. An editorial assistant at the RTS or Chambers earned at least £150 a year, rising to around £350 for the more senior positions.[100] As well as editorial assistants, newspapers employed salaried journalists, though they were paid less. Very occasionally, success might allow a writer to give up the day job to concentrate on his own creative writing. Dickens, for instance, gave up his post as political journalist on the *Morning Chronicle,* yet Trollope continued to work for the post office long after his novels became successful.[101] He eventually gave it up only when he was sure he had amassed enough savings to care for his family even if writing ceased to be remunerative. Very few of those who wrote for the RTS were in this sort of position. Thomas Milner had had a certain success as a writer, but his hand was forced by the ill health that prevented him continuing as a Congregational minister at the early age of forty.[102] Thomas Dick, however, did make the planned decision to retire from school-teaching and write full-time. He had prudently waited until he had two successful books, and some savings.[103] The majority of full-time writers, including the others who wrote for the RTS, had acquired their profession from necessity.

---

98. Black to Alexander, *ca.*1831, quoted in Ross, *W. Lindsay Alexander,* 42–43.

99. Brock, "Brewster as Scientific Journalist."

100. For RTS editor's salary, USCL/RTS FCM, 18 December 1850. On salaries at W. & R. Chambers, see Cooney, "Publishers for the People," 67–70.

101. Bonham-Carter, *Authors by Profession,* 69–70; Cross, *Common Writer,* chap. 3; Glendinning, *Trollope.*

102. RLF 1385.2, Milner to RLF, n.d. [1855].

103. RLF 1241.1, Dick's application form, 11 January 1850. See also Astore, "Observing God," 38–42.

Writing was an especially likely option for single women on the death of their father, brother, or other male relative. Teaching, governessing, and writing were virtually the only genteel options available to middle-class women who needed to earn money. Although women are estimated to have accounted for nearly 20 percent of writers, they almost all wrote novels, children's books, or poetry, for which an advanced education was less necessary.[104] This is apparent from the RTS records, where women were frequently the authors of children's tracts and books, but more rarely of works for adults. Natural history was a common topic for children's works, and botany in particular was often written by women.[105] Two of the three botany volumes in the "Monthly Series" (*Wild Flowers of the Year,* and *Garden Flowers of the Year*) were written by Anne Pratt, who also wrote botany for the SPCK. She had begun to write while still living with her parents, but after her father's death in the mid-1840s, she made her living from school-teaching and writing on botany. The RTS did also have a rarer example of a woman who wrote on natural philosophy. Eliza W. Payne never wrote for the "Monthly Series," but she produced a set of children's tracts, and later books, on physics and chemistry.[106]

Most of the female "Monthly Series" writers wrote on historical topics, which were more likely to have been part of their education. Copley, for instance, wrote a *Life of Lady Russell* (vol. 19, 1847), while Selina Bunbury wrote on the *History of Protestantism in France* (vols. 29 and 38, 1848–49). Bunbury had begun to write when she was seventeen (*ca.*1820), because her clergyman father lost his "large estates in Ireland" after "a ruinous Chancery suit, of about forty years' duration."[107] Although Bunbury had apparently not shown "any previous inclination or talent for writing," it became her way of helping the family finances. She continued to write "anonymously, and successfully, in periodicals and otherwise," for the next twenty years.[108] Although her sisters married, Bunbury seems to have remained at home, and would have expected to be supported after her father's death in the mid-1840s by her brother Robert, an evangelical clergyman. Robert Bunbury had just received his first living at Swansea (£291), and their first cousin Walter Shirley had just become the Bishop of Sodor and Man. Unfortunately for Selina Bunbury, as she explained to the Royal Literary Fund in 1848, "In a brief space of time, my

---

104. Cross, *Common Writer,* 167.
105. Shteir, *Cultivating Women.*
106. Her first book, based on the tracts, was [Payne], *Peeps at Nature.*
107. RLF 1089.12, printed appeal for Bunbury.
108. RLF 1089.1, application form, 4 January 1844.

Father, Mother, brother and cousin have gone to the grave."[109] The money she inherited from her mother was "insecurely vested" and lost.[110] Writing now became Bunbury's main source of income, rather than the additional aid it had previously been. She managed to support herself and several extended family members for the remaining thirty-five years of her life.

Women were not alone in being forced to write for a living. Kitto's deafness precluded most jobs, but when he returned from an expedition to Persia at the age of twenty-nine (1833), he was employed on a salary of £192 a year as an editorial assistant to Charles Knight, to help with the publications of the Society for the Diffusion of Useful Knowledge.[111] By the time he lost that job, during Knight's financial troubles in 1841–42, Kitto had plenty of experience and contacts in the publishing world. He decided to become a full-time writer, drawing on his personal knowledge of the Holy Land. He struggled to support his family in this way for the next twelve years. Martin, as we have seen, had begun his writing career in natural history while working in the Museum of the Zoological Society, where he had been appointed in 1830. After cutbacks at the museum in the late 1830s, he lost his job, but managed to get a commission from the publisher Whitehead to produce a *Natural History of Quadrupeds,* which came with an annual salary.[112] Unfortunately, as Martin's referee explained to the RLF, "One volume of the work was scarcely completed when the firm became insolvent and Mr. Martin was again left without resources."[113] This was why Martin was forced into freelance natural history writing for his remaining twenty-five years.

These writers all managed to survive on their literary income for substantial lengths of time. Yet their dissatisfaction with writing as a sole source of income was apparent from their frequent hopes of finding an additional regular income, however small. Such a resource would relieve much of the stress of being a writer by providing, as Kitto put it, something "on which I may be able to fall back in time of need; and which may be to me as a staff to rest on in my sufficiently perilous career."[114] Martin occasionally benefited from some financial help from a relative, but it was no replacement for the "official situation, humble though the salary might be," which he sought

---

109. RLF 1089.18, Bunbury to RLF, 23 October 1848.

110. RLF 1089.12, printed appeal for Bunbury.

111. Ryland, *Memoirs of John Kitto,* 530–38, 580.

112. RLF 1315.3, Martin to RLF, 11 April 1853 and 1315.7, Waterhouse to RLF, 13 April 1853.

113. RLF 1315.7, Waterhouse to RLF, 13 April 1853.

114. RLF 1115.6, Kitto to RLF, 13 December 184[9?].

among the London museums of natural history.[115] One of Kitto's ideas was to be appointed warden to the new cemetery being established at Woking, where he had moved in the late 1840s because the rents were cheaper than in Islington.[116] Bunbury wanted to hire a house in Cheltenham where she would act as a companion to elderly ladies, but she was unable to find the money to rent the house.[117] Nor were Kitto or Martin any more successful.

There was no doubt in the minds of these minister-writers and professional writers that literary work could produce worthwhile financial benefits. For the part-time writer, the actual amount was perhaps not that important—the £30 or £35 received for a Monthly Volume was simply a welcome addition to one's income, however much it happened to be. For the professional writers, the issue was much more urgent, although it still varied with the circumstances of individual writers. Bunbury, for instance, felt that 1848 had been a good year, for she earned £150 from her two Monthly Volumes, several SPCK works, and various contributions to periodicals.[118] At this point in time, Bunbury was supporting just herself and a sister. Kitto, on the other hand, had a wife and six children in 1845. He thought that £660 a year would be "fair," but that £330 was "a miserable pittance."[119] His estimate would not have been thought unreasonable, for the *North British Review* suggested in 1850 that a writer with a wife and six children might need to earn £600 a year.[120] The incomes that the spinster Bunbury and the family man Kitto hoped to achieve are similar to those of the ministers, indicating the similarity of their social positions.

Actually achieving those target incomes was a far from easy task for writers, even though George Henry Lewes argued in *Fraser's Magazine* that British writers were much better off than those in France or Germany, since even those who were only in the "ordinary current" were able to make "incomes *averaging* 300*l.* a-year, some less, of course, some more."[121] Lewes estimated the range of realistic incomes for a writer at £200 to £1,000 a year, and J. W. Kaye in the *North British Review* concurred with this, claiming that "many men . . . in London, Edinburgh, and other parts of the country" earn from £300 to £1,000 a year, and that "some, with very little effort,

---

115. RFL 1315.11, Martin to RLF, 16 April 1853.

116. Ryland, *Memoirs of John Kitto*, 685.

117. RLF 1089.22, Bunbury to RLF, 4 February 1851.

118. RLF 1089.18, Bunbury to RLF, 23 October 1848.

119. This relates to the *Cyclopaedia of Biblical Literature* (1845), see Eadie, *Life of John Kitto*, 335; RLF 1115.2, Kitto to RLF, 27 October 1845.

120. [Kaye], "Pendennis," 360.

121. [Lewes], "Condition of Authors," 286.

earn . . . considerably more."[122] In reality, what any writer outside the select group of famous novelists could earn was enormously variable, and there were plenty of writers at the lower end of the scale. Nevertheless, published estimates like these encouraged potential writers by countering what *Chambers's Journal* called the "general sense of the wretched nature of a purely literary life."[123]

How much the writer would earn and how quickly the money would be forthcoming depended on the particular arrangement made between publisher and writer. "Author's risk" publishing was one possibility, but although some ministers might be willing to accept reputation rather than money as a reward, most writers needed the money. And the quickest way to get it was to sell the copyright to the publisher. This turned writers into mere producers of words, who had no further interest in their manuscripts once they had been paid. The publisher was then free to print it in any format he wished, as many times as he wished, with any revisions he wished. While writers who aspired to a literary reputation might be uncomfortable with giving the publisher such power, others could be more practical. As one of Chambers's writers conceded, "In writing for you, as I said before, one works for money, & not for fame; and if you purchase my wares, I think you have a right to do what you please with them."[124] The potential disadvantage for writers was that the sum they received bore no relation to the later success of the work. If it failed, the writer did not suffer; but if it was an enormous success, he did not gain. Thus, Thomas Dick explained to the Royal Literary Fund that he was slipping into poverty even though his best-known work, *The Christian Philosopher* (1823), had reached its twelfth edition, and his RTS *Solar System* had sold over eighty thousand copies.[125] Dick had sold his copyrights, and thus, he wrote, "I derive no pecuniary benefit whatsoever from the sale of my works however extensive it may be."[126] Occasionally, publishers made discretionary payments to writers whose works had sold particularly well, and some of Dick's American publishers did so, but such generosity was rare.[127]

In retrospect, Dick would have preferred to have had a shared-profits agreement, where the publisher paid for the production and distribution, and

---

122. [Kaye], "Pendennis," 348.

123. "The Authors of Calamities," *Chambers's Journal*, 27 February 1847, 129.

124. Catherine Crowe, quoted in Cooney, "Publishers for the People," 62, n2.

125. Given available evidence for sales figures from the RTS, the eighty thousand copies was probably around forty thousand for each of parts I and II.

126. RLF 1241.2, Dick to RLF, [1850].

127. Astore, "Observing God," 240.

shared the profits (or losses) with the writer. Under such an agreement, a writer would get a share of one-third or one-half in the success of his work. The obvious disadvantage with this arrangement was that the money would be slow to come in, in contrast to the immediate payment under purchase of copyright. Thus, writing in 1845 of her *Rides in the Pyrenees*, which was published "on the plan of division of profits," Bunbury said that it had yet to yield her much "pecuniary remuneration" even though it had been well received.[128] Although shared profits was the most common arrangement, the slowness of payment is probably why it was not regularly used by writers who were at the subsistence margin.[129] A further disadvantage, as a sceptical *New Quarterly* reviewer pointed out in 1854, was that it relied on the honesty of the publisher, for it was he who controlled the accounts books. It would be too easy for a publisher to claim that there were no profits to be shared, as the Dublin publisher and RTS agent William Curry was accused by novelist Charles Lever of doing.[130] The most appropriate publishing arrangement involved balancing the writer's urgency for money with a realistic estimate of the likely success of the work. Writers with a track record of successful works might do well out of a shared-profits arrangement, but other writers would be grateful for the quick and certain income from purchase of copyright.

The payment for copyright depended on the length of the work, the publisher's usual rate per sheet (or per column), and the publisher's assessment of the quality of the work, which might lead him to adjust that rate. The literary quarterlies routinely paid more per sheet than most weekly or monthly periodicals, while Thackeray discovered after *Vanity Fair* (1847–48) that an improved reputation could double the rate a writer was offered.[131] Even at the RTS, the basic rate of £10 a sheet could be increased to twelve guineas for famous preachers or in recognition of particular effort, but it could also be reduced for RTS employees who wrote for publication in their spare time.[132] Although the RTS rate was on a par with other periodicals, it was applied equally to books. Chambers did the same thing, which is why the payments

---

128. RLF 1089.11, Bunbury to RLF, 5 March 1845.
129. On the popularity of shared profits, see "Authors and Publishers," *New Quarterly Review* 3 (1854): 12.
130. Ibid., 12–15. On Lever and Curry, see Sutherland, *Victorian Novelists and Publishers*, 90–93. On Curry's RTS connection, see RTS, FCM, 10 April 1844.
131. Bonham-Carter, *Authors by Profession*, 61.
132. USCL/RTS CCM, 20 January 1847. Twelve guineas a sheet were paid to the Revd. Hugh Stowell and Dr. Moore. See USCL/RTS CCM, 22 July 1840 and 17 October 1849. On rates for RTS staff and their relatives, see USCL/RTS CCM, 17 March 1847 and 1 January 1842.

for books of both these publishers were lower than those of, for instance, Murray or the SDUK.[133] The RTS and Chambers rarely paid over £120 even for their longest works.[134] They were both specialists in improving publications for the working classes, and the need for the published works to be as cheap as possible mitigated against higher payments for writers. Fortunately, the RTS was not competing with the big literary publishers to catch or keep successful writers, so its lower book payments did not drive its writers away.[135] The relatively low remuneration did mean, however, that it would be well-nigh impossible to make a living as a professional writer by writing for the RTS alone.

Fragile Equilibrium

For observers watching the success of Dickens or Thackeray, the potential rewards of literature might have appeared great, but for most writers, the financial gains were small and irregular. It was difficult to maintain a household, and virtually impossible to save for the future, so relatively small upsets could easily destroy the fragile financial equilibrium of a moderately successful writer. Writers generally came from the middling classes of society, and frequently felt they had to keep up at least the appearance of this status even when their income barely allowed it. One of the consequences of "keeping up appearances" was that, although Martin and his wife had been struggling from the early 1850s, it was not until his final illness at the end of the decade that his friends realised how badly off the couple actually were.[136] Only one referee had commented to the RLF, in 1854, that "I know he has long struggled to maintain his respectability."[137] This was Andrew Ramsay, who, being an editorial assistant himself (to Charles Knight), was perhaps more aware of the realities of a literary life than the natural history men could be.

Fraser's Magazine claimed that a writer had to be "very unlucky or very 'impracticable', if he do not earn an income which will support him and

---

133. For a discussion of the cost of volumes in the libraries of Murray and the SDUK, see Bennett, "Revolutions in Thought," 160–61. For Chambers, see Cooney, "Publishers for the People," 94–95.

134. Cooney, "Publishers for the People," 196–97.

135. Although, later in the century, at least one best-selling writer (Hesba Stretton) complained, see Rickards, " 'Living by the Pen.' "

136. RLF 1315.22, Owen to RLF, 20 January 1859; 1215.23, Gould to RLF, 2 February 1859.

137. RLF 1315.16, Ramsay to RLF, 21 June 1854.

his family."[138] But of course, like other people, writers occasionally made bad financial investments or acted as security for unreliable friends.[139] Sometimes, they just had sheer bad luck. In 1848, Bunbury was living with one of her sisters in Liverpool. The sister had just had to close her school, due to the economic depression. Fortunately, this was one of Bunbury's fairly successful years, and in August she went to the Bank of England to withdraw enough funds to see herself and her sister through the winter. She told the Royal Literary Fund that "on returning [I] was beset by four thieves and robbed in a moment of the entire. The notes were stopped at the Bank, but I have had many letters ["of credit"?] and from time to time they were presented in a total and paid."[140] She and her sister were forced to borrow money from a "kind lady" in order to live.[141]

Bad luck could not be avoided, but the *North British Review* additionally accused writers of being "desperately bad arithmeticians. They are not clever at £:s:d. We believe them to be as honest as their neighbours, but they are certainly more careless. . . . The same pen will rarely write articles and square accounts."[142] The reviewer believed this explained why literary men seemed to be so much worse off than other professionals with similar incomes.[143] Whether or not she could do arithmetic, Bunbury admitted, "I was not able to lay up any part of the sums I received." She believed it was because she was "obliged to write generally for the moment."[144] Kitto was no better at saving, as he was routinely living off publishers' advances, due to his "want of capital."[145] Writers had no way to predict their income accurately, so advance budgeting was difficult, and most seem to have barely survived from one payment to the next. This meant that if bad luck did befall them, they had few or no resources on which to draw. Kitto and Milner both sold parts of their libraries in attempts to raise money. This was a desperate measure for, as Kitto noted, "the books . . . are most essential to my future labours, which it has

---

138. [Lewes], "Condition of Authors," 288.

139. On the mis-investment of Bunbury's legacy from her mother, see RLF 1089.12, printed appeal on behalf of Bunbury. On Milner ill-advisedly standing as security, see RLF 1385.1, Milner's application form, 7 July 1855; 1385.2, Milner to RLF, [July 1855].

140. Partially illegible in MS. RLF 1089.18, Bunbury to RLF, 23 October 1848.

141. In a later recollection, Bunbury mentioned the loss of £400, although this seems a generous amount for the subsistence of two single women for a winter. See RLF 1089.92, Bunbury to RLF, 31 May 1881.

142. [Kaye], "Pendennis," at 360–61.

143. Ibid., 357.

144. RLF 1089.2, Bunbury to RLF, 4 January 1844.

145. RLF 1115.8, Kitto to RLF, 3 February 1849.

taken me many long years to get . . . together, and which once lost I may not hope to recover."[146] Dick sold his best telescope for similar reasons.[147] Shortly thereafter, in further desperation, he "let, on a rent, the principal part of the house that he has occupied and . . . retire[d] with his family to the Attics."[148]

After such last-ditch attempts had been made, Kitto explained, "I had no resource for the subsistence of my household but the contracting of some debts, the pressure of which now lies heavily upon me, and threatens to break up my domestic establishment."[149] Tradesmen would give credit, but not for ever, and not without limit. This was one reason Mary Jane Martin particularly welcomed her husband's RLF grants, for "ready money *in hand* giv[es] great advantage in every kind of purchase."[150] The absolutely last resort, because of the necessary publicity, was for friends of the writer to advertise his poverty and start a public subscription for his relief. Subscriptions for Dick and Kitto were announced in the final years of their lives, and were intended as much to provide future support for the bereaved dependants as for the writer himself. Kitto's subscription raised £1,800, which paid his debts and funeral expenses, and left enough to secure an income of around £60 a year for his family.[151]

Saving and bad luck were problems for all writers, as, indeed, for all those with low, irregular incomes. The challenges they posed were particularly severe if they happened at times of difficulty in the family, such as illnesses or deaths. Martin, for instance, supported his aged mother. Although her death did free him of that responsibility, the short-term need to pay medical and funeral bills strained his resources.[152] Deaths sometimes brought unexpected additional burdens. When one of Dick's married daughters and her husband both died, the care of their orphaned children fell to the grandparents. The savings Dick had put aside for his old age rapidly disappeared with five young children to care for, and this was why he ended up living in the attic.[153] Bunbury looked after a seemingly regular stream of dependent family members, including frail sisters and orphaned nephews and nieces . They were the cause of most of her applications to the RLF. Yet, since the grants she received

---

146. Ibid.

147. Astore, "Observing God," 51.

148. RLF 1241.15, Meffan to RLF, 14 July 1853.

149. RLF 1115.8, Kitto to RLF, 3 February 1849.

150. RLF 1315.47, M. J. Martin to RLF, 30 October 1853.

151. Eadie, *Life of John Kitto*, 372n. For Dick's subscription, see RLF 1241.10, Lowe to RLF, 27 March 1851.

152. RLF 1315.2, Martin to RLF, 8 April 1853.

153. RLF 1241.2, Dick to RLF, [1850].

amounted to only £375 over forty years, she was actually doing remarkably well in the long run. It was just at the points of sudden change in her family that her economy was overstretched.[154] Although minister-writers were in the same income bracket as these professional writers, they had slightly more financial security and would benefit from the support of their entire congregations in illness or old age. By the middle of the nineteenth century, denominational charitable funds were just beginning to be set up as an additional support for ministers.[155] Few of them, therefore, ended up appealing to the RLF, and they had more chance of weathering the problems of a literary life. They may have suffered from the occupational hazards of literature, such as publishers' bankruptcies and work-related illnesses, but they were affected less than the full-time writers.

Publisher's bankruptcy might seem as improbable as being beset by robbers, but it was not uncommon in the mid-nineteenth century. In 1841, Kitto recorded, "the only publishing house with which I had up to that time become connected [that is, Knight], fell into difficulties."[156] Martin suffered two publishers' bankruptcies in the early part of his career as a writer, that of Baldwin, Cradock & Joy in 1837–38, and then that of Whitehead & Co. in 1840. It happened to Milner an unfortunate three times: W. S. Orr in 1854, Freeman of Fleet Street in 1857–58, and W. & R. McPhun of Glasgow in the mid-1870s.[157]

Milner described the effects of Orr's bankruptcy in detail in his letter to the RLF in 1855:

> I then accepted a commission from Messrs. Orr to produce a "Natural History of the British Isles," as an introductory volume to a series of six, to be called the British Naturalist, in which McGillivray's Birds were to reappear. I spent eight months upon the work—never received a sixpence in advance upon it—contracted a heavy debt for books—went with the knowledge of Mr. Orr into the country to recruit my health and finish my task as to be ready for publication by 1855—and within ten days of my leaving London early in October, that house failed, and I was ruinously impoverished.[158]

---

154. RLF 1089.18, Bunbury to RLF, 23 October 1848; 1089.67, Bunbury to RLF, 3 July 1867; 1089.88, Jebb to RLF, [1878]; 1089.92, Bunbury to RLF, 31 May 1881.

155. Kenneth Brown, *Nonconformist Ministry*, 160–61, 196.

156. RLF 1115.2, Kitto to RLF, 27 October 1845.

157. RLF 1385.12, Quinton to RLF, 6 May 1858; 1385.22, Milner's application form, 5 February 1881.

158. RLF 1385.2, Milner to RLF, [July 1855]. Orr's bankruptcy is discussed in William Chambers, *Memoir of Robert Chamber*, chap. 13.

Milner had undertaken a substantial amount of research and writing for which he had not yet been paid, and suddenly had no expectation of being paid. He continued:

> The consequence to me has been, that instead of receiving as I expected about £250 for the volume, with the commencement of this year, I have not had a farthing, and must wait three years for what the winding up of the business will bring.—I have the expenses to meet—and I have endeavoured to meet them by depriving myself of the bread that perisheth.[159]

Not only was Milner left unpaid for his work, but he had debts to pay for the purchase of specialist books for his research, and he was starving himself to meet them. Although there were legal procedures for the payment of creditors after a bankruptcy, as Milner was aware, they were extremely slow and unlikely to yield full payment. The stress and the additional work Milner took on in an attempt to make up his losses soon took their toll. By late 1855, he was no longer able to work due to nervous stress and paralysis of his arm.[160]

Publishers' bankruptcies had clear financial implications for writers, and Milner's case shows that they could injure health, but they also had more general effects on publisher–writer relations. A spate of bankruptcies, as in 1847–48 or again in 1853–54, affected perceptions of the state of the trade, even though available data suggests that it continued to grow throughout both "crises."[161] Publishers became more careful about taking on new projects, something that writers often bemoaned when unable to place their works. In the winter of 1848–49, both Kitto and Bunbury found it difficult to get manuscripts accepted, and commented on "all the adverse circumstances of this year," and that it was "a time of such depression in the book trade."[162] Again, in 1853, Martin found the state of the trade such that "for months and months, I have received no order of any great importance from any publisher."[163] Bankruptcies also deprived writers of their trade connections just as much as deaths.

Illness was the other major cause of financial trouble reported by the RTS writers, due to the associated expenses and the lost opportunities for writing.

---

159. RLF 1385.2, Milner to RLF, [July 1855].
160. USCL/RTS CCM, 19 December 1855; RLF 1385.2, Milner to RLF, [July 1855].
161. Eliot, *Patterns and Trends in British Publishing*.
162. RLF 1089.18, Bunbury to RLF, 23 October 1848; RLF 1115.8, Kitto to RLF, 3 February 1849.
163. RLF 1315.3, Martin to RLF, 11 April 1853.

Figure 5.4. Writers often found ways to write in difficult conditions. In this case, it is imprisonment for debt, rather than illness, but Captain Shandon nevertheless continues to work on the *Pall Mall Gazette,* as his publisher (and family) looks on. From Thackeray, *Pendennis,* i, opp. 320.

Even when they were not personally ill, a writer's work might be severely restricted by the presence of illness, particularly for women writers, who were often expected to attend in the sickroom. If writers became ill themselves, they frequently found ways to keep working, as long as they remained clear-headed and conscious (fig. 5.4). Bunbury corrected proofs while bedridden, and if a suitable assistant could be found, dictation might be an option.[164] Martin's wife did take dictation, but Milner's wife was herself an invalid and unable to help.[165] He employed an amanuensis, but found the cost "very crippling."[166] Work of any sort was impossible if a writer suffered a serious

---

164. RLF 1089.22, Bunbury to RLF, 4 February 1851.
165. RLF 1315.28, M. J. Martin to RLF, May 1860.
166. RLF 1385.1, Milner's application form, 7 July 1855; 1385.2, Milner to RLF, [July 1855].

illness, as Milner did in his seventies when, as he would write, "a seizure of an apoplectic kind threw me headlong from the top of the stairs to the bottom, with the usual result of perfect insensibility and complete helplessness on my part."[167]

Apoplexy was (probably) not an occupational hazard for writers, but nervous illnesses and eye strain were certainly linked to overlong hours of reading and writing. Milner, Martin, and Bunbury all had problems with their hands and wrists, as a consequence of the repetitive effort involved in continual writing. In 1844, Bunbury reported that her continued writing had "brought on an affection of the nerve of the right arm, which renders its use at all times rather difficult, and sometimes deprives me of that use for a couple of months at a time."[168] She used her left hand to write some of her shorter works, but by 1853, she had to report "the loss, I fear permanently, of the use of the right arm. I trust to acquire more facility in writing with the left." Her doctor reported that "the nerve of the arm [was] injured by the constant action of writing, [and] the pain is at times most acute."[169] Since she was still complaining of an injured right arm a decade later, one suspects that she kept trying to use it, and thus aggravated the injury so that, unlike Milner, she did not recover fully. Bunbury was able to write quite legibly with her left hand, but she complained, "I cannot accomplish the amount of work I have hitherto done."[170]

The *North British Review* noted, "Rest and recreation, fresh air and bodily exercise, are essential to an author, and he will do well never to neglect them."[171] Admirable sentiments, no doubt, but long hours indoors at the desk were necessary to make a living (fig. 5.5). The *North British* reckoned that it was this unhealthy lifestyle that made writers prematurely old, adding, "At an age when other men are in the possession of vigorous faculties of mind and strength of body, they are often used-up, enfeebled, and only capable of effort under the influence of strong stimulants."[172] When he was an editorial assistant, Kitto walked from his house in Islington to Knight's offices near St. Paul's, and back, each day. But by the mid-1840s, he was working at home all day.[173] After several years of this, he began to suffer from severe headaches

---

167. RLF 1385.23, Milner to RLF, 4 February 1881. He only partially recovered.
168. RLF 1089.2, Bunbury to RLF, 4 January 1844.
169. RLF 1089.27, Bunbury to RLF, 1 November 1853.
170. Ibid.
171. [Kaye], "Pendennis," 359.
172. Ibid.
173. Ryland, *Memoirs of John Kitto*, 536, 552–53.

Figure 5.5. Arthur Pendennis, writing at his desk. From Thackeray, *Pendennis,* i, opp. 314.

and "neuralgic affection," as well as being very overweight. His doctor ordered two hours, or six miles, of walking as his daily exercise. Kitto commented to a friend, "Think of that for a man who has almost lost the power of putting one leg before another!"[174] While Kitto was merely obese, Martin suffered from "complicated disorders" in his late fifties, which included, as well as "heart disease" and asthma, "gouty affection of the *whole system,* the *head* and *stomach* alternately with the limbs."[175] He was often unable to hold a pen, since his hands "discharge[d] portions of chalk attended with ulceration."[176] The chalky discharges were another symptom of gout. Although gout was usually associated with a patrician lifestyle, a significant causal factor was lack of exercise.

Few writers could afford to stop working to recuperate, so when Milner wanted to convalesce on the North Yorkshire coast, he sought an RLF grant.[177] In the absence of grants or saving, writers felt forced to work through their illness, or to start work before they were fully recovered. This often led to a relapse, as one of Kitto's referees explained: "Nine months ago he informed me that his physician had ordered him to abstain altogether from

174. Ibid., 624.
175. RLF 1315.28, M. J. Martin to RLF, May 1860.
176. RLF 1315.42, M. J. Martin to RLF, 18 November 1862. Milner also had medical problems arising from his lifestyle. See RLF 1385.3, Aspray to RLF, 9 July 1855.
177. RLF 1385.24, Milner to RLF, [*ca.*Sept. 1880].

literary work, for some time. But he could *not* and did not: and the result is, that he is now prostrated."[178] His wife, Annabella, explained that this pattern had repeated itself several times over the previous three years. Kitto would struggle to complete a work, and just manage it before being "overtaken by utter prostration thus leaving his family without the means of support, until, by the blessing of God, health be re-established." Annabella informed the RLF in 1854 that if Kitto recovered from his current illness, she planned "to get him from home," to prevent him working.[179]

A long illness was expensive and exhausting, and might leave the survivors unable to fend for themselves. Letters from Mary Jane Martin and her referees detailed the final stages of William Martin's illness and its effect on her. In 1860, when Martin was "completely prostrated by illness" and "in the greatest agony," Mary Jane wrote to the RLF:

> Unless some kind and generous hand can be found to aid us, [we] *must end in utter destitution*, since a guinea or two now and then, as health permits, with the help afforded by the Royal Literary Fund, and my own *earnest* but weak and *most inadequate* struggles *as a woman* to keep our position and supply the sufferer's wants, alone interferes, to prevent [this].[180]

Martin's condition did not improve, and by 1863 Mary Jane had admitted to giving up "a hope (long clung to) of more than solace and alleviation."[181] When he died the following year, leaving her "destitute of present supplies and future support," Mary Jane was worn out by almost three years of constant sickroom attendance.[182] Her referee wrote to the RLF that "Mrs Martin herself professes considerable literary abilities but, from her increasing years and diminished health consequent upon her husband's long illness it is not to be expected that for the present at least these can be in any way available to her."[183] The Martins had received £120 in grants during his illness, and Mary Jane Martin was allowed a further £50 on his death, £15 of which was to defray funeral expenses and the rest to help support her. In 1867, her

---

178. RLF 1115.16, Horne to RLF, 4 March 1854.
179. RLF 1115.15, A. Kitto to RLF, 6 March 1854. They went to the spa town of Cannstadt, where he died six months later of a "neuralgic affection." RLF 1115.19, press cuttings from *The Times*.
180. RLF 1315.28, M. J. Martin to RLF, May 1860.
181. RLF 1315.47, M. J. Martin to RLF, 30 October 1863.
182. RLF 1315.54, M. J. Martin to RLF, [March 1864].
183. RLF 1315.55, Gould to RLF, 27 February 1864.

friends tried to get her a civil list pension, but the outcome of that attempt is unrecorded.[184]

William Martin was sixty-six years old when he died, which was almost exactly the average age at death for writers reported by William Guy to the Statistical Society in 1859.[185] This was at a time when the average lifeexpectancy among the British population as a whole was around thirty-seven years.[186] Nonetheless, Guy's figures showed that writers were shorter-lived than other professionals, especially ministers, by three or four years.[187] He attributed the reduced life expectancy to their sedentary lifestyle, and he also noted that married (male) writers lived for five or six years longer than their unmarried counterparts, thus bearing out the importance of female assistance.[188] In fact, apart from Kitto and Martin, most of the RTS professional writers lived rather longer than Guy would have predicted. Milner died at seventy-five, Bunbury at seventy-nine, and Dick at eighty-three years. Guy was probably right about ministers, though, for Kennedy, Stoughton, and Angus all passed eighty-six years.[189]

The long lives of some of these writers and minister-writers emphasise how important it was to provide for old age. All three of the long-living ministers were able to retire in their last years through the generosity of their congregations and their grown-up families. But Milner, Bunbury, and Dick were all writing till the very ends of their lives, under the increasing infirmities of old age. Bunbury discovered that it was not just failing eye sight and a paralysed right arm that hindered an elderly writer from earning a living, for the tastes of the publishers and the reading public had changed over the course of her writing career.[190] She had specialised all her life in high-toned novels and travel books; but by the 1860s, sensation novels were in demand. Bunbury could not and would not write such works. Her reputation as a novelist had dwindled away, and many of her earlier publishers had died. She

---

184. RLF 1315.59, Murray to Blewitt, 27 November 1867.
185. Guy, "On the Duration of Life," 343. This figure was based on the members of Guy's sample who were born in the eighteenth and nineteenth centuries. Almost half of his sample were from earlier centuries.
186. Daunton, *Progress and Poverty*, 575, table 1.c.
187. Guy, "On the Duration of Life," 359–60.
188. Ibid.
189. Angus died at age eighty-six, Kennedy at eighty-seven, and Stoughton at ninety.
190. Sutherland (*Victorian Novelists and Publishers*, 153–59) suggests that the longest literary career of the nineteenth century was that of Harrison Ainsworth, who was an active writer for sixty years. Bunbury's career lasted sixty-three years.

was still writing in the early 1880s, but felt uncertain of making her way with new publishers amid "the multitude of present writers."[191]

The image of the Christian writer that was promoted by the Religious Tract Society, and even by some of the writers themselves, was that of a special writer, committed to their task of spreading the Christian message through printed matter, and dedicated to this by a sense of vocation rather than a need for money. Yet even among the minister-writers, money played an important role. So too did the reality of physical effort, which produced strained eyes, paralysed wrists, and nervous breakdowns. From the point of the view of the publishers, writers could often be considered as just one more cog in the machinery of book production, tightly linked to editors, printers, and distributors through the work they were paid to carry out. The rhetoric of the ideal Christian writer was supposed to accentuate the difference between writers and the other cogs, yet this difference was not as great as it seemed, once the role of writing in the lives of the writers has been uncovered. Nevertheless, despite sometimes feeling like dependent parts of a great machine, writers did have a significant amount of control over their lives when things were going well in their careers. Some, at least, were extremely capable of choosing their projects and publishers to suit their current needs and interests.

---

191. 1089.92, Bunbury to RLF, 31 May 1881.

VI

Reinterpreting Science

THE REVEREND Edwin Sidney was a Norfolk clergyman and domestic chaplain to Viscount Hill. The author of several works on agricultural science, Sidney also lectured annually at the Royal Institution in the 1840s, corresponded with the Cambridge botany professor John Stevens Henslow, and assisted Michael Faraday with his ozone measurements.[1] In July 1845, the Religious Tract Society (RTS) asked him to write a volume on "corn plants and their destroyers" for the "Monthly Series," and this duly appeared as the twelfth volume, *The Blights of the Wheat, and their Remedies* (1846). The Society acknowledged Sidney's scientific credentials by allowing his name to appear on the preface of the book and in the advertisements for it. Over the next few years, Sidney proposed a further four volumes for the series, on "The Fungi infecting Houses," "The Philosophy of Food and Nutrition," "Agriculture," and "Idiots."[2] The first and last of these were rejected outright. The other two were indeed published by the Society, but only the one on agriculture was judged suitable for the "Monthly Series," the other being issued as an independent volume. Both of these works were unusual for undergoing significant authorial revisions before publication. The editorial team found Sidney's works unsuitable "for general readers" and urged him to "explain everything as clearly as possible."[3] Even after several revisions of the agriculture work, the editor explained to the committee that "from its scientific and somewhat technical character he felt some difficulty as to the propriety

---

1. [Sidney], *Blights of the Wheat,* iii. For information regarding Sidney's Royal Institution involvement, my thanks to Frank James. On the ozone measurements, see James, *Correspondence of Michael Faraday,* iv, letter 2534.

2. USCL/RTS CCM, 17 July 1847, 15 September 1847, 17 April 1850, and 19 January 1853. Sidney was involved with the administration of lunatic asylums and gave several lectures on the subject.

3. USCL/RTS CCM, 18 April 1849 and 20 June 1849.

of introducing it into the series."[4] Sidney, it seems, had trouble adapting his literary style to the presumed needs of the Society's intended audience.

The RTS committee usually exercised its power of editorial control by outright rejection, but Sidney was particularly pro-active in volunteering to make revisions. This involved a large commitment of his time, as each writing or rewriting took a year or so to complete. Sidney must also have had contacts within the RTS, as he was able to have his response to an unfavourable reader's report presented to the committee at the same meeting as the report itself, thus avoiding rejection.[5] The *Philosophy of Food and Nutrition in Plants and Animals* (1849) was completely revised once, to reduce the number of engravings needed and render the work more comprehensible to the general reader. Sidney volunteered to supervise the work through the publication process himself, and several times wrote to reassure the committee about his commitment to making the work clearer. Even so, the work was still deemed unsuitable for the "Monthly Series." It described the workings of the digestive systems of animals, and the acquisition of nutrients by plants. This included much discussion of internal anatomical structures and far more technical language than was usually found in the Monthly Volumes. Readers were expected to come to terms with descriptions of the "medullary sheath" and "exogenic stems," the processes of "exosmosis" and "endosmosis," and the fixation of ammonia.[6] Sidney also insisted on a large number of wood engravings, such as that in figure 6.1, which were intended to elucidate his text, but equally made it more inaccessible. The volume sold at 2*s*.6*d*., rather than 6*d*.

Perhaps because of this failure to reach the audience he sought, Sidney was even more determined the next time round. He completely revised his original manuscript on agriculture, and when the committee was still only willing to accept it for publication on the same terms as the *Philosophy of Food and Nutrition*, Sidney declared himself willing to revise it yet again to make it suitable for the "Monthly Series." Despite the editor's continuing uncertainty about the final result, the committee sanctioned its appearance in the Series as *The Field and the Fold* (vol. 98, 1854).

The problems that Sidney encountered through his need to use technical language and illustrations might have been expected to apply to many of the writers on the sciences. Yet they did not. Judging by the titles of his proposed

---

4. USCL/RTS CCM, 21 September 1853.
5. USCL/RTS CCM, 19 February 1851.
6. Sidney, *Philosophy of Food*, all in chap. 2.

tally from the bark to the heart-wood, and to generate adventitious leaf-buds. The wood lies upon the

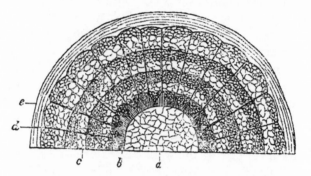

HORIZONTAL SECTION OF THE STEM OF AN EXOGEN.

VERTICAL SECTION OF THE STEM OF AN EXOGEN.

medullary sheath, and it consists of concentric rings,
formed outside the first, and over each other; and
therefore this stem is called *exogenous*, or stem from
without. Each separate layer is generally the result of one year's growth; and so the age of an
exogenous plant is usually, in latitudes sufficiently
northern, determined by their number; but, of course,
in latitudes where the period of rest is not distinctly marked, as in hot climates, the rule cannot

Figure 6.1. Sidney's work was filled with detailed diagrams, often showing structures only visible
through a microscope, such as this cross-section of a plant stem. From Sidney, *Philosophy of Food and
Nutrition*, 19.

volumes, Sidney intended to adapt and expand his discourses to the Royal Institution into Monthly Volumes, despite the great differences in audience for the two.[7] It was also Sidney's first experience of writing on the sciences for a popular audience, as his previously published works had been sermons and biographies. Thus, although there is no doubting his commitment to expressing himself in popular language, we can well imagine that he was more used to writing about the sciences in the technical language that he used at the Royal Institution, and found the transition more difficult than he expected.

Most of the other writers who published on the sciences in the "Monthly Series" had more experience writing for a popular audience, and few of them had claims to personal scientific expertise. Thomas Milner, for instance, had a definite commitment to writing on astronomy and the geological and geographical sciences (although he also wrote also on history), and was a fellow of the Royal Geographical Society.[8] Yet he was not in the habit of addressing expert audiences, and he already had experience of writing at a popular level. John Kennedy wrote on volcanoes, but he was not, nor made any pretence to be, an expert geologist or vulcanologist. He wrote about volcanoes in the same way as he wrote about the river Jordan: without ever having seen either of them. Of the other writers who wrote volumes on the sciences, William Higgins was a science lecturer, and Thomas Dick, William Martin, and Anne Pratt had extensive experience as writers. Of these, Martin had the greatest claims to scientific expertise, thanks to his eight years at the Zoological Society's museum, but he also had almost as many years' experience as a full-time popular science writer.

As Sidney's problem illustrates, the same scientific facts could be presented in different ways for different audiences, and an effective writer was one who chose the appropriate presentation. Those who made successful livings from writing on the sciences, as Martin and Milner both did, were well aware of the need to adapt to the requirements of different publishers and projects. This could involve decisions on suitable vocabulary, but it might also mean using a different argument, organising the material differently, or choosing

---

7. Sidney delivered Friday evening discourses that were intended for men of science rather than for the general public. See reports in *Athenaeum*, 25 May 1844, 481 ("On the diseases of wheat"); 24 May 1845, 518 ("On the electricity of plants"); 29 May 1847, 576 ("On the parasitic fungi of inhabited houses"); and 10 June 1848, 583 ("On the motion of the sap in flowering plants").

8. He was elected in 1849, proposed by George O'Gorman and Thomas Lee, Certificate of Election, Royal Geographical Society.

which moral (if any) to draw. It was crucial for writers to get these issues right for each publisher, since failure to do so would probably mean rejection. It was all very well for Sidney, with his £500-a-year parish, to spend three years writing and revising a single Monthly Volume, but for any writer more desperate for money, missing the publisher's requirements so badly was not an option.

Martin and Milner wrote for a range of publishers in addition to the RTS, and one of the most striking ways in which they had to adapt their writing styles was the extent of the Christian sentiments they expressed in their works. Just as the RTS was known to be an evangelical publisher, W. & R. Chambers and the SDUK were known to favour works written in a secular style, and no writer with any sense would try to place exactly the same work with the different publishers. Of course, many writers who wrote for the RTS were sufficiently evangelically committed that they would not have considered writing for a secular publisher in the first place. None of the ordained RTS writers wrote for either Chambers or Knight, although they were willing to write for John Cassell, the temperance campaigner-turned-publisher, and, if Anglican, for the Society for Promoting Christian Knowledge. The professional writers may have shared the deep commitment to faith, but they had a greater need to find publishers for their works and could not be quite so selective. Bunbury wrote for Chambers, while Martin and Kitto both wrote for Knight.[9]

The whole point of the RTS's involvement in secular publishing was to demonstrate that subjects like history or the sciences could and should be presented alongside Christianity, as part of the same worldview. The RTS feared that the same basic discoveries that its writers strung together in a Christian framework could equally well be strung together by others who ignored, or even attacked, religion. The variation in Christian tone between the writers of the "Monthly Series" was a small-scale illustration of the potential variety in the presentation of the sciences. Between them, Thomas Milner and William Martin wrote sixteen of the Monthly Volumes, including many of the ones on the sciences, and they also authored almost forty books for other publishers. Considering the range of works they wrote, for which publishers, and at which stages of their lives sheds light on the way in which writers managed their literary careers. It also shows how versatile they were

---

9. RLF 1089.21, Bunbury's application form, 4 February 1851; 1089.72, Bunbury's application form, 24 October 1871.

in re-using and adapting the same material to different ends, reinterpreting the sciences for different contexts.

FOREVER THE MINISTER

Thomas Milner (1808–*ca*.83) was born in Derby, and studied for the Congregational ministry at Glasgow. He may have returned to Derby for a short time, but by his late twenties, he had the charge of a congregation in Northampton. He married, and his daughter was born when Milner was twenty-six years old. Two sons followed over the next ten years. By this time, Milner had begun to suffer ill health, and at the age of forty he was forced to give up his ministry. He already had several publications to his credit, and decided to support his young family by becoming a full-time writer. Around this time, he moved to London, first to Norwood and latterly to Brixton, perhaps to be nearer to his publishers and to libraries for research. Despite some difficult times in the mid-1850s, Milner did manage to bring up his family successfully. His daughter became a teacher until her marriage; one son entered a merchant's office; the other emigrated to New Zealand.[10] It seems plausible that the sons helped support their father in his old age, since he wrote relatively little after the children left home and his wife died.

As might be expected of someone who chose the ministerial vocation at the age of sixteen, Milner was utterly committed to using his writings as part of his ministry. Most of the writing a minister did was in some way related to his profession, as he wrote sermons, lectures, and addresses for his congregation and the public, and perhaps lecture courses for theological students.[11] His published works were frequently derived from some of these writings, such as volumes of sermons, tracts on contemporary problems, reviews of recent theological works, printed versions of lectures, or textbooks based on college teaching.[12] Milner's early publications were typical products of a young minister (see exhibit 6.1). His first work was on the history of the church, followed by a biography of an eminent divine, a volume of sermons, and a work of devotion, all of which were perfectly in keeping with his sacred vocation. Finding a publisher for such works, let alone getting paid for them, was

---

10. RLF 1385.16, Milner to RLF, 25 June 1868; 1385.22, Milner to RLF, 5 February 1881.

11. Urwick, Stowell, and Angus were heads of theological colleges in the 1840s, and Kennedy and Stoughton were professors at New College, London in the 1870s.

12. By midcentury, most of the Nonconformist denominations had established training colleges for their ministries. See Kenneth Brown, *Nonconformist Ministry*, chap. 2.

Exhibit 6.1. Thomas Milner's publications

This list does not include subsequent editions or revisions and is based on Milner's letters to the RLF and library catalogues.

History of the Seven Churches of Asia (Derby, 1830)

Life, Times and Correspondence of Isaac Watts (London: Simpkin, 1834)

Sermons on Special Occasions (Northampton, 1837)

Sanctuary and Oratory, or illustration and records of devotional duty (London: Ball, 1837)

A letter to the Rev W Wales, in reply to that gentleman's sermon, entitled "The repair of the temple the duty of the people" (Northampton: Cordeux & Sons, 1838)

Astronomy and Scripture; or, some illustrations of that science, and of the solar, lunar and terrestrial phenomena of Holy Writ (London: John Snow, 1843)

The Elevation of the People, moral, instructional, and social (London: John Snow, 1846)

The Gallery of Nature; a pictorial and descriptive tour through creation, illustrative of the wonders of astronomy, physical geography, and geology (London: W. S. Orr, 1846)

Life of Cyrus (London: RTS, 1847)

The Caves of the Earth; their natural history, features and incidents (London: RTS, 1847)

The History of Rome; from the earliest times to the fall of the empire. For schools and families (London: RTS, 1848)

Descriptive Atlas of Astronomy and Physical and Political Geography [with August Petermann] (London: W. S. Orr, 1849)

Lives of Eminent Anglo-Saxons I (London: RTS, 1850)

Lives of Eminent Anglo-Saxons II (London: RTS, 1850)

Universal Geography (London: RTS, 1850)

Babylon and the Banks of the Euphrates (London: RTS, 1851)

Nineveh and the Tigris (London: RTS, 1851)

Mines and Mining (London: RTS, 1851)

Australia: its scenery, natural history and resources (London: RTS, 1853)

Life of Alexander the Great (London: RTS, 1853)

Australia: its settlements (London: RTS, 1853)

History of England to 1852 (London: RTS, 1853)

The Baltic, its gates, shores and cities, with a notice of the White Sea (London: Longman, 1854)

The Crimea, its ancient and modern history: the Khans, the Sultans and the Czars (London: Longman, 1855)

"Natural History of the British Isles" (London: W. S. Orr, 1855, but unpublished due to bankruptcy)

Russia: its rise and progress, tragedies and revolutions (London: Longman, 1856)

The Ottoman Empire: the sultans, the territory and the people (London: RTS, 1857)

Library of Biblical Literature (London: Freeman, 1856–57, 3 volumes, but only 2 volumes published due to bankruptcy)

Our Home Islands: their natural features (London: RTS, 1857)

Our Home Islands: their productive industry (London: RTS, 1858)

The Heavens and the Earth: familiar illustrations of astronomy (London: RTS, 1859)

Our Home Islands: their public works (London: RTS, 1860)

The Gallery of Geography (London: Chambers, 1864)

Half Hour Readings for Sunday Afternoons (London: RTS, 1874)

The British Islands: their physical geography and natural history (London: RTS, 1874)

far from straightforward. Denominational networks might help, particularly in getting articles accepted by periodicals. Another possibility was to work with the local printer, since the minister's reputation in his own town might command a circulation for his sermons or his thoughts on a pamphlet war, even though those views would be of little interest outside the area. Several of Milner's early works were thus published in Derby and Northampton, and he did not get a major London publisher till he had several works to his name.

Tracts and sermons did not generate much money, and they were only moderately successful at bringing the writer's name to the attention of the religious world. Books were much better at achieving both these aims. It is entirely possible that Milner had published rather more than appears in the list in exhibit 6.1, but that only books were deemed worthy of mention.[13] The problem with books, of course, was that they took months to produce, while sermons had to be written every week no matter whether they were to be published or not. The biographies of evangelical ministers commonly detail the busy and complex schedules of their week, during which it is almost incredible that they found time to write anything other than their essential sermons and lectures. The following account of life as a Congregational minister in Edinburgh was William Alexander's response to a suggestion that he should spend more time in pastoral visiting. It equally illustrates the difficulty of finding time to write:

> Now, when it is considered that I have three discourses a week to prepare and deliver, that I am often called besides to preach, sometimes at home, sometimes at a distance; that I have church meetings, prayer meetings, deacons' meetings, committee meetings, and public meetings to attend; that I have baptisms to perform in the houses of members, funerals to attend; that I have to converse with numerous applicants for church fellowship; and that I have many calls on my time besides which I cannot prevent,—I leave it to the good sense of any candid man to say whether, even supposing I never were to enjoy the luxury of reading a book, or to occupy myself in literary exertion, or to spend an hour with my family and friends, it be possible for me [to do more visiting].[14]

It is hardly surprising that many ministers lacked the time or inclination to pursue any writing beyond the discourses they had to write as part of their professional duties. It is quite impressive that Milner managed to produce four

---

13. The bibliography is based on Milner's own account of his publications and library catalogue records.

14. Ross, *W. Lindsay Alexander*, 137.

volumes, only one of which was sermons, in his first decade as a minister. Any minister who was going to make a habit of writing for the press—and most of the ordained RTS writers did make it a lifelong habit—must have been expert at time management.[15]

Milner may have become interested in the sciences as a consequence of training at Glasgow, where the university professors gave regular lectures on natural philosophy and related subjects. Although intending to become a minister, he might nevertheless have attended some of their lectures. His first published work on the sciences was written while he was still an active minister. *Astronomy and Scripture* (1843) was written with the explicit intention of illustrating "the Relation between the chief facts of Astronomy, and the general testimony of Scripture." He claimed that it was "written popularly, being intended for the use of those classes of young persons who revere the word of God, and seek an acquaintance with His works."[16] The opening chapters of the book discussed ancient and medieval attitudes to the heavens, and dismissed them as superstitious or idolatrous. After describing the astronomical discoveries of Copernicus, Kepler, and Galileo, there followed chapters describing the planets, sun, moon, stars, and comets, among which were interspersed chapters on solar, lunar, terrestrial, and stellar phenomena recorded in Scripture. The aim was to explain the scriptural accounts by means of modern astronomy, and thus "promote the interests of Religion and Science."[17] This was a defence of astronomy for believers, not a defence of religion for astronomers. It was written for those who were familiar with the Scriptures and had faith in them, but were worried by apparent contradictions between the inspired word and what they knew of astronomy. Milner was completely confident that there could be no genuine contradictions, since the heavens were made by the same deity who revealed himself in the Bible.

One of the most potentially difficult areas of astronomy for Christians in the 1840s was the nebular hypothesis. The observations of William Herschel had shown that nebulae existed in different shapes (fig. 6.2), and it had been suggested, principally by the eminent French mathematician and physicist Pierre-Simon Laplace, that these were in fact different developmental stages, and that nebulae eventually evolved into stellar systems.[18] William Whewell

---

15. On the benefits of a minister being also a writer, see "The Pulpit: its relation to literature," *British Banner*, 17 January 1849, 41.

16. Milner, *Astronomy and Scripture*, v.

17. Ibid.

18. Numbers, *Creation by Natural Law*.

Figure 6.2. The nebula in Orion. From Milner, *Gallery of Nature,* 185.

had coined the term "nebular hypothesis" in his *Bridgewater Treatise on Astronomy and General Physics* in 1833, but dismissed any claims that such a hypothesis alone could explain the origin of the universe.[19] God would still be needed as the ultimate origin. When Milner wrote *Astronomy and Scripture,* the hypothesis had not yet gained the notoriety that it would acquire a year later when it was used as a key plank in the argument of the *Vestiges of the Natural History of Creation,* and became even more strongly linked with a progressive universe in which God played no role.[20] For Milner, however, a progressive universe did not rule out the possibility of divine control. While Lord Rosse built an enormous telescope at Parsonstown, in Ireland, to try to undermine the hypothesis by showing that nebulae were in fact clumps of distant stars, Milner had no problem admitting that "the varieties of aspect under which the nebulae appear—diffused—winding—and globular—certainly favour the idea that they are all passing from one stage of construction to another."[21] He used a common image of development to illustrate his point, comparing the different classes of nebulae to the different stages of a man's life, just as the *Vestiges* author did in a different context.[22]

---

19. Schaffer, "Nebular Hypothesis," 135.
20. Robert Chambers, *Vestiges,* esp. chaps. 1–2.
21. Milner, *Astronomy and Scripture,* 367. On Rosse, see Schaffer, "On Astronomical Drawing."
22. James A. Secord, *Victorian Sensation,* 101–2.

Milner believed that the association in the public mind of the nebular hypothesis with Laplace and his religious infidelity had often caused it to be dismissed without due consideration, which he wished to redress.[23] Although he did not claim that the hypothesis was anything more than probable, he sought to convince his readers that "there is nothing . . . in the hypothesis, if it were proved to be true, that need disquiet the religious mind."[24] He maintained that it involved "no new principle under the sun," and that the action of God was as obvious in a gradual developmental scheme of creation as in the older idea of instant creation.[25]

> Supposing the material of our globe to have congregated gradually, and the vast edifice to have been prepared by slow degrees like an oak from an acorn, we are as capable of saying, in relation to the formation of primordial elements, and their unerring direction to a designed end, "Lo, on these things worketh God," as upon the contrary theory, that every separate object in the beautiful and harmonious system of the universe, was fashioned in the twinkling of an eye.[26]

In this passage, as in the earlier one about the development of man, Milner used only the image of the development of an organism—of man from child, and oak from acorn—and was not implying anything about the evolution of species. If the nebular hypothesis were true, for Milner it would not involve a rejection of the God of the Bible, but a re-imagining of his creative acts as recorded in Genesis. Indeed, Milner continued to argue for the compatibility of the nebular hypothesis with Christianity in works written after *Vestiges,* when he might have been expected to dissociate himself from a now notorious hypothesis. The larger scope of his later *Gallery of Nature* (1846) permitted him more space to discuss the hypothesis. Certain passages were clearly derived from the earlier work, sometimes word for word with only minor revisions, and although the discussion was filled out with more detail, the argument itself was identical.[27]

In *Astronomy and Scripture,* Milner had also argued that the existence of noted infidels among men of science, such as Erasmus Darwin, Voltaire, and Laplace, did not mean that the sciences themselves were infidel. Plenty of people were infidels who knew nothing of the sciences, while the piety of

---

23. Milner, *Astronomy and Scripture,* 367.
24. Ibid., 371.
25. Ibid., 370.
26. Ibid., 371.
27. Compare, in particular, Milner, *Astronomy and Scripture,* 366–67, with Milner, *Gallery of Nature,* 188–89; Milner, *Astronomy and Scripture,* 371, with Milner, *Gallery of Nature,* 190–91.

other men of science, such as Newton and Boyle, demonstrated that faith need not be compromised by the sciences.[28] Particular discoveries would not make a person lose faith, nor should their truth value be judged on the faithfulness, or otherwise, of the man of science with whom they were associated. He was thus taking the same line that the RTS would take in deciding to launch its publishing programme on secular subjects. The difference was that Milner was making the argument explicit, and he could do that because he was a minister writing for an audience of young Christians. The RTS works, however, were mimicking secular works and did not wish to scare off their potential readers with disquisitions on the relationship of science with faith.

Since Milner was writing for a Christian audience, he not only had to consider whether the sciences were antagonistic to faith, but whether the Scriptures were antagonistic to the sciences, as a minority of Christians claimed, urging their fellow believers to avoid them. Milner admitted that some passages of Scripture could be read as discouraging Christians from studying natural phenomena, referring to the sciences as "philosophy and vain deceit" (Colossians 2:8), and "science falsely so called" (I Timothy 6:20).[29] But he interpreted those passages as applying to Arabic philosophy and medieval astrology, and argued that, in fact, the Scriptures encouraged the study of the works of God.

> Nature is a scroll written with a demonstration of the power and wisdom of the Almighty; and he who takes the record in hand, and endeavours to decipher the inscription, is acting far more like a rational, accountable, and religious being, than he who suffers it to remain unstudied and neglected. The Scriptures speak with no unfriendly voice of the inductive philosophy, but rather enjoin its cultivation.[30]

Although Milner used the term "demonstration," he was not claiming that nature could prove the existence or attributes of God, in the strict natural theological sense. A demonstration could be either a proof or a display of something already known, and for Milner, nature displayed truths about God already known from Revelation—truths that might nevertheless become better known if demonstrated in a visible manner. The easy combination of the adjectives "rational, accountable, and religious" implies that evangelical

---

28. Milner, *Astronomy and Scripture*, 38–39.
29. Ibid., 39.
30. Ibid.

religion was in fact entirely comfortable with the rational investigation of nature that was pursued by men of science.[31]

Milner's first foray into astronomy writing might have remained an exception. Certainly his contemporaries who remained Congregational ministers, such as John Kennedy and John Stoughton, published only a few works on nonreligious topics (mostly for the RTS), and ultimately became well respected for their scholarly works on apologetics and the history of Congregationalism. In their cases, the few nonreligious works emerged from the Nonconformist habit of giving a weekday evening lecture to the congregation in addition to the Sunday sermon. Kennedy was also involved with a literary society at the Stepney meeting house, while the young Stoughton had joined the newly founded Windsor and Eton Literary and Scientific Institute.[32] These organisations gave the ministers further opportunities to produce extended pieces of writing on secular topics.

Kennedy, for instance, lectured to the Stepney society on "the Holy Land, arctic exploration, volcanic phenomena, and ethnology, with special reference to the unity of the race and the primitive condition of mankind."[33] Although not intended for publication, such lectures might eventually find their way into print, and in Kennedy's case they were the cause of his introduction to the RTS. Having heard of his lectures to the Stepney literary society, his friend Joseph Angus invited him to address the students at the local Baptist college. The lecture was attended by Angus's brother-in-law, Joseph Gurney, who was "so struck by the valuable information contained in the lecture, and the lucidity with which it was conveyed, that he asked Kennedy to write for the RTS on *The Jordan and the Dead Sea*."[34] The lecture on volcanoes also became a Monthly Volume, and he wrote on arctic exploration in the first number of the *Leisure Hour*.[35] He also wrote again on ethnology, for Cassell's "Library" of sixpenny volumes, which issued from 1850. With so little biographical material on Milner, we do not know if he too gave weekday lectures, but from the tone of *Astronomy and Scripture* it could quite appropriately have been

---

31. On the similarity between Enlightenment natural philosophy and evangelicalism, see Bebbington, *Evangelicalism in Modern Britain*, 57–60; Bebbington, "Science and Evangelical Theology."

32. Kennedy, *Old Highland Days*, 249; Georgina K. Lewis, *John Stoughton*, 48.

33. Kennedy, *Old Highland Days*, 249.

34. Ibid., 249–50.

35. [J.K.], "Sir John Franklin's First Journey in the polar regions," *Leisure Hour* 1 (1852): 10–12.

delivered orally to an audience drawn from his congregation, before being turned into a published work.

The breadth of subjects covered in Kennedy's lectures is also indicative of the sort of preparation that was involved in preparing a lecture. None of these subjects were ones on which Kennedy himself was an expert, but they were all subjects about which he could learn enough from a library. Most minister-writers were enthusiastic in amassing as many books as they could, but few were able to afford an extensive personal collection. Their personal and denominational networks came in very useful in a practical way, giving them access to the shelves of friends and colleagues. Stoughton recorded being delighted to find "a large collection of books" under the "hospitable roof" of his congregation member, Thomas Coombs.[36] Kennedy and Stoughton both used the British Museum library and had access to the Nonconformist Dr. Williams's Library and those of the several denominational training colleges.[37] Kennedy was even known to borrow from Mudie's circulating library for his researches.[38] When Milner lived in Northampton, he could not have been a regular user of the London institutional libraries, but he would presumably have had similar personal and ministerial networks that would allow him to borrow books. By the 1850s, when he was resident in London and had become a fellow of the Royal Geographical Society, he was able to borrow from its library.[39]

Milner's second work on the sciences was the *Gallery of Nature*. It was issued in parts of sixteen pages by London publisher William S. Orr, and copious wood engravings (fig. 6.3) decorated Milner's text. This work was aimed at a far wider audience than *Astronomy and Scripture*, as is indicated both by its publication by a London publisher and by its serial issue. It seems that Milner was approached by Orr at short notice, perhaps after the original writer pulled out.[40] In its finished form, the *Gallery* contained three major sections on astronomy, physical geography, and geology. The astronomy section in the *Gallery* owed much to *Astronomy and Scripture*, but the other two sections appear to have been written afresh. In their turn, however, those

---

36. Stoughton, *Recollections*, 81.
37. Georgina K. Lewis, *John Stoughton*, 100.
38. Kennedy, *Old Highland Days*, 269.
39. Milner's one surviving letter to the Royal Geographical Society concerns the return of a book he had borrowed. See Royal Geographical Society Archives, Milner to RGS, 11 May 1852.
40. Milner, *Gallery of Nature*, iii.

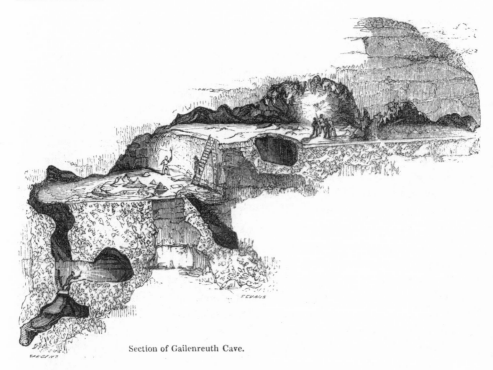

Section of Gailenreuth Cave.

Figure 6.3. The group of interconnected caverns at Gailenreuth. This was one of many images in the *Gallery of Nature* that stretched across the page and was surrounded by the text. From Milner, *Gallery of Nature*, 255.

sections were used as the basis of later writings in geology and geography. For example, the *Gallery*'s description of caverns containing animal remains reappeared in the RTS Monthly Volume *Caves of the Earth* (1847). In both instances, Milner discussed German caverns, and began with an anecdote describing how one such cavern, Bauman's Höhle, got its name.[41] He then used the examples of the caverns of Gailenreuth, Zahnloch, and Kühloch. In both cases, he cited the investigation of Kühloch by Oxford geologist William Buckland, who calculated that the cave contained the bones of at least two and a half thousand animals, suggesting around a thousand years of continuous occupation.[42]

---

41. The account is almost word for word: compare [Milner], *Caves of the Earth*, 109 (4 lines up) to 110 (five lines down), with Milner, *Gallery of Nature*, 254 (lines 19 to 23 down).

42. Milner, *Gallery of Nature*, 255; [Milner], *Caves of the Earth*, 110–11. Only in the latter case are the figures attributed to Buckland.

The *Gallery of Nature* was still written in a Christian framework, as indicated by the subtitle's description of it as "a pictorial and descriptive tour through creation." But its audience was different than that for *Astronomy and Scripture*, and consequently its religious spirit is extremely toned down in comparison. Milner did not use his prefatory advertisement to expand on the theological implications of the subtitle (he rather apologised for errors resulting from the rush in which the work was prepared), and the explicit discussions about the relative merits of faith and the sciences that were a feature of the previous book do not appear in the new one.[43] The discussion of the nebular hypothesis, being based on that in *Astronomy and Scripture*, was obviously very similar, but when Milner came to consider the relative ages of the earth and of mankind, he was relatively restrained. This potentially contentious issue was dealt with in four pages, in which the various evidences were described, but Milner did not dwell on the religious implications, since the *Gallery* was intended for a broad nonpartisan audience.

The idea that the earth had changed its appearance since its creation had been debated by geologists since the late eighteenth century, and the evidence for geological change raised awkward questions for the Genesis account. By the time Milner was writing, an ancient and changing earth was hardly contentious among practising geologists, evangelicals or not.[44] What that meant for the history of life on earth was still deeply problematic, especially when works like *Vestiges* argued for a long evolutionary history for mankind. Milner could hardly avoid discussing the age of the earth in his geological works. Using the same argument that he applied to the nebular hypothesis, Milner argued that even if the earth was more than six thousand years old, as seemed probable, this would have no significant consequences for Christian faith. Just as the gradual development of the solar system from a nebula was consonant with an overseeing God, so too was the development of the earth itself. There was plenty of evidence that the earth was old and that it had undergone major changes during its history, but since this had all occurred before the arrival of mankind, it could easily be regarded as God's way of preparing the earth for its intended occupants.[45] Like most

---

43. Milner, *Gallery of Nature*, iii.

44. The minority of Scriptural Geologists excepted. On the various evangelical positions on geology, see Clement, "Sifting Science," chap. 3; Yule, "Impact of Science," 328; Brooke, "Natural Theology of the Geologists." For a survey of how marginal Scriptural Geology was, see Stilling, "Scriptural Geology." See also Shortland, *Hugh Miller*.

45. Milner, *Gallery of Nature*, 784–88. William Martin had used the same argument in *Natural History of Mammiferous Animals*, 336.

people in the 1840s, Milner assumed that humans had been on the earth for only six thousand years, no matter how old the earth itself was. The first definitely human fossils (of Cro-Magnon man) were not discovered until 1868.[46]

When Milner returned to the issue again, in *Caves of the Earth*, he adopted a broadly similar narrative, but used a stronger Christian tone with more scriptural references, particularly in the introduction and conclusion. It was not, however, as clearly devotional as the tone he had used while addressing an explicitly Christian audience in *Astronomy and Scripture*, since that would not have suited the RTS's requirements. In the *Gallery* version of the passage about skeletons in the cavern of Kühloch, Milner suggested simply that the bears had lived there "previous to a great inundation in a by-gone time," as had various other animals, such as rhinoceros and elephant, which were now "confined to more southern latitudes."[47] The equivalent passage in *Caves of the Earth* led Milner to note that "conclusions of great interest and importance have been drawn from the circumstances noticed," and to devote a further three pages to discussing the implications of this evidence of flood and climate change.[48] He did not doubt that there was "a great diluvial catastrophe," and although, in accordance with contemporary geological practice, he did not explicitly claim that this was the Mosaïc Flood, he later conflated the two floods in order to discourse on the moral lessons of the Mosaïc Flood.[49] Milner reminded his readers that not a sparrow falls to the ground without God's will, so that all the changes of the earth, no matter how many or how large or small, should be read as actions of God. He invited his readers to see the existence of those large "natural convulsions which are occasionally fatal to life upon an extensive scale," such as the diluvial catastrophe, as "acts of the universal government of God, the instruments of his righteousness."[50] This allowed him to lead into a short discussion of the delinquency and rebellion of mankind, thus preparing the way for the later discussion of the importance of the Atonement for salvation, which he, like all RTS writers, had to include somewhere in every work to be published by the Society.

The examples provided from these three of Milner's works on the sciences show that he was able to reuse substantial sections from one work to another.

---

46. Bowler, *Invention of Progress*, 100–2.

47. Milner, *Gallery of Nature*, 255.

48. [Milner], *Caves of the Earth*, 111.

49. Although formerly a supporter of the diluvial theory, William Buckland had rejected it in his *Bridgewater Treatise* in 1833. See Topham, "Infinite Variety of Arguments," 106.

50. [Milner], *Caves of the Earth*, 113.

This made the process of composition easier, since he was not starting from scratch each time. As we shall see, William Martin was also able to do this. Since the books were for different publishers and served different audiences, the basic outline of a work on, say, geology could be reshaped to suit those different needs. Although the list of examples used might be the same and they might be presented in the same order, the narrative tone and the extent to which lessons were explicitly drawn could make the works very different. These three works also illustrate a range of styles that might all be called Christian. *Astronomy and Scripture* was very obviously devotional and aimed at an audience of believers. It would not have been suitable for the RTS secular publishing campaign. On the other hand, the *Gallery of Nature* was so faintly religious that the RTS required more obvious Christian input for *Caves of the Earth*. The other volumes in the "Monthly Series" suggest that the committee probably did not require as strong a Christian tone as Milner actually gave it, but it is hardly surprising that Milner the ex-minister erred on the side of stronger Christian tone.

By the time he wrote the *Gallery of Nature*, Milner was already unwell and was having trouble carrying out his ministerial duties. His success with the *Gallery*, combined with the ease with which he was acquiring new commissions from the RTS, may have suggested the viability of authorship as an alternative career, and showed him that it would be possible to continue to support his wife and children even if he had to abandon his chosen calling. Milner's life certainly changed as a consequence of that decision, as can be seen by the number and range of publications he produced throughout the late 1840s and 1850s, and which contrast with the typically ministerial productions of his earlier years. As a minister, Milner had never received more than £150 a year, but this was supplemented by his wife's life interest in some property, which amounted to between £100 and £120 a year.[51] This allowed the Milners to support their family at a standard of living similar to other ministers, and to writers like Bunbury and Kitto. Although Mrs. Milner became a permanent invalid a year after her husband became a full-time writer, he was initially well able to support his family by his writings. He published regularly with the RTS, a mixture of short and medium-length works, along with the occasional more substantial work with Orr. It is not clear how Milner became involved with the RTS, but he probably knew someone on the

---

51. RLF 1385.1, Milner's application form, 7 July 1855; 1385.2, Milner to RLF, [*ca.*7 July 1855]; 1385.16, Milner's application form, 25 June 1868.

committee or staff, as he was one of the first writers applied to at the launch of the "Monthly Series."[52]

At the beginning of his literary career, Thomas Milner had two advantages. First, he had the support of his wife's annual income, which, although not large enough to support the family, provided an assurance of regular funds and reduced the strain on Milner. Earning £150 a year, rather than £270, was a far easier task. Bunbury, as we have seen, thought £150 a year a reasonable achievement. Second, Milner had set up a good balance between long and short works. This was a serious matter for writers. Was it better to spend a year writing one long book and receive a substantial payment at the end of it, or to spend the time writing several short books and receive a series of smaller payments? A long book was tempting, as it would generally bring a significantly higher sum for copyright. But it took longer to produce, which meant longer until any money was forthcoming, and meanwhile, there was rent to pay and mouths to feed. At a time of frequent publishers' bankruptcies, it was also more risky. This was why Bunbury wrote so many short works for the RTS, SPCK, and Chambers, despite her personal desire to write "longer and more prepared works."[53]

While a long work was an exception for Bunbury and indeed for Milner, it was the norm for John Kitto. This strategy gained Kitto a sound reputation as a scholar, and as proof of this, he was elected to the Society of Antiquaries, and awarded an honorary D.D. by the University of Giessen.[54] Kitto solved the cash flow problem by requesting advances on the copyright payment while he was completing the work, and his reputation was sound enough that he was granted them.[55] Nevertheless, he ran into trouble because he was a terrible judge of how long projects would take, and this was exacerbated by his tendency to write serious works where research and accuracy were essential. When he undertook the *Cyclopaedia of Biblical Literature* (1845), Kitto believed that the agreed payment was a reasonable one. But the project turned out to involve, in his words, "*twice* the time and labour which I had supposed sufficient for it, and ... that which might have been a fair remuneration for the labour of 18 months became a miserable pittance when spread over three

---

52. USCL/RTS CCM, 13 November 1844.
53. RLF 1089.2, Bunbury to RLF, 4 January 1844.
54. Ryland, *Memoirs of John Kitto*, 594–96.
55. On advances, see "The Authors of Calamities," *Chambers's Journal*, 27 February 1847, 129; Sutherland, *Victorian Novelists and Publishers*, 112.

years."[56] The *Cyclopaedia* brought him his greatest fame as a scholar, but it also convinced him to think more seriously about writing "less ponderous works than have hitherto occupied my time" in the hope that "I may yet be able to bring up my family in comfort."[57] In contrast, with his publications for the RTS and Orr, Milner seemed to have got the balance between long and short works just about right.

Despite these advantages, a string of unfortunate circumstances in the mid-1850s brought the Milner family near to breaking point. First of all, Milner acted as security for an acquaintance who defaulted on his debts. Through this "confidence misplaced in another," Milner became liable for the debt.[58] He worked particularly hard through 1852 and succeeded in repaying the amount. Then, in late 1854, he was hit by the bankruptcy of Orr, as described in the previous chapter, and was deprived of £250 expected payment. In addition, his writing hand and wrist were beginning to trouble him. His youngest son was still at school, but his daughter was now old enough to contribute to the family finances by becoming a teacher.[59] As he had done in 1852, Milner tried to work ever harder to recoup the loss caused by Orr's bankruptcy, and proposed to the RTS an ambitious plan of four volumes on the British Isles, to be followed by four more on the Empire.[60] He also got a commission from Longman for a series of books related to recent events in the Crimea.[61] By mid-1855, his surgeon described him as "suffering from a right hand disabled by incessant activity, and great nervous debility."[62] He continued to try to work, and in winter of 1855–56 suffered something close to a mental breakdown. The RTS was sufficiently concerned about the likelihood of him finishing the works to which he was committed that the committee sent one of the editors to Brixton to enquire after him. John Henry Cross reported that Milner "had been suffering lately from pecuniary trials which incapacitated him for literary work," but that he intended to honour his commitments.[63] When the manuscripts did appear, two months later than promised, they were

56. RLF 1115.2, Kitto to RLF, 27 October 1845.
57. RLF 1115.8, Kitto to RLF, 3 February 1849.
58. RLF 1385.2, Milner to RLF, [*ca.*7 July 1855].
59. Ibid.
60. USCL/RTS CCM, 20 September 1854 and 18 October 1854.
61. No correspondence with Longman's survives, but the payments are recorded in the Miscellaneous Expenses ledger (A3) from 1854–56, Longman's Archives, Reading University Library. My thanks to Michael Bott.
62. RLF 1385.3, Aspray to RLF, 9 July 1855.
63. USCL/RTS CCM, 19 December 1855.

in need of substantial revisions. The committee, presumably judging that Milner was in no fit state, sent the manuscripts to someone else for revision.[64]

The next few years were difficult for Milner and his family, although he was more fortunate than Kitto. He did recover his health, finish his commissions for the RTS and Longmans, and continue his life. He avoided being locked into the spiral of working until too ill and then restarting work before his health was fully returned, which, as Kitto's case showed, could be fatal. Like Kitto, he got support from the RLF and advances from his publishers, but unlike him, he had a smaller family, some financial backup, and a number of small projects. Milner was hit by a publisher's bankruptcy again in 1857, but this time the loss was less severe. By the end of the 1850s, he was back in his stride. Apart from the *Gallery of Geography,* however, he wrote relatively few new works in the 1860s. By this time, his children had left home, reducing the burden on his finances. He continued to write for the periodicals, and his commitment to Christian tone was still evident in his choice of journals. He contributed to the SPCK's *People's Magazine,* the *Christian Witness,* and the *Christian World Magazine.* He also made revisions to the *Gallery of Nature,* which was now published by Orr's former partners, W. & R. Chambers, and was reissued until at least 1880. The fact of Chambers's involvement provides another indication of the mildness of the Christian tone in the *Gallery.*

Milner and his wife were by now growing older, and old age brought different problems to writers. Due to her own ill health, his wife had never been able to do as much to assist her husband as other wives did, but the annual income that came through her property was help of a different kind. When she died of typhus in 1868, Milner lost that financial backup, as well as incurring the costs of illness and funeral.[65] Milner himself remained in reasonable health until the mid-1870s, when he moved, first to Dover and then back to Derby, to escape the heat and bustle of London. Although his daughter had been widowed, she and her children were supported by her brothers, and were thus no burden to Milner.[66] Since Milner did little writing in his later years, it seems probable that he too was being at least partly supported by his sons. In 1879, he suffered an apoplectic fit and a serious fall, from which he never fully recovered, dying in or around 1883.[67]

---

64. USCL/RTS CCM, 19 March 1856.

65. RLF 1385.16, Milner's application form, 25 June 1868.

66. RLF 1385.22, Milner's application form, 5 February 1881; 1385.23, Milner to RLF, 4 February 1881.

67. RLF 1385.23, Milner to RLF, 4 February 1881; 1385.24, Milner to RLF, [autumn 1880].

Writing for Both Sides

William Martin (1798–1864) did not set out to be a full-time writer any more than Thomas Milner did. Martin's father was a natural history illustrator, and his son was trained in natural history, with the intention of becoming an apothecary. In his early thirties, he applied successfully for the position of superintendent of the museum of the Zoological Society. The society had been founded only in 1826, and when it employed Martin four years later, it was still in the early stages of organising its collection of live animals in the Zoological Gardens, and was starting to acquire preserved specimens and skeletons that needed a home. It was this collection that Martin looked after for eight years, during which time it became a fully fledged museum with premises in Leicester Square.[68] The museum provided Martin with a regular annual income of £100 a year, as well as the subject matter for his first publications.[69]

As with ministers, but in a rather different sense, a certain amount of writing was part of Martin's job. He wrote a daily report on his activities in the museum, as well as on those of the man employed to preserve and mount birds, John Gould.[70] He also performed dissections of dead animals from the Zoological Gardens, and reported on these to the meetings of the Zoological Society. These reports later appeared in the society's *Proceedings.* Since he was responsible for ordering and labeling all of the society's nonliving specimens, Martin had the opportunity to examine many new specimens, including some from Charles Darwin's *Beagle* collection, which occasionally turned out to be of scientific interest.[71] He was given permission by the society to write up the reports on these specimens, and in one case was allowed to name a new genus of insectivorous mammals (fig. 6.4).[72]

Martin was committed to seven consecutive hours a day to the Zoological Society, but outside those hours (presumably), he found time to pursue

---

68. Martin is not mentioned in either of the histories of the Zoological Society, doubtless because he was overshadowed by John Gould's later fame. See Scherren, *Zoological Society of London,* 33, 53–54; Mitchell, *History of the Zoological Society,* 97–98.

69. ZS MC, 20 October 1830, 44; also 20 April 1836, 418.

70. Only one volume survives, Zoological Society, Museum Report Book, 1833.

71. Martin reported on *Beagle* specimens in *Proceedings of the Zoological Society* 5 (1837): 3, 11.

72. The genus was *Echinops,* whose members are similar to hedgehogs. Permission granted ZS MC, 5 April 1837 (reference is to the common name of the specimen, "sokina"); report communicated to the society, 13 February 1838, see *Proceedings of the Zoological Society* 5 (1838): 17–19; published in *Transactions of the Zoological Society* 2 (1841): 249–56.

Figure 6.4. The new genus of insectivorous mammal named by William Martin: *Echinops.* From *Transactions of the Zoological Society* 2 (1838): 250.

additional literary work, as is clear from the list of his publications in exhibit 6.2.[73] He became a regular contributor to two of the new instructive penny periodicals of the early 1830s, writing on natural history for both the SDUK *Penny Magazine* and the RTS *Weekly Visitor.* He also wrote two volumes on natural history with reference to Scripture for the RTS, and three volumes on menageries for the "Library of Entertaining Knowledge," probably at the request of the editor of the *Penny Magazine,* Charles Knight, who was having trouble finding the time to write them himself.[74] The menageries volumes functioned as a guide to the Zoological Gardens, and the Zoological Society granted the SDUK permission to have the volumes sold by the "cakewoman at the Elephants' Stand."[75]

In the 1830s, therefore, Martin wrote as part of his job, which might or might not lead to publication, and he also earned some extra money by writing for the SDUK and RTS. Writing for money was an optional extra in his life. This all began to change in 1836. The Zoological Society museum

---

73. ZS MMC, 16 April 1836; MC, 20 April 1836.

74. Martin claimed to have written three volumes of the LEK. See RLF 1315.8, List of Works 1833–[*ca.*1853]. The SDUK archives list the names of the writers of most of the treatises of the LEK (though only of the first *Menageries* volume) and do not mention Martin, nor is he mentioned elsewhere in the archives; but I see no reason to disbelieve Martin's claim to have written the volumes. On the *Menageries* volumes, see SDUK Archives, Entertaining Knowledge Committee Minutes, 1831–33 (especially 6 May 1831); Publications Committee Minutes, 1833–38 (esp. 28 February 1833, 4 March 1833, and 23 March 1836).

75. ZS MC, 7 September 1831.

Exhibit 6.2. William Martin's publications

This list does not include subsequent editions or revisions and is based on Martin's letters to the RLF and library catalogues.

Menageries, 3 volumes of "Library of Entertaining
  Knowledge" (London: Knight for the SDUK, early 1830s)
*Popular Introduction to the study of Quadrupeds, or of the class Mammalia, with a notice of those mentioned
  in Scriptures* (London: RTS, 1833)
Introduction to the study of Birds, with a particular notice of the Birds mentioned in Scripture (London:
  RTS, 1835)
*A General Introduction to the Natural History of Mammiferous Animals, with a particular view of the
  physical history of man, and the more closely allied genera of the order Quadrumana, or monkeys* (London:
  Wright & Co., 1841)
Popular History of Reptiles, or introduction to the study of class Reptilia, on scientific principles (London:
  RTS, 1842)
(editor) C. G. Barth, *Scripture Natural History containing a description of quadrupeds, birds, reptiles,
  amphibia, fishes, molluscous animals, corals, plants, trees, precious stones and metals, mentioned in
  the Holy Scriptures* (London: RTS, 1843)
History of the Dog (London: Knight, 1845)
History of the Horse (London: Knight, 1845)
Our Song Birds (London: RTS, 1846)
Our Domestic Fowl (London: RTS, 1847)
Articles on zoology for *National Cyclopaedia of Useful Knowledge* (London: Knight, 1847–51)
Comparison of Structure in Animals: the hand and the arm (London: RTS, 1848)
Pictorial Museum of Animated Nature (London: Knight, 1848–49)
British Fish and Fisheries (London: RTS, 1849)
The Ox (London: Knight, 1849)
Poultry (London: Knight, 1849)
The Sheep (London: Knight, 1849)
The Hog (London: Knight, 1849)
(editor) Robert Mudie, *Feathered Tribes of the British Isles* (London: Bohn, 1849)
The Senses and the Mind (London: RTS, 1850)
Wonders of Organic Life (London: RTS, 1852)
A General History of Humming-Birds, or the Trochilidae (London: Bohn, 1852)
Some volumes of "Books for the Country" (1850s)
Natural History of Quadrupeds (London, 1853)
Natural History of the Class Mammalia (London, 1858)

Martin contributed papers to the *Proceedings* and *Transactions* of the Zoological Society of London between 1833–38. He also wrote 122 articles for the *Penny Magazine,* six hundred articles for the *Visitor* and *Leisure Hour* magazines, and for *Recreative Science.*

had been in its new premises in Leicester Square for eighteen months, and the society had regularised its staffing procedures. Gould the taxidermist, now on a salary, was given charge of the bird collections. More crucially, additional staff were taken on. In keeping with its better premises, the museum was to have a curator, a man of higher social status than Martin, who was to be "a competent Zoologist in all its branches; of agreeable manners and address, to have the control and direction of all the persons employed in the Museum department."[76] The curator was to have a clerk, and an assistant. George Waterhouse was appointed in April 1836, and Martin became the assistant curator.[77] Notwithstanding Gould's departure to Australia, the Zoological Society soon found this to be an expensive establishment, and consequently decided to discontinue the offices of assistant curator and assistant secretary. With effect from January 15, 1839, Martin was out of a job.[78]

Writing suddenly became a much more important part of Martin's life. He had not chosen to give up his paid job, and unlike Milner, he did not have a backup income to support him through difficult times. One advantage he did have was that he and his wife and mother were accustomed to living on £100 a year, whereas Milner and his family were used to £270 a year. Martin left no accounts of his routine as a writer, but it probably involved longer hours than his paid job had. Most professional writers worked from early in the morning till late in the evening every day, just to earn enough to survive. Selina Bunbury regularly started work before 7 AM, while John Kitto claimed to work from 4 AM until 11 PM.[79] Family members, especially wives and daughters, were often drafted in as researchers or copyists, and although Martin had no children, his wife, Mary Jane, did help.[80] In addition to taking dictation and nursing him through his illnesses, she kept the household "with strict economy."[81] Gould spoke of Mary Jane Martin with great respect. He claimed that she also displayed "considerable literary abilities," which makes one wonder whether she contributed more to the writing process than simply taking dictation.[82]

Martin's years at the Zoological Society served him well for the rest of his life. The personal connections he had made with other members of staff and with the society's committee (which included comparative anatomist Richard Owen) remained strong. Waterhouse, Gould, and Owen were all still writing references for him twenty-five years after he had ceased to work for the society. He had also gained enormous knowledge and expertise in natural

---

76. ZS MMC, 18 March 1836.
77. ZS MMC, 4 April 1836 and 9 April 1836; MC, 20 April 1836.
78. ZS MMC, 26 January 1838; MC, 1 August 1838.
79. RLF 1089.11, Bunbury to RLF, 5 March 1845; Ryland, *Memoirs of John Kitto*, 552–53.
80. Kitto's wife went to the British Museum for him. See Ryland, *Memoirs of John Kitto*, 536, 551.
81. RLF 1315.2, Martin to RLF, 2 April 1853.
82. RLF 1315.55, Gould to RLF, 27 February 1864.

history, which supplied him with the subject matter for all his publications. His publications were much more tightly focused than those of Milner, who ranged over history, geography, and the sciences, and they suggest a different manner of working. Where Milner relied strongly on the contents of libraries, Martin knew the animal kingdom inside out. Despite no longer being part of the mainstream scientific world, Martin remained aware of what was going on and was able to update his works or take advantage of particular events.[83] For instance, in 1843, writing in the *Visitor* on the rhea, he referred to one of his earlier books, published eight years previously, and noted how little had then been known. One major difference was that it was now known that there were, in fact, two different species of rhea, thanks to Darwin's observations.[84] Similarly, when Gould displayed his magnificent collection of hummingbirds at the Zoological Gardens in 1851, Martin was determined to take advantage of the opportunity. He suggested a book on hummingbirds to the RTS, which turned him down, although he did get a three-page article with illustrations in the *Leisure Hour*.[85] He had greater success with publisher H. G. Bohn, who agreed to take a volume that was explicitly presented with "reference to the collection of J. Gould, FRS &c now exhibiting in the Gardens of the Zoological Society of London."[86] This volume was by far the most lavishly illustrated of any of Martin's works, for publishers such as the RTS and Knight were committed to low-priced books, and used wood engravings for illustrations. Bohn, however, allowed fifteen coloured illustrations (fig. 6.5), which brought home the brilliance of the little birds in a way that wood engravings could not match.

In late 1837, the Zoological Society had determined to allocate explicit duties in the museum to the three senior members of staff. Waterhouse, as the most senior, was given specific responsibility for the mammal collection, despite his own fondness for beetles. Gould, obviously, was given the birds, which left Martin with "Fishes, Reptilia, Mollusca and Radiata."[87] Yet, when it came to published works, Martin wrote most frequently on mammals and

---

83. He was never a Fellow of the Zoological Society, although he was elected to the Linnean Society in 1831, possibly due to his father's connections there. Certificate of Election (1 February 1831, signed by N. A. Vigors, T. Bell, and E. T. Bennett), Linnean Society Archives.

84. "On two species of Rhea, or south American Ostrich," *Visitor* (Feb. 1843): 75–77. The reference is to [William Martin], *Study of Birds*.

85. USCL/RTS CCM, 21 May 1851; "Winged Gems," *Leisure Hour*, 22 April 1852, 263–66.

86. [William Martin], *History of Humming-Birds*, title page.

87. ZS MMC, 29 December 1837.

Figure 6.5. Martin's works were rarely as lavishly illustrated as this example from his *General History of Humming-Birds* (opp. 168), which contained fifteen of these (originally colour) plates.

birds, rather than on the lower animals. He wrote one volume on fish and one on reptiles, and only a few periodical articles on the radiata (starfishes, sea urchins), although they did feature in his works covering the whole animal kingdom.[88] It could easily be the case that publishers were more interested in books on mammals and birds than on starfish, and that Martin was catering to the market demands. It may also be true that Martin himself preferred mammals and birds, but when he was no longer in charge of the whole museum, found himself relegated to the lower groups.

Having a specific subject area at the tips of your fingers made it easier for full-time writers to work quickly. They might need some research to verify facts, but they could form the outline of their work without having to embark on research trips to the British Museum library. Martin's life before becoming a full-time writer served him well in that way, as did Kitto's, for he produced book after book on the history, geography, and peoples of the Holy Land. Bunbury, as a woman, did not have this sort of career-related experience, but she still wrote many of her nonfiction works from experience. Her particular forte was the travel narrative, which she based on her own

---

88. "The star fish and sea urchin," *Weekly Visitor*, 22 December 1835, 465–66; "Observations on the starfish, sea urchin, and other echinodermata," *Visitor* (May and June 1843): 168–69, 223–24.

journeys, undertaken with some of her more wealthy relatives and friends.[89] This became difficult when, after the deaths of her parents and brother, she was no longer able to afford to travel abroad so often to acquire new experiences to write about. She appealed (successfully) to the Royal Literary Fund for a grant to enable her to visit to Finland and perhaps Russia.[90]

Since Martin wrote on a relatively restricted range of subjects, it is hardly surprising that he often wrote works that had much in common with his previous works. Take mammals, for instance. Martin wrote three works specifically on mammals, and they also featured in the *Menageries* volumes, the *Scripture Natural History*, and the *Museum of Animated Nature*. Then there were the short books on the ox, horse, and dog, as well as all the articles in periodicals. In the *Visitor*, in April and May 1833 alone, he wrote articles on the dormouse, the mole, the lyre bird, the maned anteater, the jerboa, the porcupine, the pangolin, and the llama.[91] The similarity of subject matter allowed Martin to recycle material from one work to another on an extensive scale. The sets of facts that might be reused fell into two groups, of different scientific status. Zoologists needed to be able to identify individual specimens as members of a species, so the formal description of a species (such as that of the tench, in fig. 3.6) was extremely important. This was something a writer could not change significantly, as it was fundamental to systematic taxonomy that those words constituted a true description of the species. Works intended for a wider audience, however, usually had more than just the formal description of the animal. There were usually details relating to the habitat in which it lived, its behaviour, and its relationship with humans (say, as food or as sport). Here, a writer had more opportunity to exercise his narrative powers, with a greater range of information and anecdote from which to select.

For instance, Martin discussed domestic fowl in books (not to mention periodical articles) three times in the 1840s: for the "Monthly Series," as *Our Domestic Fowls* (vol. 20, 1847); in the "Poultry" section of Knight's "Farmer's Library"; and in the *Museum of Animated Nature*, also issued by Knight. The "Farmer's Library" was a set of chunky reference works containing practical and useful information on each of the main categories of domesticated animals found in Britain. As well as sections on the economic value of fowls, and their

---

89. See, for instance, the explanation of her first travels abroad, which were undertaken to meet up with family friends in Paris, as recounted in Bunbury, *My First Travels.*

90. RLF 1089.34, Bunbury to RLF, 1 April 1856.

91. *Weekly Visitor* (April–May 1833): 127–28, 129–31, 133, 137–38, 145–46, 153–54, 169–70, and 177–78.

Figure 6.6. Knight's "Farmer's Library" was intended as a reference work, and its use of illustrations and different fonts makes it easy to find the start of each new entry, such as this one for Sonnerat's jungle fowl. From William Martin, "Poultry," 506.

treatment and management, there were separate entries on the individual species, each with a wood engraving (fig. 6.6). The *Museum of Animated Nature* was a serial publication for a more general readership that aimed to provide a printed version of the experience of "the greatest National Museums" in zoology.[92] Each eight-page number cost 3*d.* and contained four pages of wood engravings, with the remaining pages providing the "labels" for each specimen.

Martin did not suffer from Edwin Sidney's problem of using technical language in popular works, even though his paper in the *Transactions of the Zoological Society* indicated that he was perfectly able to express himself in

92. [William Martin], *Museum of Animated Nature*, i, 1.

standard zoological technical language, in Latin, when need be. He stated in the introduction to the RTS volume, "We shall endeavour to treat the subject in a popular and interesting manner, divesting scientific details of that obscurity which, from the use of technicalities, the general reader too frequently complains is thrown around them."[93] To this end, he used common terms (such as "breast, belly and thighs") for fowl anatomy, and, in the "Farmer's Library" volume, for instance, explained what "sub-serrated ridge" meant. When he quoted from authorities who used more technical language, he inserted a simpler term in parenthesis. Thus, while quoting Owen on fossil sloths, in his RTS volume on *Structure in Animals*, Martin glossed Owen's use of "brachial" as "upper-arm," and "flexed" as "bent."[94]

One of the great concerns with domestic fowl was the history of their domestication and the identification of the original wild species. The wild stock was believed to be from the Indian subcontinent, so Indian fowl received special attention. Sonnerat's jungle fowl was one of the contenders. Martin's three descriptions of the male of this species are compared in exhibit 6.3, and were very nearly identical, which shows how little freedom a writer had when dealing with the formal description of a Sonnerat's jungle fowl. The RTS description was slightly shorter (at the extremes of comb and tail), and the "Farmer's Library" description was marginally more detailed (the comb, the location of the purple tail feathers). There were also slight differences in orthography, most obviously between the two descriptions for Knight (reflection/reflexion, gray/grey). The selection of colour adjectives varied slightly, with the feet being either "yellow" or "yellowish," and the tail being variously "deep rich glossy green," "rich deep green," and "deep rich refulgent green." But it is clear that, try as he might, there are only so many ways that a writer could express the colour of a jungle fowl's tail and retain accuracy.

The *Museum* was supposed to be a visual experience, with only minimal text to support the illustrations. Sonnerat's jungle fowl had three illustrations, but the text consisted only of the announcement, "This splendid bird, of which many specimens have lived long in the menagerie of the Zool. Soc., is celebrated for its high courage and prowess, and is in great request among the cock-fighters of Hindostan," followed by the description of the male and female of the species.[95] Nor was there much connecting narrative, except

---

93. [William Martin], *Our Domestic Fowls*, 20.

94. [William Martin], *Comparison of Structure in Animals*, 45–46.

95. [William Martin], *Museum of Animated Nature*, ii, 391. Images are numbers 1732–34, on pages 392–93.

Exhibit 6.3. Three descriptions of Sonnerat's jungle fowl

IN *OUR DOMESTIC FOWLS* (RTS, 1847), P. 33:

The comb of the male is large with its margin serrated. The wattles are rather ample. The hackles of the neck, and lower part of the back, and the wing coverts on the shoulder, have the shafts expanded into a thin cartilaginous, or rather horny plate, of a bright golden yellow, with a rich metallic gloss. The plumage on the middle of the back, the breast, and under parts generally is a deep grey, each feather having a paler margin. The tail is of a deep rich glossy green, with varied metallic reflections. Bill and legs yellow.

IN THE *MUSEUM OF ANIMATED NATURE* (KNIGHT, 1848–49), P. 391:

The comb is only slightly indented. The wattles are large and double. The hackles (though they scarcely come under this term) of the neck, of the wing and tail-coverts dark greyish, with bright golden orange shafts dilating into the centre and towards the tip into a flat horny plate. Feathers of the middle of the back, breast, belly, and thighs deep rich grey, with paler shafts and edges. Tail generally rich deep green: the feathers which immediately succeed the hackles are rich purple, with a pale yellow edge; those next in succession are golden-green, with grey edges, and all are glossed with brilliant metallic reflexions. Bill, legs and feet yellow.

IN *POULTRY*, FOR KNIGHT'S "FARMER'S LIBRARY" (1849), PP. 506–7:

The comb is large, with a sub-serrated ridge, that is the ridge is but slightly dentated, in comparison with the comb of the *gallus Bankiva*. The wattles are large and double. The hackles of the neck, the wing coverts on the shoulders, and the tail coverts are dark grayish, with bright golden orange shafts, dilating in the centre and towards the tip into a flat, horny, and very glossy plate. The feathers of the middle of the back, breast, belly, and thighs, are of a deep rich gray, with paler shafts and edges. The tail is of a deep rich refulgent green, but the feathers which immediately succeed the hackles of the lower part of the back, and lie against the sides of the tail, are rich purple with a pale yellow edge, those next in succession are golden green with gray edges, and all are glossed with brilliant metallic reflections. Bill, legs, and toes yellowish.

between the sections on the major classes of animal. The other two works, however, were primarily textual. Again, both mentioned the splendour of the plumage, the bravery and use in cockfighting, and the presence of specimens on view to visitors in the Zoological Gardens, but the variation in the structure of the narrative illustrates how Martin told the same facts in different ways, reinterpreting the jungle fowl for different audiences.

The RTS entry began with a description of the country and habitat of the fowl, its size and appearance, and its bravery in combat. The descriptions of the male and female were then followed by quotations from other writers recounting the behaviour of Sonnerat's in the wild, and how it was captured for cockfighting. This entry therefore started out by introducing a splendid bird to the reader, and followed up with further anecdotes about it. In contrast, the entry in the "Farmer's Library" started by arguing that the term "Sonnerat's jungle-fowl" as commonly used was inaccurate, for it confused two separate species. It then described the true Sonnerat's fowl. Again, the bravery of the male and its use in cockfighting were noted, leading to a discussion of how the wild cocks were caught for this purpose. It ended by noting the presence of living specimens at the Zoological Gardens. In contrast to the RTS entry, this one was drier and more matter of fact. It made no attempt to interest the reader in the species before launching into the details, but rather assumed that the reader would be interested and would expect certain information to be included. Although there was narrative at the beginning of each chapter, the bulk of the Knight volume was set up as a reference work, unlike the continuous prose of the RTS volume.

The RTS and Knight volumes were arranged differently, but they both recounted the same details and used the same illustrative quotations. Sonnerat's jungle fowl was first described by Colonel William Sykes, of the East India Company, in a letter to the Zoological Society in 1832, and Martin quoted from this account in both his works. In the RTS volume, the Sykes quotation appeared after the formal description simply as further information about the fowl in the wild, but in the Knight volume, it opened the account, since it provided the evidence for the contention that two different species had often been confused under the one name.[96] Both entries mentioned the fighting skills of the Sonnerat's cock, and used the same quotation from Daniel Johnson's *Sketches of Indian Field-Sports, as followed by the Natives of India* (1822) to describe how the fowl were beaten toward a line of suspended nooses, in which their heads were caught, allowing them to be captured alive.[97] In the Knight volume this followed a simple statement that the cock "is anxiously sought after by the cock-fighters in Hindustan."[98] In contrast, in the RTS volume, Martin led up to the Johnson quotation by including two others describing the prowess of the cocks and their ability to elude skilled

96. [William Martin], *Our Domestic Fowls*, 33–35; William Martin, "Poultry," 506.
97. [William Martin], *Our Domestic Fowls*, 36–37; William Martin, "Poultry," 507.
98. William Martin, "Poultry," 507.

huntsmen.[99] Both accounts concluded by dismissing Sonnerat's claim that his eponymous fowl was the sole original wild stock of all domestic fowl.[100]

These examples illustrate how Martin was able to recycle not only the formal and relatively unalterable description of the species, but also many of the points to be discussed, along with their illustrative quotations. They also show that the manner in which the points were arranged, and the specific role played by the quotations, could be varied, so that the publications that resulted were adapted to meet the needs of the general reader or of the reader in search of information on a specific subject.

In addition to the zoological contacts and expertise he gained while working for the Zoological Society, Martin acquired contacts in the world of publishing. His two main outlets during the 1830s were Charles Knight and the RTS, and they remained his main publishers through the 1840s. Having those contacts meant that even though Martin's contract and salary with Whitehorne was suddenly terminated, his transition from part-time to full-time writing was relatively easy. No evidence survives of how Martin became involved with these two publishers, but he must have been well established with the RTS by 1833, as he had a very prominent place in the relaunched *Weekly Visitor*. His article on the crocodile took the front page of the first issue (fig. 6.7), and he averaged an article in each subsequent issue for at least the first six months. Like the crocodile, many were front-page illustrated articles.[101] Martin was probably an Anglican, and his long connection with the RTS suggests a commitment to evangelicalism, particularly as he wrote for the Society in the days before he had to do so out of financial necessity.[102] The Society did try to ensure that it only engaged evangelical writers.

Given Martin's evangelical commitment, that he would choose Charles Knight as his other main publisher initially seems strange. In the 1830s, Knight was closely associated with the SDUK, whose publications were always religiously neutral. When the RTS launched the "Monthly Series" and presented it as an answer to secular publishers, as well as to the infidel press, the publications of Knight and the SDUK were ranged there alongside Chambers. After the demise of the SDUK, Knight did claim that he wished to infuse his publications with a greater Christian tone, but many evangelical

99. [William Martin], *Our Domestic Fowls*, 35–36.

100. Ibid., 40–41; William Martin, "Poultry," 507.

101. Of the eight articles listed earlier, for April–May 1833, six were front-page articles.

102. His 1861 application to the RLF was accompanied by a reference from the Reverend John B. Honnywill, a retired Anglican clergyman. See RLF 1315.37, Honnywill to RLF, [June 1861]. This is the only surviving evidence for Martin's religious affiliation.

Figure 6.7. Martin wrote this article on the crocodile for the very first issue of the *Weekly Visitor* (1833): 1.

commentators judged his attempts and found them lacking—probably because many of his publications were reissues of SDUK works. Knight reorganised his business after the financial troubles of 1848–49, and concentrated on government printing contracts, so we cannot tell how much longer (or whether) Martin would have continued to write for him once the RTS had declared war on the secular press. During the previous fifteen years, however, he seems to have had no qualms about writing for both sides.

Martin may have first learned about the SDUK from the several members of the Zoological Society who were also involved with it. In particular, Nicholas Vigors was a member of the museum committee to which Martin reported, and was also active on the SDUK's committees. It could have been Vigors who recommended Martin to Knight, when the latter was trying to complete the *Menageries* volumes. Martin wrote over a hundred articles for the *Penny Magazine*, and he also wrote for Knight separately from the SDUK business.

After Knight's financial troubles, Martin did not find another publisher who could provide him with such regular work. He managed to place the *General History of Humming-Birds* because he had already edited an edition of Robert Mudie's *Feathered Tribes of the British Isles* for Bohn, but that was his only work with that house. Martin's book projects with the RTS also dried up in the mid-1850s, so the onset of the illness that would eventually kill him may have been affecting his productivity. Yet, it is notable that even during health, Martin had only rarely undertaken full-length book commissions. Most of the volumes for Knight and the RTS were short books, which appeared in cheap series, and the *Museum of Animated Nature* was a serial. He also wrote around one periodical article a week. The *Penny Magazine*, *Visitor*, and *Leisure Hour* were certainly the most important periodicals for him (he claimed to have written over six hundred articles for the RTS periodicals), but he also wrote for *Hogg's Instructor*, the *Home Companion*, the *Illustrated London News*, and *Recreative Science*.[103] It could be that Martin had realised that shortish works were the best way of generating a regular income, or he may have been scared off long works by his bad experience with Whitehorne's commission at the very start of his professional writing career. He may simply have been an exception to the general rule by which, according to *Chambers's Journal*, the professional writer always "aspire[d] to labours of a higher kind." *Chambers's* believed that most writers wished to write large-scale theoretical and synthetic works, but that "the necessity of bread forbids."[104] Martin does not seem to have made much effort to move away from short works of popular instruction. His familiarity with the learned natural history circles, of course, would have made it clear to him that he would be unlikely to be taken seriously as a scholarly writer, when Owen and others so obviously regarded him only as an industrious workman.[105]

Martin proved able and willing to suit the different requirements of his publishers. When writing for the RTS (before the "Monthly Series"), he employed a strongly religious style, in keeping with the requirements of a

---

103. RLF 1314.20, Martin's application form, 31 January 1859; 1315.27, Martin's application form, 4 June 1860. He averaged forty articles a year over his whole career, but that includes his time of illness when he was doing very little.

104. "The Authors of Calamities," *Chambers's Journal*, 27 February 1847, 130.

105. RLF 1315.11, Owen to RLF, 11 April 1853.

Society that did not yet regard publishing on secular subjects as part of its remit. When writing for Knight, Martin was usually producing works that were similar to reference works and were supposed to be secular in style. The introduction was usually the only opportunity for connected narrative in such a work (there was typically no conclusion), and Martin kept this secular. His work for Knight meant that, in the mid-1840s, Martin was unusual among the RTS writers in having extensive experience of writing in the two different styles that the RTS sought to fuse. He was well suited to create the desired Christian tone, and his success is indicated by the number of volumes he wrote for the "Monthly Series," including the one on *British Fish and Fisheries*.

Martin's earliest RTS volumes, the introductions to the quadrupeds and birds mentioned in Scripture, had been presented as part of sacred knowledge, since they provided information that would help readers to interpret the Bible. The *Popular History of Reptiles* was the third in the series, despite not carrying the subtitle "those mentioned in Scriptures."[106] The obvious Christian sentiments of these works meant that they had a restricted audience compared to that intended for the later "Monthly Series." *Reptiles* was priced at 6*s.*, which, although not dear in general terms, was regarded as expensive by the RTS committee, and the volumes sold slowly. It was not until 1848 that the quadrupeds volume finally sold its first print run, fifteen years after first publication.[107] These were the "expensive and scientific" works from which the committee had considered removing the Society's imprint.[108]

These works illustrate Martin's most strongly Christian style, which was different from that used by Thomas Milner in *Astronomy and Scripture*. Although both were aimed at believers, Milner was writing scripture exegesis, whereas Martin was writing theology of nature. The *Reptiles* volume, for instance, used many of the tropes familiar from natural theologies and gloried in the plenty and variety of species, pointing out evidence of divine wisdom in everything from the adaptation of tortoises to their environment, to the epiglottis of the crocodile (which allows it to breathe while submerged, hidden from its prey).[109] Yet there were also significant differences. It was the *wisdom* of God, and occasionally his beneficence or power, that the natural world was said to illustrate—not his existence. And crucially, in both introduction and conclusion, where the most explicitly natural theological

---

106. [William Martin], *Popular History of Reptiles*, 1.
107. USCL/RTS FCM, 19 April 1848.
108. USCL/RTS FCM, 26 June 1844.
109. [William Martin], *Popular History of Reptiles*, 93, 101–3.

language was to be found, Martin made clear the inadequacies of natural theology as a basis for true religion. Thus, in the introduction, he argued that the study of nature tended to humble us, and that this was in keeping with our history on earth, but we need not fear, because God has promised salvation. The story of the Fall and the promise of the Atonement were thus added to the evidences of the natural world, and the reader was urged to remember, "To this atonement we must be led not by the light of science, but by the Spirit of God whose gracious influences will not be sought in vain."[110]

Martin's works for Knight illustrate his other writing capability, although they might initially be taken to illustrate *lack of style* rather than an alternative style, since they tended to be dry, instructional, reference-type works. If the writer's remit was to describe all the important species of domestic fowl, there was not much opportunity to introduce religious sentiments, evangelical or otherwise. The account given earlier of the descriptions of Sonnerat's jungle fowl in the two Knight publications was complete—there were no religious sentiments hidden there. In contrast, the RTS *Our Domestic Fowls* began by announcing that Genesis was the only available history of early man, and proceeded to use the Bible as a historical source on the domestication of animals.[111] From there, it was not too great a step to ask why some animals were so easily domesticated, and to reply that it was evidence of "the wisdom and goodness of Divine Providence."[112] The discussion of Sonnerat's jungle fowl, including the dismissal of its claims to be the sole wild stock, was part of a discussion of the origins of domestic fowl. The section concluded with the admission that, although we are "in the dark as to the time and circumstances of its subjugation and dispersion," it seems that, "from a casual and little-noticed expression in the first Book of Kings..., as early as the days of Solomon, the domestic fowl was kept in Judaea."[113] Martin had also discussed the history of domestication in the introductory section to the "Farmer's Library," but there he used a majority of non-scriptural sources. Genesis was mentioned, but not until two pages in, and then only briefly, as one source among many.[114] Again, we see how the same or similar arguments and examples could be presented in a different manner.

---

110. Ibid., 14.
111. [William Martin], *Our Domestic Fowls*, 5 ff.
112. Ibid., 18.
113. Ibid., 41.
114. William Martin, "Poultry," 495.

Despite Martin's undoubted ability to write in styles that suited both evangelical and secular publishers, it was of no avail if he was too ill to write. As shown in the previous chapter, the last ten years of his life were a catalogue of appeals to the RLF as he became increasingly ill. Periodical articles were now all he could write, and then only with the help of his wife. Although Martin appears to have written no more books for the RTS, he continued to write for the *Leisure Hour,* and he also showed his continuing commitment to presenting science in a Christian framework by contributing to a new journal in the early 1860s. *Recreative Science* was launched in 1860, and was a short-lived popular science journal that aimed "at every step [to] recognize, in hope and faith and love, the Source of things created, and point the mind of the student to the great Benefactor, by whose will the worlds sprung into being."[115] His half dozen articles for this journal were his last works, but, as Mary Jane Martin pointed out, such work barely paid for food.[116]

WHEN they were asked to write for the Religious Tract Society's new campaign against the cheap secular and infidel publishers, both Thomas Milner and William Martin had strong credentials in writing for a popular audience and in a Christian manner. Martin had more experience, but it was probably Milner who had come closest to the necessary style in the *Gallery of Nature,* since Martin's non-RTS works were decidedly secular in tone. Both writers had two main publishers for whom they wrote, as one publisher, particularly when that one was the RTS, would not have generated enough money to live on. Having a variety of outlets, particularly in terms of length and subject matter, helped the writer's domestic economy to run more smoothly. It also meant that they had to be able to adapt to the different needs of the publishers, most noticeably concerning religious spirit or lack thereof.

Milner and Martin were both capable of taking the same basic facts and anecdotes, and weaving them together in different ways, producing an interpretation of the sciences adapted to a particular publisher and his intended audience. Yet, the fact that Martin had been persuaded to write in a secular tone for certain publishers indicates that even some evangelicals occasionally forgot that omitting religion did not signal neutrality, but rather a deliberate decision to turn one's back on salvation. It was central to the RTS campaign that

---

115. "The endeavour," *Recreative Science* 1 (1860): 2.
116. RLF 1315.28, M. J. Martin to RLF, May 1860.

subjects such as the sciences were not inherently secular or infidel. That they sometimes appeared that way was a consequence of the interpretation of those who were communicating scientific knowledge to its wider publics. By employing Martin, Milner, and other writers to portray the sciences in a Christian tone, the RTS sought to demonstrate that it was the style of interpretation alone that was giving the sciences a bad name. The appropriate interpretation, of course, was that which linked the sciences inextricably with salvation.

Postscript

PRINT became the first mass medium in the late 1840s and 1850s. One of the consequences was the development of new publishing genres to cater to the needs of the new consumers of print. Fiction may have been the most obvious growth area, but informative works also benefited from the general increase in demand. Nonfiction presented specific problems for publishers. The lack of formal education of most readers meant that the publications had to be written in easily understood language, yet this should not compromise the basic promise of accuracy and truth which a nonfiction work claimed to provide. But even the very truth claims of nonfiction were problematic, because somewhere there was a line between the narration of true facts that were generally accepted, and the addition of the writer's own personal interpretation of those facts. The location of that boundary was tricky, particularly in those sciences that dealt with deep history, where so much depended on the interpretation of a small amount of surviving evidence.

For instance, an account of the history of the earth might present as fact that the earth was much older than six thousand years and had undergone significant changes during its history. This "fact" was, of course, based on a host of other "facts," such as the appearance of the earth's surface and the existence of fossils. The fact that volcanic eruptions could change the face of the earth was something that could be seen to happen, but the "fact" that the earth was old could not be "seen" in the same way. That had to be deduced from other "facts," and it was possible to debate the validity of such a deductive chain. Equally, it would be possible to argue, from the "facts" of a long and changing earth history and the nebular hypothesis, that the universe was not divinely created and overseen. For midcentury evangelicals, there was a point somewhere along this particular chain of interpretation where the conclusions ceased to be generally accepted, and should not be legitimately presented as fact.

Infidel publishers relished the opportunity to present a whole sequence of facts and reasoning as an attack on religious faith, and this was obviously a type of publishing that evangelicals opposed. Nevertheless, despite the vociferous evangelical opposition to them, the outright infidel publications were still a minority at midcentury. Of more serious concern were the secular publishers, not least because this group was not just small and short-lived enterprises, but included publishers in the heart of the respectable book trade. The secular publishers generally avoided making explicit theological conclusions, one way or the other. But by so doing, they incurred the censure of evangelicals for suggesting that the sciences did not impinge on faith. The idea that faith and the sciences (or any other area of knowledge) could be separated simply did not fit with the all-pervading nature of the evangelical experience. Most evangelicals were happy with the idea of presenting nonfiction to the mass audience, including the latest scientific discoveries. But they wanted to ensure that there was a theological interpretation laid on those discoveries, and that it was a Christian interpretation.

For organisations such as the Religious Tract Society, a major problem with the flood of cheap publications lay in disciplining readers. When works were read in the middle-class home, in the parish library, or in the Sunday school, there were systems of authority to ensure that readers interpreted the works "correctly"—as well as the censorship that would have kept out many of the potentially corrupting works in the first place. Such systems of authority could control only a small proportion of the mass audience, and beyond them, different methods of disciplining readers were needed. This was why it was necessary to develop a Christian variant of the new genre of popular science publishing, in which the "Christian tone" of the narration could attempt to control readers' interpretations. While it could not function as effectively as a teacher's supervision, it limited the range of interpretations open to the reader, by making it more difficult to read an infidel message against the Christian tone.[1] What the reader would do with a "correct" Christian reading of the sciences was not discussed. It was always assumed that having once seen the proper way of viewing the sciences, it would be difficult or impossible to return to a non-Christian perspective. In other words, although the press could lend its power both to Good and Evil, when given a fair hearing, Good would win the day.

The RTS considered its programme of secular publishing with a Christian tone to have been a great success, and, as the Reverend Dr. Samuel Green

---

1. On the creativity of readers, see Fish, *Is There a Text in This Class?;* on the constraints placed on readers, see Jauss, *Aesthetic of Reception;* Eagleton, *Literary Theory,* chap. 2.

noted in the centenary history, "popular science has had a prominent place."[2] At the end of the nineteenth century, the Society's annual reports described such publishing as a routine subsidiary "to that which is directly evangelis-tic and religious." Christian tone could be applied to any subject, "whether in prose or poetry, whether treating of science or history, whether dealing with fact or fiction, with study or with sport." While Christian tone in the 1840s had been something that was still under development and was not explicitly defined, by the 1880s the Society could describe its secular works as "permeated by Christian principle; always on the side of pure morals; . . . not obtrusively religious, but using all its influence on the side of Christ; lively and interesting, and yet not sensational in any bad sense of the word; truth teaching, but not dull; elevating, but yet attractive."[3] The success of the RTS secular publishing programme could be dated back to the "Monthly Series" and the *Leisure Hour*.

One of the soundest reasons for considering these projects to be a success had nothing to do with convincing readers of the inseparability of science and salvation. The new publications came at an extremely opportune moment for the Society's finances. Not only did its income recover from a slump in the late 1830s and early 1840s, but it entered a period of sustained growth, as is clear from figure P.1. When the Society's sales income finally peaked in 1885, it stood at over £180,000 a year, three times what it had been in 1850. Such a massive increase in sales was made possible by the broader appeal of the new publishing programme, which targeted the spending power of the middle and lower-middle classes. The zenith of the programme was arguably the *Boy's Own* and *Girl's Own Papers*, launched in 1879 and 1880, which were voted the most popular periodicals among adolescents in 1888, and boosted the sales income to its heady heights.[4] Although the benevolent income of the Society did double over the same period (to around £12,000 in 1885), it was dwarfed by the sales income, and it was the latter that made possible a vastly expanded system of charitable grants to tract and Christian literature societies all over the world. The annual value of these grants grew from around £10,000 in the 1850s to over £40,000 in the 1880s. Over the course of this period,

---

2. Samuel G. Green, *Story of the Religious Tract Society*, 125.

3. RTS Report (1889): 11–12.

4. Salmon, *Juvenile Literature*, 15, 23. The stories of the papers are told in Cox, *Take a Cold Tub, Sir!* and Forrester, *Great-Grandmama's Weekly*.

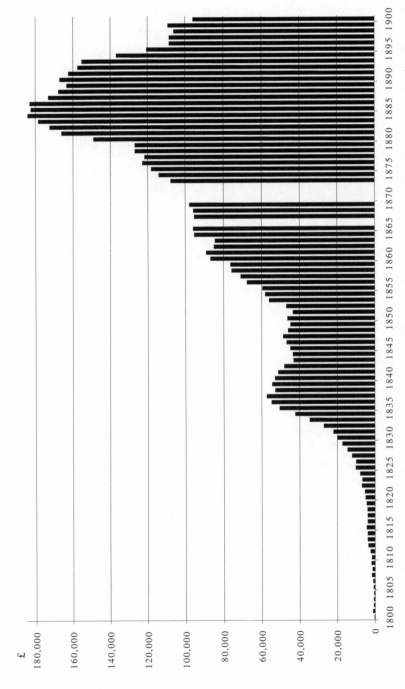

Figure P1. Annual sales income of the RTS over the nineteenth century. The figures for income, grants, and circulations were printed in the annual reports, most of which survive. Notice the period of sustained growth that followed the launch of the "Monthly Series" and *Leisure Hour.*

Table P.1. Surviving sales figures for the "Monthly Series"

Date	Sales	Volumes issued so far	Average sales per volume
31 March 1847	153,469 in last 12 months	16	9,592 in last 12 months
31 March 1850	645,622	52	12,416 to date
31 March 1854	148,320 [×10]	99	14,982 to date

Source: RTS Report (1847): 116–17; USCL/RTS CCM, 18 September 1850 and 21 June 1854.

Note: The 1854 figure must be out by a factor of ten, so the average is calculated on an assumed total sales of 1,483,200.

the Society reformulated itself from a middle-class society evangelising the working-classes to a British society bringing Christianity and literacy to the world. The fact that the extensive overseas activities were substantially funded by the commercial success of the British publishing operation was hidden behind the success of the mission.[5]

There seems no doubt that the new publishing programme was a financial success for the Society—but money was not the primary reason it was undertaken. The programme was supposed to reach a wide range of readers, from educated families to working-class artisans, and convince them both of the importance of conversion and also of the impossibility of considering the sciences outside a Christian worldview. Although the committee certainly had access to more complete figures at the time, only a few sales figures survive, and are given in tables P.1 and P.2. The "Monthly Series" figures show that the volumes did generally sell their large initial print runs of fifteen thousand within a few years, and that sales held up, with old volumes still selling as the newer ones were issued. The total sales for the Series must have been much larger than the ones shown here, as the volumes were kept in print until the early 1880s. The best-seller details given in the Society's *Jubilee Memorial* (1850) showed that, of the sixteen volumes that had been in print

---

5. When sales incomes began to fall in the 1890s (and continued to do so into the twentieth century), the grant programme was threatened. The committee initially tried to get through what it thought was a brief bad spell by using funds from the capital reserves, but by the early 1900s they were forced to curtail the grant programme. It was tied much more closely to the benevolent income, with contributions from the trade fund when possible (as had been the case prior to the post-1850 expansion), and more attention was devoted to encouraging the auxiliaries in their fund-raising efforts. The decline can be attributed in part to increased competition consequent on the changes in the publishing trade in the 1890s (see Eliot, *Patterns and Trends in British Publishing*, 13–14), to the unquantifiable effects of secularisation (see Hewitt, *Let the People Read*, 73, and compare Chadwick, *Secularization of the European Mind*), and to the decline of evangelicalism as a major force in British religion (see Wolffe, *Evangelical Faith and Public Zeal*, introduction).

Table P.2. Surviving sales figures for the *Leisure Hour*

Date	Sales	Source
January 1852	At least 50,000	*Christian Spectator* (Jan. 1852): 682
January–February 1852	83,000 for No. 1	Executive Committee, 2 March 1852
	64,500 for No. 4	
	54,000 for No. 9	
March 1852	70,000	*Christian Spectator* (March 1852): 697
1852	60,000	Finance Committee, 26 Sept. 1855
May 1855	80,000	Annual Report (1855)
September 1855	67,500	Finance Committee, 26 Sept. 1855
May 1856	77,500	Annual Report (1856)

for more than two years, only two had not sold ten thousand copies to break even, while eight had sold over twenty thousand copies.[6] These figures are far better than any known for equivalent series. Meanwhile, the *Leisure Hour* was achieving sales of almost eighty thousand a week by 1856, which is as good if not better than *Chambers's Journal.*[7] Neither Chambers nor the RTS, however, could match the 125,000 copies a week sold by the *Family Herald,* let alone the 450,000 of the *London Journal.*[8] The RTS was glad to receive news that the *Leisure Hour* sold three times as many copies as the atheistic *Reasoner* in an infidel book shop in Southampton, but success in one shop was not enough to increase circulation to the extent the Society really wanted.[9] The circulations of both periodical and book series were high enough to be counted a success—they did significantly better than break even—but they were not high enough to have included more than a small fraction of the working classes among their readership.

When Thomas Pearson commended the "Monthly Series" for being a step in the right direction, he had suggested that it would succeed: "It has too much been forgotten that the people will have entertaining literature. It is by entertaining literature of a depraved kind that the evil is wrought, and it must be by entertaining literature of a healthy Christian tone that the evil must be counteracted."[10] Yet the solidly respectable but unexciting adjectives used by reviewers to describe the "Monthly Series" call Pearson's

---

6. William Jones, *Jubilee Memorial,* app. V.

7. Cooney, "Publishers for the People," 98.

8. Ibid., 103; Anderson, *Printed Image,* 14.

9. USCL/RTS ECM, 13 July 1852; "The Leisure Hour," *Christian Spectator* (July 1852): 733.

10. Pearson, *Infidelity,* 509.

assessment of its entertainment value into question. The works were variously described as "a good sixpenny worth of solid information," "like most of the books in this series—a far better book than it seems," and "very interesting and truly instructive."[11] The *Leisure Hour*, too, received critical praise, being described as "cheap and interesting," a "marvel of cheapness," "attractive and . . . improving," and "more solid, more in earnest in its work, and more trustworthy."[12] The RTS works were classified as valuable contributions to cheap, wholesome literature—but this is far from the same thing as "entertaining." It seems eminently plausible that many potential readers would not have regarded the RTS publications as "entertaining," particularly in comparison with other available publications.[13]

As the *British Quarterly Review* noted, the *Leisure Hour* "eschews the objectionable or doubtful features that are cultivated by its contemporaries. There are no answers to correspondents, real or fictitious; no contributions to gaping credulity, no bad jokes, no stale anecdotes, no axiomatic philosophy."[14] The absence of jokes, anecdotes, and letters pages, in addition to the moral tone of all the fiction that it contained, would have made it obvious to potential readers that the *Leisure Hour* was not quite in the same genre as *Reynolds's Miscellany* or the *London Journal*, however much it tried. The *British Quarterly* reviewer recommended:

> To attain the influence enjoyed by some of its inferior contemporaries, it must take up part of the ground occupied by them, which may be done without the slightest compromise of its higher aims. By an occasional sprinkling of lighter matter, an excursion now and then into the more "primrose paths" of literature, poetry, criticism, and miscellaneous pictures of society, there is no doubt that the *Leisure Hour* might extend the circle of its readers, and thus materially improve its means of usefulness.[15]

The balance between "higher aims" and "primrose paths" was critical, as the inclusion of the latter was essential to conveying the publication, and its message, to the desired readership. Yet, the inclusion of too much fictitious or trivial content would compromise theRTS's claim to be a moral and Christian

---

11. *Baptist Magazine* 44 (1852): 496; *British Quarterly Review* 6 (1847): 557; *Evangelical Magazine* ns 25 (1847): 25.

12. *Christian Guardian* 44 (1852): 46; *Englishwoman's Magazine* 7 (1852): 320; *Baptist Magazine* 44 (1852): 229; *British Quarterly Review* 29 (1859): 344.

13. Anderson, *Printed Image*, chap. 3.

14. "Cheap Literature," *British Quarterly Review* 29 (1859): 344.

15. Ibid.

publisher. It was conceivable that publications that carried even a small amount of Christian content to a mass audience, even if it was surrounded by sensational gossip, would ultimately be more effective than the *Leisure Hour* could hope to be, but it was highly unlikely that the committee and subscribers of the RTS would agree to publish such a periodical. The inclusion of fiction of any sort in the *Leisure Hour* was already a move away from the traditional objection to nontruthful narratives, and marks an acceptance of the fact that fiction sold periodicals. By the time of the *Boy's Own Paper,* the RTS had become willing to make more concessions to the public taste for excitement and adventure, but that willingness came only after three decades of experience with secular publishing.

At the time when the "Monthly Series" and the *Leisure Hour* were being produced, the Society was determined to avoid all the defining characteristics of "trash," and this meant that the RTS publications were recognisably different from those with which they had to compete.[16] This was compounded by the Society's commitment to good quality writing and editing. Quarterly reviewers praised the *Leisure Hour* for its production quality, and noted that it formed an exception to the general rule among the cheap periodicals, where editorial work was generally "discharged with culpable slovenliness."[17] It was because of the Society's high principles, which prevented it from producing a work that really resembled the cheap, corrupting, and immoral publications, that the "Monthly Series" and *Leisure Hour* were more effective against the so-called neutral publications than against the corrupting infidel publications that were the other part of the official target. Similar reasons explain why none of the philanthropic publications, whether Christian or secular, were able to gain the enormous circulations they craved. As the anonymous author of *The Power of the Press* pamphlet had pointed out, "in all that relates to mechanical or commercial production, whether as to price or style, journals of this class take the acknowledged lead in our periodical literature."[18] That "acknowledged lead" meant that it was not difficult to tell the difference between an issue of *Chambers's Journal* or the *Leisure Hour,* on the one hand, and *Reynolds's Miscellany* or the *London Journal,* on the other.

Although the circulations for the "Monthly Series" and *Leisure Hour* were not as high as the RTS would have liked, they were still high enough to suggest that at least *some* working-class readers were being reached. I have not attempted to assess the successof the publications in convincing those

---

16. Ibid.   17. Ibid., 330–31, 339.   18. *Power of the Press*, 20.

readers that science and salvation were inevitably intertwined. Even if it were possible to track down the tens of thousands of readers of the RTS publications, and discover what (if anything) they thought on reading those works, it would not affect my argument. It does not matter if few readers were instantly converted to evangelicalism. Probably few were. More may have been convinced by the argument against the separation of science and faith. But for many more readers, the "Monthly Series" must have been influential for being the cheapest, most widely distributed source of introductory treatises on the sciences (and other secular knowledge) available in the 1840s and 1850s. It therefore reached places and readers that other series did not, and presented them with a particular version of Christian natural knowledge. As modern studies of media effects reveal, the press may not affect its readers as directly as writers or publishers might wish, but it does affect what they know and how they think about it.[19] Readers of evangelical popular science did not have to accept its messages wholeheartedly, but its mere presence, as one of few sources of cheap information on the sciences, made its particular presentation influential.

When the RTS began its new scheme of publishing on secular subjects with a Christian tone, it claimed to be trying to reach an audience of adults and children from the working and middle classes. A few of the surviving copies of Monthly Volumes bear evidence of having been in a small circulating library, run by a bookseller or shopkeeper. Of course, not all copies were so fortunate. Those now in the University of Leeds library were bound in pairs in marbled boards, with leather spines and corners, and gilt detail. The edges of the pages were decorated with a speckled red pattern, and look as though their owner never opened them.[20] However, we do know that William Buckland, the Oxford geology professor, was a keen reader of the *Leisure Hour*, though he can hardly be said to have needed its call for harmonising the sciences with faith.[21] And a Welsh labourer, John Jones, found a copy of the Welsh translation of Dick's *Solar System* in his preacher's library, and recollected, "It was comparatively easy to understand." Its writer and publisher would have been pleased to know that it gave him "many a sublime thought," and that he later bought his own copy.[22]

---

19. Curran and Seaton, *Power without Responsibility*, 263.

20. The Reverend Dr. V. Kenna owned (at least) thirty-four volumes of the Series. They are at shelf-mark "Early Education REL" in the Special Collection at Leeds University.

21. Gordon, *Life of William Buckland*, 269.

22. Quoted in Astore, "Observing God," 231, and from information from Anne Secord.

The RTS publications did reach a varied audience, which included some members of the working classes, but never on quite the scale that had been dreamt of. As the Society came to realise, it was usually only a few particularly skilled, dedicated, and solvent members of the working classes who read improving publications. Instead, the Society discovered a large audience of readers hitherto unprovided for—people outside the restricted circle of RTS subscribers for whom the Society had previously provided books, but people who would still be counted among the middle and lower-middle classes. These were the people whose purchases saved the Society's finances, and they were also the people whom publishers like Chambers and Knight were reaching. The publications that had been started primarily to fight the infidel press among the working classes ended up proving their worth against the secular press among the lower-middle classes. Once they realised this, the RTS editorial staff were able to develop a more sophisticated understanding of the multifarious reading audiences of Britain, which they had previously conceived in terms of "people like us" and "the working classes." The general difficulties that all philanthropic publishers had in reaching working-class audiences indicates just how difficult it was, at midcentury, to sell cheap improving nonfiction to the recently literate working classes who were happily reading fiction and so-called trash.

It should be clear by now that evangelicals undoubtedly took an interest, and even an active involvement, in the sciences. They were not all determined to dismiss the findings of science to defend a literal interpretation of Genesis. It could be argued that in the early days of the evangelical revival, evangelicals paid little attention to the sciences, but once evangelicalism was well established in the mainstream of British religious life, its followers had time and opportunity to concern themselves with things other than doctrine. The prominent position occupied by the sciences in the RTS publishing programme, from the 1840s onward, indicates that the sciences were regarded as eminently worthy of study. The evangelical ambivalence toward natural theology is irrelevant here, as it was perfectly possible to be interested in nature for reasons other than the desire to prove the existence of God. An understanding of some aspects of the natural world could be an exegetical aid, and the study of nature could provide striking illustrations of truths already known from Revelation. Evangelicals could thus find the sciences to be a useful devotional exercise. They could also acknowledge that the sciences provided useful information for the temporal life, and would be of interest to readers of all backgrounds for reasons that had nothing to do with devotion. Works such as the "Monthly Series" aimed to take advantage of that interest, and although they did carry an injunction to conversion, their main aim was to demonstrate that there was nothing about the sciences that was contradictory to Christianity, when both were properly interpreted. It was thus hoped that Christian works of popular science could undercut the spiritually dangerous presentations of science found in other popular works.

Although the RTS did not initially publish on the most up-to-date sciences, such as physiology, electromagnetism, or organic chemistry, its publications were not simply compilations from old works of natural history. Few, if any, of its writers could fairly be described as hacks. Even those who were dependent on writing for their sole income were able to retain some independence from their publishers, managing (for most of the time) to play the trade successfully, writing for different publishers as it suited their personal literary careers. Most of them, particularly those who wrote on the sciences, did have a substantial amount of knowledge of their subject area, and in a few cases were sufficiently actively involved to have some claim to expertise. In fact, those of the Society's writers who came closest to the unoriginality of hack writing, by compiling directly from other people's works, were some of the ordained writers, although they clearly did not deserve the description in other senses.

In carrying out their ambitions, the committee and staff of the RTS had to negotiate their way through a host of tensions. The one we would label "science and religion" seems the most obvious, but it may actually have been the least important. The major tension appears to have been that between the spiritual mission of the Society and the commercial world of publishing, or between the spiritual and temporal worlds. The Society itself embodied both these facets in its structure, with the separate benevolent and publishing wings. As with the British and Foreign Bible Society, the subscribers generally saw, and were presented with, the benevolent activities.[23] For them, the RTS was a religious organisation dedicated to evangelisation throughout Britain and the world. That it carried out this mission through a publishing business was secondary. For the committee and staff in Paternoster Row, the Society was a commercial publishing operation that had to respond to market demands and contemporary trends within the book trade just like any other publisher. The committee knew that the purpose of their organisation was evangelisation and that they were stewards of the Lord's wealth, but they also believed that the best way to achieve their aims was by being careful businessmen, not

---

23. Howsam, *Cheap Bibles*, 203–5.

enthusiastic amateurs. Yet although this attitude grounded their actions on the Society's behalf, the annual reports and the *Christian Spectator* hid the commercial reality behind the dutiful appearance of a religious society, in order to gain support from the evangelical community.

The same tension also underlies the actions of the Society's editors and writers. The editors had to work out how to balance the need to appear similar to the competing secular publications with the requirement to provide Christian tone. Meanwhile, the writers were presented, by both the RTS and themselves, as people with a spiritual vocation to write for Christ. This image hid the important role that such writing played in the domestic economy of the writers, and disguised the physical labour involved. The manner in which these tensions were resolved, or at least put into temporary equilibrium, was at a practical, day-to-day level, for these decisions affected the selection of publications by the Society, the mixture of contents in its periodicals, and the writer's choice of subject matter and publisher.

From the way it has been presented in the historical literature (and, indeed, in much literature for the general reader), the tension between "science and religion" often seems like a philosophical one: is it possible for these two bodies of knowledge, these two systems of authority, to co-exist, or does one defeat the other? This is what we see in the debates over the reception of Darwinism, and it also characterises much of the discussion of natural theology in the earlier part of the nineteenth century. From these discussions, it seems as though the main consequence of one's deciding such a question was whether or not one remained a confessed Christian, and whether or not one accepted a particular scientific result. But religion is no more a simple matter of the acceptance (or not) of particular doctrines than science is only about theories. Both have practical sides, and this should affect the histories we tell of science and religion.

One obvious practical consequence of a decision about the relative merits of science and religion is the continuation (or not) of church-going and other religious observances. But, as historians of religion are well aware, explicitly religious practical activities are but the tip of the iceberg.[24] For the faithful, religion was an all-pervading influence that affected every aspect of life, from church-going to the choice of leisure activities and the operation of a business concern. Even for those who were not religious, religion could be a significant influence, whether this was due to the beliefs of social superiors or through the

---

24. For two very different examples, see Hempton, *Religion and Political Culture,* chap. 3, and Garnett, "Evangelicalism and Business."

creative selection of parts of orthodox religious practice for personal purposes (such as the use of certain church ceremonies as rites of passage).[25] This was certainly true of evangelicalism by the middle of the nineteenth century. The evangelical beliefs of members of the government and those lobbying them produced a reduction in the length of the factory day and restrictions on the opportunities for Sunday trading, no matter whether the people affected were confessed evangelicals or not. On a more personal scale, even non-evangelicals were influenced by the use of conversion narratives in describing life histories and by the example of active involvement in social work.

This awareness of the practical implications of religious faith has yet to be generally combined with studies of practice in the sciences. The evangelicals discussed here illustrate that evangelical beliefs about how the sciences should be presented were manifested in practical activities such as writing and publishing. In fact, it is probable that most of these evangelicals did not spend a lot of time worrying about the ideal philosophical relationship between "science and religion," but just got on with writing about the sciences. The idea that the relationship between science and religion was something that actually needed thinking about—rather than being taken for granted—was only starting to become obvious to evangelicals in the years leading up to midcentury. From the way that many of the RTS writers wrote about the sciences, it is clear that they were all starting from the assumption that the sciences were perfectly in keeping with evangelical ambitions for salvation. Because these people were writers, however, they had to think through and justify their position more thoroughly than most of their contemporaries did.

The evangelicals of the RTS are not only notable for showing how closely linked the practices of science and of religion could be, but for showing how this was true outside the small circle of the expert gentlemen of science. The gentlemen of science have been the focus of many studies concerned with nineteenth-century science and religion, largely because they were clearly involved with science and often left evidence of their involvement (or not) in religious affairs. Fewer ministers left evidence of their involvement in the sciences. The very fact that gentlemen of science were experts in their fields made them very closely involved with weighing up the strength of the evidence of new discoveries in the sciences, and deciding how, or if, such discoveries affected their religious beliefs. Since the gentlemen of science have tended to leaveexplicit statements about science and religion for historians

---

25. For example, Williams, *Religious Belief and Popular Culture*.

to work on, studies of the involvement of science and religion at a practical level, such as that of Michael Faraday's Sandemanianism, are rare.[26] Thus, examining the interactions between science and faith outside the scientific community provides a perfect opportunity to concentrate more closely on practical activities. Conversely, studying practical activities such as writing and publishing is one of the few ways to uncover attitudes to science and faith in the wider community, due to the relative lack of more theoretical writings on the subject.

The Religious Tract Society's achievement with its new programme of publications at midcentury lay in adapting older traditions of Christian writing about nature to meet the situation created by recent innovations in printing technology. The result was that the newly emerging genre of popular science publishing existed in Christian as well as secular variants. One of the striking things that is being uncovered by historical studies of late-nineteenth-century popular science publishing is that the Christian variant remained strong, even at a time when the majority of practising men of science had adopted a secular tone.[27] The later-nineteenth-century Christian popular science writers did not have to work as self-consciously as their midcentury predecessors to create their Christian tone, as they were working within a genre that by then had been well established. As expert science become more professionalised, the role of popular science in forming the public understanding of science became increasingly important. The continuing activities of Christian writers clearly demonstrate that the Christian popular science discussed in this book had a future, and that giving due consideration to the attitudes of the wider community, rather than just the experts, will produce a rather different picture of the relationship between science and religion in the nineteenth century.

---

26. Cantor, "Reading the Book of Nature."
27. Lightman, "'The Voices of Nature'"; Lightman, "The Story of Nature"; Lightman, "The Visual Theology of Victorian Popularizers."

APPENDIX A
Biographical Sketches of RTS Writers and Staff

The following information on the key writers and staff of the Religious Tract Society comes from the files of the Royal Literary Fund; from entries in the Clergy Lists, Baptist Handbooks, and Congregational Year Books; from biographies and obituaries; and from the following sources:

DNB: *Dictionary of National Biography* (ed. L. Stephen, 1885–1901)

DEB: *Dictionary of Evangelical Biography* (ed. D. M. Lewis, 1995)

Boase: *Modern English Biography* (ed. F. Boase, 1892–1921).

BBA: *British Biographical Archive* (ed. L. Baillie, 1984)

William Lindsay Alexander (1808–84)
Congregational minister

Son of a Baptist wine merchant, Leith, Edinburgh; studied at Edinburgh University and St. Andrews University, where he joined the Congregational church. Trained for ministry at Glasgow Theological College, 1827–28. Tutor at Blackburn Theological College, 1828–31. Began to study medicine at Edinburgh (1831), and also considered a literary career. Ordained 1834, minister of North College Street church, Edinburgh, 1834–77. Professor of theology (1854), and principal (1877) of Edinburgh Theological College, retired 1881. Member of Old Testament Revision Company. Married Miss Marsden, 1837, 8 surviving children. Author of at least 15 published works. Editor of *Scottish Congregational Magazine*. D.D. (St. Andrews), LL.D. (Edinburgh), FRSE.

Monthly Volumes:

Iona (vol. 57, Aug. 1850)

The Ancient British Church: Being an Inquiry into the History of Christianity in Britain Previous to the Establishment of the Heptarchy (vol. 76, Mar. 1852)

Sources: James Ross, *W. Lindsay Alexander* (1887). Also DNB, DEB, BBA

Joseph Angus (1816–1902)

Baptist minister

Son of Baptist farmer, Northumberland; studied at King's College London and Edinburgh University; trained for ministry at Stepney College (1835); then returned to Edinburgh (M.A. 1837). Minister of New Park Street Chapel, Southwark (1838); principal of Stepney College, later Regent's Park College (1849–93). Secretary of Baptist Missionary Society from 1840. President of Baptist Union in 1865. Served on New Testament Revision Company. Married Amelia Gurney (sister of Joseph Gurney, q.v.), 1841, 10 children. Author of at least 16 published works. Editor of *The Freeman*. D.D. (Brown University).

Monthly Volume:

The Bible in Many Tongues (vol. 92, July 1853)

Sources: DNB, DEB, BBA. Obituaries in *The Times* and *Baptist Handbook*

Charles D. Bell (1819–98)

Anglican clergyman

Son of landowner in Co. Derry; studied at Trinity College, Dublin (B.A. 1842, later M.A., B.D., D.D.); ordained 1844. Curate of Mapton in Arden, 1843–45; curate of St. Mary's, Reading, 1845–47; curate of St. Mary-in-the-Castle, Hastings, 1847–54; perpetual curate of St. John's chapel, Hampstead 1854–61; vicar of Ambleside, 1861–72; vicar of Rydal, 1872; rector of Cheltenham, 1872–95. Canon of Carlisle, 1869. Author of at least 25 published works.

Monthly Volume:

The Life of Calvin (vol. 100, Aug. 1855)

Sources: BBA. Obituary in *The Times*

Selina Bunbury (1803–82)

Anglican novelist and travel writer

Daughter of Church of Ireland clergyman; lived with parents until their deaths in the mid-1840s, then lived with various relatives in Liverpool (a sister), Cheltenham, Oxford (a cousin), and died in Cheltenham (staying with a nephew). Despite having no source of income outside writing, managed to travel to France, Italy, Sweden, Finland, and Russia. Remained unmarried. Author of at least 30 major works, and numerous smaller ones for RTS, SPCK, and Chambers. Contributed to *Christian Examiner, Fraser's Magazine*, the *Cornhill Magazine*.

Monthly Volumes:

History of Protestantism in France to the Reign of Charles IX (vol. 29, Apr. 1848)

The History of Protestantism in France, from the End of the Reign of Charles IX to the Revocation of the Edict of Nantes (vol. 38, Jan. 1849)

Sources: BBA, RLF archive

Esther Copley (1786–1851, née Beuzeville)
Anglican, then Baptist, writer

Daughter of a merchant, born in Kent, lived in Oxford until 1839, and thereafter in Eythorne, Kent. Married the Reverend Hewlett, an Anglican curate, and on his death, married William Copley, a Baptist minister in Oxford (1827). Author of at least 8 major works, and numerous small ones for RTS. Founding editor of *Visitor*.

Monthly Volume:

The Life of Lady Russell (vol. 19, June 1847)

Sources: DEB, BBA

John Edmund Cox (1812–90)
Anglican clergyman

Born in Norwich; studied at Oxford University (B.A. 1836, later M.A., B.D., D.D.); ordained 1837. Curate of Aldeby, Norfolk, 1837–43; curate of St. Mary's Southtown, Great Yarmouth, 1842–44 (also gaol chaplain); curate of Stepney, 1844–47; vicar of St. Helen's Bishopsgate, London, 1849–87; died in Bath. Also chaplain to United Grand Lodge of Freemasons, Royal Society of Musicians, British Society of Musicians, and the West Middlesex Volunteer Regiment. Chairman of Poor Clergy Relief Society. Author of at least 11 published works. FSA.

Monthly Volumes:

The Life of Luther (vol. 10, Sept. 1846)

The Life of Cranmer, the First Protestant Archbishop of Canterbury (vol. 33, Aug. 1848)

Sources: BBA, Boase

John Henry Cross (ca. 1804–76)
RTS editorial assistant

Born in London; joined RTS as reader in 1833, and gradually took on responsibility for the children's works. Served as children's editor from 1853 until he retired in poor health in 1875. Author of over 600 works for the RTS. Edited the *Child's Companion* and *Tract Magazine*. Died in Brixton.

Source: Boase

Thomas Dick (1774–1857)

Secession Church of Scotland writer

Son of a Secession Church linen manufacturer, Dundee; studied at Edinburgh University, 1794; teacher at Orphan's Hospital, at Leven, in Perthshire; licensed preacher, 1801; teacher at Secession school in Methven 1807–17; teacher in Perth 1817–27. Retired from teaching after success of the *Christian Philosopher*. Married (1) Elizabeth Aedie, 1804, 3 surviving children; (2) Euphemia Young, 1830; (3) Elizabeth Glegg, 1841. Wrote on theology, astronomy, and education; lived at Broughty Ferry near Dundee. Author of at least 11 major works. Editor of *Educational Magazine* and *Journal of Christian Philanthropy*. LL.D. (Union College, New York), Fellow of Royal Astronomical Society.

Monthly Volumes:

Solar System, Part I (vol. 6, May 1846)

Solar System, Part II (vol. 9, Aug. 1846)

The Atmosphere, and Atmospheric Phenomena (vol. 31, June 1848)

The Telescope and Microscope (vol. 67, June 1851)

Sources: William J. Astore, *Observing God* (2001), DNB

Henry Dunckley (1823–96)

Baptist minister turned journalist

Born in Warwick, trained for ministry at Accrington College, Lancashire, and at Glasgow University (B.A. 1846, later M.A., LL.D.). Minister of Great George Street church, Salford, 1848–55. Married Elizabeth Wood, 1848, 5 children. Began to write for the *Manchester Examiner and Times* in 1854, and resigned his charge to become editor, 1855–89. Author of many items of journalism, and at least 5 books.

Monthly Volumes:

Money: A Popular Treatise on Its Nature, History and Uses (vol. 84, Nov. 1852)

Successful Men of Modern Times (vol. 96, Nov. 1853)

Sources: DNB, BBA

David Jonathan East (d. 1903)

Baptist minister

Trained for ministry at Stepney College (1836); pastor at Leamington, Arlington, and Waltham Abbey. Principal of Calabar College, Jamaica, 1852–92; deacon at Beechen Grove Church, Walford, 1892. Involved with Baptist Missionary Society.

Monthly Volume:

The Crusades (vol. 42, May 1849)

Source: DEB

Robert Ferguson (1806–75)
Congregational minister

Born in Glasgow to Church of Scotland parents; trained for Congregational ministry at Glasgow Theological College and Hoxton College. From 1831, minister at Haddington, Leicester, and Finchingfield; at Stepney, London, 1836; Brickfields chapel, Stratford; George Street chapel, Ryde, 1849–59; Portland chapel, St. John's Wood, 1859–65. Author of at least 10 works. Edited *Eclectic Review* and *Free Church of England Magazine*. Secretary of the British and Foreign Sailors Society; founder of the Congregational Pastors' Retiring Fund. LL.D. and D.D. (Jefferson College), FSA.

Monthly Volume:

Life and Times of John de Wycliffe (vol. 71, Oct. 1851)

Sources: BBA, obituary in *Congregational Year Book*

Edward William Grinfield (1785–1864)
Anglican clergyman

Born in Bristol, son of a Moravian minister; studied at Oxford (B.A. 1806); ordained 1808; studied law. Minister at Laura Chapel, Bath 1820; preacher at Kensington; founded and endowed (£1,000) a lectureship on the Septuagint at Oxford 1859; died in Brighton. Married. Author of at least 26 works, including several polemical pamphlets.

Monthly Volume:

The Jesuits: An Historical Sketch (vol. 68, July 1851)

Source: DNB

Joseph Gurney (1804–79)
Baptist, parliamentary shorthand writer, RTS trustee

Born in London, son of a parliamentary shorthand writer; became parliamentary shorthand writer, 1822, succeeding to father's official position in 1849, retired 1872. Became committee member of RTS in 1829, trustee in 1845, and treasurer in 1875. Treasurer of Regent's Park Baptist College. Married (1) Emma Rawlings; (2) Harriet Tritton. Author of various works for RTS. Editor of RTS *Annotated Paragraph Bible*, 2 vols. (1850–60) and *Revised English Bible* (1877).

Sources: DNB, Boase

Thalia Susannah Henderson (b. post-1818, fl. 1853)
Congregational

Daughter of Ebeneezer Henderson (1784–1858), Congregational minister at Sheen Vale (had previously been missionary, and missionary tutor). Father was honorary secretary of RTS, and of British Society for Propagating the Gospel among the Jews.

Monthly Volume:

The Greek and Eastern Churches (vol. 87, Feb. 1853)

Source: none. Father is in DNB, and his memoir was written by TSH

William Mullinger Higgins (fl. 1833–68)
Science lecturer

Lecturer on experimental philosophy at Guy's Hospital. Author of at least 13 works on the sciences. FGS.

Monthly Volume:

James Watt and the Steam Engine (vol. 75, Feb. 1852)

Sources: BBA

William Jones (1795–1855)
RTS general secretary

Born Battersea; clerk to an attorney; attorney at law. Became itinerant Independent preacher, 1820; committee member of RTS, 1820. Corresponding secretary for RTS, 1823–55; general secretary, 1842. Married, 3 sons. Wrote numerous tracts for RTS.

Source: William Henry Jones, *Memorials of William Jones* (1857)

William Henry (Rich) Jones (1817–85)
Anglican clergyman

Born London, eldest son of William Jones (q.v.); studied at King's College, London and at Oxford (B.A. 1840). Curate of St. Andrew's Holborn, 1841; rector of St. Martin-in-the-Fields, 1842; incumbent of St. James's, Curtain Road, Shoreditch, 1845; vicar of Bradford-on-Avon, 1851 to death. Rural dean of Potternene, 1861–73; Canon of Salisbury (1873). Married (1) unknown; (2) Miss Rich, 4 children. Wrote on archaeology. FSA.

Monthly Volume:

The Life of Alfred the Great (vol. 46, Sept. 1849)

Source: DNB

John Kennedy (1813–1900)
Congregational minister

Born Aberfeldy, son of Congregational minister; studied at King's College, Aberdeen and Edinburgh University; trained for ministry at Glasgow Theological College. Pastor of Blackfriars, Aberdeen, 1836; minister at Stepney, 1846. Professor of apologetic theology, New College, 1871–76; retired to Hampstead 1882. Director of London Missionary Society from 1843, and of British and Foreign Schools Society from 1850; involved in Liberation Society, British and Foreign Bible Society, and Evangelical Alliance. Chairman of Congregational Union in 1872. Married Helen Blackie, 1846, 7 children. Author of at least 19 major works and numerous smaller ones for RTS (1850 until death). Edited *Christian Witness* and *Evangelical Magazine.*

Monthly Volumes:

The Jordan and the Dead Sea (vol. 55, June 1850)

Idumaea; With a Survey of Arabia and the Arabians (vol. 61, Dec. 1850)

Volcanoes: Their History, Phenomena, and Causes (vol. 74, Jan. 1852)

Sources: John Kennedy, *Old Highland Days* (1901)

John Kitto (1804–54)
Anglican writer

Born in Plymouth, son of a stonemason; apprenticed to father, 1814; became deaf after accident, 1817; in the workhouse, 1819–22; librarian to a private gentleman; involved with Plymouth Brethren. Trained at Church Missionary College to become missionary printer, 1825; posted to Malta, 1827. Engaged on private expedition to Persia, 1829–33. Returned to England, left Brethren. Editorial assistant to Charles Knight, 1833–41; then full-time writer. Moved variously from Islington, to Woking, to Camden Town in search of cheaper rents. Died in Cannstadt while taking the waters for his illness. Married Annabella Fenwick, 1833, 9 children. Author of at least 22 works, as well as many periodical articles. Founder editor of *Journal of Sacred Literature.* FSA, D.D. (Giessen).

Monthly Volumes:

Ancient Jerusalem (vol. 12, Nov. 1846)

Modern Jerusalem (vol. 15, Feb. 1847)

The Tahtar Tribes (vol. 36, Nov. 1848)

The Court of Persia (vol. 40, Mar. 1849)

The People of Persia (vol. 45, Aug. 1849)

Sources: DNB, DEB, John Edwards Ryland, *Memoirs of John Kitto* (1856); John Eadie, *Life of John Kitto* (1857)

William Freeman Lloyd (1791–1853)
Probably Anglican, RTS editor

Born in Gloucestershire, to pious parents. In some sort of commercial career in Oxford and London. Secretary of Sunday School Union from 1810. Joined committee of RTS, 1816, became editor 1825, retired 1847. Author of 5 major works and numerous small works for RTS and SSU. Editor of *Sunday-School Teachers' Magazine, Youth's Magazine*, the *Child's Companion*, and the *Weekly Visitor*.

Source: BBA

Benjamin Luckock (1792–1846)
Anglican missionary and clergyman

Ordained in London, 1821; missionary in West Indies, 1821–41; on his return, variously curate at Worcester, Lincoln, and London; assistant minister, St. Paul's Chapel, Lissom Grove, 1846. Twice married, at least 2 children. Author of a volume of sermons and a volume of poetry.

Monthly Volume:

Jamaica, Enslaved and Free (vol. 4, Mar. 1846)

Source: RLF archive

Samuel Manning (1822–81)
Baptist minister

Son of a mayor of Leicester, who became a Baptist; short business career in Liverpool; trained for ministry at Bristol Baptist College and Glasgow University, 1846. Minister at Sheppard's Barton, Frome, Somerset, 1846–61. Member of Baptist Missionary Society committee; book editor of RTS, 1863, and secretary 1876. Author of many volumes for RTS, including successful travel series. Originated *Boy's Own Paper*, edited *Baptist Magazine*. LL.D. (Chicago).

Monthly Volumes:

Life and Times of Charlemagne (vol. 78, May 1852)

Remarkable Escapes from Peril (vol. 90, May 1853)

Sources: DNB, DEB

William Charles Linnaeus Martin (1798–1864)
Anglican natural history writer

Born Burton-on-Trent, the son of a natural history illustrator; apprenticed to an apothecary. Superintendent of museum of Zoological Society of London, 1830–39. Thereafter, full-time writer, living in Hammersmith and Lewisham. Married Mary Jane Uppadine, 1825, no children. Author of at least 18 major works, 45 papers in the *Proceedings* of the Zoological Society, and a thousand periodical articles. Fellow of Linnean Society.

Monthly Volumes:

Our Song Birds (vol. 5, Apr. 1846)

Our Domestic Fowls (vol. 20, July 1847)

Comparisons of Structure in Animals: The Hand and the Arm (vol. 28, Mar. 1848)

British Fish and Fisheries (vol. 49, Dec. 1849)

The Senses and the Mind (vol. 51, Feb. 1850)

Wonders of Organic Life (vol. 79, June 1852)

Sources: DNB, RLF archive

James Goodeve Miall (1805–96)
Congregational minister

Born in Portsmouth, son of a schoolmaster; trained for ministry at Hoxton Academy, 1824–26. Minister at Framlingham, 1826; at St. Neots, 1832; at Salem Chapel, Manor Row, Bradford, 1837 until retirement in 1875. Served as chairman of Congregational Union, 1861. Married Miss Mackenzie ca. 1832, 7 children. Author of at least 8 volumes.

Monthly Volumes:

Life's Last Hours; or, The Final Testimony (vol. 44, July 1849)

Remarkable Delusions; or, Illustrations of Popular Errors (vol. 72, Nov. 1851)

The Inquisition (vol. 89, Apr. 1853)

Paris: Ancient and Modern (vol. 99, Mar. 1854)

Source: Boase

James Henry Millard (ca. 1825–after 1881)
Baptist minister

Trained for ministry at Stepney College and University College London; commenced ministry in 1845. Minister in Huntingdon, ca. 1849–54, later movements uncertain but became pastor of Maze Pond, Borough, London in 1858 and of Green Lane Chapel, Derby in 1880.

Monthly Volumes:

Life and Times of Leo X (vol. 54, May 1850)

Lives of the Popes, from the Rise of the Roman Church to the Age of Gregory VII (vol. 64, Mar. 1851)

Lives of the Popes, from the Age of Gregory VII to the Dawn of the Reformation (vol. 73, Dec. 1851)

Lives of the Popes, Part III (vol. 81, Aug. 1852)

Lives of the Popes, Part IV (vol. 85, Dec. 1852)

Source: *Baptist Handbook* entries

William Haig Miller (1812–91)
Banker

Employed at National and Provincial Bank from 1835, becoming head of the Advance Department, retired 1879. Lived in Islington. Joined RTS editorial department as part-time assistant in 1849. Was asked to become editor in December 1850, but declined in April 1851. Author of at least 8 major volumes, and others for the RTS. First editor of the *Leisure Hour*.

Monthly Volumes:

The French Revolution: Sketches of Its History (vol. 23, Oct. 1847)

Life of Napoleon Bonaparte (vol. 37, Dec. 1848)

Source: Boase

Thomas Milner (1808–83)
Congregational minister turned writer

Born in Derby; trained for ministry at Glasgow University (M.A.). Minister in Northampton, ca. 1826; retired due to ill-health, 1847. Thereafter, full-time writer on astronomy, geology, and geography, living in Norwood and then Brixton. Retired to Derby, in poor health, in 1877. Married (before 1833), 3 children. Author of at least 37 volumes, and numerous smaller works. Fellow of Royal Geographical Society.

Monthly Volumes:

The Life of Cyrus (vol. 16, Mar. 1847)

The Caves of the Earth: Their Natural History, Features, and Incidents (vol. 24, Nov. 1847)

Lives of Eminent Anglo-Saxons, Illustrating the Dawn of Christianity and Civilization in Great Britain, Part I (vol. 53, Apr. 1850)

Lives of Eminent Anglo-Saxons, Illustrating the Dawn of Christianity and Civilization in Great Britain, Part II (vol. 58, Sept. 1850)

Babylon, and the Banks of the Euphrates (vol. 62, Jan. 1851)

Nineveh and the Tigris (vol. 63, Feb. 1851)

Mines and Mining (vol. 66, May 1851)

Australia: Its Scenery, Natural History, and Resources; With a Glance at Its Gold Fields (vol. 93, Aug. 1853)

The Life of Alexander the Great (vol. 94, Sept. 1853)

Australia and Its Settlements (vol. 95, Oct. 1853)

Source: BBA

George ("Old Humphrey") Mogridge (1787–1854)
Evangelical writer

Born in Birmingham and apprenticed at the age of 14; began to contribute to periodicals in his twenties; became a full-time religious writer. Married. First wrote for RTS in 1814; over 150 works for the Society by his death, many written as "Old Humphrey"; wrote numerous other works, including nine as "Peter Parley."

Source: obituary in *Christian Spectator*

William Newnham (1790–1865)
Doctor (and phrenologist)

Born in Surrey, the son of a doctor; studied at Guy's Hospital and Paris; general practitioner in Farnham, Surrey, ca. 1811–56. Member of the British Medical Association and the Royal Society of Literature. Married (1) Unknown, 1812; (2) Caroline Atkinson, 1821, 6 surviving children. Apart from medical works, author of at least 10 volumes.

Monthly Volume:

Man, in His Physical, Intellectual, Social, and Moral Relations (vol. 14, Jan. 1847)

Source: DNB

William Lowndes Notcutt (d. before 1871)
Botanist

Born in Ipswich (grandfather had been a chemistry lecturer at Hackney College); lived variously in Fakenham, Daventry, and Cheltenham. Author of at least 4 volumes, and contributor to several larger botanical works.

Monthly Volumes:

The Geography of Plants (vol. 52, Mar. 1850)

The Palm Tribes and Their Varieties (vol. 77, Apr. 1852)

Source: BBA

John D. Owen (1788–1867)
Anglican clergyman

(Identification is uncertain—the following details are for a Reverend John Owen who lived in Leicester at the time that a Reverend J. D. Owen, of St. Mary's Leicester, wrote for the RTS.)

Born in Cardiganshire, the son of Calvinistic Methodist parents; trained at Ystrad Meurig; ordained (Anglican) 1812. Curate of Hirnant, Montgomeryshire 1811–13; unknown locations; vicar of Thrussington, Leicestershire, 1845. Rural dean, 1853.

Monthly Volume:

Schools of Ancient Philosophy (vol. 32, July 1848)

Source: DEB

Anne Pratt (1806–93)
Anglican, botanist and schoolteacher

Born in Chatham, daughter of a wholesale grocer; lived with parents until their deaths, mid-1840s; settled in Dover, 1849, as schoolteacher. Married John Pearless, 1866. Author of at least 17 works, and probably more for RTS and SPCK.

Monthly Volumes:

Wild Flowers of the Year (vol. 3, Feb. 1846)

Garden Flowers of the Year (vol. 17, Apr. 1847)

Plants and Trees of Scripture (vol. 47, Oct. 1849)

Sources: DNB, Margaret Graham, "A Life among the Flowers of Kent."

Edward Smith Pryce (fl. 1840–60)
Minister

Lived in Gravesend in 1850–52. Author of at least 4 works.

Monthly Volumes:

Ancient Egypt: Its Monuments and History (vol. 59, Oct. 1850)

Tyre: Its Rise, Glory and Desolation, with Notices of the Phoenicians Generally (vol. 80, July 1852)

Edited William Scoresby's (q.v.) *Account of the Arctic Regions and Northern Whale Fishery* (1820) into Monthly Volumes on:

The Arctic Regions: Their Situation, Appearances, Climate and Zoology (vol. 39, Feb. 1849)

The Northern Whale-Fishery (vol. 41, Apr. 1849)

John Allan Quinton (fl. 1848–58)
Possibly Baptist, RTS editorial assistant

A printer's compositor from Ipswich, who won an RTS essay competition for working men, on the topic of the Sabbath. Joined RTS editorial department in 1849, as assistant to J. H. Cross (q.v.). Was still working there in 1858.

Jonathan Edwards Ryland (1798–1866)
Baptist man of letters and translator

Born in Northampton, the son of a Baptist minister and college tutor; studied at Bristol Baptist College and Edinburgh University. Taught mathematics and classics at various locations in Leeds, Bradford, and Bristol, settled in Northampton in 1835. Married Frances Buxton, 1828. Translated scholarly works from German; wrote for periodicals; edited the *Eclectic Review*. M.A. (Brown University).

Wrote/translated Monthly Volumes on:

> *Life of Martin Boos, a Roman Catholic Clergyman in Germany* (vol. 26, Jan. 1848)

> *Life of John Kaspar Lavater* (vol. 43, June 1849)

Source: DNB

William Scoresby (1789–1857)
Whaler captain turned Anglican clergyman

Born in Whitby, the son of a whaler captain; served on whaling boats; studied at Edinburgh University in the winter months, 1806–09; whaler captain out of Whitby and Liverpool. Studied at Cambridge University (B.A. 1825); ordained. Curate of Bessingby, near Bridlington Quay, 1825; chaplain of Mariner's church, Liverpool, 1827; incumbent of Bedford chapel, Exeter, 1832; vicar of Bradford, 1839; retired in 1847 in poor health. Married (1) Miss Lockhart, 1811, 2 sons; (2) 1828; (3) 1849. Lived at Torquay. Carried out scientific researches on his whaling voyages and in later travels. Author of 6 major works, and around 90 other works. FRSE, FRS, Member of the French Institute.

His *Account of the Arctic Regions and Northern Whale Fishery* (1820) was turned (with his permission) into Monthly Volumes by Edward Smith Pryce (q.v.):

> *The Arctic Regions: Their Situation, Appearances, Climate and Zoology* (vol. 39, Feb. 1849)

> *The Northern Whale-Fishery* (vol. 41, Apr. 1849)

Sources: DNB, Robert Scoresby-Jackson, *Life of William Scoresby* (1861)

Edwin Sidney (ca. 1798–1872)
Anglican clergyman

Born in Gloucester; studied at Cambridge University (B.A. 1821); ordained. Curate of Acle, Norfolk, 1821–46; rector of Cornard Parva 1846–72; domestic chaplain to Viscount Hill, 1843–72. Twice select preacher at Cambridge; annual lecturer at the Royal Institution for 10 years; supporter of the Asylum for Idiots. Author of at least 11 works.

Monthly Volumes:

The Blights of the Wheat, and Their Remedies (vol. 11, Oct. 1846)

The Field and the Fold (vol. 98, Jan. 1854)

Source: DNB

George Smith (1803–70)
Congregational minister

Raised in Bristol; studied privately; preached in "Tent Missions" near Bristol, 1820; town-mission work in Liverpool, 1823. Ordained 1827. Minister of Heath Street Chapel, Liverpool, 1827; minister of new Tabernacle, Plymouth, 1833; of Trinity Chapel, Poplar, London, 1842. Director of London Missionary Society; secretary of Anti-Slavery Society, of Irish Evangelical Society, of Congregational Union, and honorary secretary to Christian Witness Fund. Also involved with British and Foreign Bible Society. Married, with children. Author of at least 4 works. D.D. (Glasgow).

Monthly Volume:

The Origin and Progress of Language (vol. 34, Sept. 1848)

Source: obituary in *Congregational Year Book*

Miss Stokes (probably Emily, but maybe Jane)
Daughter of George Stokes (q.v.)

Monthly Volume:

Sketches of the Waldenses (vol. 8, July 1846)

George Stokes (1789–1847)
Wealthy Anglican layman

Lived in Colchester, then Cheltenham. Joined RTS committee in 1818, became trustee in 1825. Worked voluntarily in RTS editorial department, as co-editor with W. F. Lloyd (q.v.). Retired in 1846. Married, at least 2 daughters. Wrote numerous works, of all lengths for the RTS, including a commentary on the Bible.

Source: memoir appended to RTS Report (1848)

John Stoughton (1807–97)
Congregational minister

Born in Norwich, the son of an admiral; worked in a lawyer's office; trained for the ministry at Highbury College, 1828. Co-pastor at Windsor, 1833; pastor at Hornston Street, Kensington, 1843–74. Professor of historical theology at New College, 1872–84; retired to Ealing, 1884. Involved with Evangelical Alliance, and served as chairman of Congregational Union in 1856. Married Miss Cooper, 1836, 4 surviving children. Author of at least 26 volumes, including several on the history of Congregationalism.

Monthly Volumes:

Glimpses of the Dark Ages; or, Sketches of the Social Condition of Europe, from the Fifth to the Twelfth Century (vol. 2, Jan. 1846)

The Dawn of Modern Civilization; or, Sketches of the Social Condition of Europe, from the Twelfth to the Sixteenth Century (vol. 18, May 1847)

Our English Bible (vol. 35, Oct. 1848)

London in the Olden Time; or, Sketches of the Great Metropolis, from Its Origin to the End of the Sixteenth Century (vol. 60, Nov. 1850)

London in Modern Times; or, Sketches of the Great Metropolis during the Last Two Centuries (vol. 65, Apr. 1851)

Venice: Past and Present (vol. 88, Mar. 1853)

Switzerland: Historical and Descriptive (vol. 91, June 1853)

Sources: DNB, John Stoughton, *Recollections of a Long Life* (1894); Georgina K. Lewis, *John Stoughton* (1898)

William Hendry Stowell (1800–58)
Congregational minister

Born on the Isle of Man; studied at Blackburn Academy. Minister at North Shields, 1821–34; pastor of Congregational church at Masborough, 1834–49. Principal of the Rotherham Independent College, 1834–50; president of Cheshunt College, 1850–56; died London. Involved with Evangelical Alliance. Married Sarah Hilton, 1821, children. Author of at least 11 works; editor of the *Eclectic Review.*

Monthly Volumes:

The Life of Julius Caesar (vol. 1, Dec. 1845)

The Life of Mohammed (vol. 22, Sept. 1847)

The Life of Sir Isaac Newton (vol. 69, Aug. 1851)

Sources: DNB, DEB, William Stowell, *Life and Labours of William Hendry Stowell* (1859)

Charles Tomlinson (1808–97)
Anglican, science writer

Raised in Salisbury; became clerk, later teacher; attended some lectures at the London Mechanics' Institute; began to write on science, especially for SPCK; moved to London, 1842, to write. Appointed lecturer in experimental science at King's College. In retirement, became a noted Dante scholar. Married Sarah Windsor, ca. 1834. Contributed to periodicals, and author of at least 23 works. FRS, Fellow of the Chemical Society, on the council of the British Association for the Advancement of Science.

Monthly Volume:

The British Nation: Its Arts and Manufactures (vol. 70, Sept. 1851)

Source: Mary Tomlinson, *Life of Charles Tomlinson* (1900)

William Urwick (1791–1868)
Congregational minister

Born in Shrewsbury; trained for ministry at Hoxton Academy, 1812. Pastor at Sligo, 1816; at York Street chapel, Dublin, 1826. Professor of dogmatic and pastoral theology, Dublin Theological Institute, 1832–52. Secretary to the Irish Congregational Union. Involved in the Irish Home Mission, the Dublin City Mission, the British and Foreign Bible Society, and the Evangelical Alliance. Married Sarah Cooke, 1818, 5 surviving children. Author of at least 14 major works, and at least 13 others. D.D. (Dartmouth College).

Monthly Volume:

Dublin (vol. 82, Sept. 1852)

Sources: DNB, William Urwick, *Life and Letters of William Urwick* (1870)

Alfred Westwood
RTS writer

A friend of RTS committee member Dr. Bull. Westwood was not a doctor or a minister.

Monthly Volume:

Good Health: The Possibility, Duty and Means of Obtaining and Keeping It (vol. 56, July 1850)

James Whitehorne (fl. 1845–62)
RTS editorial assistant

Member of RTS committee, who became editorial assistant to W. F. Lloyd (q.v.) in 1845. General editor, 1853–62.

Dr. Wilkinson
Doctor

A doctor from Islington. Possibly James John Garth Wilkinson (1812–99), yet he was a homeopathic doctor and a Swedenborgian.

Monthly Volume:

> *Eminent Medical Men* (vol. 25, Dec. 1847)

Charles Williams (1796–1866)
Congregational minister, turned RTS editor

Born in London, the son of an engine factory foreman; worked with father, then became bookseller's assistant in Piccadilly, rising to manager. Trained for the ministry at Hoxton Academy; minister at Newark upon Trent; at Salisbury, 1833. Moved to London, 1835; became RTS editorial assistant, 1838; dismissed, 1850. Returned to ministry, in St. John's Wood; then pastor at Sibbertoft, Northamptonshire, till death. Married Miss Smeeton, ca. 1827, at least 2 children. Author of at least 75 works, mostly for RTS.

Monthly Volumes:

> *Magic, Pretended Miracles, and Remarkable Natural Phenomena* (vol. 30, May 1848)
>
> *Characters, Scenes, and Incidents of the Reformation, from the Rise of the Culdees to the Times of Luther* (vol. 48, Nov. 1849)
>
> *Characters, Scenes, and Incidents of the Reformation, from the Times of Luther to the Close of the Sixteenth Century* (vol. 50, Jan. 1850)
>
> *Caxton, and the Art of Printing* (vol. 83, Oct. 1852)

Sources: DNB, obituary in *Congregational Year Book*

Daniel Wilson (1816–92)
Baptist, later Anglican, antiquary

Born in Edinburgh, son of a wine merchant; studied briefly at Edinburgh University; tried to make literary career in London; returned to Edinburgh, 1842, and concentrated on archaeology. Professor of history and English literature at Toronto University, 1853, and president of the university, 1881. Secretary to Society of Scottish Antiquaries, 1845; served as president of Canadian Institute, 1859 and 1860. Married Margaret Mackay, 1840, 1 child. Author of at least 11 volumes, as well as learned papers. Knighted 1888.

Monthly Volumes:

> *Old Edinburgh* (vol. 86, Jan. 1853)
>
> *Modern Edinburgh* (vol. 97, Dec. 1853)

Sources: DNB, DEB

Appendix B

Volumes of the "Monthly Series"

When published, the volumes were undated and almost all anonymous. The Monthly List of Publications, which survives, with annotations, in the RTS archive makes it possible to identify publication dates and writers. What follows is based on this listing. Text in parentheses indicates a transcription of the writer's name as annotated on the listing. Works where the author was identified on the original are denoted by an asterisk.

Dec. 1845   1. *The Life of Julius Caesar* (Rev. W. H. Stowell, Rotherham, York)

Jan. 1846   2. *Glimpses of the Dark Ages; or, Sketches of the Social Condition of Europe, from the Fifth to the Twelfth Century* (Rev. J. Stoughton, Kensington)

Feb. 1846   3. *Wild Flowers of the Year* (Miss Pratt, Chatham)

Mar. 1846   4. *Jamaica, Enslaved and Free* (the late Rev. B. Luckock, Blanford Square)

Apr. 1846   5. *Our Song Birds* (Mr. Martin, Hammersmith)

May 1846   6. *Solar System, Part I* (Thomas Dick, LL.D., Broughty Ferry, near Dundee)

June 1846   7. *The Task, and Other Poems* by William Cowper, Esq.*

July 1846   8. *Sketches of the Waldenses* (Miss Stokes)

Aug. 1846   9. *Solar System, Part II* (Dr. Dick, Broughty Ferry)

Sept. 1846 10. *The Life of Luther* (Rev. J. E. Cox, Oliver's Terrace, Mile End)

Oct. 1846   11. *The Blights of the Wheat, and Their Remedies* (Rev. E. Sidney, Acle, Norwich)

Nov. 1846   12. *Ancient Jerusalem* (Dr. Kitto, Woking)

Dec. 1846   13. *Philosophy of the Plan of Salvation* by an American Citizen* [viz., James Barr Walker]

Jan. 1847   14. *Man, in His Physical, Intellectual, Social, and Moral Relations* by W. Newnham, Esq.* (of Farnham, Surrey)

Feb. 1847   15. *Modern Jerusalem* (Dr. Kitto, Woking)

Mar. 1847   16. *The Life of Cyrus* (Rev. T. Milner, Northampton)

Apr. 1847   17. *Garden Flowers of the Year* (Miss Pratt, Chatham)

May 1847   18. *The Dawn of Modern Civilization; or, Sketches of the Social Condition of Europe, from the Twelfth to the Sixteenth Century* (Rev. J. Stoughton, Kensington)

June 1847   19. *Life of Lady Russell* (Mrs. Copley, Eythorne)

July 1847   20. *Our Domestic Fowls* (Mr. W. Martin, Zoological Society)

Aug. 1847   21. *Truth, and Other Poems* by Wm. Cowper, Esq.*

Sept. 1847   22. *The Life Of Mohammed* (Rev. W. H. Stowell, Rotherham)

Oct. 1847   23. *The French Revolution: Sketches of Its History* (Mr. W. H. Miller, Islington)

Nov. 1847   24. *The Caves of the Earth: Their Natural History, Features, and Incidents* (Rev. T. Milner, Northampton)

Dec. 1847   25. *Eminent Medical Men* (Dr. Wilkinson, Islington)

Jan. 1848   26. *Life of Martin Boos, a Roman Catholic Clergyman in Germany* (translated by Mr. Ryland, Northampton)

Feb. 1848   27. *Self-Improvement* (from Todd's Student's Guide) [viz. John Todd, *The Student's Manual: designed, by specific directions, to aid in forming the intellectual and moral character and habits of the student* (1835)]

Mar. 1848   28. *Comparisons of Structure in Animals: The Hand and the Arm* (Mr. Martin, Hammersmith)

Apr. 1848   29. *History of Protestantism in France to the Reign of Charles IX* (Miss Bunbury, Faulkner St., Liverpool)

May 1848   30. *Magic, Pretended Miracles, and Remarkable Natural Phenomena* (Rev. C. Williams)

June 1848   31. *The Atmosphere, and Atmospheric Phenomena* (Dr. Thomas Dick, Broughty Ferry, near Dundee)

July 1848   32. *Schools of Ancient Philosophy* (Rev. J. Owen, Vicarage of St. Mary's, Leicester)

Aug. 1848   33. *The Life of Cranmer, the First Protestant Archbishop of Canterbury* (Rev. J. E. Cox)

Sept. 1848   34. *The Origin and Progress of Language* (Rev. G. Smith, Poplar)

Oct. 1848   35. *Our English Bible* (Rev. J. Stoughton, Kensington)

Nov. 1848   36. *The Tahtar Tribes* (Dr. Kitto, Woking)

Dec. 1848   37. *Life of Napoleon Bonaparte* (Mr. W. H. Miller, Islington)

Jan. 1849   38. *The History of Protestantism in France, from the End of the Reign of Charles IX to the Revocation of the Edict of Nantes* (Miss S. Bunbury, Liverpool)

Feb. 1849   39. *The Arctic Regions: Their Situation, Appearances, Climate and Zoology* by Captain Scoresby FRSE* (condensed by Rev. S. Pryce, Gravesend)

Mar. 1849   40. *The Court of Persia* by J. Kitto, D.D.*

Apr. 1849   41. *The Northern Whale-Fishery* by Captain (now Rev. Dr.) Scoresby FRSE* (prepared by Rev. S. Pryce, Gravesend)

May 1849   42. *The Crusades* (Rev. D. J. East, Waltham Abbey)

June 1849	43. *Life of John Kaspar Lavater* (translated from several works by Mr. Ryland, Northampton)
July 1849	44. *Life's Last Hours; or, The Final Testimony* (Rev. J. G. Miall, Bradford, York)
Aug. 1849	45. *The People of Persia* by J. Kitto, D.D., FSA*
Sept. 1849	46. *The Life of Alfred the Great* (Rev. W. H. Jones, Hoxton Square)
Oct. 1849	47. *Plants and Trees of Scripture* (Miss Pratt, Dover, Castle House Academy)
Nov. 1849	48. *Characters, Scenes, and Incidents of the Reformation, from the Rise of the Culdees to the Times of Luther* (Rev. C. Williams)
Dec. 1849	49. *British Fish and Fisheries* (Mr. Martin, Hammersmith)
Jan. 1850	50. *Characters, Scenes, and Incidents of the Reformation, from the Times of Luther to the Close of the Sixteenth Century* (Rev. C. Williams)
Feb. 1850	51. *The Senses and the Mind* (Mr. Martin, Lewisham, late of Hammersmith)
Mar. 1850	52. *The Geography of Plants* (Mr. Notcutt, Fakenham)
Apr. 1850	53. *Lives of Eminent Anglo-Saxons, Illustrating the Dawn of Christianity and Civilization in Great Britain, Part I* (Rev. T. Milner, Norwood)
May 1850	54. *Life and Times of Leo X* (Rev. J. H. Millard, Huntingdon)
June 1850	55. *The Jordan and the Dead Sea* (Rev. J. Kennedy, Stepney)
July 1850	56. *Good Health: The Possibility, Duty and Means of Obtaining and Keeping It* (Alfred Westwood, Esq., through Dr. Bull [an RTS committee member])
Aug. 1850	57. *Iona* by the Rev. Dr. W. Lindsay Alexander, D.D., Fellow of The Society of Scottish Antiquaries* (Edinburgh)
Sept. 1850	58. *Lives of Eminent Anglo-Saxons, Illustrating the Dawn of Christianity and Civilization in Great Britain, Part II* (Rev. T. Milner)
Oct. 1850	59. *Ancient Egypt: Its Monuments and History* (Rev. S. Pryce, Gravesend)
Nov. 1850	60. *London in the Olden Time; or, Sketches of the Great Metropolis, from Its Origin to the End of the Sixteenth Century* (Rev. J. Stoughton, Kensington)
Dec. 1850	61. *Idumaea; With a Survey of Arabia and the Arabians* (Rev. J. Kennedy, Stepney)
Jan. 1851	62. *Babylon, and the Banks of the Euphrates* (Rev. T. Milner, Norwood)
Feb. 1851	63. *Nineveh and the Tigris* (Rev. T. Milner, Norwood)
Mar. 1851	64. *Lives of the Popes, from the Rise of the Roman Church to the Age of Gregory VII* (Rev. J. H. Millard, Huntingdon)
Apr. 1851	65. *London in Modern Times; or, Sketches of the Great Metropolis during the Last Two Centuries* (Rev. J. Stoughton, Kensington)
May 1851	66. *Mines and Mining* (Rev. T. Milner, Norwood)
June 1851	67. *The Telescope and Microscope* (Dr. Dick, Broughty Ferry)
July 1851	68. *The Jesuits: An Historical Sketch* (Rev. E. Grinfield, Brighton)
Aug. 1851	69. *The Life of Sir Isaac Newton* (Rev. Dr. Stowell, Cheshunt)

Sept. 1851 70. *The British Nation: Its Arts and Manufactures* (Mr. C. Tomlinson, 12 Bedford Place, Hampstead Rd)

Oct. 1851 71. *Life and Times of John De Wycliffe* (Rev. Dr. Ferguson, Ryde)

Nov. 1851 72. *Remarkable Delusions; or, Illustrations of Popular Errors* (Rev. J. Miall, Bradford)

Dec. 1851 73. *Lives of the Popes, from the Age of Gregory VII to the Dawn of the Reformation* (Rev. J. H. Millard, Huntingdon)

Jan. 1852 74. *Volcanoes: Their History, Phenomena, and Causes* (Rev. J. Kennedy, Stepney)

Feb. 1852 75. *James Watt and the Steam Engine* (Mr. Higgins, Cheshunt)

Mar. 1852 76. *The Ancient British Church: Being an Inquiry into the History of Christianity in Britain Previous to the Establishment of the Heptarchy* by William Lindsay Alexander, D.D. FSSA* (Edinburgh)

Apr. 1852 77. *The Palm Tribes and Their Varieties* (Mr. Notcutt, Fakenham)

May 1852 78. *Life and Times of Charlemagne* (Rev. S. Manning, Frome)

June 1852 79. *Wonders of Organic Life* (Mr. W. Martin, Lewisham Rd., Greenwich)

July 1852 80. *Tyre: Its Rise, Glory and Desolation, with Notices of the Phoenicians Generally* (Rev S. Pryce, Gravesend)

Aug. 1852 81. *Lives of the Popes, Part III* (Rev. J. H. Millard, Huntingdon)

Sept. 1852 82. *Dublin* (Rev. Dr. Urwick, Dublin)

Oct. 1852 83. *Caxton, and the Art of Printing* (Rev. C. Williams, St. John's Wood)

Nov. 1852 84. *Money: A Popular Treatise on Its Nature, History and Uses* (Rev. H. Dunckley, Salford)

Dec. 1852 85. *Lives of the Popes, Part IV* (Rev. J. H. Millard, Huntingdon)

Jan. 1853 86. *Old Edinburgh* (Mr. D. Wilson, 12 Graham St., Edinburgh)

Feb. 1853 87. *The Greek and Eastern Churches* (Miss Henderson, East Sheen, late of Highbury)

Mar. 1853 88. *Venice: Past and Present* (Rev. J. Stoughton, Kensington)

Apr. 1853 89. *The Inquisition* (Rev. J. G. Miall, Bradford, York)

May 1853 90. *Remarkable Escapes from Peril* (Rev. S. Manning, Frome)

June 1853 91. *Switzerland: Historical and Descriptive* (Rev. J. Stoughton, Kensington)

July 1853 92. *The Bible in Many Tongues* (Rev. Dr. Angus, Stepney College)

Aug. 1853 93. *Australia: Its Scenery, Natural History, and Resources; With a Glance at Its Gold Fields* (Rev. T. Milner)

Sept. 1853 94. *The Life of Alexander the Great* (Rev. T. Milner)

Oct. 1853 95. *Australia and Its Settlements* (Rev. T. Milner)

Nov. 1853 96. *Successful Men of Modern Times* (Rev. H. Dunckley, Pendleton)

Dec. 1853 97. *Modern Edinburgh* (Mr. D. Wilson, 12 Graham St., Edinburgh)

Jan. 1854 98. *The Field and the Fold* (Rev. E. Sidney, Cornard, Suffolk)

Mar. 1854 99. *Paris: Ancient and Modern* (Rev. J. Miall, Bradford)

Aug. 1855 100. *The Life of Calvin* (Rev. C. D. Bell, Hampstead)

REFERENCES

Adams, Thomas, and Nicholas Barker. "A New Model for the Study of the Book." In *A Potencie of Books: Books in Society,* edited by Nicholas Barker, 5–43. London, 1993.

Allen, David. *The Naturalist in Britain.* Harmondsworth, 1978.

———. "Tastes and Crazes." In *Cultures of Natural History,* edited by Nicholas Jardine, James A. Secord, and Emma Spary, 394–407. Cambridge, 1996.

Altick, Richard D. *The English Common Reader: A Social History of the Mass Reading Public, 1800–1900.* Chicago, 1957.

———. "From Aldine to Everyman: Cheap Reprint Series of the English Classics, 1830–1906." *Studies in Bibliography* 11 (1958): 3–25.

———. "Nineteenth-Century Bestsellers: A Third List." *Studies in Bibliography* 39 (1986): 235–41.

Amory, Hugh. "De Facto Copyright?: Fielding's 'Works' in Partnership, 1769–1821." *Eighteenth-Century Studies* 17 (1984): 449–76.

Anderson, Patricia. *The Printed Image and the Transformation of Popular Culture 1790–1860.* Oxford, 1991.

Astore, William J. "Observing God: Thomas Dick (1774–1857), Evangelicalism and Popular Science in Victorian Britain and Antebellum America." D. Phil. diss., University of Oxford, 1995.

———. *Observing God: Thomas Dick, Evangelicalism, and Popular Science in Victorian Britain and America.* Aldershot, 2001.

Augustine. *The City of God against the Pagans.* Loeb ed., 1965.

"Authors and Publishers." *New Quarterly Review* 3 (1854): 9–17, 143–50.

"The Authors of Calamities." *Chambers's Edinburgh Journal* (27 February 1847): 129–31.

Barnes, James J. *Authors, Publishers and Politicians: The Quest for an Anglo-American Copyright Agreement.* London, 1974.

[Barth, C. G.] *Scripture Natural History; Containing a Description of Quadrupeds, Birds, Reptiles, Amphibia, Fishes, Insects, Molluscous Animals, Corals, Plants, Trees, Precious Stones and Metals, Mentioned in the Holy Scriptures.* Translated by John Ryland and William Martin. London, 1843.

Battiscombe, Georgina. *Shaftesbury: A Biography of the Seventh Earl, 1801–85.* London, 1974.

Bebbington, David W. *Evangelicalism in Modern Britain: A History from the 1730s to the 1980s.* London, 1989.

———. "Science and Evangelical Theology in Britain from Wesley to Orr." In *Evangelicals and Science in Historical Perspective,* edited by David N. Livingstone, D. G. Hart, and Mark A. Noll, 120–41. Oxford, 1999.

Beer, Gillian. *Darwin's Plots: The Evolutionary Narrative in Darwin, George Eliot and Nineteenth-Century Fiction.* London, 1983.

Ben-David, Joseph. *The Scientist's Role in Society: A Comparative Study.* London, 1984.

Bennett, Scott. "John Murray's Family Library and the Cheapening of Books in Early Nineteenth-Century Britain." *Studies in Bibliography* 29 (1976): 139–66.

———. "Revolutions in Thought: Serial Publication and the Mass Market for Reading." In *The Victorian Periodical Press,* edited by J. Shattock and M. Wolff, 225–57. Leicester, 1982.

Bickersteth, Edward. *Domestic Portraiture; or, The Successful Application of Religious Principle in the Education of a Family, Exemplified in the Memoirs of Three of the Deceased Children of the Rev Legh Richmond, with Introductory Remarks.* 6th ed. London, 1843.

Binney, Thomas. "Authorship." *Exeter Hall Lectures on Behalf of the YMCA,* vol. 9. London, 1854.

Bonham-Carter, Victor. *Authors by Profession.* London, 1978.

"Booksellers." *Chambers's Edinburgh Journal* (6 February 1847): 88.

Bowler, Peter J. *The Invention of Progress: The Victorians and the Past.* Oxford, 1989.

Brent, Richard. *Liberal Anglican Politics: Whiggery, Religion and Reform, 1830–1841.* Oxford, 1987.

Brewer, John. *The Pleasures of the Imagination: English Culture in the Eighteenth Century.* London, 1997.

Brief Observations on the Political and Religious Sentiments of the Late Rev Dr Arnold, as Contained in His Life by the Rev Arthur Penrhyn Stanley, Extracted from the Record Newspaper. London, 1845.

Brock, William H. "Brewster as Scientific Journalist." In *"Martyr of Science": Sir David Brewster, 1781–1863; Proceedings of a Bicentennial Symposium,* edited by Alison Morison-Low and John R. R. Christie, 37–44. Edinburgh, 1984.

Brooke, John Hedley. "Natural Theology and the Plurality of Worlds: Observations on the Brewster–Whewell Debate." *Annals of Science* 34 (1977): 221–86.

———. "The Natural Theology of the Geologists." In *Images of the Earth,* edited by Ludmilla Jordanova and Roy Porter, 39–64. Chalfont St. Giles, 1979.

———. *Science and Religion: Some Historical Perspectives.* Cambridge, 1991.

Brooke, John Hedley, and Geoffrey Cantor. *Reconstructing Nature: The Engagement of Science and Religion.* Edinburgh, 1998.

Brooke, John Hedley, and R. Hooykaas. *New Interactions between Theology and Natural Science: Natural Theology in Britain from Boyle to Paley.* Milton Keynes, 1974.

Brougham, Henry. *A Discourse of Natural Theology, Showing the Nature of the Evidence and the Advantage of the Study.* London, 1845.

Brown, Kenneth. *A Social History of the Nonconformist Ministry in England, 1800–1930.* Oxford, 1988.

Brown, P. A. H. *London Publishers and Printers c. 1800–1870.* London, 1982.

Bunbury, Selina. *My First Travels: Including Rides in the Pyrenees, Scenes during an Inundation at Avignon, Sketches in France and Savoy, Visits to Convents and Houses of Charity, etc. etc.* 2 vols. London, 1859.

Burkhardt, F., and S. Smith, eds. *The Correspondence of Charles Darwin.* 13 vols. Cambridge, 1985–2002.

Cantor, Geoffrey N. "Reading the Book of Nature: The Relation between Faraday's Religion and His Science." In *Faraday Rediscovered: Essays on the Life and Work of Michael Faraday, 1791–1867,* edited by David Gooding and Frank A. J. L. James, 69–81. Basingstoke, 1985.

Cardwell, D. S. L. *The Organisation of Science in England.* London, 1972.

Carpenter, William. *Scripture Natural History; or, A Descriptive Account of the Zoology, Botany and Geology of the Bible.* London, 1828.

Carpenter, William B. *Zoology: A Systematic Account of the General Structure, Habits, Instincts and Uses of the Principal Families of the Animal Kingdom, as Well as of the Chief Forms of Fossil Remains.* 2 vols. Edinburgh, 1842.

Chadwick, Owen. *The Secularization of the European Mind in the Nineteenth Century.* Cambridge, 1975.

Chambers, Robert. *Vestiges of the Natural History of Creation, and Other Evolutionary Writings.* Edited by James A. Secord. Chicago, 1994.

Chambers, William. *Memoir of Robert Chambers with Autobiographical Reminiscences.* New York, 1872.

Chapman, John W. "The Commerce of Literature." *Westminster Review* n.s. 1 (1852): 511–54.

"Cheap Literature." *British Quarterly Review* 29 (1859): 313–45.

Clarke, William K. L. *A History of the SPCK.* London, 1959.

Clement, Mark. "Sifting Science: Methodism and Natural Knowledge in Britain 1815–70." D. Phil. diss., University of Oxford, 1996.

Cooney, Sondra Miley. "Publishers for the People: W. & R. Chambers—The Early Years, 1832–50." Ph.D. diss., Ohio State University, 1970.

Cooter, Roger. *The Cultural Meaning of Popular Science: Phrenology and the Organization of Consent in Nineteenth-Century Britain.* Cambridge, 1984.

Cox, Jack. *Take a Cold Tub, Sir!: The Story of the* Boy's Own Paper. Guildford, 1982.

Cross, Nigel. *The Royal Literary Fund 1790–1918: An Introduction to the Fund's History and Archives, with an Index of Applicants.* London, 1984.

———. *The Common Writer: Life in Nineteenth-Century Grub Street.* Cambridge, 1985.

Cruikshank, George. *The Comick Almanack: An Ephemeris in Jest and Earnest, Containing Merry Tales, Humorous Poetry, Quips and Oddities.* 2 vols. London, 1870.

Curran, James, and Jean Seaton. *Power without Responsibility: The Press and Broadcasting in Britain.* 4th ed. London, 1991.

Curwen, Henry. *A History of Booksellers, the Old and the New.* London, 1873.

Darnton, Robert. "Philosophers Trim the Tree of Knowledge." In *The Great Cat Massacre and Other Episodes in French Cultural History,* edited by Robert Darnton, 185–207. New York, 1985.

———. "What Is the History of Books?" In *The Kiss of Lamourette,* edited by Robert Darnton. London, 1990.

Darton, F. J. Harvey. *Children's Books in England: Five Centuries of Social Life.* 3rd ed. Edited by Brian Alderson. Cambridge, 1982.

Daunton, Martin. *Progress and Poverty: An Economic and Social History of Britain, 1700–1850.* Oxford, 1995.

Davidoff, L., and C. Hall. *Family Fortunes: Men and Women of the English Middle Class, 1780–1850.* London, 1987.

Desmond, Adrian. "Artisan Resistance and Evolution in Britain 1819–1848." *Osiris* n.s. 3 (1987): 72–110.

———. *Huxley: The Devil's Disciple.* London, 1994.

———. *Huxley: Evolution's High Priest.* London, 1997.

Desmond, Adrian, and James Moore. *Darwin.* London, 1991.

[Dick, Thomas]. *The Atmosphere, and Atmospheric Phenomena.* London, 1848.

Dooley, Allan C. *Author and Printer in Victorian England.* Charlottesville, 1992.

[Dunckley, Henry]. *Money: A Popular Treatise on Its Nature, History, and Uses.* London, 1852.

Eadie, John. *Life of John Kitto, D.D., FSA.* Edinburgh, 1857.

Eagleton, Terry. *Literary Theory: An Introduction.* Oxford, 1983.

Eliot, Simon. *Some Patterns and Trends in British Publishing, 1800–1919.* London, 1994.

———. "Some Trends in British Book Production, 1800–1919." In *Literature in the Market Place: Nineteenth-Century British Publishing and Reading Practices,* edited by John O. Jordan and Robert L. Patten, 19–43. Cambridge, 1995.

———. "*Patterns and Trends* and the *NSTC*: Some Initial Observations, Part I." *Publishing History* 42 (1997): 79–104.

———. "*Patterns and Trends* and the *NSTC*: Some Initial Observations, Part II." *Publishing History* 43 (1998): 71–112.

Erickson, Lee. *The Economy of Literary Form: English Literature and the Industrialisation of Publishing, 1800–1850.* Baltimore, 1996.

Feather, John. "The Publishers and the Pirates: British Copyright-Law in Theory and Practice, 1710–1775." *Publishing History* 22 (1987): 5–32.

———. *A History of British Publishing.* London, 1988.

———. *Publishing, Piracy and Politics.* London, 1995.

Fish, Stanley. *Is There a Text in This Class? The Authority of Interpretive Communities.* London, 1980.

Fison, Margaret (Mrs. William). *Colportage: Its History and Relation to Home and Foreign Evangelisation.* London, 1859.

Forrester, Wendy. *Great-Grandmama's Weekly: A Celebration of the "Girl's Own Paper," 1880–1901.* Guildford, 1980.

Frasca-Spada, Marina, and Nicholas Jardine, eds. *Books and the Sciences in History.* Cambridge, 2000.

Fyfe, Aileen. "The Reception of William Paley's *Natural Theology* in the University of Cambridge." *British Journal for the History of Science* 30 (1997): 321–35.

———. "Copyrights and Competition: Producing and Protecting Children's Books in the Nineteenth Century." *Publishing History* 45 (1999): 35–59.

———. "Industrialised Conversion: The Religious Tract Society and the Development of Popular Science Publishing in Victorian Britain." Ph.D. diss., University of Cambridge, 2000.

———. "Publishing and the Classics: Paley's *Natural Theology* and the Nineteenth-Century Scientific Canon." *Studies in History and Philosophy of the Sciences* 33 (2002): 733–55.

———. Introduction to [Charles Williams], *Wonders of the Waters* [1842]. Bristol, 2003.

———. "Periodicals and Book Series: Complementary Aspects of a Publisher's Mission." In *Culture and Science in the Nineteenth-Century Media,* edited by Louise Henson, Geoffrey Cantor, and Sally Shuttleworth. Aldershot, 2004.

Garnett, E. Jane. " 'Gold and the Gospel': Systematic Beneficence in the Mid-Nineteenth Century." In *The Church and Wealth,* edited by W. J. Sheils and D. Wood, 347–58. Oxford, 1987.

———. "Evangelicalism and Business in Mid-Victorian Britain." In *Evangelical Faith and Public Zeal: Evangelicals and Society in Britain, 1780–1980,* edited by John Wolffe, 59–80. London, 1995.

Gaskell, Philip. *A New Introduction to Bibliography.* Oxford, 1972.

Gillespie, N. C. "Divine Design and the Industrial Revolution: William Paley's Abortive Reform of Natural Theology." *Isis* 81 (1990): 214–29.

Glendinning, Victoria. *Trollope.* London, 1992.

Gordon, Mrs. *The Life and Correspondence of William Buckland, D.D. FRS.* London, 1894.

Gosse, Edmund. *Father and Son: A Study of Two Temperaments* [1907]. Edited by A. O. J. Cockshut. Keele, 1994.

Gosse, Philip H. *Natural History: Fishes.* London, 1851.

Graham, Margaret. "A Life among the Flowers of Kent." *Country Life* 161 (1972): 1500.

Green, Ian. *Print and Protestantism in Early Modern England.* New York, 2000.

Green, Samuel G. *The Story of the Religious Tract Society for One Hundred Years.* London, 1899.

Griffin, Robert J. "Anonymity and Authorship." *New Literary History* 30 (1999): 877–95.

Griffin, Robert J., ed. *The Faces of Anonymity: Anonymous and Pseudonymous Publication from the Sixteenth to the Twentieth Century.* London, 2003.

Guy, William A. "On the Duration of Life as Affected by the Pursuits of Literature, Science and Art: With a Summary View of the Duration of Life among the Upper and Middle Classes of Society." *Journal of the Statistical Society* 22 (1859): 337–61.

Haines, Sheila R. "Am I My Brother's Keeper? Victorian Tract Societies and Their Work, 1840–1875." D.Phil. diss., Sussex University, 1979.

Harding, Anthony J. *Coleridge and the Inspired Word.* Montreal, 1985.

Hempton, D. A. *Religion and Political Culture in Britain and Ireland.* Cambridge, 1996.

Hewitt, Gordon. *Let the People Read: A Short History of the United Society for Christian Literature.* London, 1949.

[Higgins, William Mullinger]. *James Watt and the Steam Engine.* London, 1852.

Hilton, Boyd. *The Age of Atonement: The Influence of Evangelicalism on Social and Economic Thought, 1795–1865.* Oxford, 1988.

Hindley, Diana, and Geoffrey Hindley. *Advertising in Victorian Britain, 1837–1901.* London, 1972.

Hinton, D. A. "Popular Science in England, 1830–1870." Ph.D. diss., Bath University, 1979.

Howsam, Leslie. *Cheap Bibles: Nineteenth-Century Publishing and the British and Foreign Bible Society.* Cambridge, 1991.

Jackson, M. V. *Engines of Instruction, Mischief and Magic: Children's Literature in England from Its Beginnings to 1839.* Aldershot, 1989.

Jacyna, L. S. "Immanence and Transcendence: Theories of Life and Organisation in Britain, 1790–1835." *Isis* 74 (1983): 311–29.

James, Frank A. J. L., ed. *The Correspondence of Michael Faraday.* 4 vols. London, 1991–.

Jauss, Hans Robert. *Toward an Aesthetic of Reception.* Translated by Timothy Bahti. Minneapolis, 1982.

Jenyns, Leonard. *The Zoology of the Voyage of HMS* Beagle, *under the Command of Captain Fitzroy, RN, During the Years 1832 to 1836. Published with the Approval of the Lords Commissioners of Her Majesty's Treasury. Edited and Superintended by Charles Darwin. Part IV. Fish.* London, 1842.

Jeremy, David J., ed. *Business and Religion in Britain.* Aldershot, 1988.

Johns, Adrian. *The Nature of the Book: Print and Knowledge in the Making.* Chicago, 1998.

Jones, M. G. *Hannah More.* Cambridge, 1952.

Jones, William. *The Jubilee Memorial of the Religious Tract Society: Containing a Record of Its Origin, Proceedings, and Results. AD 1799 to AD 1849.* London, 1850.

Jones, William Henry. *Memorials of William Jones of the Religious Tract Society, Compiled from His Private Papers and Other Authentic Documents.* London, 1857.

Jordan, John O., and Robert L. Patten, eds. *Literature in the Market Place: Nineteenth-Century British Publishing and Reading Practices.* Cambridge, 1995.

[Kaye, J. W.] "Pendennis: The Literary Profession." *North British Review* 13 (1850): 335–72.

Kennedy, John. *Old Highland Days: The Reminiscences of Dr John Kennedy, with a Sketch of His Later Life by His Son, Howard Angus Kennedy, with Twenty-Two Portraits and Illustrations.* London, 1901.

Kitteringham, Guy Stuart. "Studies in the Popularisation of Science in England, 1800–1830." Ph.D. diss., University of Kent, 1981.

Klancher, Jon P. *The Making of English Reading Audiences, 1790–1832.* Madison, 1987.

Knickerbocker, Driss Richard. "The Popular Religious Tract in England 1790–1830." D.Phil. diss., University of Oxford, 1981.

Knight, Charles. *Passages of a Working Life During Half a Century: With a Prelude of Early Reminiscences.* 3 vols. London, 1873.

Knight, David. *The Age of Science: The Scientific Worldview in the Nineteenth Century.* Oxford, 1986.

Knight, Frances. *The Nineteenth-Century Church and English Society.* Cambridge, 1995.

Laquer, T. W. *Religion and Respectability: Sunday Schools and Working-Class Culture, 1780–1850.* New Haven, 1976.

[Lewes, George Henry]. "The Condition of Authors in England, Germany and France." *Fraser's Magazine* 35 (1847): 285–95.

Lewis, Donald M. *Lighten Their Darkness: The Evangelical Mission to Working-Class London, 1828–1860.* London, 1986.

Lewis, Georgina K. *John Stoughton D.D.: A Short Record of a Long Life.* London, 1898.

Lightman, Bernard. " 'The Voices of Nature': Popularising Victorian Science." In *Victorian Science in Context,* edited by Bernard Lightman, 187–211. Chicago, 1997.

———. "The Story of Nature: Victorian Popularizers and Scientific Narrative." *Victorian Review* 25 (1999): 1–29.

———. "The Visual Theology of Victorian Popularizers of Science: From Reverent Eye to Chemical Retina." *Isis* 91 (2000): 651–80.

Lindberg, David, and Ronald L. Numbers, eds. *God and Nature: Historical Essays on the Encounter between Christianity and Science*. Berkeley, 1986.

Livingstone, David N., D. G. Hart, and Mark A. Noll, eds. *Evangelicals and Science in Historical Perspective*. Oxford, 1999.

"L. N. R." *The Book and Its Story; a Narrative for the Young*. 11th ed. London, 1858.

Martin, R. H. *Evangelicals United: Ecumenical Stirrings in Pre-Victorian Britain 1795–1830*. Metuchen, N.J., 1983.

[Martin, William]. *Introduction to the Study of Birds, with a Particular Notice of the Birds Mentioned in Scripture*. London, 1835.

———. *General Introduction to the Natural History of Mammiferous Animals; with a Particular View of the Physical History of Man, and the More Closely Allied Genera of the Order Quadrumana, or Monkeys*. London, 1841.

[———]. *Popular History of Reptiles, or Introduction to the Study of Class Reptilia, on Scientific Principles*. London, 1842.

[———]. *Our Domestic Fowls*. London, 1847.

[———]. *Comparison of Structure in Animals: The Hand and the Arm*. London, 1848.

[———]. *Pictorial Museum of Animated Nature*. London, 1848–49.

[———]. *British Fish and Fisheries*. London, 1849.

———. "Poultry." In *The Farmer's Library*, edited by Charles Knight, 491–603. London, 1849.

[———]. *The Senses and the Mind*. London, 1850.

———. *A General History of Humming-Birds, or the Trochilidae: With Especial Reference to the Collection of J Gould, FRS &c Now Exhibiting in the Gardens of the Zoological Society of London*. London, 1852.

[Masson, David]. "Present Aspects and Tendencies of Literature." *British Quarterly Review* 211 (1855): 157–81.

Mayhew, Henry. *London Labour and the London Poor; a Cyclopaedia of the Condition and Earnings of Those That Will Work, Those That Cannot Work, and Those That Will Not Work*. 2 vols. London, 1851.

Miller, Hugh. *The Old Red Sandstone; or, New Walks in an Old Field*. Edinburgh, 1841.

Milner, Thomas. *Astronomy and Scripture; or, Some Illustrations of That Science, and of the Solar, Lunar and Terrestrial Phenomena of Holy Writ*. London, 1843.

———. *The Gallery of Nature, a Pictorial and Descriptive Tour through Creation, Illustrative of the Wonders of Astronomy, Physical Geography, and Geology*. London, 1846.

———. *The Caves of the Earth: Their Natural History, Features, and Incidents*. London, 1847.

Mitchell, P. Chalmers. *Centenary History of the Zoological Society of London*. London, 1929.

Morrell, Jack B. "Brewster and the Early British Association for the Advancement of Science." In *"Martyr of Science": Sir David Brewster, 1781–1863; Proceedings of a Bicentennial Symposium*, edited by Alison Morison-Low and John R. R. Christie, 25–30. Edinburgh, 1984.

Morrell, Jack B., and Arnold Thackray. *Gentlemen of Science: Early Years of the British Association for the Advancement of Science*. Oxford, 1981.

Mortenson, Terence J. "British Scriptural Geologists in the First Half of the Nineteenth Century." Ph.D. diss., Coventry University, 1996.

305

Myers, Greg. "Science for Women and Children: The Dialogue of Popular Science in the Nineteenth Century." In *Nature Transfigured: Science and Literature, 1700–1900,* edited by John Christie and Sally Shuttleworth, 171–200. Manchester, 1989.

———. *Writing Biology: Texts in the Social Construction of Scientific Knowledge.* Madison, Wis., 1990.

Neuburg, Victor E. *Popular Literature: A History and a Guide.* Harmondsworth, 1977.

"New and cheap forms of popular literature." *Eclectic Review* 22 (1845): 74–84.

Newnham, William. *Man, in His Physical, Intellectual, Social and Moral Relations.* London, 1847.

Nord, David Paul. "The Evangelical Origins of Mass Media in America, 1815–1835." *Journalism Monographs* 88 (1984): 1–30.

———. "Free Grace, Free Books, Free Riders: The Economics of Religious Publishing in Early 19th-Century America." *Proceedings of the American Antiquarian Society* 106 (1996): 241–72.

[Notcutt, William Lowndes]. *The Geography of Plants.* London, 1850.

Nowell-Smith, Simon. *International Copyright Law and the Publisher in the Reign of Queen Victoria.* Oxford, 1968.

Numbers, Ronald L. *Creation by Natural Law: Laplace's Nebular Hypothesis in American Thought.* Seattle, 1977.

———. *The Creationists: The Evolution of Scientific Creationism.* New York, 1992.

Ó Ciosáin, Niall. *Print and Popular Culture in Ireland, 1750–1850.* London, 1997.

O'Brien, Susan. "Eighteenth-Century Publishing Networks in the First Years of Transatlantic Evangelicalism." In *Evangelicalism: Comparative Studies of Popular Protestantism in North America, the British Isles, and Beyond, 1700–1990,* edited by Mark A. Noll, David W. Bebbington, and George A. Rawlyk, 38–57. Oxford, 1994.

Paley, William. *Natural Theology; or, Evidences of the Existence and Attributes of the Deity, Collected from the Appearances of Nature.* London, 1802.

[Patmore, Coventry]. "Popular Serial Literature." *North British Review* 7 (1847): 110–36.

[Payne, Eliza W.]. *Peeps at Nature; or, God's Works and Man's Wants.* London, 1850.

Pearson, Thomas. *Infidelity: Its Aspects, Causes and Agencies; Being the Prize Essay of the British Organization of the Evangelical Alliance.* London, 1853.

Pickering, Andrew, ed. *Science as Practice and Culture.* Chicago, 1992.

The Power of the Press: Is It Rightly Employed? London, 1847.

[Pratt, Anne]. *Wild Flowers of the Year.* London, 1846.

[———]. *Garden Flowers of the Year.* London, 1847.

Pugh, S. D. (Mrs. John). *Phrenology Considered in a Religious Light; or, Thoughts and Readings Consequent on the Perusal of "Combe's Constitution of Man."* London, 1846.

Raven, James, ed. *Free Print and Non-Commercial Publishing since 1700.* Aldershot, 2000.

Raven, James, Helen Small, and Naomi Tadmor, eds. *The Practice and Representation of Reading in England.* Cambridge, 1996.

"Review of Dr. Paley's *Natural Theology.*" *Edinburgh Review* 1 (1802): 287–305.

"Review of *Kosmos* and *Vestiges.*" *Westminster Review* 44 (1845): 152–202.

Rickards, Suzanne L. G. "'Living by the Pen': Hesba Stretton's Moral Earnings." *Women's History Review* 5 (1996): 219–38.

Roberts, Michael. "Geology and Genesis Unearthed." *Churchman* 112 (1998): 225–55.

Rose, Jonathan. "Rereading the English Common Reader: A Preface to the History of Audiences." *Journal for the History of Ideas* 53 (1992): 47–69.

———. *The Intellectual Life of the British Working Classes.* New Haven, 2001.

Rosman, Doreen M. *Evangelicals and Culture.* London, 1984.

Ross, James. *W. Lindsay Alexander, D.D., LL.D: His Life and Work, with Illustrations of His Teaching.* London, 1887.

Russell, Colin A. *Science and Social Change, 1700–1900.* London, 1983.

Ryland, John Edwards. *Memoirs of John Kitto, D.D., FSA, Compiled Chiefly from His Letters and Journals. With a Critical Estimate of Dr Kitto's Life and Writings by Professor Eadie, D.D., LL.D.* Edinburgh, 1856.

Salmon, Edward. *Juvenile Literature As It Is.* London, 1888.

[Sargent, George Etell]. *The Story of a Pocket Bible.* London, 1859.

Saunders & Otley. *Advice to Authors, Inexperienced Writers, and Possessors of Manuscripts, on the Publication of Books Intended for General Circulation or Private Distribution, with Select Specimens of Printing.* London, ca. 1853.

Schaffer, Simon. "The Nebular Hypothesis and the Science of Progress." In *History, Humanity, and Evolution,* edited by James R. Moore, 131–64. Cambridge, 1989.

———. "On Astronomical Drawing." In *Picturing Science, Producing Art,* edited by Caroline A. Jones and Peter Galison, 441–74. London, 1998.

Scherren, Henry. *The Zoological Society of London: A Sketch of Its Foundation and Development.* London, 1905.

Schmoller, Hans. "The Paperback Revolution." In *Essays in the History of Publishing, in Celebration of the 250th Anniversary of the House of Longman, 1724–1974,* edited by Asa Briggs, 283–318. London, 1974.

Schofield, R. S. "Dimensions of Illiteracy in England, 1750–1850." In *Literacy and Social Development in the West: A Reader,* edited by Harvey J. Graff, 201–13. Cambridge, 1981.

Scoresby, William. *The Northern Whale-Fishery.* London, 1849.

Scoresby-Jackson, Robert. *The Life of William Scoresby.* London, 1861.

Secord, Anne. "Corresponding Interests: Artisans and Gentlemen in Nineteenth-Century Natural History." *British Journal for the History of Science* 27 (1994): 383–408.

———. "Science in the Pub: Artisan Botanists in Early Nineteenth-Century Lancashire." *History of Science* 32 (1994): 269–315.

———. *Artisan Naturalists: Science as Popular Culture in Nineteenth-Century England.* Chicago, 2004.

Secord, James A. "Behind the Veil: Robert Chambers and *Vestiges.*" In *History, Humanity, and Evolution,* edited by James R. Moore, 165–94. Cambridge, 1989.

———. *Victorian Sensation: The Extraordinary Publication, Reception and Secret Authorship of Vestiges of the Natural History of Creation.* Chicago, 2000.

———. Introduction to Samuel Clark. *Peter Parley's Wonders of the Earth, Sea and Sky* [1837]. Bristol, 2003.

[Sedgwick, Adam]. "Natural History of Creation." *Edinburgh Review* 82 (1845): 1–85.

Shortland, Michael, ed. *Hugh Miller and the Controversies of Victorian Science.* Oxford, 1996.

Shteir, Ann B. *Cultivating Women, Cultivating Science: Flora's Daughters and Botany in England 1760–1860.* London, 1996.

[Sidney, Edwin]. *The Blights of the Wheat and Their Remedies.* London, 1846.

———. *The Philosophy of Food and Nutrition in Plants and Animals.* London, 1849.

Sivasundaram, Sujit P. " 'Nature Speaks Theology': Colonialism, Cultivation, Conversion and the Pacific, 1795–1850." Ph.D. diss., University of Cambridge, 2001.

Smith, Harold. *The Society for the Diffusion of Useful Knowledge, 1826–46.* Halifax, Nova Scotia, 1974.

Spinney, G. H. "Cheap Repository Tracts: Hazard and Marshall Edition." *Transactions of the Bibliographical Society* 2nd series, 20 (1940): 295–310.

Stanley, Arthur Penrhyn. *Life and Correspondence of Thomas Arnold D.D.* 2 vols. London, 1844.

Stilling, Rodney L. "Scriptural Geology in America." In *Evangelicals and Science in Historical Perspective,* edited by David N. Livingstone, D. G. Hart, and Mark A. Noll. Oxford, 1999.

[Stokes, George]. "The Bound Publications of the RTS, III." *Christian Spectator* (1841): 33–35.

[———]. "On the Union of General and Scriptural Knowledge." *Christian Spectator* (1844): 89–90.

Stott, Anne. *Hannah More: The First Victorian.* Oxford, 2003.

Stoughton, John. *Recollections of a Long Life.* London, 1894.

Stowell, William. *A Memoir of the Life and Labours of William Hendry Stowell, D.D.* London, 1859.

Suleiman, Susan R., and Inge Crosman, eds. *The Reader in the Text: Essays on Audience and Interpretation.* Guildford, 1980.

Sutherland, John. *Victorian Novelists and Publishers.* London, 1976.

Thackeray, William M. *Pendennis.* London, 1848–50.

[Tomlinson, Charles]. *The British Nation: Its Arts and Manufactures.* London, 1851.

Tomlinson, Mary. *The Life of Charles Tomlinson, by His Niece.* London, 1900.

Topham, Jonathan R. "Science and Popular Education in the 1830s: The Role of the *Bridgewater Treatises*." *British Journal for the History of Science* 25 (1992): 397–430.

———. " 'An Infinite Variety of Arguments': The *Bridgewater Treatises* and British Natural Theology in the 1830s." Ph.D. diss., University of Lancaster, 1993.

———. "Beyond the 'Common Context': The Production and Reading of the *Bridgewater Treatises*." *Isis* 89 (1998): 233–62.

———. "Science, Natural Theology, and Evangelicalism in Early Nineteenth-Century Scotland: Thomas Chalmers and the *Evidence* Controversy." In *Evangelicals and Science in Historical Perspective,* edited by David N. Livingstone, D. G. Hart, and Mark A. Noll, 142–74. Oxford, 1999.

———. "Scientific Publishing and the Reading of Science in Early Nineteenth-Century Britain: An Historiographical Survey and Guide to Sources." *Studies in History and Philosophy of Science* 31A (2000): 559–612.

———. "The *Wesleyan Methodist Magazine* and Religious Monthlies in Early Nineteenth-Century Britain." In *Science in the Nineteenth-Century Periodical: Reading the Magazine of Nature,* edited by Geoffrey Cantor, Gowan Dawson, Graeme Gooday, Richard Noakes, Sally Shuttleworth, and Jonathan R. Topham. Cambridge, 2004.

——. Forthcoming. "Science, Natural Theology and the Practice of Christian Piety in Early Nineteenth-Century Religious Magazines." In *Science Serialized: Representations of the Sciences in Nineteenth-Century Periodicals,* edited by Geoffrey Cantor and Sally Shuttleworth. Cambridge, Mass.

Turner, Frank M. "The Victorian Conflict between Science and Religion: A Professional Dimension." *Isis* 69 (1978): 356–76.

Twyman, Michael. *Printing 1770–1970: An Illustrated History of Its Development and Uses in England.* London, 1999.

Urwick, William. *The Life and Letters of William Urwick, D.D. of Dublin.* London, 1870.

van Wyhe, John M. "Phrenology's Nature and the Spread of Popular Naturalism in Britain, c. 1800–1850." Ph.D. diss., University of Cambridge, 2001.

——. *Phrenology and the Origins of Victorian Scientific Naturalism.* Aldershot, 2004.

Vincent, David. *Bread, Knowledge and Freedom: A Study of Nineteenth-Century Working-Class Autobiography.* London, 1982.

——. *Literacy and Popular Culture: England 1750–1914.* Cambridge, 1989.

——. *The Rise of Mass Literacy: Reading and Writing in Modern Europe.* Oxford, 2000.

Weedon, Alexis. *Victorian Publishing: The Economics of Book Production for a Mass Market, 1836–1916.* Aldershot, 2003.

Williams, Sarah C. *Religious Belief and Popular Culture in Southwark c. 1880–1939.* Oxford, 1999.

Wolffe, John. "The Evangelical Alliance in the 1840s: An Attempt to Institutionalise Christian Unity." In *Voluntary Religion,* edited by W. J. Sheils and D. Wood, 333–46. Oxford, 1986.

——. *The Protestant Crusade in Great Britain, 1829–60.* Oxford, 1991.

Wolffe, John, ed. *Evangelical Faith and Public Zeal: Evangelicals and Society in Britain 1780–1980.* London, 1995.

Wosh, Peter J. *Spreading the Word: Bible Business in Nineteenth-Century America.* Ithaca, 1994.

Yapp, G. W., ed. *Official Catalogue of the Educational Exhibition Held in St Martin's Hall, July 4, 1854.* London, 1854.

Yarrell, William. *A History of British Fishes.* 2nd ed. 2 vols. London, 1841.

Yeo, Richard. *Encyclopaedic Visions: Scientific Dictionaries and Enlightenment Culture.* Cambridge, 2001.

Young, Robert M. *Darwin's Metaphor: Nature's Place in Victorian Culture.* Cambridge, 1985.

Yule, John David. "The Impact of Science on British Religious Thought in the Second Quarter of the Nineteenth Century." Ph.D. diss., University of Cambridge, 1976.

Index

advertising: change in style of, 166–69; for *Leisure Hour,* 171, 179–80; for "Monthly Series," 62, 74–75, 166–67, 171

Ainsworth, Harrison, 222n190

Alexander, William Lindsay, 147n29, 193, 205; account of life as Congregational minister, 231–32; biographical sketch, 277; consideration of literary career, 206; first stipend, 205; *Iona,* 145

Alfred the Great. See *Life of Alfred the Great* (Jones)

America, RTS relations with. *See* United States, RTS relations with

American Monthly Volumes, 164

American Sunday School Union, 163–64

Ancient Jerusalem (Kitto), 170

anecdotes, use of in narrative, 117, 133–34

Anglicans, as RTS writers, 195

Angus, Joseph, 197, 198, 236; age at death, 222; *Bible Handbook,* 145; biographical sketch, 277

apocalypse, 23, 24

Arnold, Thomas, 63, 100–3, 104

Arthur, William, 147n30

Ashley, Lord (later Earl of Shaftesbury), 64

astronomy, 20; nebular hypothesis, 3, 18, 19–20, 239; *Solar System* I and II (Dick), 65, 164, 182, 211, 271; *The Telescope and Microscope* (Dick), 164

Astronomy and Scripture (Milner), 232–36, 260; defense of astronomy for believers, 232; devotional tone, 236–37, 240, 241; idea that faith not compromised by science, 235–36; on nebular hypothesis, 234–35

Athenaeum, 99

Atmosphere and Atmospheric Phenomena, The (Dick), 113, 164, 165

atonement: absence in SPCK works, 123, 136; in *British Fish and Fisheries,* 122; in *Caves of the Earth,* 241; in evangelical tracts, 29, 108; inclusion in Monthly Volumes, 110, 113, 117–18, 118n33; role in evangelical theology, 21, 111

Augustine, St., 84

authorship: image of as a profession, 188; noble ideal of *vs.* underlying reality of trying to make a living from it, 186. *See also* writers, professional

"author's risk" publishing, 211

auxiliary societies, RTS, 32, 33, 176–78; Glasgow, 178

Baldwin, Cradock & Joy, 45, 216

ballads, 27, 28, 43

ballad seller, illustration of, 28

Baptist Magazine, 145, 157–58, 159

Baptist Missionary Society, 25

Baptists, 21, 24, 29; as RTS writers, 195, 198

Barth, Christian Gottlob, *Scripture Natural History,* 95, 96

Bauman's Höhle, 238

Bell, Charles D.: biographical sketch, 278; *Life of Calvin,* 65, 151, 152

Bell & Daldy, 73

Benevolent Income of RTS, 36–37, 265, 267n5

Bentham, Jeremy, 102

Bentley, Richard, "Standard Novels and Romances," 50

Bible: difficulty of reading for working classes, 27; episodes involving fish in *British Fish and Fisheries,* 121–22, 123; exemption from paper taxes, 45; Protestant emphasis on access to, 10; as Word, 8

"Bible Christians," 26